P9-AOI-434

CUSHING of GETTYSBURG

CUSHING of GETTYSBURG

The Story of a Union Artillery Commander

KENT MASTERSON BROWN

THE UNIVERSITY PRESS OF KENTUCKY

Frontispiece: Cadet Alonzo Hereford Cushing, c. May 1861, in the furlough uniform of a West Point Cadet. On the forage cap is a wreath bearing the letters "U.S.M.A." Alonzo had the photograph taken for his mother and brother William. Wisconsin Historical Society.

Scholarly publisher for the Commonwealth, serving Bellarmine College, Berea College, Centre College of Kentucky, Eastern Kentucky University, The Filson Club, Georgetown College, Kentucky Historical Society, Kentucky State University, Morehead State University, Murray State University, Northern Kentucky University, Transylvania University, University of Kentucky, University of Louisville, and Western Kentucky University.

Editorial and Sales Offices: Lexington, Kentucky 40508-4008

Library of Congress Cataloging-in-Publication Data

Brown, Kent Masterson, 1949-
Cushing of Gettysburg : the story of a Union artillery commander / Kent Masterson Brown.

p. cm.
Includes bibliographical references (p.) and index.
ISBN 0-8131-1837-9 (alk. paper)
1. Gettysburg (Pa.), Battle of, 1863. 2. Cushing, Alonzo Hereford, 1841-1863. 3. Soldiers—United States—Biography. 4. United States—History—Civil War, 1861-1865—Artillery operations. 5. United States. Army—Artillery—Biography. I. Title.
E475.53.B85 1993
973.7'349—dc20 93-19602

This book is printed on recycled acid-free paper meeting the requirements of the American National Standard for Permanence of Paper for Printed Library Materials. ♾

To Capt. Henry Pell Brown, Sr., AUS
(1917–1972)
636 Tank Destroyer Battalion
(Oran, Tunisia, Salerno, Anzio, Rapido River,
Monte Casino, Rome, Southern France)

A heroic artilleryman and a wonderful father

. . . I will always remember

DOC

Contents

Maps

Acknowledgments

A journey to Gettysburg twenty-seven years ago sparked my interest in the life of Lt. Alonzo Hereford Cushing. Like so many visitors to that great national military park, I was awestruck by the sights at the "angle." I wondered then what manner of man would hold that position in the face of such an overwhelming enemy thrust.

To tell the story of Lt. Alonzo Cushing necessitated the help of many, many wonderful people and institutions. That help began with the sincere interest of two devoted old soldiers: my father, Capt. H. Pell Brown, Sr., and my godfather, Col. Frank B. von Borries, both experienced military scholars. It was furthered by the companionship of three of Kentucky's greatest historians, among my dearest friends, who took an active interest in the Cushing story: Hambleton Tapp, Holman Hamilton, and J. Winston Coleman. Though they are all gone now, I will always carry their memory with me as well as their thoughts and inspiration.

No more startling discovery was made for this work than my locating Alonzo Cushing's letters in an old trunk in the attic of the Chautauqua County Historical Society in Westfield, New York, in 1977. To all the wonderful people who helped me then and whose tireless efforts at preserving the history of Chautauqua County contributed so much to making this work possible—and, I hope, to making Alonzo Cushing himself live in these pages—I give my deepest thanks. I especially thank Christopher C. Hanks, Mary N. Vere, Roderick and Priscilla Nixon, and Dallas K. Beal for their help, encouragement, and hospitality.

Fredonia, New York, Alonzo Cushing's hometown, has a very fine public library and regional museum, made so not only by its marvelous collections but by the helpful, generous, and patient people who work there. Margaret Gregory, Betty Schroeder, Ann M. Fahnestack, and Donna Karoson provided me with innumerable newspaper clippings, local histories, maps, and assorted documents and photographs that enabled me to relate Alonzo's life in Fredonia more understandably and thoughtfully.

In Wisconsin, as in New York, there were those who made a critical difference to the writing of this story. No two people did more to provide me with information on the Cushings in Wisconsin than my dear friends Margaret E. Zerwekh and her late husband, Kenneth Zerwekh, of Delafield. They supplied a stream of significant documents and resources that I would have overlooked had they not been there to offer help. Like my friends in Chautauqua County, the Zerwekhs are highly dedicated to the history of their country and generous in sharing their time and great knowledge.

I searched for seventeen years to locate Henry Brown's painting of the death of Lieutenant Cushing. The Zerwekhs brought its whereabouts to my attention, and its owner, Richard Groseclose of Hartsville, Wisconsin, kindly allowed my use of it. What a difference that painting made in accurately telling of Alonzo Cushing's appearance and last moments.

Charles L. Sanford of Beloit, Wisconsin, a collateral descendant of the Cushings, has a remarkable collection of family manuscripts relevant to the Cushing story. And no account of the Cushings in early Putnam, Ohio, could possibly be told without reference to Larry Sanford's documents and photographs. Larry is a sound and thoughtful historian as well as a truly generous one.

I am indebted further to the State Historical Society of Wisconsin and Margaret Gleason, Kathleen A. Kubach, and Josephine L. Harper. As well, I am deeply appreciative of the help provided by the Ohio Historical Society and Tauni Graham.

No record of a Civil War soldier would be complete without information from the vast resources of the National Archives, and no one makes the otherwise overwhelming experience of using them easier than my friend Michael P. Musick, a dedicated scholar and researcher. I also thank Robert W. Krauskopf, Timothy K. Nenninger, and Elaine C. Everly of the National Archives for the help they gave me.

The vast resources of the United States Military Academy, too, were opened to me by a host of helpful people: Kenneth Rapp, Joseph M. O'Donnell, Alan C. Aimone, and Judith A. Sibley. I am most grateful.

I am also indebted to others. Thomas J. Harrison, Kathy Harrison, Robert Prosperi, and the Gettysburg National Military Park; Ted Alexander, Paul Chiles, and the Antietam National Military Park provided valuable information and documents relating to those great battles and Cushing's role in them. Gordon Cotton of the Old Courthouse Museum at Vicksburg, Mississippi, was my key to tracing the records of Judge Houghton to Larry Sanford and to understanding something of Houghton's life in Vicksburg. Judith A. Schiff and Yale University helped me in my quest for information contained in the Gen. Alexander Stewart Webb Papers, and Peter Dummy and the Massachusetts Historical Society helped make available to me the Col. Paul J. Revere papers. Richard L.

Leisenring of Kanona, New York, graciously copied for me the diary and letters of Col. Patrick O'Rorke, and my friend Brian C. Pohanka of Alexandria, Virginia, provided helpful information about Capt. James McKay Rorty.

No research on an American military figure is complete unless it finally passes through the United States Army Military History Collection at Carlisle Barracks, Pennsylvania, where Richard J. Sommers's help in producing this manuscript was profound.

I thank my good friends Craig Caba of Enola, Pennsylvania, Carlo W. D'Este of New Seabury, Massachusetts, Jane Orient, M.D., of Tucson, Arizona, Paul and Pat DeHaan of Kalamazoo, Michigan, and Richard H. Knight, Jr., of Nashville, Tennessee. I thank as well the Office of the Prothonotary, Gettysburg, Adams County, Pennsylvania; the Offices of the Register of Deeds of Milwaukee and Waukesha Counties, Wisconsin; the Muskingum County Recorder's Office, Zanesville, Ohio; the University of Wisconsin at Milwaukee; and Gettysburg College, the Library of Congress, the Cincinnati Free Public Library, the New York Public Library, and the Margaret I. King Library of the University of Kentucky for all their help and assistance.

My dear friends Charles Roland and Gary Gallagher read the manuscript and provided able, thoughtful, and necessary suggestions for its improvement. For their time and assistance I am most grateful.

This work would never have been completed but for the encouragement of Kenneth Cherry and his staff at the University Press of Kentucky. For his and their belief in me and the project, I am deeply indebted.

Prologue: "In the Midst of Life We Are in Death"

The date on the duty roster read July 12, 1863. Across the Plain at the United States Military Academy at West Point the lovely elm and chestnut trees stood motionless. Dull gray clouds covered the sky, and occasional thunder gave promise of a summer cloudburst.[1]

The news of Gen. Robert E. Lee's defeat at Gettysburg and Gen. Ulysses S. Grant's victory at fortress Vicksburg had captured the attention of all the cadets. Victory would prove elusive, however, for Lee would slip across the Potomac River on July 13 and 14, and then would begin another phase of the ghastly struggle which would ultimately maim some of those now wearing cadet gray. In the West, the Union would suffer defeat at bloody Chickamauga in September, and the war in that theater would drag on for nearly two more years.

The war, and the deep personal losses it brought about, was also having a very immediate impact upon the Corps. From their summer camp along the Plain near Fort Clinton, the cadets had followed the long lists of casualties—some of them graduates of the academy—printed in the newspapers. They had heard and read of rumblings of civil disorder in New York City over the recent draft. The Corps of Cadets had even been readied in anticipation of attacks by draft rioters on West Point and the Cold Spring Iron Foundry across the Hudson River. The cadets were "under arms"; they had been issued ball cartridges and some cadets were on picket duty along the roads leading to the post. The Republic had descended into chaos, it seemed.[2]

Inside the quaint, stone Greek revival Cadet Chapel which had been built in 1836, with its gracious Doric columns and Roman arch windows, beneath the black marble shields bearing the names of revered Revolutionary War generals which adorned its simple walls, gathered the Corps of Cadets in the center pews. The cadets wore gray dress coats with white linen collars, white waist and shoulder belts with black cartridge and cap boxes and bayonet scabbards; cocky black shakos bearing brass castle emblems rested in their arms. Cadet officers held their swords.[3]

In the chapel the aspiring soldiers found an oasis of peace and quiet; an atmosphere of dreaminess and calm, far away, it seemed, from the turbulent world. The academic staff was seated in pews alongside the walls on either side. Some were in black civilian attire; army officers, in their blue uniforms with impressive gold epaulets. Seated with the academic staff was a notable member of the class of June 1861, Lt. and Bvt. Maj. Charles Carroll Parsons, 4th United States Artillery, who had fought heroically at Shiloh, Perryville, and Stones River and had returned to the academy as a professor of geography, history, and ethics. Various local citizens sat at the front along with the superintendent of the academy, Lt. Col. Alexander Hamilton Bowman, class of 1825; the commandant of cadets, Maj. and Bvt. Col. Henry Boynton Clitz, 12th United States Infantry, class of 1845, who had won brevets at the battle of Cerro Gordo in the Mexican War and at Gaines's Mill, Virginia, in June 1862; and Navy Assistant Paymaster Milton Buckingham Cushing. Seated nearby was the venerable Lt. Gen. Winfield Scott, a Virginian by birth and education, who for a number of years had lived at West Point. Six feet, five inches tall and of enormous frame but riddled with infirmities, the white-haired old hero of Chippewa, Lundy's Lane, Veracruz, and Mexico City and former general-in-chief of the U.S. Army—a man one year older than the Constitution itself—was a commanding presence in his blue uniform with its gold bullion facings and epaulets. The post band occupied the loft. Behind the chancel the national colors, proudly bearing stars representing all the states in the Union—even those in rebellion—hung in the still, humid air. The cadets' rifles were stacked in front of the simple house of worship.[4]

The clock in the tower of the Academy Building next door announced that it was 5:00 P.M. Solemn music was played by the post band. Eyes were fixed on Professor Robert W. Weir's great, suggestive painting of the figures representing "Peace" and "War" which was mounted in the circular space over the chancel and bore the solemn admonition from Proverbs: "Righteousness exalteth a nation; but sin is a reproach to any people." Church services had been held in the chapel earlier in the day, for it was Sunday. West Point, in accordance with Special Orders Number 16, issued July 11, 1863, had gathered to bury one of her sons who had recently been killed in action. Such occasions had been rare, even after two years of bloody civil war.[5]

Honored that day was the splendid life and heroic death of Lt. and Bvt. Capt. Alonzo Hereford Cushing. Only nine days before—on July 3 at Gettysburg—he had secured for himself a place in history which few men of his military rank attain. On the front page of the July 6 *New York Times*, the nation had read the story of Cushing's heroic death, written down the morning after the battle by a special correspondent on the battlefield:

> Captain Cushing, Company A, Fourth Regular Artillery, was killed and his battery suffered severely. The gallantry of this officer is beyond praise. Severely wounded early in the afternoon, he refused to leave his post beside his guns, but continued to pour grape and canister into the advancing columns of the rebels until they had reached the very muzzles of his pieces, and sure of their capture, were attempting to turn them upon our forces, when they were driven off by our infantry. At this moment, Capt. Cushing received his death wound, and fell lifeless to the earth. Heaps of corpses and wounded in front of his battery this morning told a terrible tale of the effectiveness of its fire.[6]

Just two summers before, Cushing, then a twenty-year-old captain in the Corps of Cadets, had been seated in the Cadet Chapel on the Sunday before his graduation with all the members of his graduating class, and heard the cadet choir sing the traditional commencement hymn, which began, "When shall we meet again," and ended with the prophetic words, "Never, no never." Now he was dead. The young cadets had heard stories of Alonzo Cushing, and the twenty-seven who made up the class of 1864 fondly remembered him from their days as plebes.[7]

The cadet escort and pallbearers slowly moved up the aisle carrying the flag-draped, wooden soldier's casket and gently placed it on the catafalque. There was silence. The Reverend John W. French, D.D., Chaplain, 5th United State Infantry, and professor of English at the academy, dressed in his black cassock and white surplice, stood up and recited from the *Book of Common Prayer* of the Episcopal Church: "I am the resurrection and the life, saith the Lord: he that believeth in me, though he were dead, yet shall he live: and whosoever liveth and believeth in me, shall never die." The congregation read from the Psalms; French read the Lesson from the First Epistle of St. Paul to the Corinthians, chapter 15.[8]

French quietly walked to the lectern. He asked that his words be blessed, and then he addressed the large gathering. "But a few days since," he said, "the honors of war were here given over the bier of a member of this military family, who had been absent for years. Today the institution takes to her arms a form mangled in battle, on which, within two years, rested her parting benedictions. The sight of a son brought back to his father's house for burial touches the heart. Around him the rooms which looked on his infancy and boyhood are eloquent with a thousand memories. This scene is similar. A beloved pupil, here but yesterday, is brought back from a field of glory that his bier may be encircled by ties and affections only second to those of the family and of nature. Such affections fold around him now, as does that flag which he defended." Drawing upon biblical passages recounting the role of the soldier, French continued: "We honor him who now lies before us, in the midst of his military kindred—younger and elder brothers—for duty well done; not in the routine of peace, though for that the true soldier should receive the affection which he gives to duty, but in the appropriate sphere of war, and on that theatre which secures the eye and the applause of history—the battlefield—our pupil, our friend, our comrade, fought and fell. In position by the key-stone of the battle, and under the concentrated and deadly fire of the enemy, he served his guns admirably. Wounded repeatedly, he continued to act, resisting a most determined onset, till his death shot came." Concluding, French remarked: "There is glory for the brave fallen soldier. To deny it we must oppose the reason and the sentiment of mankind. But in God's eye, there is a glory rising far above all which is human."[9]

Capt. and Bvt. Maj. Francis Asbury Davies, 16th United States Infantry, an 1856 graduate of West Point who had won his brevet rank for gallantry at the Second Battle of Bull Run and had returned to the academy to teach, directed the pallbearers, escort, post band, the chaplain and his sergeant, the Corps of Cadets, citizens, academic staff, Paymaster Cushing, the superintendent and the commandant, and General Scott out of the chapel and into the long procession to the West Point Cemetery.[10]

The drummers of the post band, their drums muffled and draped in black crape, beat a slow, melancholy cadence. Leading the procession, the flag-draped casket was borne on a caisson and limber drawn by six horses, a fitting last journey for the remains of the brave young artilleryman. The casket was followed by a riderless horse, carrying the full equipment of a trooper but with the trooper's boots reversed in the stirrups, led by a solitary cadet on foot. The Corps of Cadets marched slowly in a column of platoons with arms reversed. The solemn procession marched past the Academy Building, the 1855 Barracks, the superintendent's, the commandant's and the professors' homes, and into the West Point Cemetery just beyond the north gate of the academy.[11]

Within the historic cemetery, Dr. French delivered the graveside prayers, the words with special meaning at that hour: "Man that has been born of a woman, hath but a short time to live, and is full of misery. He cometh up, and is cut down, like a flower; he fleeth as it were a shadow, and never continueth in one stay. In the midst of life we are in death." Charles Parsons must have had deep thoughts about it all. He fondly recalled Cushing as a cadet; he could visualize Cushing's last hours, for he had been a battery commander who, in desperate struggle at Perryville, had had his command completely overrun by the attacking enemy.

At war's end, Parsons would give up the army blue and become an ordained Episcopal minister.[12]

General Scott, massive in size, stood erect, bareheaded, at the grave. Alonzo Cushing's grandfather, a volunteer in the Chautauqua County, New York, militia, had followed Scott in the fighting near Buffalo during the War of 1812, and Cushing's father had moved his family to the Wisconsin Territory after Scott helped secure peace in the region by overcoming the Sauk warrior Black Hawk. The old general, known in the army as "Old Fuss and Feathers," knew Alonzo's prominent uncles and cousins from Ohio and Massachusetts well. In fact, he likely had helped the lad secure an appointment to West Point just about seven years before, and had known Alonzo throughout the young man's years at the academy. Scott's career spanned many years, and it had profoundly affected the lives of three generations of Cushings. General Scott would die in less than three years, and his final resting place would be only about twenty paces from Cushing's grave site in the West Point Cemetery.[13]

The congregation—the former general-in-chief, the field grade officers, professors, cadets, and civilians—standing before the grave, recited the Lord's Prayer. The Corps of Cadets then lined up in columns and, on command, fired three crisp volleys that resounded up and down the busy Hudson River. The ceremony was over. The last earthly remains of Lt. and Bvt. Capt. Alonzo Hereford Cushing were lowered into the grave. Nearby, Milton Cushing, Alonzo's oldest full brother, wept. The air was still. As the smoke cleared, the Corps of Cadets reassembled in a column of platoons and marched back to the summer encampment on the Plain. The service had had a profound effect upon them.[14]

In death the heroic Alonzo Cushing, a lad born of solid New England, Puritan stock, was united with fellow West Point comrades and kindred spirits: Lt. George Augustus "Little Dad" Woodruff; Lt. Justin E. Dimick; brilliant Col. Patrick Henry "Paddy" O'Rorke, the academic leader of Alonzo's class; and the brave Brig. Gen. Edmund "Ned" Kirby and Lt. Charles E. Hazlett. He was united in death as well with his father and infant brother and sister and two half brothers and two half sisters, all victims of disease and economic chaos.

Cushing unselfishly had devoted his life to his family and his country. That life he had sacrificed heroically at a critical hour of his country's history. He was now but a memory. Tales of his life and death would be told and retold by aged veterans and would be memorialized in paintings—including a massive cyclorama of the Battle of Gettysburg—and on granite monuments and bronze tablets. The place where he died would become the single most visited site in all of the nation's military parks.

And, like the tales of the young warriors of Homer, the story of Alonzo Hereford Cushing's death would find a place as well in epic poetry. Stephen Vincent Benet—whose grandfather, Lt. Stephen Vincent Benet, was the librarian at West Point during the Civil War and was present at Cushing's funeral—probably best recalled the youthful artilleryman's last moments in his epic poem, *John Brown's Body:*

> There was a death-torn mile of broken ground to cross,
> And a low stone wall at the end, and behind it the Second corps.
> And behind that force another, fresh men who had not yet fought.
> They started to cross that ground. The guns began to tear them.
>
> From the hill they say that it seemed more like a sea than a wave,
> A sea continually torn by stones flung out of the sky,
> And yet, as it came, still closing, closing and rolling on,
> As the moving sea closes over the flaws and rips of the tide.
>
> You could mark the path that they took by the dead that they left behind,
> Spilled from that deadly march as a cart spills meal on a road,
> And yet they came on unceasing, fifteen thousand no more,
> And the blue Virginia flag did not fall, did not fall, did not fall.
>
> They halted but once to fire as they came. Then the smoke closed down
> And you could not see them, and then, as if cleared again for a breath,
> They were coming still but divided, gnawed at by blue attacks,
> One flank half-severed and halted, but the centre still like a tide.
>
> Cushing ran down the last of his guns to the battle-line.
> The rest had been smashed to scrap by Lee's artillery fire.
> He held his guts in his hand as the charge came up the wall
> And his gun spoke out for him once before he fell to the ground.[15]

1

"His Mother Is Poor but Highly Committed"

Deep snow blanketed the stark southern Wisconsin countryside, outlining the hardwood trees and burdening the boughs of the towering evergreens. A bitter cold wind was blowing against the crude log house as Mary Barker Smith Cushing went into labor. Her sister Cordelia Pearmain, herself eight months pregnant, was at Mary's bedside to comfort her. Then, on a cold, dark January 19, 1841, Mary gave birth to a fourth son. Mary and her husband, Milton Buckingham Cushing, agreed to name the child Alonzo Hereford Cushing in honor of Milton's brother and sister-in-law, Alonzo and Margaret Hereford Cushing of Gallipolis, Ohio, whose financial help had provided the proud but impoverished parents with their humble home in the Wisconsin wilderness.[1]

Alonzo's parents both hailed from old Puritan Massachusetts families. The progenitor of the Cushings in America, Matthew Cushing, had settled in Hingham, Massachusetts, in 1638 with an entourage led by the Reverend Robert Peck of the Parish of Hingham, England. The Smiths had arrived in Massachusetts somewhat earlier than the Cushings. On her mother's side, Mary descended from John and Priscilla Alden of the *Mayflower*. The Smiths eventually settled the town of Pembroke. The Cushings and the Smiths over the years produced a prodigious number of clerics, teachers, lawyers, judges, and statesmen. During the American Revolution over two hundred Cushings served in the patriot armies, and the Smiths produced a comparable number.[2]

The Cushings and the Smiths, like other families who traced their lineage to the great Puritan exodus from England, looked back upon their early ancestors in America as the ones who, with piety and divine inspiration, were the founders of the great new Republic. They looked upon themselves, consequently, as an elite class of people. Clannish, they preferred living in communities of descendants of Puritans. They were fiercely Protestant and deeply suspicious of those who practiced the Roman Catholic faith or who hailed from non-English-speaking countries where Catholicism was the dominant religion. Both the Cushings and the Smiths were staunch Baptists. In every respect they were nativists as well.

What brought the Cushings to the Wisconsin wilderness was both the yearning to find land and fortune and the economic chaos of the times. The family's westward movement began with Alonzo Cushing's grandfather, Zattu Cushing, who was born in 1770 at Plymouth, Massachusetts. After the financial collapse of his family during the Revolution, Zattu apprenticed as a ship's carpenter in Boston, then journeyed to Saratoga County, New York, where, at a place called Ballston Spa, he unsuccessfully tried farming. While there he met Rachel Buckingham, the oldest of twelve children of Ebenezer and Esther Buckingham, who had moved there from Connecticut. Zattu and Rachel were married in 1792. That same year they moved west to Oneida County, New York, where Zattu attempted farming again. In Oneida County, five children were born to the Cushings: Lucinda in 1794, Walter Bradely in 1796, Lydia in 1798, Milton Buckingham (Alonzo's father) in 1800, and Zattu, Jr., in 1802.[3]

After helping to construct a ship on Lake Erie, Zattu determined to move again. This time he selected property held by the Holland Land Company in what became Chautauqua County, New York. In February 1805, after a perilous journey made partly on sleds pulled by oxen across frozen Lakes Ontario and Erie, Zattu and his family settled along Canadaway Creek in the town of Pomfret. The journey with his family almost ended in disaster when the ice on Lake Erie began to break up during a thaw. Blowing an old dinner horn, Zattu managed to alert some men on the shore, who safely guided the Cushing family to the mouth of Eighteen Mile Creek in present-day Chautauqua County. The village that grew up around the Cushing home became known as Fredonia. There, Zattu and Rachel had three more children: Catherine Putnam in 1808, Alonzo in 1810, and Rachel in 1813.[4] Zattu had journeyed to western New York as a Baptist missionary, and now he established the first Baptist church in Chautauqua County. Further, although he had no formal education, he ultimately became the first county judge, a position he held for fourteen years.[5]

During the War of 1812 Zattu joined the local militia, helped defend the settlements, and fought in the disastrous Battle of Buffalo in 1813. Among the commanders of American forces at Buffalo and Niagara was newly commissioned Brig. Gen. Winfield Scott, who by war's end had become a national hero for his victories at Chippewa and Lundy's Lane.[6]

Rachel Buckingham Cushing died in 1816. A year later Zattu married Eunice Elderkin of Ostego County, New York. To that marriage were born four more children: Judson in 1818, Addison in 1820, Sarah in 1821, and Frank in 1825. After retiring from the bench and entering into various business pursuits, Zattu Cushing died in 1839.[7]

The year before the Cushings moved to western New York, Rachel's mother and father and nine of her brothers and sisters—Stephen, Ebenezer, Jr., Bradley, Milton, Elizabeth, Alvah, John, Matilda, and Pamelia—had moved to land in Ohio along the Muskingum River which had just been opened for settlement by the Ohio Company. The village that grew up around the Buckingham homes became known as Putnam in honor of Gen. Rufus Putnam, who, along with other Massachusetts Revolutionary War heroes such as Col. and Bvt. Brig. Gen. Benjamin Tupper and Maj. Winthrop Sargent, had founded the Ohio Company and claimed lands themselves nearby. The village became a haven for New England Puritan families, and it took on the appearance of a New England town, architecturally and socially. Across the Muskingum River from Putnam was the growing town of Zanesville along the famous Zane's Trace.[8]

In 1819 Alonzo Cushing's father, Milton Buckingham Cushing, then nineteen years old, entered Hamilton Literary and Theological Institute, a Baptist college in Hamilton, New York, which grew to become Madison College and eventually Colgate University. He wanted to become a doctor. But because he suffered from tuberculosis, a disease he may have contracted from his mother, he was unable to complete his schooling, although he often referred to himself in later life as "Dr. Cushing."[9] With the nation still in a deep depression after its second war with England, Milton journeyed to Putnam, Ohio, to find work among his mother's brothers and sisters. Arriving there in 1820, he was given a job by Esther Cooley Buckingham, the widow of his uncle, Stephen Buckingham, in her late husband's dry goods store. Within a year the store became known as M.B. Cushing & Co.[10]

On November 25, 1823, Milton, twenty-three years old, married Abigail Browning Tupper, the granddaughter of both Benjamin Tupper and Rufus Putnam. Four children were born to Milton and Abigail: Benjamin Tupper in 1825, Edward Anselm in 1827, Rowena Sophia in 1829 and Abigail Elizabeth in 1833.[11] Early in the marriage Milton discovered that his wife too was tubercular. Highly infectious, tuberculosis often spread through entire families, transmitted from one member to another in the cramped quarters of their houses. The disease was deadly: some people died shortly after contracting it; others were able to live with it for many years, but they slowly wasted away under its debilitating symptoms. Sadly, every member of the Cushing household contracted the disease: each of Milton's and Abigail's children would die of tuberculosis before reaching the age of thirty.[12]

Milton, it seems, was always in need of money. His uncle Ebenezer

Buckingham, Jr., continually provided him with the necessary capital to operate the dry goods store and even helped provide the Cushings with a home on the second floor of the lovely old "Stone Academy" on Jefferson Street in Putnam; the lower floor was rented out for use as a school and meeting hall. In 1830 Milton's sister Rachel journeyed to Putnam from Fredonia. She helped Milton in his dry goods business and lived with his family in the Stone Academy. In 1832 she marred Edward W. Tupper, Abigail Cushing's brother.[13]

In the year of his sister's marriage, Milton formed a partnership in the dry goods business with his cousin Catharenus Putnam Buckingham, the son of Ebenezer, Jr. Catharenus was an 1829 graduate of West Point, and the engineer of the famous covered second "Y" bridge between Zanesville and Putnam. The partnership of Cushing & Buckingham was short-lived, however. "The merchantile business," wrote Buckingham years later, "which I had commenced did not promise to be either pleasant or profitable but not desiring to close it out at once [probably out of respect for his poor, struggling cousin] I made an arrangement [with a clerk in the business] to have half of my share of the profit."[14]

Like so many individuals of Puritan ancestry, Milton was interested in education and sent his children to boarding schools at early ages. As well, he was a staunch abolitionist; he and many of his neighbors used their homes as stations on the underground railroad. He was one of the founders of the Muskingum County Emancipation Society as well as the local temperance society. Joining Milton in the abolition and temperance activities was his cousin Catharenus.[15]

In November 1833, just after giving birth to her fourth child, Milton's wife died of tuberculosis. The newborn daughter, Abigail Elizabeth, died of tuberculosis a little more than eight months later. Mother and daughter were buried in what became known as Woodlawn Cemetery in Putnam.[16] With three sickly children to care for and his business failing, Milton determined to move to Columbus, Ohio, a town with more economic promise than Putnam, after borrowing the sum of $7,000 from another cousin, the Reverend Goodsell Buckingham. In Columbus, Milton established another dry goods store.[17] And in Columbus, Milton met Mary Barker Smith, a young lady who was then teaching at her own female seminary. She had moved to Ohio with her sister Elizabeth, who had married John Gillman Pillsbury, from their family home in Salem, Massachusetts.[18] Born in 1807 to Elisha Smith and Mary Butler Bass Smith, Mary was an extraordinary young woman. Somewhat small in stature, with a full and rather round face, she radiated kindness and compassion. She had a keen intellect, having received an award for scholarship in the Boston female schools in 1822.[19]

Two of Mary's first cousins, Joseph Smith and Albert Smith, would play important roles in her life and the lives of her children. Joseph Smith, by 1835, was a commander in the U.S. Navy and commandant of the Boston Navy Yard; he would become a captain in 1837 and, later, an admiral. Albert Smith was a graduate of Brown University and had served as United States marshall for the state of Maine. He would be elected to the state legislature and then to Congress. Gen. Winfield Scott and Sen. Daniel Webster would select him to assist in tracing the northeastern boundary of the United States, and he would become a highly respected lawyer in Washington, D.C.[20]

Milton Buckingham Cushing fell in love with Mary Barker Smith, and the two were married in the Baptist Church in Columbus on June 12, 1836. Milton was thirty-six years old and Mary was twenty-nine. The next year, on April 30, Mary gave birth to her first child, Milton Buckingham Cushing, Jr.[21] In 1837 another of Mary's sisters, Cordelia Miller Smith also moved to Columbus, where she married an Englishman by the name of William Robert Pearmain.[22] That year the nation's banking system collapsed. Milton lost virtually everything he owned, and the panic of 1837 ushered in a long, disastrous depression.

Milton had followed the opening of the Wisconsin Territory with great interest and now looked to it as a refuge. With the defeat of the Sauk warrior Black Hawk, Gen. Winfield Scott had secured treaties with the Indians which opened up the new lands for settlement, and there had already been a rush of settlers to the area.[23] Milton wrote to his brother and sister-in-law, Alonzo Cushing and Margaret Hereford Cushing, of Gallipolis, Ohio, asking if they could help him purchase some land in the new territory. Alonzo had migrated to Gallipolis, from Fredonia, New York, in 1830, following his brother Zattu, Jr., and had become a successful lawyer there. Now he and his new wife agreed to help.[24]

Milton and Mary and all the children set out toward Wisconsin Territory in 1838 in the company of William and Cordelia Pearmain. They hoped to escape creditors until they could find land on which they could subsist and until they were on their feet again. The Cushings and Pearmains sojourned along the way in Chicago and then in Milwaukee, where Mary gave birth, on August 22, 1838, to her second child, a son named Howard Bass Cushing.[25] In 1839 the Cushings finally settled a 250-acre tract purchased by Milton's brother and sister-in-law from the lands being sold by the territorial government of Wisconsin to raise funds for the construction of the Milwaukee and Rock River Canal project. The property was located along the north bank of the Bark River in the shadow of the Kettle Mountain range, in a valley between Lakes Nagawicka and Nemahabin. There the Cushings built a log cabin along the Territorial Road connecting Milwaukee and Madison, giving Alonzo and

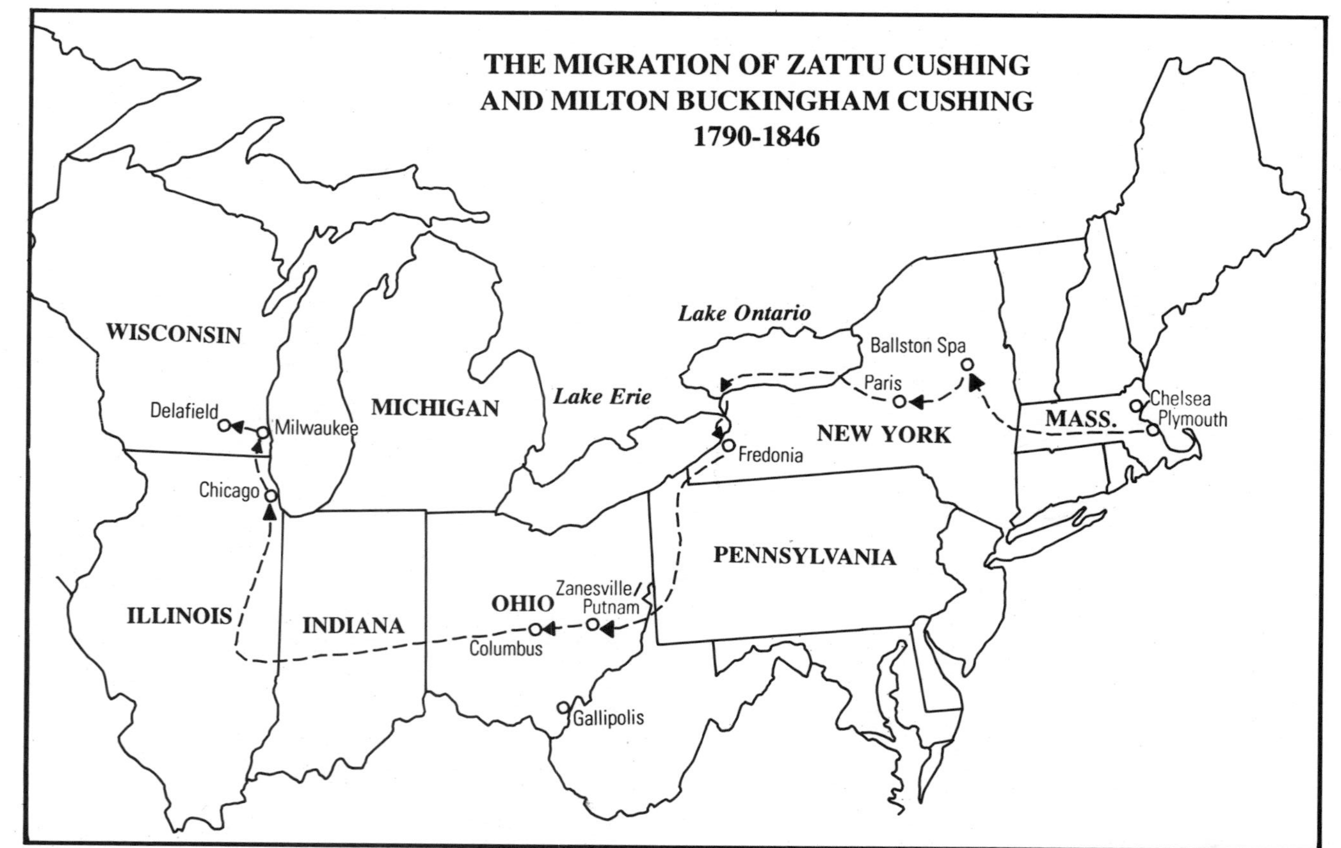
THE MIGRATION OF ZATTU CUSHING
AND MILTON BUCKINGHAM CUSHING
1790-1846
WISCONSIN
Delafield
Milwaukee
Chicago
MICHIGAN
Lake Erie
Lake Ontario
Ballston Spa
Paris
Chelsea
Plymouth
MASS.
NEW YORK
Fredonia
PENNSYLVANIA
ILLINOIS
INDIANA
OHIO
Zanesville/
Putnam
Columbus
Gallipolis

Margaret Cushing a mortgage for the full price of the land and taking title to it themselves.[26]

The countryside was elegant. The soil was a rich loam, beneath it a firm bed of limestone. The area was well watered; springs, creeks, rivers, and lakes abounded. Forests of white and red oak, maple, basswood, ash, elm, cherry, and black walnut covered the land. The lakes region would become a haven for settlers seeking the best of farming and grazing lands.[27] The little crossroads hamlet of largely New England settlers of Puritan ancestry which grew up around the Cushings' and Pearmains' cabins soon became known as Delafield, a name that Cushing family tradition claimed was given to the cluster of log homes by Mary Cushing in honor of the owner of the first grist mill.[28]

Other members of the Cushing and Smith families joined Milton and Mary in Wisconsin. Milton's brother Walter migrated there from Fredonia. Mary's sister Jane Reed Smith arrived shortly after the Cushings had settled their land and soon married another Massachusetts settler named John Henry Batchelder, a dentist (the Batchelders, though, soon returned to Massachusetts).[29] A third son, named Walter, was born to the Cushings in December 1839 but died of tuberculosis only days later. Little Walter was buried near the log cabin.[30]

By the time of Alonzo's birth in 1841, the population of Wisconsin had grown to nearly 31,000. Besides native-born Americans from New England, New York, the old Northwest, and Kentucky, the Territory received a large influx of German, Norwegian, Canadian, English, Irish, Welsh, and Scottish settlers, many of them recent immigrants to America. This great mix of nationalities was something vastly new and probably disturbing to nativists like Milton and Mary.[31] Delafield was growing, too. Nelson P. Hawk had opened a tavern there in 1840 (though the nearest sundry store was in Prairieville, twelve miles east), and the Territorial Road through the town had been vastly improved. Soon the territorial legislature set off Delafield as a township, and on January 5, 1842, Milton Cushing was elected chairman of the local Board of Supervisors.[32]

Mary became pregnant again. On November 4, 1842, she gave birth to the couple's fifth son, William Barker Cushing. Little did Milton and Mary realize, in their impoverished circumstances on the Wisconsin frontier, the undying fame their two little sons, Alonzo and William, would bring to the Cushing name.[33] Like most of their neighbors, they settled in the Wisconsin wilderness to escape the woes of the nation's economic collapse. But the depression was long-lived; the nation would not actually come out of its economic decline until well into the late 1840s. Milton was never able to rebound; his family remained impoverished.[34]

The Pearmains soon decided to leave Wisconsin; they had given up on life on the frontier. The two families bade one another goodbye; the

Pearmains headed back to Massachusetts; and Mary Cushing, virtually penniless, with a desperately sick husband and six children (Milton's oldest son from his first marriage had returned to Ohio), remained on the Wisconsin frontier.[35] Milton's health was seriously declining. The rigors of the frontier, coupled with his inability to earn the money to repay what he owed his cousin and his brother and sister-in-law, finally caused him to sell his Delafield property. On April 14, 1843, he and Mary Cushing, without having paid off the note to Alonzo and Margaret Cushing, sold their Wisconsin homeplace to a Kentuckian named Alfred L. Castleman, and another portion of the land to an Albert Alden from Maine. Mary, however, refused to walk away totally from the one piece of land dearest to her, the grave of her infant son, Walter. She purchased back from Mr. Castleman the little gravesite—six feet by four feet—for the sum of ten dollars. Only a loving mother could possibly have known and understood the inestimable value of the deed to such a tiny parcel of earth.[36]

In the fall of 1843 the Cushings moved to Milwaukee, where Milton secured a position as a clerk of the County Board of Supervisors.[37] They remained in Milwaukee until late spring of 1844, when for some reason unclear in history, they determined to return to Chicago. The family always claimed that Milton sought to enter the practice of medicine there, but he was clearly too ill to do so. Chicago was probably nothing more than the first step on the Cushings' way back east.[38]

The year he left Wisconsin for Chicago ushered in another loss for Milton, although he did not know it at the time. It had been over nine years since he had borrowed the $7,000 from his cousin, Goodsell Buckingham, back in Putnam, Ohio, and he had failed to make any payments on that debt. On March 4, 1844, the Reverend Buckingham, then living in Morgan County, Ohio, filed suit against Milton in the Muskingum County Court of Common Pleas, asking for the full amount of the loan plus interest and costs. On September 13, 1844, a judgment was entered against Milton in the amount of $7,562.22, and on June 9, 1845, three parcels of property that he owned in Putnam, Ohio—including the property where he and his cousin Catharenus had operated their dry goods store—were sold at a sheriff's auction on the steps of the Muskingum County Court House.[39]

Meanwhile, life had become difficult indeed for Mary and the children. They probably found living space in a boardinghouse in noisy and dirty Chicago. Milton was ill; there was little money to buy food and clothing; and to add to Mary's burden, she became pregnant again. On October 1, 1845, she gave birth to a daughter, Mary Rachel. But Mary Rachel, like little Walter, became ill shortly after birth. Milton believed that she had a "certain kind of consumption"; Mary thought the child "inherited" the ailment from her father. Mary Rachel had, in fact, contracted tuberculosis and died in September 1846. Not long after the birth of Mary Rachel, Mary had become pregnant again, for the seventh time.[40]

Alonzo's half-siblings had gone their own ways by then. Benjamin Tupper Cushing, when he was about sixteen years old, had left the family and journeyed back to Columbus, Ohio. He worked briefly in the office of the *Columbus State Journal* and then enrolled in Marietta College. After graduating, he studied law in the Cincinnati offices of none other than Salmon Portland Chase. Edward Anselm Cushing set out on his own in 1845; Rowena Sophia, two years younger than her brother Edward, left the family shortly after their return to Chicago. Both went back to Zanesville, Ohio, where Edward embarked upon the study of medicine.[41]

The year 1846 was tumultuous. By that fall the nation, which had slowly been coming out of the depression, was plunged into a war with Mexico. Milton's health worsened. He had very likely never been able to work at any form of employment after he returned to Chicago; his tuberculosis had become too advanced, so he determined to seek a change in climate. To "take a cure" for consumption in those days often involved a journey to a warmer climate. Milton knew of only one such place where he could go—Vicksburg, Mississippi, where Lawrence Sterne Houghton, his sister Lydia's son, was living. Born in 1815 in what became Fredonia, New York, Lawrence had worked in the dry goods store of Cushing & Buckingham in Putnam in 1831 and 1832. Then he had left Ohio and journeyed back to Fredonia, but in 1833 he had moved to Leavenworth, Indiana, where he taught school. From there he had journeyed to Vicksburg. His late father had practiced law in Vicksburg and was buried there. Lawrence had entered the practice of law, served as postmaster and as justice of the peace, and was an up-and-coming citizen of the thriving Mississippi River town. He had married Jane Catharine Billings, a native of Moro, in Saratoga County, New York. By 1846 the couple had three children, one born that spring. The Houghtons lived in a fine old two-story frame house on the northeast corner of Randolph and Locust Streets. They offered Milton the opportunity to restore his health in their home and Milton agreed to go.[42] After giving his wife what little money he had available, he bade farewell to her and the children. Alonzo, then just over five years of age, kissed his father goodbye. It was the last time he would ever see him.

It appears that Milton first headed back to Delafield, Wisconsin, on horseback in order to try to collect money still due him from the sales of his real estate. Whether he was successful or not is unknown. He finally traveled to Cassville, Wisconsin, where he boarded a steamboat for the long down-river trip to Vicksburg.[43]

Instead of remaining alone in Chicago, Mary determined to travel all the way to Chelsea, Massachusetts, so that she and the children might be among the family she had left behind almost twelve years before, and have her baby there. Milton probably agreed to meet Mary and the children in Massachusetts, and then they would move back to Fredonia, New York. Like the Pearmains, they had determined to go "home." In Chelsea and Fredonia they could rely upon family help and support. Milton and Mary clearly had given up on life in the West.[44]

Virtually all of Mary's family were living back in Massachusetts. Her mother, Mary Butler Bass Smith, was living in Chelsea, as were Cordelia and William Pearmain, and their then three children. Mr. Pearmain was engaged in the auction business. Mary's sister Jane Reed Smith and her husband, Dr. John H. Batchelder, were living in Salem with their four young children. Dr. Batchelder continued to practice dentistry. Margaret Sprague Smith, a sister whom Mary had not seen in over twelve years, had married a Joshua Loring in 1834, and five children had been born to the couple. The Lorings lived in Boston, where Joshua was engaged in the banking business. Elizabeth and her husband, John G. Pillsbury, had returned from Columbus to Lowell, Massachusetts, and Elizabeth was pregnant with the couple's first child.[45]

Mary, pregnant and with four little children at her side, set out across the country. During the long journey, Mary and her children one night sought lodging in a little hostelry. In the morning, she carefully counted her money and found that very little was left. She went to the innkeeper's office and quietly asked for her bill. Her youngest son, four-year-old William, with Alonzo alongside, was clinging to her dress. Little William sensing that his mother was very depressed and worried, exhorted the innkeeper, "You mustn't charge my muver much money. She hasn't very much!"[46]

The only correspondence between Mary and Milton Cushing that is known to exist is a letter written by Milton to his wife on Sunday, November 29, 1846, from Patch Grove, Wisconsin. By then he apparently had heard from his sons and daughter in Ohio of the loss of his property in Putnam. By late November 1846, he had returned to Wisconsin, from Vicksburg, ostensibly to try to collect payment still owed him by Alfred L. Castleman for the sale of the Wisconsin homeplace, and to see if he could broker some real estate in the western part of the state. Hearing of the arrival of some letters from his wife, Milton had traveled over twenty-two miles in an open buggy in freezing temperatures to the post office at Cassville, Wisconsin. "Obtaining your letters," he wrote to Mary, "I stopped to read them, and before I got through I was warm enough."[47]

Mary, it seems, had been to visit a psychic in Boston by the name of "Mrs. Freeman." Unable to communicate with her husband, she had sought out the "clairvoyant" in an effort to find out about Milton's state of health. She was deeply troubled by her husband's failure to write. Mary's use of the "clairvoyant" was the only means of quelling her yearning for information about her husband. Mrs. Freeman, it seems, had informed Mary that Milton was traveling for reasons of health, that his "mind was much exercised," and that the medicine he was using was like "poison to him." Mary had written to her husband repeating the psychic's findings. Milton, in his letter to Mary, attempted to put her concerns to rest, but in doing so, he provided evidence of his own deteriorating medical condition. He referred to his condition as "a species of incipient consumption . . . having its chief seat in the liver," which manifested itself in frequent and prolonged attacks of high fever marked by paroxysms of chills and sweating. He coughed incessantly. For it he took "Wistar's Balsam of Wild Cherry," a "resinous substance" which he claimed "braced" his system, and a stronger and still more bracing tonic, called "Osgood's Cholagoque" as well. In the letter, Milton revealed not only his love for his wife and family but his concern for their safety and his firm reliance upon his religious faith to carry them through their trials. He apparently had not heard from Mary until he arrived in Cassville. Commenting on her long trip to Massachusetts, Milton wrote, "But thanks be to God, I know the main facts about which I was most anxious, your own and the children's safety and health. This afforded great relief to my overburdened mind, and was an occasion of great rejoicing and devout thanksgiving to the Father of Mercies and the Redeemer of Men."[48]

Milton Cushing finally set out on a long journey to be reunited with Mary and the childen. From Wisconsin he traveled by steamboat to Gallipolis, Ohio, in order to visit his brothers Alonzo and Zattu and their wives. Milton had not been able to repay his brother and sister-in-law fully for the land they had purchased for him in Wisconsin. Maybe Mr. Castleman had given Milton all or part of the money due him; at any rate, Milton's visit to Gallipolis was an effort by him to repay Alonzo and Margaret some or to provide some assurance to them of the status of his Wisconsin land, and also to determine from his lawyer brother whether anything could be salvaged from all his losses in Putnam. He most likely intended to straighten out his business affairs with his cousin Goodsell as well before heading toward Chelsea, Massachusetts.

By the time he arrived in Gallipolis, however, Milton was terribly ill, thin, and emaciated; a persistent cough wracked his frail body. The journey and the stress had been too much for him. He obtained a room in a hotel, probably the American House Hotel on First Street, a hostelry that catered to river travelers. Then on April 22, 1847, forty-seven-year-old Milton Buckingham Cushing, in the final throes of tuberculosis, died in his hotel room. Far away from Mary and his children, Milton's extraordinarily sad life had come to an end.[49]

Mary, Alonzo, and the rest of the children, it appears, were still in Chelsea at the time of Milton Cushing's death. They had arrived in October 1846, and on January 1, 1847, Mary had given birth to a daughter whom she named Mary Isabel.[50] Whatever property the Cushings had obtained was gone. Much of it had been sold in order to afford the basic necessities of life for Mary and the children during Milton's long illness. By the time Mary learned of her husband's death, his last earthly remains had already been buried, according to his earlier request, in Fredonia, New York. She was penniless and grief-stricken.

Milton had long counseled Mary that in the event of his death, she and the children should return to his hometown of Fredonia, where they would find comfort among the many members of the Cushing family still residing in the town. Mary had promised that she would raise the children in his old hometown if that was his wish. Always the devoted wife and mother, Mary remembered her promise, and against the advice of her sisters she resolved to keep it. Thus, in the summer of 1847, Mary Barker Smith Cushing and her five children arrived in Fredonia, determined to live near the final resting place of her husband and to provide her children with the advantages that a close and loving greater family would give them.[51]

The move proved to be a fortunate one. When six-year-old Alonzo Hereford Cushing first arrived at his father's hometown in 1847, five of his father's brothers and sisters still lived in and around Fredonia, as did Eunice Elderkin Cushing, the widowed second wife of Judge Zattu Cushing. Lucinda, Milton's oldest sister, had married a William Barker of Fredonia, and had five children. Lydia C. Cushing, the widow of Daniel Sterne Houghton, in 1826 had married Dr. Squire White, a native of Guilford, Vermont, who had become the first licensed physician in Chautauqua County, New York. Three children had been born to the Whites, and the family would become very close to Mary and her children. Of the four children born to Lydia and her first husband, all had reached adulthood by 1847, and two daughters were living in nearby Dunkirk, New York: Martha Rachel, married to William F. Wheeler; and Henrietta Eliza, married to Laurens Risley. Milton's sister Catherine had married Philo Hull Stevens of Harpersfield, New York, and seven children had been born to that marriage. Addison Cary Cushing and his wife, Elizabeth, had one child born just that May. Frank Cushing, a lawyer in Fredonia, was still single, although he was courting Minerva Risley, daughter of Gen. Elijah Risley. Sarah Buckingham, sister to Alonzo's grandmother, Rachel Buckingham Cushing, and her husband, Benjamin Sprague, after living in Putnam, Ohio, had also moved to Chautauqua County, New York. The couple had raised five children, some of whom lived nearby. Thus, a large number of Cushings, Barkers, Whites, Stevenses, Risleys, Buckinghams, and Spragues embraced Mary and her five children. Alonzo quickly came to know all his aunts, uncles, and cousins around the growing little community, and Fredonia became his hometown as it had been his father's and grandfather's.[52]

Mary Cushing's financial plight was still desperate, and some of the Cushing family—as had some members of the Smith family in Chelsea—asked her to allow them to adopt her children, believing she simply could not adequately care for them. To those offers Mary gave a quick but polite rebuff; she was determined to keep her family together. With some assistance from her late husband's family and by working as a seamstress, she obtained a small frame house on Green Street. There she opened a select, private primary school—a "dame school"—where, for a modest tuition, she taught many of the young children of the community as well as her own. By doing so, Mary not only saved the family money but guaranteed her children's steady academic proficiency. Those were years of hardship for Mary and her children—it was said that for months they lived on nothing more than "pudding and molasses"—but her teaching did provide for the family.[53]

The village of Fredonia was a quaint, typical nineteenth-century American town. By 1847 it had become a thriving center of business and culture, thanks in large part to its proximity to Lake Erie and the great Erie Canal. It had grown up along the banks of Canadaway Creek and around Judge Zattu Cushing's house. Main Street crossed Canadaway Creek not far from the center of town. Where Main Street intersected Temple Street there was a lovely village green known as Barker Common. There stood the First Baptist Church, the Presbyterian Church of Fredonia, and, nearby, Trinity Episcopal Church. On either side of Main Street lived Alonzo's aunts, uncles and cousins. Dr. Squire White's home stood on Main Street not far from Green Street. Francis Smith Edwards, a local lawyer and the husband of Dr. White's daughter Julia, lived on Dunkirk Street. Alonzo's Uncle Addison had lived in Zattu's handsome old home on Eagle Street nearby, but he had sold it to George White, Zattu's grandson and son of Dr. Squire White and his wife, Lydia Cushing. The Risleys lived in prominent homes along lovely Garden Street on the other side of town. On East Main Street was the grocery and drug store of Devillo A. White, another son of Dr. White; next to it was the dry goods store of Alonzo's uncle, Philo H. Stevens. Close by the Barker Common, at the corner of Main and Center Streets, stood the handsome three-story building that housed the *Fredonia Censor*, a newspaper founded by Henry C. Frisbee in 1821 and, in 1847, operated by Willard M. McKinstry and his family. There were a number of noted hostelrys: the Mansion House, the Erie Hotel, Abell Tavern, Mulford's Hotel, and the Scott Tavern where General Lafayette had been entertained in 1825.[54]

Alonzo quickly learned all about his grandfather Zattu, whose large house stood just south of Green Street, and he must have heard Eunice, Zattu's widow, tell of the early days on the New York frontier. The Cushings joined the First Baptist Church of Fredonia situated just off the town common. It was, for all practical purposes, the congregation Zattu had founded. There, every Sunday, Wednesday, and holiday, they heard their Green Street neighbor, the Reverend Arnold Kingsbury, deliver his "powerful preaching."[55]

Fredonia, like many New York towns, was thoroughly New England and Puritan. All up and down Main Street were the residences and shops of people who bore such New England names as Buckingham, Hinckley, Putnam, Doolittle, Kimble, Rowley, Havens, Dickinson, Franklin, Stevens, and, of course, Cushing. Alonzo, like most Americans of New England ancestry then, would grow up knowing a hometown that was truly homogeneous in its race, religion, politics, ideals, and values. Although life along the Wisconsin frontier and in Chicago had brought the Cushings into daily contact with those who spoke with Irish, German, and Scandinavian accents, they had always sought out those with ancestry like their own. In Fredonia it was the same as in Chelsea or Salem, Massachusetts, or Putnam, Ohio, for that matter. If the Cushings heard an Irish or German accent spoken, it was probably by someone's servant or laborer. Although impoverished, Mary Cushing and her children were proud of their ancestry and of the community of New England Puritans like themselves.

By the fall of 1847 the War with Mexico had ended, but for a young lad like Alonzo, the stories of the great campaigns and battles must have been stirring. He must have heard about Zachary Taylor and his victories at places named Monterrey and Buena Vista, and about Winfield Scott's forces pushing into the very streets of Mexico City. Aunts and uncles reminded the lad that his grandfather Zattu had fought with General Scott near Buffalo during the War of 1812, and that but for the old general the Wisconsin Territory might not have opened for settlers when it did.

As Alonzo and his brothers grew older, their mother expected them to help supplement the family earnings. Milton, Jr., worked in White's grocery and drug store, and Howard worked as a "devil" in the *Fredonia Censor* office nearby. The younger boys, Alonzo and William, helped local farmers bring in their herds and did odd jobs around town for modest pay, all of which was turned over to their mother to help defray the family's living expenses.[56] The Cushing family was closely knit; each member supported the others. The difference in ages, though, caused the boys to pair off: Milton and Howard, being older, played and were schooled together; Alonzo and William became inseparable companions. All the brothers adored their little sister, Mary Isabel. Reflecting upon her childhood, Mary Isabel once said of Alonzo and William: "One trait, I think, was very remarkable in our family—the respect and courtesy manifested toward each other. I never received a reproof or heard an impatient word from either of my brothers. They always displayed toward each other and my mother and myself the same courtesy they would show a commanding officer. The petting and love I received was enough to have spoiled me for life for contact with the world."[57]

Without doubt, Mary Isabel's recollections are a tribute to her mother. In spite of poverty and loss, she taught and trained her children well. She was a proud woman, and she instilled in Alonzo and his brothers and sister a soaring pride in their family and in themselves. Mary Cushing was a tower of strength though rather short in stature; those who knew her found her "quiet and unassuming, . . . bright and witty in conversation," and always well informed about the events of the day. She was a voracious reader and loved to read and write poetry. Puritan that she was, Mary was attentive to her church duties. Her faith dominated everything she did, day in and day out. Moral teaching to her went hand in hand with Bible reading, and she imparted both to her children every day of their lives with her. She brought them up, wrote one granddaughter, "to have faith in the power of prayer." Her children adored her. To them she was always known as "Little Ma."[58]

As he grew older, Alonzo increasingly disliked the name Alonzo; he preferred being called Allie or Lon by his family and friends. Because of his dark complexion and dark auburn hair, his brothers and sisters—particularly Will—often called him "Indian." The nickname was apparently given to Alonzo by his half brother Edward, probably while the family was living in the Wisconsin Territory, where the Sauk, Fox, Winnebago, and Pottawatomi Indians still roamed.[59] Milton, Jr., being the oldest, was intimidating to his little brothers. His propensity to jump on playful Alonzo and William earned him the nickname "Pouncer." Howard was called "Howie" or "How," and Mary Isabel was called "Sis" by her brothers.[60]

Little William was known in the family as Billy, Will, or (another nickname bestowed by Edward) "Bill Coon." One day in Chicago, while his mother was busy with household chores, William climbed into a clothes press, took his father's stovepipe hat, placed it on his head, and set off to "see the world." He was soon missed at home, and the whole household began a search for him. Neighbors reported seeing him running as fast as he could, holding the tall hat on his head. It was thirty-six hours later that his frantic half sister Rowena found him in a little house near the Chicago River, where a kind sailor had carried him after rescuing the boy from Lake Michigan; William had fearlessly walked off a pier into the turbulent water. Sleeping quietly in the bed of the good sailor's wife,

William was grasped by his teary-eyed half sister. "The wiver went and the steamboat went, and I wanted to go too," he exclaimed. Unfortunately, the little lad, when he was rescued from the water, had not told the sailor his real identity but instead said that his name was Bill Coon. From that day on, the nickname stuck.[61]

When Lon was old enough, he attended Miss Julia Moore's Select School. Almost a model child, he was attentive and worked hard from the start; if he was ever in trouble with his mother or anyone else, it was rarely. Lon grew up looking after the interests of his mother. He became, as well, a kind of father figure to his young brother and sister even as a very young child.[62] William, on the other hand, though a hard worker in school and attentive to his mother and family, was rambunctious, hot-tempered, and a kind of roughneck. He seems to have feared nothing. One trait emerged: he was a leader of sorts even as a child. Although one year younger than Lon, William was often the one who led. He soon joined his brother at Miss Julia Moore's Select School and quickly became the "captain" of a group of small boys—which at times included Lon—named the "Muss Company." He "drilled" his "company" to rush out of school, regardless of time or classes, whenever he mounted the schoolyard fence and gave a whistle. On more than one occasion, the signal was given during classtime, to the astonishment of the teacher, who in some way had incurred William's strong displeasure. The teacher came to the Cushing household one evening and informed Mary of her son's antics. Mary, as one could imagine, put her foot down. Her discipline, however, did not end the boy's insatiable appetite for trouble.[63]

One of Lon's and Will's good friends early in their days in Fredonia was little David Parker, who was the same age as William; the two were close companions. One day the two boys, having played some classroom prank, were ordered to stay after school. Will was incensed. After a few minutes he and David Parker darted out of the classroom. Miss Moore ordered some of the older boys to catch them and bring them back. Running as fast as they could, the two little fugitives soon came to a board fence. From the top of it, Will turned around and tried to kick his pursuers. In doing so, he fell backward and broke his arm. Although he had managed to make his escape from school, his refuge, unfortunately, was in the office of his uncle, Dr. Squire White. There, in pain, Will's arm was reset. One can only imagine the scolding the boy received when his uncle brought him back in the buggy to his Green Street home.[64]

Will's escapades did not end there. On another occasion, while standing in front of Devillo White's grocery store, he was approached by a man with whom he had had an altercation of some sort before. "I've got you now," yelled the man, "and I'll give you a good spanking." William immediately jumped up on a barrel containing ax and hoe handles, seized an ax handle, and struck the man on the side of the head, felling him to the ground! It was a shocking display, to say the least.[65]

Lon worried about his brother. He fretted about his pranks and his punishments. The older he grew, the more his concern became evident. Lon never wanted Will to do anything but what made his mother proud. Often he would lecture his brother in an effort to get him to behave, but to no avail; Will was headstrong and rebellious. He would eventually grow up and lose his yen for boyish pranks, but along the way he would suffer serious setbacks. His brother Lon, as always, would be there to comfort and console him and encourage him to pick up the pieces and try again. Small wonder Mary Cushing once wrote that Will "always looked up to and worshipped Alonzo."[66]

After the war with Mexico the United States added to its great domain the largest amount of territory since the Louisiana Purchase, but with new lands came an old problem: the expansion of slavery. The problem became acute with the discovery of gold in the Sacramento Valley of California in January 1848. There was such a rush of fortune hunters to the region that statehood for California was sought the following year. When the territorial legislature in California approved a constitution that prohibited slavery, the South fumed. Zachary Taylor had been elected to the presidency in 1848. He recommended the immediate admission of California to the Union in December 1849 with its "free" constitution, as well as the organization of the New Mexico and Utah territories without reference to slavery. Southerners talked of secession; Taylor lashed back. Then, Sen. Henry Clay of Kentucky presented a compromise on the floor of the United States Senate on January 27, 1850. The compromise was accepted. The nation would remain intact for eleven more years.[67]

In the Cushing household, news of the great compromise was followed with interest. Lon undoubtedly had heard his mother speak of his father's and uncles' efforts back in Putnam, Ohio, to secret fugitive slaves to freedom through the underground railroad. In fact, one of his father's cousins, Sarah Sturges Buckingham, daughter of Ebenezer, Jr., and Eunice Buckingham, married the Reverend George Beecher, son of Lyman Beecher and brother of Henry Ward Beecher and Harriet Beecher Stowe (who would publish *Uncle Tom's Cabin* in 1852), probably the most noted abolitionist family of the age. Lon, must have heard as well that Dr. James Pettit, who lived on Chestnut Street in Fredonia and who manufactured an "eye salve" that was sold at White's store, used his home as a station on the underground railroad. Dr. Pettit was president of the large and active local antislavery society. In the Cushing household there was no equivocation on the issue of slavery. To them, the institution was morally wrong.[68]

The people of western New York took time away from the momentous issues that threatened to divide the nation for a brief while in the spring of 1851. Dignitaries and common folk alike swarmed into Fredonia and Dunkirk to celebrate the opening of the New York & Erie Railroad. Chartered in 1832, the newly completed railroad connected Piermont, New York, on the west bank of the Hudson River north of New York City, with Goshen, Middletown, Port Jervis, Binghamton, Owego, Elmira, Corning, and Dunkirk. The long rail line, with its connections up the Hudson to Newburgh, New York, and south to Jersey City, New Jersey, it was said, would make the "old" Erie Canal obsolete.[69]

Back in Putnam, Ohio, Lon's half brothers and half sister had struggled to establish themselves. Benjamin had never married; having passed the bar in 1848, he had attempted practicing law in Columbus, but like his father at that age, he had not been well enough to endure the rigors of the law practice. What had sustained him was his love of writing poetry and prose, at which he had become most accomplished. Edward, who had become a physician of considerable talent in Putnam, had married Mary Burr of Wilmington, North Carolina. By 1850, the couple had a son named Edward. The two promising young men, tragically, did not live to fulfill everyone's predictions of greatness. The Cushing household learned that Benjamin Tupper, after an extended trip to the Atlantic coast to "take the cure" for his tuberculosis, had died in Putnam in 1850. Less than two years later, Mary and her children would hear of the death of twenty-five-year-old Edward, also of tuberculosis. Rowena, after living in Putnam for several years and marrying an Asa A. Brown, had moved to Wilmington, North Carolina. In 1858 she too would die of tuberculosis at the age of twenty-nine.[70]

Mary's own children were growing up. The older ones began to seek life's fortunes. By 1854, Milton, Jr., though not well, left Fredonia and journeyed to Fitchburg, Massachusetts. There, assisted by Mary's sisters and their families and putting to use his training under his cousin Devillo White, he was learning to become a pharmacist. Howard, sickly himself, moved back to Chicago. There was opportunity in that fast-growing city. His experience working as a printer's devil for the *Fredonia Censor* had been decisive; he wanted to enter the newspaper business. On the Wisconsin frontier and in Chicago, Mary had had as many as seven children under her roof at one time; she was now down to three.[71]

Soon Lon was old enough to attend the Fredonia Academy. The school was a special place to the Cushings. Zattu had encouraged its development in 1826, the year of its founding. The academy building, located at the corner of Temple and Church streets, was a simple two-story frame structure with a central bell spire. So excellent was the instruction at the academy that it drew students from all over western New York. In fact, by 1839 there were students from Canada and thirteen states and territories. Many of the out-of-state students were the children of families that had moved away from western New York years before. Some of the Academy's graduates had gone on to the best schools in the East. At the time Alonzo attended classes at the academy, there were just under two hundred male and 125 female students. The "Female Department" was separately operated, having its own principal and instructors and classrooms. Tuition was four dollars per term, and students were instructed in reading, writing, surveying, English, grammar, geography, history, rhetoric, composition, logic, natural and moral philosophy, and the French, Latin, and Greek languages. Religious exercises were held every day at the beginning of classes, and students were required to attend public worship every Sunday. Although the boys' and girls' classes were separated, recitations were delivered and compositions were read by all the students together every Friday afternoon.

Lon performed well at the academy. As all students were expected to do, he attended classes for six hours each day, then went home to study for up to five hours every evening. He began to learn self-discipline and the merits of hard work.[72] When not attending classes, Lon worked in Devillo White's grocery and drug store, as his brother Milton had done. William, like his brother Howard, worked in the office of the *Fredonia Censor* across the street. What money the boys earned was turned over to Mary and used for necessities.[73]

One week each summer Lon got to spend on the Silver Creek, New York, farm of Ellen Cumming Cushing, known as "Fanny," the second wife of his Uncle Addison. Lon looked forward to the little respite with great relish every year; it was something of a "vacation," even though he earned his keep there by assisting his aunt and uncle on the farm. Work was often turned into play, however, as wagon trips were diverted for purposes of picking berries, and field chores became times of frolic and fun.[74] At home during the summer months, Lon enjoyed the company of friends and, as he grew older, the company of young ladies as well. One summer evening he escorted Julia Greenleaf, for whom he seemed to show special affection, down to the Stoddard's mill pond near Canadaway Creek behind the town. He had asked her to take a row in "a forlorn old scow," which, apparently, was much patronized by the young people of Fredonia. When Lon and Julia reached the bank, they found that someone had untied the boat and set it adrift. Since there was no other boat, the two sat down on the bank, wondering if someone had tricked them out of their row. Soon they heard a wild whoop in the distance and saw Will Cushing waving an oar and shouting, "Next time you want to row, do not forget to ask your friends."[75]

Not long after the attempted boat ride, Lon asked Julia to accompany him to a Methodist prayer meeting. The Methodists were known as the most strict of all the religious denominations in Fredonia; card playing and dancing were forbidden by them. With her own stern adherence to piety, it is not surprising that Mary Cushing encouraged her children to attend Methodist services. On this occasion, as expected, Will offered to accompany his brother and Julia. Lon quickly declined the "pleasure" of Will's company. William, it seemed, acceded with some grace, and Lon thought he at last had Julia to himself. After the two young people were seated in the meeting house, Will slipped into the sanctuary and took a seat behind them. When the first hymn was being sung, Lon and his girlfriend were shocked to hear Will's familiar voice shouting out rather personal remarks to the tune of the hymn. The sexton heard the commotion, grabbed the rambunctious lad, and in front of the entire congregation—and to Lon's complete embarrassment—led William out of the meeting house.[76]

Few years before the Civil War were more turbulent than the year 1854. In January, Stephen A. Douglas, as chairman of the Senate Committee on Territories, reported a bill to organize the Territory of Nebraska which called for permitting the people of the new territory to decide the slavery issue for themselves. The proposal caused an explosion of emotion. Northerners were outraged; there were cries from them not to enforce the fugitive slave law in retaliation. Southerners responded to Yankee, abolitionist rhetoric with invective unlike anything heard before. The territory was divided into Kansas and Nebraska in an unsuccessful attempt to pacify both sides. In February, a new Republican Party was organized in Ripon, Wisconsin, to rally both old line antislavery Whigs and angry Democrats against the proponents of the Kansas-Nebraska bill. In spite of the storm, the bill passed both houses of Congress on May 25, 1854, and President Franklin Pierce signed it into law. By midsummer Kansas had become a battleground in the wake of the rush to populate the territory by those favoring both sides of the slavery debate. Gangs of Free-Soilers and proslavery "border ruffians" fought pitched battles over settlement rights and political differences.[77]

The year 1854 proved to be one of reaction for the Cushings wholly apart from the questions of slavery and secession. Beginning in the 1840s, immigrants from Ireland, Germany, and Eastern Europe had poured into the United States in the wake of famine, economic failure, and political upheaval overseas. In Ireland, nearly every potato harvest between 1845 and 1855 failed. As potatoes were the staple food of the island, the famine resulted in over one million deaths and an exodus of nearly two million Irish to America. Many arrived in the New World impoverished and starved or dreadfully ill. Equal numbers of Germans, uprooted by revolutions, crop failures, and the economic collapse of many German states, poured into America. For the most part, the new immigrants brought

Cadet Captain Alonzo Hereford Cushing, West Point class of June 1861, at about the time of his graduation. United States Military Academy.

Left: Judge Zattu Cushing, whose portrait is displayed in the Chautauqua County, New York, Courthouse. Darwin R. Barker Library and Museum. *Right:* Mary Barker Cushing, known as "Little Ma." Wisconsin Historical Society.

An ambrotype of Rowena Sophia Cushing, half-sister of Alonzo, c. 1856, the only known likeness of any of the children of Milton Buckingham Cushing and Abigail Browning (Tupper) Cushing. Larry Sanford Collections, Beloit, Wisconsin.

Three of Alonzo's brothers also served in the Civil War. *Above left:* Lt. Howard Bass Cushing, 4th United States Artillery, c. 1865. United States Military History Institute. *Above right:* Lt. Milton Buckingham Cushing, Jr., U.S.N. Wisconsin Historical Society. *Right:* Lt. Comm. William Barker Cushing, U.S.N., c. 1864. National Archives.

Main Street, Fredonia, New York, c. 1867, showing the Dudley and Centre Block buildings. The complex housed Devillo A. White's grocery and drug store, where Alonzo worked (second door from the left), and Philo H. Stevens's dry goods store (third door from the left). Darwin R. Barker Library and Museum.

Commodore Joseph Smith, above, and Gen. Winfield Scott, right. Both from Library of Congress.

Above: The Cadet chapel (right) and the Library and Post Headquarters at West Point. *Below:* West Point, c. 1859, as seen from Fort Putnam. To the left is the 1850 Barracks. The long building with the square tower at right is the Academy Building. Behind it the roof of the Cadet Chapel and the Library and Post Headquarters are visible. Across the Plain is the West Point Hotel. Both from United States Military Academy.

Three of Alonzo Cushing's West Point classmates.

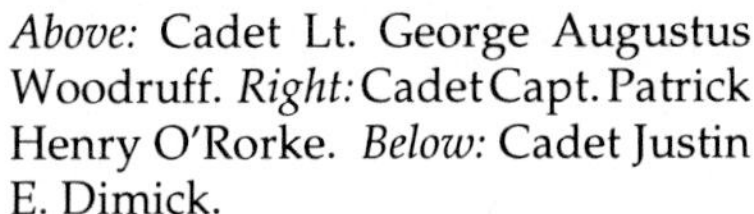

Above: Cadet Lt. George Augustus Woodruff. *Right:* Cadet Capt. Patrick Henry O'Rorke. *Below:* Cadet Justin E. Dimick.

Photos from United States Military Academy.

Three other fellow West Point cadets. *Above:* Cadet Capt. Edmund Kirby, class of May 1861. *Right*: Cadet Charles Edward Hazlett, class of May 1861. *Below:* Cadet George Armstrong Custer, class of June 1861. All from United States Military Academy.

The grave of Lt. Col. Alonzo Hereford Cushing (left) in the West Point Cemetery. The stone was erected by his mother. Construction of the large memorial to Gen. John Buford at right severely damaged Cushing's gravesite. Col. Frank B. von Borries Collections, Lexington, Kentucky.

with them their Catholic faith; some radicals from Germany and Eastern Europe brought as well the political philosophies of such thinkers as Friedrich Engels and Karl Marx. Most native-born Americans were deeply apprehensive of these new citizens. A visit from a rather tactless papal nuncio had convinced many that the nation was in danger of interference from Rome. The impoverished state of the new immigrants in America's growing cities precipitated widespread crime and violence, and it did not take long for riots to break out. Among native-born Americans, particularly New England Puritans like the Cushings, anti-Catholic and anti-foreign feelings ran rather high.[78]

As a consequence of the heavy immigration and the rise of the number of practicing Catholics in the nation, native-born Protestants formed the secret "Order of the Star Spangled Banner," complete with an elaborate ritual and discipline. To inquiries about the organization, members universally responded, "I know nothing." Soon secretly nominated "Know-Nothing" or American Party candidates appeared on election ballots across the country, and their strength at the polls proved to be surprisingly great.[79]

Since waves of immigrants, largely Irish and German, poured into New York City, New York state was ripe for the Know-Nothings. Populated largely by native-born Americans, many of whom had migrated there from New England, the state was thoroughly Protestant. Many New Yorkers, descendants of early Puritan settlers, adhered to the precepts of very conservative religious sects. The faith of native-born New Yorkers of German or Dutch ancestry had been formulated early in the Reformation, and they carried deep-seated fears of papal influence. Ever since the opening of the Erie Canal, the religious conservatism particularly of those living in what was called the "Burned-over District" had been augmented by the myriad of preachers and preachings making their way through the area, each preacher and sermon, it seemed, more fundamental than the previous one.

In 1854 lawyer Francis Smith Edwards, a kinsman with whom the Cushings were very close, was nominated by the Know-Nothings to run for Congress from western New York's thirty-third congressional district. Edwards won his election to Congress handily and took his seat on March 4, 1855. Statewide, the Know-Nothings very nearly won a majority of the seats in the New York assembly; in neighboring Massachusetts they did actually capture a majority in the state legislature.[80]

Mary Cushing, like most of her greater family and many of her neighbors, embraced the principles of the Know-Nothing Party. One wonders, of course, whether Mary Cushing and those others who advocated the nativist principles of the Know-Nothing Party in 1854 recognized the irony of their position. Staunchly in favor of the abolition of slavery for the blacks, they nevertheless rallied against the "foreigners" and "Catholics." But Mary was a product of her family's history and religion. Family, church, and community were virtually one and the same to her. The massive influx of immigrants, whose religion and political philosophies were, in her mind, those against which her early Puritan ancestors had rebelled, was deeply disturbing to her.

Edwards's congressional victory caused rejoicing within the Cushing household, as a victory against "foreign" and papal influence as well as an honor to the family. His victory became a turning point for Mary Cushing's two young boys. Because of their poverty, the only way Lon and Will could continue their education beyond Fredonia Academy would be to attend West Point or Annapolis. The service academies, although egalitarian in theory, were still havens for the sons of native families of influence. That was important to Mary. Edwards's victory meant that Lon and Will, at least, would have the chance to further their education.

In 1855 Congressman Edwards asked William to accompany him to Washington to serve as a page in the House of Representatives. The day of Will's departure probably was a sad one for Lon, but Mary thought the experience would be good for William. He would get away from Fredonia; maybe he would grow up a little and become a little less rebellious. William worked in Washington with Congressman Edwards for the entire year. It was said he became universally popular with all the congressmen.[81]

Lon had worked hard at school and performed well in his final term at the Fredonia Academy. Mary asked Congressman Edwards if he could try to secure an appointment to West Point for Lon and an appointment to Annapolis for Will the following year. Edwards agreed, but determined that he would recommend them both the same year. Mary also wrote to her cousins Commodore Joseph Smith and Albert Smith, seeking their assistance. Joseph, since 1846, had been serving as chief of the Bureau of Navy Yards and Docks in Washington, D.C., a most prestigious position in the Navy Department. Albert had become a prominent lawyer in Washington. Both were close friends of the army's General-in-Chief Winfield Scott.[82]

Will returned from Washington and re-enrolled in the Fredonia Academy in the fall of 1856, and Lon, even though he had completed his course studies at the Academy in May, signed up for another term.[83]

But a presidential election dominated the news in that year. More important, Congressman Edwards was up for reelection. In November the Democratic presidential candidate, James Buchanan, was swept into office; the Know-Nothings were crushed and Edwards was defeated.[84] Nevertheless, on December 1, 1856, Francis Edwards, as a lame-duck congressman, formally recommended the appointment of Alonzo Hereford Cushing to fill a vacancy in the next class of cadets at the United States Military Academy. Edwards wrote to the War Department not only giving Lon a warm personal endorsement, but informing it of the boy's family ties to both the Honorable Caleb Cushing (then U.S. attorney general) and Commodore Joseph Smith. "His mother is poor," wrote Edwards, "but highly committed and her son will do honor to the position." Albert and Joseph Smith and their friend General Scott apparently provided the necessary additional assistance on behalf of Lon's application.[85]

Lon spent an anxious Christmas awaiting news, and finally, in late January 1857, the long-awaited notice arrived: he had been conditionally appointed a cadet on January 16 (all appointments to the United States Military Academy were conditional then). With the announcement came a circular over the printed name of Secretary of War Jefferson Davis which stated that only about one-third of those who entered the academy actually would be graduated, and that unless the appointee had an aptitude for mathematics and science, he should not accept the appointment. Lon was unshaken. Mary was overjoyed. Taking with them the printed acknowledgment and acceptance to be signed by the applicant and his parent or guardian and returned to the secretary of war. Lon and his mother walked downtown to the office of cousin Allen Hinckley, a justice of the peace, to acknowledge and accept the appointment officially in Hinckley's presence.[86] When the time came to sign the document, Lon, reflecting his dislike for the name Alonzo—and, undoubtedly to his mother's complete displeasure—penned the name "Alfred A. Cushing." Mary dutifully inscribed her name to the acceptance as "Alfred's" mother. Allen Hinckley must have been somewhat puzzled as he certified the "genuineness" of the signatures.[87]

The Cushings were soon doubly indebted to Francis Edwards that winter for, through his assistance and that of Mary's cousins, William was conditionally appointed a midshipman in the entering class at the United States Naval Academy.[88] Mary had been able to secure for her two young sons the opportunity for superlative educations. Of all things in life outside of her children's religious faith and devotion to family, their education was the most important to her.

For the two young boys, the spring of 1857 brought days of soaring pride as well as growing apprehension about what was ahead for them at West Point and Annapolis. As always, it seemed, Lon's first concern was whether he would make his mother and family proud of him. As he wrote to Congressman Edwards: "I hope I may be able to do honor to the position."[89]

2

"I Am Boning Everything"

Finally the day came for Lon and William to leave Fredonia. They had visited everyone they knew, bidding good-bye to all. Cousin George White drove the two boys in his carriage, along with Mary and Mary Isabel, the three miles to the New York & Erie Railroad depot at Dunkirk.[1] As the train chugged and hissed into the depot, Lon and Will bade farewell to their dear mother and sister. The boys were well on their way to restoring to the Cushing family that great sense of accomplishment it had known in earlier generations. The old pioneer, Zattu, certainly would have been proud, as would their father Milton.

The train rumbled east to Corning and Elmira and then passed through southern New York state, just above the Pennsylvania border, all the way to Middletown, Goshen, and Piermont, where Lon and Will got off. The boys mutually pledged that they would stay in touch. Lon, with almost fatherlike sternness, reminded his brother to behave himself, study hard, and not let the family—or himself—down. With warm goodbyes, Will took a train south to Baltimore and Annapolis, Maryland. Lon, sixteen years old and on his own for the first time in his life, obtained passage aboard a steamboat for the short trip up the Hudson to West Point.

The Hudson, busy with commercial vessels plying their way between New York City and Albany, presented an awe-inspiring spectacle to the young lad. Before long the boat entered that part of the river known as the "Highlands," where the mountains, forests, and overhanging cliffs were serene and majestic. After a while Lon heard other passengers cry out, "There is West Point!" Straining to catch a view of the famous citadel, he spied the great red, white, and blue garrison flag fluttering in the distance. He looked at the hills around West Point and the great river ahead. This was where Lon's great, great-uncle, Brig. Maj. Nathaniel Cushing, as well as Gen. Rufus Putnam and Col. and Bvt. Brig. Gen. Benjamin Tupper, had helped keep the Hudson free from British control during the Revolution. He had heard so much about those illustrious members of his family.

The steamboat pulled alongside West Point's south dock, and Lon, carpetbag in hand, boarded a horse-drawn bus in the company of other newly arrived cadet candidates. The long gravel road wound past the stone Riding Hall and up the precipitous bluff along the summit of which sprawled the great stone academy buildings. When the bus reached the summit, Lon could see the Plain and, to his left, the domed Library-Post Headquarters. Ahead were the giant Academy Building and the 1850 Barracks with its gothic turrets; farther on was the Mess Hall. Nestled between the Academy Building and the Library was the Cadet Chapel with its simple Greek revival portico and four fluted Doric columns, "the only one of all the buildings enthroned with tenderness in a cadet's memory." Across the Plain, on the edge of the bluff, was the West Point Hotel. Row upon row of white tents were set up along the edge of the Plain near the site of old Fort Clinton for the cadets' summer encampment.[2]

Lon reported for duty in the Library-Post Headquarters building where he provided the post adjutant, Lt. James B. Fry, 1st United States Artillery, with the necessary information: his name, age, parents' names and residence, and so on. There, it seems, Lon's use of the name "Alfred" ended forever; on rigid questioning, he informed the adjutant that his real name was Alonzo. The new candidate, in the company of other new arrivals, then followed an orderly outside, past the Chapel and the Academy Building, and into the cold, dark, austere 1850 Barracks. Lon was met by several cadet officers who yelled at him: "Stand at attention!" The cocky "yearling" cadets tongue-lashed him for not tucking in his chin and squaring his shoulders; they referred to him and the other new arrivals as "animals." Life at West Point had begun in earnest for young Alonzo Hereford Cushing.[3]

Lon was assigned to a barracks room with three other candidates. The room had a small fireplace with a white-painted wooden mantel. There was only one window. On one wall was a gun rack; against the other wall was a clothes press. The room was otherwise devoid of furniture; the new candidates were to sleep on blankets spread on the floor. One cadet candidate would write later, "My bones ached in the morning as if I had been pounded all night."[4]

Lon's first two weeks at West Point were spent drilling, studying, and attending daily instruction from upper-class cadets in preparation for the entrance examinations. After drill instructions, the candidates were marched to the Mess Hall behind the Academy Building for their meals. They undoubtedly presented a rather ridiculous sight, dressed in all sorts and kinds of civilian clothes, including hats, and wherever they went there would be a sizable number of cadet officers, smartly dressed in their gray coats with three rows of shining brass bell buttons glistening down their chests, counting cadence and reminding the stumbling candidates of their humble station in life. Cadet Candidate William H. Harris wrote to his father, Ira Harris, the newly elected Republican senator from New York, that he and his fellow candidates "drilled three times a day for an hour to an hour and one-half each," which, he complained, "gets rather tiresome."[5]

Lon underwent a physical examination by the Medical Board and then finally, before the Academic Board—which comprised the superintendent, Maj. Richard Delafield; the commandant, Col. William J. Hardee; and seven professors—he was put through the rigors of the academic entrance examination. He was asked to read passages aloud, perform mathematics problems at the blackboard, and take dictation to test his ability to spell. Following this nerve-racking experience he was marched across the Plain to the cadet summer camp and assigned to a tent.[6]

On June 20, 1857, Special Orders No. 90 were read aloud by the post adjutant to the assembled candidates. Sixty-eight of them, including Lon, had been found qualified for admission. On July 1, Lon and the others who had passed the entrance examinations were admitted to the United States Military Academy as plebes; they would not be formally sworn in as cadets until they had successfully passed the semiannual oral examinations in January. The new plebes formed the class of 1862.[7] At the time Lon was admitted, the academic course was five years in length. The five-year program had been inaugurated as an experiment by former Secretary of War Jefferson Davis, and under it the classes of 1859, 1860, and 1861 would be graduated. Lon and his classmates, however, as a result of the outbreak of the Civil War, would experience an abbreviated year as First Classmen: they would be relieved from duty at West Point after a two-month "fifth year" which began on May 6 and ended on June 24, 1861.[8]

As a plebe, Lon busied himself with his duties at summer camp. He was paid thirty dollars a month, and out of this meager sum he acquired his uniforms and accoutrements—shoes; gray swallowtail dress coat; white cross-shoulder belts; black shako with pompon; trousers; cartridge and cap boxes, and weapons. Anything remaining out of his pay was credited to his account at the academy. Upon graduation, he would turn much of his account over to his mother, just as he had done with whatever money he had earned as a boy in Fredonia.[9]

Lon quickly learned the meaning of the various drumbeats that signaled the events of each and every day at West Point. When the morning gun announced reveille, the cadets rolled out of bed to the sound of a long roll from the drummers. They were then drummed to breakfast, sick call, and assembly. Twice a day the commands of the post adjutant were heard above the drum rolls calling the cadets to drill. After supper, to the drummers' cadence, the cadets returned to their quarters. Even "lights out" was yelled by the guards over the sound of a drumbeat.

Like all plebes, Lon received his share of demerits early on. The first recorded against him were dated July 16, 1857, when he was given two for "repeatedly failing to come to an order properly at parade." Two days later, he was "late at parade." By summer's end he had accumulated fourteen "skins," as they were often called. The worst infraction occurred while on guard duty shortly after ten o'clock at night, August 21, when he was cited for "not coming to arms post when addressed by [the] officer of the day."[10]

With the end of summer camp, classes began in earnest. The cadets moved back into the barracks, two to a room. Iron bedsteads with mattresses were brought in; the days of sleeping on the floor were over. A washstand, table, two straight chairs, two water buckets, and a lamp finished out the quarters. The accommodations were austere but nevertheless palatial compared with those of the first two weeks in June.[11]

The emphasis of instruction at West Point was on subjects necessary to the art of military engineering. Mathematics (algebra, geometry, and calculus), engineering, French (because most great military engineering treatises were written by French officers), and English formed the core of a curriculum that was filled out with drawing, Spanish, philosophy, chemistry, and practical military studies. Class records indicate that Lon struggled academically during his Fifth Class year, but he passed his midyear orals, which was all that mattered to him at the time. Before Post Adjutant Fry and Charles Drake, clerk of the Orange County Court in Goshen, New York, Lon and his classmates were administered the oath of allegiance on February 6, 1858.[12]

The upper classes contained many notable personalities who would play pivotal roles during the Civil War. In the class of 1858 were Cadets Horace Porter, James H. Wilson, Alanson M. Randol, Stephen Dodson Ramseur, Alexander C.M. Pennington, and Wesley Merritt. Another member of that class was Lon's cousin Samuel Tobey Cushing of Providence, Rhode Island. In the class of 1859 were Cadets Norman J. Hall, Edwin H. Stoughton, and Joseph Wheeler.[13]

Even though a common sufferer of hazing like all plebes, Lon became close with many upperclassmen. One of those he grew to admire was Edmund Kirby, nicknamed "Ned," a native of Brownsville, New York, who was the youngest son of Mexican War veteran Bvt. Col. and Paymaster Edmund Kirby. Kirby became a cadet corporal in 1858 and sergeant major the following year; in 1860 he would be named a lieutenant and then a captain in the Corps.[14] Kirby's classmate Charles Edward Hazlett, born in Putnam, Ohio, in 1838, also became a close friend to Lon.

Charlie Hazlett was the son of Robert and Lucy Hazlett, who had been friends and supporters of Alonzo's father in the abolition movement; Charlie's older brother John, a young lawyer in Zanesville, had taken up the abolitionist torch where Milton and his family had left off. Charlie would have known Lon's half brothers and sister, Benjamin, Edward, and Rowena, as well as his Aunt Rachel Cushing and her husband, Edward W. Tupper. And, of course, he would have known all the Buckinghams. Sandy-haired and refined-looking, Hazlett had been suspended once from the academy after being court-martialed for failing to obey direct orders. Reentering West Point in 1856, he had settled down somewhat. He liked music, and throughout his cadet years he was often reported for playing an instrument—probably a banjo—in his quarters after hours. He was doing well in both academics and military studies, however; he had been named a color corporal and went on to become color sergeant and a lieutenant in the Corps of Cadets.[15]

Another close acquaintance of Lon's was Justin E. Dimick of New Hampshire. A real discipline problem, he was the son of Mexican War veteran Lt. Col. Justin Dimick of the 1st United States Artillery, a member of the West Point Class of 1815.[16] Kirby and Hazlett would be graduated in the class of May 1861, which included such notable personalities as Cadets John Pelham, William H. Elderkin, Adelbert Ames, Emory Upton, Thomas L. Rosser, Nathaniel R. Chambliss, Robert Franklin Beckham, Orville E. Babcock, Henry R. DuPont, and Hugh Judson Kilpatrick. Dimick, however, because of academic and conduct trouble, would complete his career at West Point with Lon's class.

In Lon's class too there were those who would win eternal fame. Patrick Henry O'Rorke of New York was certainly the "brains" of the class from the beginning. Born in 1836 in County Cavon, Ireland, of medium size, "with raven-black hair and his face inclined to freckles," O'Rorke was several years older than his classmates. In fact, he was the oldest lad ever to enter the academy. His family had settled in the Irish section of Rochester, New York, known as "Dublin." He had turned down a scholarship to Rochester University because of his mother's objections to its non-Catholic administration and had apprenticed instead to learn the trade of a marble cutter. Then his local congressman, after hearing glowing remarks about the young man's academic proficiency, offered him an appointment to the academy. O'Rorke was blessed with a warm and endearing personality; he quickly became known as "Paddy" or "Pat" to his classmates, though Lon's New England Puritan background very likely restrained him from accepting the famine Irish O'Rorke at first.[17] At the other end of the academic spectrum was George Armstrong Custer from Monroe, Michigan, known to his classmates as "Fannie." Custer continually stood at the bottom of his class, a rank reserved for those called the "immortals," and courted trouble on a regular basis. Yet, as expected of a young man like Fannie Custer, he would become well liked.[18]

George Augustus Woodruff, known as "Little Dad," was reputedly one of the smallest cadets (five feet tall) ever to be admitted to the academy. Born in Marshall, Michigan, in 1840 to George and Augusta Schuyler Woodruff, Little Dad hailed from an illustrious family. His paternal great-grandfather had been a regimental commander in the Continental Army, and his mother was related to Revolutionary War Maj. Gen. Philip Schuyler of New York. Like Lon, Woodruff had been raised in a deeply religious—indeed, pious—family. Despite his small size and somewhat retiring personality, Little Dad, when the occasion demanded, easily commanded attention.[19]

Other classmates and close acquaintances of Lon's were Charles C. Parsons of Ohio; and William H. Harris of New York; Stephen C. Lyford of New Hampshire; Lawrence S. Babbitt of Massachusetts, son of Capt. and Assistant Quartermaster Edwin B. Babbitt of the class of 1825; John R. Edie of Pennsylvania; Joseph P. Farley of the District of Columbia, son of Capt. John Farley of the class of 1819; James P. Drouillard of Ohio; and James Dearing of Virginia. But probably Lon's closest friends in his class were Henry E. Noyes and Eugene Carter of Maine, James H. Lord of Pennsylvania, and Samuel P. Ferris of Connecticut. None of these cadets came from army families; rather, their backgrounds appear to have been similar to Lon's, which may well have been the initial reason for their friendship. To be sure, one reason Lon liked Noyes, Lord, Carter and Ferris was that they knew how to have a good time. None of them would star academically; more often they would rank among the "immortals" of the class. They liked to socialize and were particularly fond of playing cards; they quickly got Lon hooked on the game of whist.[20]

One gets the impression that this foursome may have distracted Lon from his studies too much. James Lord, dropped from Lon's class because of academic troubles, was readmitted but would not be graduated until June 1862. This rather small, baby-faced fellow once wagered that he could actually be reported for wearing a mustache. Lon and the others took him up on the bet, thinking he would never be able to grow one. Lord tried and was in fact caught, but he lost the gamble anyway, for he was reported for the very unmilitary offense of "trying to have some hair on [his] upper lip!"[21] Samuel Ferris would be Lon's most frequent roommate. An avid cardplayer, he would miss being last in the class only by the failure of two Southerners—George O. Watts of Kentucky and Frank A. Reynolds of Virginia—to resign before graduation and by the George Armstrong Custer hold on that position.[22]

By the end of his first year, Lon stood forty-seventh out of a class of sixty-eight members in mathematics, thirty-second in English, and fortieth in Order of General Merit. He had "earned" sixty-one demerits—at a time when one hundred demerits in any six-month period would mean expulsion from the academy. Most of Lon's delinquencies arose from his lateness at reveille, parade, or formation, or from the way he took care—or failed to take care—of his quarters. He was cited for "laughing in ranks," breaking the glass out of the window in his room, defacing his barracks door by writing on it in pencil; on one occasion, he was given a skin for "tobacco spittle" on the floor, evidence that he chewed tobacco. Many of his delinquencies arose from keeping his light burning after taps, an infraction in part necessitated by his struggle to keep up with West Point's academic demands.[23]

Following the graduation in May of the class of 1858, Lon was no longer an "animal"; he and his classmates were "yearlings" at last! In June the new cadet candidates arrived, among them a number of boys who would cross paths with Lon in the future: Samuel M. Mansfield of Connecticut, son of Col. Joseph King Fenno Mansfield of the class of 1822; Tully McCrea of Ohio; John Egan of Vermont; John Calef of Massachusetts; and Ranald S. Mackenzie of New Jersey. Lon at last had his chance to "devil" the new arrivals as he had been deviled over the previous year, and he seems to have plunged with enthusiasm into the task of making the lives of the new candidates as miserable as possible. It is hard to tell, though, who pounced on the entering candidates more quickly—Cushing or Custer. George Custer and George Watts, one night in June 1858, sneaked into the division of the barracks where the animals slept. Expecting trouble, the young cadet candidates in one room had piled tin wash basins on top of chairs in front of their door. When Custer opened the door, the metal basins fell, making a terrific racket. A deathly silence fell, and Custer later confessed that his heart "beat like an engine" in fear of being caught. The danger soon passed, and Fannie and his Kentucky friend pushed in. "Who lives here?" asked Watts. Cadet candidate Kenelm Robbins of Massachusetts cried out, "Mr. Robbins!" Watts then barked, "Good God, Mr. Robbins, come out of this!" He grabbed Robbins by the armpits, and down the hall they went. Cadet candidate Reuben A. Higgason of Mississippi was next, Custer dragging him by the ankles. The two were tormented through the wee hours. Poor Robbins returned to his room "speechless," but Higgason "opened every stop of his oath-organ, and he kept it going" apparently until reveille.[24]

Lon, quickly in the thick of things like Custer, was not as lucky. On June 14, 1858, he was found by the officer of the day terrorizing the new candidates in their barracks rooms at 3:00 A.M.! He was placed under arrest and kept under guard for five days. On June 18 he even received three demerits, as a prisoner, for not obeying orders to parade with his guard for the officer in charge. On June 19, Special Orders Number 89 announced that Cushing was "released from arrest." The experience, however humilitating, did not deter Lon from seeking more fun at the expense of the animals.[25] One cadet remembered that yearlings Cushing, Custer, Edie, Noyes, and others would gather around one of the animals from the state of Maine—probably Jared A. Smith, who was a "serious, rather broad and loggy country man"—and insist on examining the workings of the large, double-cased silver watch he always carried. The devilish yearlings would hold it to their ears, insisting that they wanted to hear it ticking. Never did they tire of having that poor boy wind that watch or explain who last repaired it. They would, almost daily, escort the young cadet candidate out to a sundial near the center campus where they would "discover" that the massive silver timepiece was not accurately keeping up with the sun's time. Each day they threatened to report the young man for "carrying a time piece that discredited the official time, and thereby reflected on [him] as [an] officer of the army." Recalled an observer, "I can see the crowd around [the candidate], and more mischievous circumstances never twinkled in a light-hearted group."[26]

Cadet candidate Morris Schaff was spotted by Lon one evening after dinner, leaning against a post in front of the barracks; he appeared lonely. Cushing was in the middle of a group of yearlings, all sporting their brass buttons and jaunty blue forage caps. He stepped in front of Schaff and asked, his prominent white teeth gleaming through his radiant smile, "What is your name, Animal?"

"Schaff," the young boy responded.

"Come right down here, Mr. Shad," said Lon. The candidate was then conducted to a room in the barracks where he was ordered by Lon and his yearling friends to debate the repeal of the Missouri Compromise with another candidate from Illinois "whose eyes," Schaff recalled, "were so large and white as almost to prolong twilight."[27]

While Schaff was sitting opposite his friend from Illinois at supper the next day, Lon—scanning the room to make sure the First Captain was not looking—hurled a boiled potato at him. The potato grazed Schaff's ear and landed with an enormous splash in the Illinois candidate's soup. Seeing the approaching "missile," the lad had closed his eyes; the splatter opened them so wide, Schaff recalled, as to display an "additional zone of white."[28] Lon's love of deviling plebes never left him. As late as six days before his graduation, he would be caught "loitering in the vicinity of a prisoner's tent" at around 7:00 P.M. during the summer encampment. Even then, he was up to no good.[29]

Custer must have reminded Lon of his brother Will. Fannie was constantly courting trouble. In a style reminiscent of William Cushing, Custer one day in Spanish class asked Professor Patrice de Janon how a

Spaniard would say "Class is dismissed." When the professor uttered the phrase in Spanish, Custer got up and led the whole class out of the room. On one occasion it is known that Fannie crept out of the barracks, stole an annoying rooster, he had heard crowing not far from the campus, returned with his prize, and plucked and cooked the bird in his barracks room fireplace. The barracks trash can was filled with feathers and bones; the officer of the day could never find the culprit who had made the mess, but Custer was given skins for keeping "bread, butter, potatoes, plates, knives and forks" in his fireplace. Cadet Tully McCrea, later a roommate of Custer's, best summed up Fannie's experience at West Point: "The great difficulty is that he is too clever for his own good. He's always connected with all the mischief that is going on and never studies any more than he can possibly help."[30]

The favorite rendezvous of the cadets was Benny Havens, a saloon near Buttermilk Falls, about one mile south of the post. The tavern had been removed from the post area some years before for selling "liquors and viands" instead of coffee to the cadets and was strictly "off limits." As one could guess, though, it had become a true institution. Custer, Dimick, Ferris, and others would often climb out of their barracks room windows after lights out and spend the evening there. George Woodruff, in 1859, carefully recorded in a notebook the story of Benny Havens, including eighteen verses of a song called "Benny Havens Oh!" which he noted was "extremely popular with all who learned the way to Benny's during the cadet life."

Come tune your voices comrades and stand up in a row
For to singing sentimentally we're going for to go
In the Army there's sobriety, promotion's very slow
So we'll sign our reminiscences of Benny Havens Oh!
    Oh! Benny Havens Oh!
    Oh! Benny Havens Oh!
So we'll sign our reminiscences of Benny Havens Oh!

Let us toast our foster father, the Republic, as
    you know
Who in the paths of science taught us upwards for
    to go,
And then the maidens of our land whose cheeks with
    roses glow
Whose smiles and tears were sung with cheers at
    Benny Havens Oh!
    Oh! Benny Havens Oh!
    Oh! Benny Havens Oh!
Whose smiles and tears were sung with cheers at
    Benny Havens Oh![31]

Another cadet whose good times got him in trouble was Justin Dimick. Entering his class in ethics before his instructor arrived, he shouted, "The virtues are what we are, the duties are what we do, what we are is more important than what we do. Thus the virtues are more important than the duties." With that, Dimick threw his textbook across the room, smashing a windowpane just as the professor, stern and unpopular Reverend John W. French, entered. "Mr. Dimick," French said, "make it your duty to pick up that glass." Dimick sheepishly obeyed, picking up the glass fragments. "Now, sir," the angry professor said, "go to the blackboard and discuss the subject of virtue." Dimick did so. Then French pronounced the inevitable: "Go to your quarters in arrest, Mr. Dimick." Dimick would be turned back in June 1858, reenter the academy only to be dismissed in March 1859, and then be reinstated again. Certainly, each time he was in trouble his cause was aided by his noted father.[32]

In the fall of 1858 the nation's attention was captured by a race for the United States Senate in Illinois. A prairie lawyer by the name of Abraham Lincoln, who had come out of obscurity ten years after a most unsuccessful single term in the House of Representatives, had challenged incumbent Stephen A. Douglas for the Senate seat. The great crisis over the expansion of slavery became concentrated on that Illinois race. Lon read the newspapers with keen interest. Know-Nothingism was all but dead and gone, but he must have been guarded about Lincoln, though to be sure, he supported Lincoln's opposition to the expansion of slavery.[33]

Lon's second Christmas and New Year were spent at the academy; the holidays were little different from those of the year before. The roast turkey at supper on Christmas day made the season stand out. Lon loved Christmas. From West Point he once wrote to his brother Will: "Christmas is near at hand and I am anxiously awaiting for the good dinner, and I am going to eat at least one pound of roast turkey, and any quantity of cranberry sauce and such things." Throughout his life, Christmas was his favorite time of year, and turkey was his favorite meal. Undoubtedly, though, Lon's thoughts mirrored those of Cadet Tully McCrea. "The joy of Christmas dinner," McCrea wrote, "depends upon where it is eaten; the greatest pleasure is in being at home, surrounded by those we love." On Christmas night and New Year's eve there were "hops" in the gymnasium. As usual, there were no girls to dance with the cadets, so the cadets danced with one another. Lon waltzed at times with James Dearing, Adelbert Ames, Peter C. Hains of Pennsylvania, and others.[34]

Amusement during the winter months was often found in sledding or skating. At times cadets could skate across the river to Cold Spring or Garrison, New York. Often Lon would journey up to old Fort Putnam, the great stone fort above the academy built under the direction of Gen.

Rufus Putnam. He would recall that his half brothers and half sisters—all of whom were dead by 1858—had been the great-grandsons and great-granddaughters of the famed Revolutionary War hero.

The cadets many times used idle moments for pleasure reading. The succession of librarians, Lts. Absalom Baird, Oliver Otis Howard, and John C. Kelton, would allow cadets to check books out on Saturday, to be returned the following Monday. George Woodruff, a voracious reader, was among the most frequent visitors to the Library from Lon's class. Cushing, Custer, and Dearing preferred lighter reading. Lon checked out his first library book on May 1, 1858, nearly one year after he had arrived at the academy. By the time of his graduation, however, he had read at least ten volumes of Scott's Waverley novels and one of Cooper's novels; in addition, he had checked out such books as Dickens's *Barnaby Rudge, Martin Chuzzlewit* and *Sketches by Boz.* Something of a romantic, Lon, like George Woodruff and Charles Hazlett, enjoyed reading *The Age of Chivalry* as well. He did have a serious side. Like many in his class, he read Bourrienne's *Napoleon,* Henry's *Campaign Sketches,* and Alison's *Marlborough.* Probably because his brother was at the Naval Academy, Lon once checked out Cooper's *Naval History*. Only once—April 30, 1861—did he receive a demerit for failing to return a book on time.[35]

Lon showed only modest academic improvement as a Fourth Classman. The class by year's end consisted of eight fewer members than it had at the end of the plebe year. Lon rose to thirty-second in mathematics and was thirty-third in French; in English he dropped to thirty-ninth, and in Order of General Merit he ranked thirty-fifth. But his demerit picture worsened; he was absent from or late at reveille or parade all too many times and seemed to have marked difficulty keeping his shoes "blackened." On May 24, 1859, he was cited for "disobedience of orders, not stepping off at command at drill after repeated orders from the Commander," a serious offense for which he was given five skins. Lon was unhappy about the charge and officially challenged the adverse report, asking that it be stricken from his record. He lost his appeal, although he did sway one vote on the review board. By year's end, he had racked up 135 demerits, more than twice the number he had received as a plebe.[36]

Lon's brother William spent his first two years at the Naval Academy in much the same manner as Alonzo did at West Point. He received ninety-nine demerits in his first year, 188 during his second, and was nearly dismissed from the academy after a midshipman who looked like him was observed climbing out of the house of a young lady in town. The guilty party finally confessed, but it was not surprising to anyone who knew him that Will had been a key suspect. Academically, he was not at the bottom of his class; he showed some promise, but it seems he was constantly sick. Small and rather thin, he suffered from what he described as "consumptive" colds and prolonged weakness that at times kept him confined in bed. He would never get any better; like his father at that same age, he apparently had begun to reveal the symptoms of tuberculosis.[37]

For Lon the end of the academic year in the early summer of 1859 meant one word: "furlough!" It was all that he and his classmates could talk about; it was all they could think about. In anticipation of their first furlough in two years, a song was composed giving ample evidence of the cadets' excitement. Little Dad Woodruff, who may have had a hand in writing the lyrics, penned them in an old scrapbook.

Oh! Furlough men have gone before,
For half a century or more,
But never went a class so fine,
As that which goes in '59.

Oh! Gay and bright, the sunbeams dance
Upon the wine-clad hills of France
Where blushing maidens make the wine
For furlough men of '59.

Oh! Bright are stars, and midnight skies,
But brighter far are women's eyes,
And brighter, softer, yet the[y] shine
On furlough men of '59.

We'll tell the cits some famous lies,
And make them stare in mute surprise;
If they our words in question call,
We'll swallow them, hats, boots, and all.

Some winter's night, when wars the gale,
Shall children list their grandsire's tale,
And hear amazed, the deeds so fine,
Performed by us in '59.[38]

On June 14, 1859, Lon's class was granted its long-awaited furlough until August 28. For the first time in two years he was able to return home to Fredonia. A proud young cadet, he put on his furlough uniform: a long blue frockcoat with its single row of brass buttons. He buttoned the coat tightly under his chin and around his neck tied a black cravat. A high-crowned, floppy blue forage cap with the brass emblem of the academy—a wreath with the letters "U.S.M.A."—fastened on the front topped off the outfit. Lon said farewell to his school friends, then retraced his route of two years before: a steamboat to Piermont, and the New York & Erie Railroad to Dunkirk.[39]

Lon's reunion with his mother and sister was heartfelt and tearful. He spent most of his furlough in the company of his family. Older and in many ways wiser than when he first left Fredonia for West Point, he told family and friends alike the horror stories of being a cadet. He visited Stoddard's mill pond, not far from his humble Green Street home, with his old schoolmates and friends, and sat with his aging aunts and uncles and young cousins telling and retelling his experiences at the great service academy. Lon was not a standout academically; he was struggling. He was proud of himself nevertheless.

William too was on leave of absence for the summer. Lon's and Will's good friend David Parker remembered the two brothers when they returned home. Will, Parker recalled, wore his "smart uniform" and in every way created a "deep impression on his old acquaintances of both sexes."[40] Lon, it seems, became somewhat enamored of one young girl in Fredonia that summer. Who she was is not known. Maybe it was Julia Greenleaf. Lon would refer to the young lady only once in a letter to his mother during the war, but unfortunately for history he failed to name her.[41]

Lon's leave ended sooner than that of his younger brother. When the time came to depart, he was taken to the train depot at Dunkirk by his mother, along with three girlfriends, including the one to whom he was paying special attention. To Lon's dismay, as he was preparing to board the New York & Erie train, he was kissed goodbye by all but the young girl of his affections! The memory of that parting lingered in his mind until the end. As the shrill whistle blew and the train lunged forward, Lon waved to his mother and his friends until Dunkirk faded into the distance.[42] One of Lon's most memorable occasions as a cadet was the cruise up the Hudson with his returning fellow classmates aboard the steamship *Old Broadway*, which he boarded at Piermont. The cadets mobbed the deck of the ship, singing songs and exchanging furlough stories about their homes, their girlfriends, and the adoration they all had received. They were feeling the last breaths of the only freedom they had experienced in two grueling years.[43]

William Cushing left Fredonia at least two days before he had to. What prompted him to do so is unclear. David Parker drove him to the Dunkirk depot, where Will purchased his ticket and checked his trunk. The train was an hour late, so the two boys went over to a "German Saloon" across the street and proceeded to get drunk. When the train finally arrived, Will had to be helped aboard by the conductor, only to discover that while he was in his drunken stupor, his ticket and pocket watch had been stolen. Even though Will had no money, an understanding conductor let him pass through to Piermont and somehow Will made it back to Annapolis in time.[44]

Lon worried about his brother. "I cannot imagine why you started off so soon for," he wrote Will. "You left home at least two days before it was necessary." Concerned about Will's studies, Lon continued: "I suppose you are now back at Annapolis preparing to study hard and just knock spots in everything. You will perhaps feel a little blue for a few days, but that feeling will soon wear off when you get to studying and I want you to do your best boning and see if you cannot acquire a good standing. Bone demerits as well as studies and don't get into any scrapes."[45]

Lon's Third Class year began at 2:00 P.M. on August 28, 1859, when he reported for duty back at the academy. Maybe the visit home had given him some needed incentive, or maybe he was growing up; in any case, 1859-60 proved to be one of his better years at the academy. "I am boning everything," Lon wrote to Will, "and keeping out of all scrapes and the consequence is that I am getting the best marks in my sections in French and Spanish and am knocking things in Drawing, and what is of more importance than all the rest put together, I have been transferred up in Analytical Mechanics already, and I have now got into a section where the keen men are. I am going to keep on boning and am coming out in a respectable place next June." It seems as though it just took Lon, a hard-working but plodding sort of student, longer to settle down and catch on than some of his classmates. In this respect, as in many others for that matter, Lon's West Point experience mirrored that of John Pelham (who would become the great cannoneer of Lee's army) in the class ahead of him.[46]

Mary had given Lon and Will each a pair of slippers to take back to school, and they became prized possessions to the boys. Lon used them while studying at night. "If I only had a dressing gown," he wrote, "I would be fixed off all right." Mary had told Lon that she planned to travel to Boston and Chelsea to visit her sisters and their families, and maybe she would visit West Point on the same trip. Lon certainly hoped so.[47] Her great news later that year was that, through the financial help of her cousin Albert Smith, she had left her Green Street home and moved into a new and more comfortable house in Fredonia. Lon was overjoyed. "Mother," he wrote Will, "is in excellent quarters now and kindly invited me to come home for a few weeks this summer and enjoy the comforts of the new place, but I informed her that it was impossible to comply with said invitation, but I hoped to be able to spend the summer at home in one year. It will be splendid won't it?"[48]

By the fall of 1859 the nation appeared to be disintegrating. John Brown, the perpetrator of the Pottawatomi Massacre in Kansas, attempted to carry out a slave insurrection. On October 16, with thirteen armed white men and five blacks, Brown seized the federal arsenal at Harpers Ferry. His gang captured the mayor of the town and took some of the leading citizens of the area hostage. Gov. Henry A. Wise of Virginia called out the state's militia and asked for federal assistance. From Washington, D.C., Col. Robert E. Lee, a former superintendent at West Point and a hero of the Mexican War, arrived with a company of marines as Brown was holding the militia at bay from inside an old engine house near the arsenal. The next day the marines battered down the engine house doors, taking Brown and his remaining defenders prisoner. On December 2, 1859, Brown was hanged near Charles Town, Virginia. Wondering whether the Union would hold together, Lon wrote to William, "If it don't hold together, the Lord only knows what we will do. Our diplomas will go to the devil in no time . . . and we might as well follow them. However, I imagine that we will weather through this winter and this damnable storm which old John Brown succeeded so admirably in kicking up and remain a free and happy country for some time to come. I think old Ossowatimie richly deserves hanging for his misdeeds, but think [Gov. Henry] Wise has rather displayed his posterior in making such an almighty fuss over it all."[49]

Lon tried to keep his mind on things other than the ominous events of the day. He and his cadet friends sought recreation whenever and wherever it could be found. Among their favorite pastimes was the game of whist. Lon and his roommate Samuel Ferris often teamed up at those games; on occasion Lon and Henry Noyes were partners. Competition was keen, and "bragging rights" were fought over. James Lord and Eugene Carter were apparently among Lon's fiercest competitors.[50]

Lon thoroughly enjoyed tobacco, too, and seemed not to care particularly in what form it came. He chewed tobacco often and relished "Havanas," but mostly he liked to smoke a pipe, and the real meerschaum that Will brought back to him from his Naval Academy Mediterranean cruise was a prized possession. Since 1857, smoking had been permitted in the barracks, but nowhere else in the Academy, but Lon was often found with tobacco in some form or other, whether it was prohibited or not. As late as June 18, 1861—only twelve days before graduation—he was given a skin for "smoking in the commissary store."[51]

Lon's Third Class year ended in June 1860, his class having lost three more of its members during the academic year. Lon's performance showed significant improvement. In philosophy he ranked tenth, in French seventeenth, in Spanish twenty-first, and in drawing twenty-third, all out of a class of fifty-seven. He had risen three files to section one in philosophy from the beginning to the end of the academic year. In Order of General Merit, Lon stood twelfth in his class.[52] Moreover, he had gotten some control of his propensity to receive demerits; he had been given only fifty-five skins for the year (one, of all things, for being "late at church"!). Lon had worked hard, though, and his class standing was evidence of his great effort.[53]

Lon had become one of the most well-liked cadets at the Academy. He was fun-loving with plebes but never mean; he was congenial, with a toothy but contagious smile and a mirthful laugh. Every cadet who in later life reminisced about Lon did so with a near reverential fondness. His hard work and good nature paid dividends. On June 16, 1860, Special Orders Number 79 named Lon a sergeant in the Corps during summer camp, and on August 28, Special Orders Number 120 named him a sergeant in the Corps for the academic year—a singular honor.[54] As a sergeant, Lon was the "commandant" of a table in the Mess Hall and an inspector of his subdivision in the barracks. What excited him most was that he was able to "walk about" the Mess Hall as much as he pleased, and could keep a light after taps as long as he wished. Lon wrote to Will: "If you come up we won't go to bed at taps but will sit up as long as we please."[55]

One individual with a commanding presence stood out among the officers and cadets. General-in-Chief of the Army Winfield Scott had made West Point his headquarters, and during parades and drill he became, for all practical purposes, the real "Commandant of Cadets." He was often seen around the post carrying out his duties. At one time he was accompanied by the visiting Prince of Wales; at other times, by his old archenemy, Sen. Jefferson Davis of Mississippi, who often journeyed to West Point on fact-finding missions. Lon must have spent many moments talking with the enormous old general. Though his great frame appeared to be bending under a myriad of infirmities and pains, Scott was kind to all who approached him, and he took an interest in Lon. In the Chapel, Lon noticed that "Old Fuss and Feathers" could pray every bit as hard as it was told he could fight. Lon and his fellow cadets deeply admired the old hero.

The Department of Tactics of the academy had been staffed by a particularly fine group of young officers. Commandant William Hardee had been graduated from West Point in 1838. Hailing from Georgia, he had been brevetted for gallantry during the Mexican War for his services at Veracruz and St. Augustine. From 1853 to 1855 he had written *Rifle and Light Infantry Tactics,* a standard text subject that would be published in Philadelphia in 1861. Hardee was most competent. The cadets thought that his son Will, though, was a brat; the little boy and his friends would often yell and throw rocks and sticks at the cadets while they were at drill.[56] In the fall of 1860 there was a change in the military command at West Point. Hardee was replaced by a somewhat retiring but extremely competent bachelor colonel who hailed from Lancaster, Pennsylvania.

John Fulton Reynolds, born in 1820, had been graduated from West Point in 1841, the year of Lon's birth. After garrison duty along the Texas frontier, Reynolds had served with Gen. Zachary Taylor in the Mexican War and had crossed the American plains twice on military expeditions. The cadets quickly came to like him. As William Harris remarked: "Col. Reynolds is generally quite popular in corps. He is living in the Commandant's house, makes himself omnipresent, but is a quiet man and being a bachelor associates with his officers more than Col. Hardee did."[57]

Other instructors in the Department of Tactics were such bright young officers as Lt. Alexander McDowell McCook of Ohio, 2d United States Infantry, class of 1851, nicknamed "A. McD."; Lt. Charles W. "Charlie" Field of Kentucky, 2d United States Cavalry, class of 1849; Lt. Robert "Bully" Williams of Virginia, 1st United States Dragoons, class of 1851; Lt. Fitzhugh Lee of Virginia, 2d United States Cavalry, class of 1856; and Lt. Charles Griffin of Ohio, 2d United States Artillery, class of 1847. Under their tutelage, Lon learned the rudiments of infantry, cavalry, and artillery tactics.[58]

Lieutenant Griffin stood out. Under his command was the West Point Battery. Organized in 1776 by none other than Col. Alexander Hamilton, and in the 1850s part of Battery F, 4th United States Artillery, it was one of the oldest units in the United States Army. During the Civil War, few companies would have a more distinguished record.[59]

For Lon and his classmates, artillery drill under Lieutenant Griffin was as dangerous as it was tedious. Once Paddy O'Rorke, holding the rammer as the number one cannoneer, nearly had his arms blown off by the premature firing of his gun.

"Mr. O'Rorke! Mr. O'Rorke! Are you all right?" exclaimed the instructor after the gun fired and O'Rorke was thrown to the ground.

Picking himself up, O'Rorke replied with amazing understatement, "I've lost my glove, sir."

"Bother your glove! Your arm, man? Is your arm all right?"

"Oh, yes sir. There's nothing wrong with my arm."

Irish Catholic though he was, O'Rorke was winning Lon's admiration more and more every day. Lon never had that close a scrape with catastrophe during artillery drill, but he did receive demerits for "not carrying trail in proper direction" on one occasion. It took hard work and drill to make a great artilleryman. Lon would learn.[60]

Among the traits Lon displayed which his classmates often recalled were fearlessness and unselfishness. They were illustrated clearly during Lieutenants Lee's and Field's riding classes in the round-roofed Riding Hall. Many cadets were injured during those sessions. "Tasting the tanbark," as the cadets called it, was a known and feared hazard. Lon's classmate and friend Joseph Farley remembered that one time the cadets drew lots for the horses. When a horse named Xantippe, "a perfect devil of a mare whose trick was to rear and fall back before one could get fairly seated in the saddle," was drawn by an unfortunate cadet, Lon stepped forward and generously offered to take Xantippe in exchange for the rather duller horse he had drawn; "Oh! I'll break the old lady of her tricks," he remarked. As he swung into the saddle, the horse reared back and fell to its side, mashing Lon's face beneath the McClellan saddle. For a while he was so bruised and swollen he was unrecognizable. "The boy, you see," wrote Farley, "was father to the man."[61]

One southerner in the academy for whom Lon had great fondness was Virginian James Dearing, who often served as Lon's dancing "partner" during the hops and appears to have been one of the regulars at games of whist. Dearing was in his barracks room one day picking on his banjo to his roommate's utter disgust. He apparently had little talent for the banjo, although he could strum the tune "Dixie," which he did often. Lon suddenly appeared at the door grinning from ear to ear. "Guess what I have?"

"Quail," said Dearing's roommate, "Quail and manna! Or did you bring something to clip banjo strings, Lon?"

Lon laughed out loud and then set down an assortment of apples he had picked the night before. "Pay me back when your box comes from home," he said, and left. Dearing, having forgotten about the banjo altogether, commenced to munch on the wonderful New York Winesaps.[62]

Storm clouds continued to gather on the national scene as the war of words between rival sections gained momentum. On November 6, 1860, the Republican Abraham Lincoln, aided by Free-Soil Democrats and large numbers of former Know-Nothings, won a plurality of national votes in the tumultuous presidential election.[63] Then one by one, beginning with South Carolina in December 1860, the southern states passed ordinances of secession, and the harbor in Charleston, South Carolina, became the flash point for the tense nation. Kentuckian Maj. Robert Anderson, an 1825 graduate of West Point, in command of the federal garrison there, had moved all his men into Fort Sumter at the entrance to the harbor as a precautionary measure. In January 1861 the unarmed relief ship *Star of the West* was fired upon and turned away by South Carolina coastal batteries without Anderson's firing a shot in return. The situation was tense militarily and politically.[64]

In Lon's class, the election of Lincoln and the secession of South Carolina precipitated the resignations of Cadets Henry S. Farley of South Carolina and Charles P. Ball of Alabama. From that point forward the division among the cadets grew. Southerners would gather in the barracks and cheer for Dixie. Cadets from northern states would gather together and cheer for the Stars-and-Stripes.[65]

On January 23, 1861, Col. Pierre Gustave Toutant Beauregard was named superintendent of the United States Military Academy, replacing Maj. Richard Delafield. Born in St. Bernard Parish, Louisiana, in 1818, Beauregard had been graduated second in the West Point class of 1838. He had served on Gen. Winfield Scott's staff during the Mexican War, winning two brevets for gallant and meritorious services. He was a superlative officer, but his southern sympathies were well known. It is a wonder he was ever named to the post. On February 8, sixteen days after he arrived, Beauregard was relieved as superintendent and old Major Delafield temporarily recalled. In March, Lt. Col. Alexander Hamilton Bowman took over as the new superintendent.[66] The cadets knew the nation was preparing for war. General Scott headed to Washington to take command of the small military force there and to help make preparations for the March inaugural of the new president. Lieutenant Griffin was ordered to assemble all the regular army dragoons and horses and prepare to take the West Point Battery to Washington. The day after Beauregard left the academy, in front of the assembled Corps of Cadets, Griffin led the old battery out of the United States Military Academy toward the capital city.[67]

A provisional government of the seceded states was organized at Montgomery, Alabama, and there Jefferson Davis was named president of the new Confederate States of America in February 1861. Southern officers in the old army began to tender their resignations in great numbers. Colonel Beauregard resigned his commission in the United States Army, accepted one as a brigadier general in the Provisional Army of the Confederate States, and took over command of the Confederate forces in Charleston harbor.[68] On April 12 the long, caustic war of words came to an end. Commanded by none other than General Beauregard, superintendent at West Point only two months before, Confederate batteries opened up on the Union garrison at Fort Sumter at dawn. On April 13 Major Anderson surrendered his garrison to the Confederates. Meanwhile, in Pensacola Bay, Florida, gallant Lt. Adam J. Slemmer, after spiking the guns at Fort Barrancas and blowing up the ammunition at Fort McRae, occupied Fort Pickens. Although they did not attack, the Confederates demanded his surrender. Slemmer (who had been Lon's first algebra instructor at West Point) refused to give up the fort. Quickly, the Lincoln administration issued a call for 75,000 volunteers for a term of three months to "suppress the rebellion."[69]

At the Naval Academy, Will had let his penchant for practical jokes get the best of him one time too many. His last rebellious episode had been directed at his Spanish professor. After the midyear examinations in 1861, Will had been found deficient in Spanish. A report had been forwarded to the Navy Department which stated that Will was "deficient" at

February semiannual examinations; that his "conduct was bad"; that his "aptitude for naval service" was "not good"; and that he was "not recommended for continuance at the Academy." Three months short of graduation, Will was ordered to leave Annapolis. He signed his resignation on March 23, 1861.[70]

News of Will's dismissal from the Naval Academy reached Lon at about the same time as news of the firing upon Fort Sumter. He had feared Will would get into trouble, but not this late in his career at Annapolis. Lon wrote to his mother: "I have been anxiously waiting for some news from home or from Washington for some time, but none reaches me. Willie for all I know may be dead, maybe in Fredonia [or] at Annapolis or a member of some voluntary military organization. . . . It is a terrible misfortune that this thing should have happened now of all times—a first classman just about to get his diploma and above all a war breaking out—many resignations in the Navy and a glorious chance for distinction and promotion."[71]

Throughout the year the cadets had felt the growing sectional rift within their own ranks. Southern cadets as well as instructors at the academy had resigned in great numbers. Within the First Class, Thomas Rosser of Virginia had been among the first, followed by John Pelham and others. In Lon's class, James Dearing resigned on April 22, 1861. Fitzhugh Lee left the academy on April 27; he was serenaded by his fellow officers the evening before; then, after tearful farewells, the cadets lined up and, waving their hats in the air, bid the popular Virginian goodbye as he passed down the road in his carriage. Largely because of resignations, Alonzo's class would be reduced to only thirty-five members by June 1861.[72]

Lon left no room for doubt about his feelings for those who were resigning. "The disunionists are rapidly resigning and my class is already reduced to about 40 members," he wrote to his mother. "I want to see every man go who has any scruples about fighting their 'Southern Bretheren.' The only thing I regret is that they are all below me in class and so I will lose instead of gaining in relative standing by their resignations. Standing is of comparative little importance in these times, however. All I want now is to graduate right away. I could not for anything stay here a whole year longer. I want to fight my 'Southern Bretheren.' They would like very well to whip us and kill us, and it is just and right that we return the compliment. Three cheers for the Stars and Stripes, American Eagle and Yankee Doodle."[73]

On May 4, 1861, the First Classmen completed examinations; two days later they were graduated, and the newly commissioned officers were ordered to proceed to the city of Washington and report to the adjutant general.[74] Lon's Second Class year had been a good one; his class standing had improved. He ended the year standing seventh in ethics, sixteenth in infantry tactics, ninth in artillery tactics, eleventh in cavalry tactics, eighth in chemistry, thirteenth in drawing, and tenth in Order of General Merit.[75] He and his classmates were First Classmen at last—but their First Class "year" would last only forty-nine days. A bill had slowly worked its way through Congress to cut the term at West Point back to four years. For almost two years Lon and his classmates had worried that the bill might not be enacted in time to benefit them; they had written their congressman and had signed petitions agitating for the passage of the legislation to shorten their term at the academy. With the outbreak of hostilities, the five-year course was finally abandoned.[76]

On May 6, when Special Orders Number 60 were read before the assembled new First Classmen, Lon was appointed a captain in the Corps of Cadets, as were Patrick O'Rorke (named First Captain), Francis U. Farquhar of Pennsylvania, and Stephen Lyford. Among the twelve cadets named lieutenants in the Corps were George Woodruff and Joseph C. Audenreid.[77] Class rings were given to the First Classmen. In those days a committee of cadets designed the ring for their own class. George Custer was one of those who helped design the ring for Lon's class. Gold with a seal cut in a flat, oval, smoky blue sardonyx stone, the ring showed an arm with a sword in the hand, interposed between the guns of a fort and a flag upon which the guns were firing. The motto inscribed on the ring read: "Per Angusta ad Augusta" (through trials to triumph).[78] The events called for a photograph! Lon dressed up in his blue furlough uniform and had his picture taken for his mother and William. That photograph of a youthful-looking Alonzo H. Cushing became the most noted one ever made of him, and a favorite in the Cushing family. It was a proud time for Lon, indeed.[79]

Probably no one was more disgusted over Will's dismissal from the Naval Academy than his uncle, Commodore Joseph Smith—"old Guts," as Will called him. But when Will journeyed to Washington, D.C., to seek his uncle's help, Smith helped him secure a position as a master's mate and an assignment aboard the forty-seven-gun screw frigate *Minnesota,* part of a blockading squadron in the Chesapeake Bay. William sailed from Washington to Fort Monroe, where he was ordered to take a captured prize, *The Delaware Farmer,* to Philadelphia. From there he journeyed to West Point for a brief visit with his brother. Upon his return to the fleet Will was sent with another captured prize, the bark *Pioneer,* from Fort Monroe to New York harbor, and he went to West Point to visit Lon again. He arrived on May 27, 1861, and on that day, Lon was given a skin for "introducing an unauthorized person into the barracks." Lon, though sorely disappointed at Will's resignation, was consoled by the fact that his brother was proving himself in the navy already and had been assured readmission to the Naval Academy, so he said.[80]

It seems that their older brother Howard Cushing, who had been working as a typesetter in the office of a Chicago newspaper called the *Farmer's Advocate,* had journeyed home to Fredonia on more than one occasion while Lon was at West Point. Howard, like so many of the Cushings, was suffering from tuberculosis; the older he grew, the more the symptoms became evident. He had returned to Chicago from Fredonia in the spring of 1861. At the time Lon was preparing to become a new First Classman, Howard joined Capt. Ezra Taylor's newly organized Battery B, 1st Illinois Light Artillery, for a term of three months. On April 21, 1861, Howard and his battery were ordered to the strategically important river city of Cairo, Illinois.[81]

Work at the academy had become particularly difficult for Lon. In a short period of time the First Classmen were drilled in military engineering, ethics, and ordnance and gunnery. Day and night they worked and crammed, all trying to learn in forty-nine days what the academy normally taught in a year. Even Fannie Custer was studying hard. "We have to study exceedingly hard now," Lon wrote. "They are putting us through nearly a whole years course in six weeks and all who are not thoroughly proficient at examination will be turned back for another year. I have to study from 5 A.M. to 11 P.M. daily, with some intermission of course for meals, drill, etc. They have even reduced our usual time of recreation—30 minutes after supper to 5 minutes. We would all be grey headed in six months if it was to continue this way. Only three or four weeks ahead however and we are willing to study hard for this length of time for the sake of graduating so soon. Then hurrah for a brush with the Rebels. In less than six weeks I shall undoubtedly have an opportunity of smelling gunpowder."[82] Finally, classes concluded, and Lon and his class of only thirty-five members took their examinations. Then grades were posted. In military engineering Lon stood ninth, in ethics seventh, in ordnance and gunnery eleventh, and in Order of General Merit twelfth. Throughout the 1860-61 academic year, Lon had only received fifty-three demerits. Altogether, his performance at West Point had been sound.[83]

On the Sunday before he was relieved from duty at the academy, Cadet Captain Alonzo Hereford Cushing attended chapel with his class. Chaplain John W. French delivered the morning sermon as usual. French had not been well; many claimed that his worry over the terrible events that were dividing the nation had been the cause of his frail health. Lon looked around the lovely Chapel. The painting of "Peace" and "War" over the chancel, the shields on the walls, and the flag behind the lectern would always live in his memory. Seated in the pews alongside the walls were the professors and instructors. At the front was Lieutenant Colonel Bowman; next to the superintendent was the commandant, Colonel Reynolds. Beside Lon sat Cadet Captain Stephen C. Lyford and Cadet Charles C. Parsons. Nearby were First Cadet Captain Patrick Henry O'Rorke, Cadet Lieutenant George Augustus Woodruff, and Cadet Justin E. Dimick. Seated there as well were the "immortals"—Cadets Henry E. Noyes, Eugene Carter, Lon's old roommate Samuel P. Ferris, and, of course, George Armstrong Custer—who, at the time, was under arrest.[84]

From the choir loft a cadet choir sang the traditional graduation hymn, titled "Unity."

When shall we meet again?
    Meet ne'er to sever?
When will Peace wreathe her chain
    Round us forever?
Our hearts will ne'er repose
Save from each blast that blows
In this dark vale of woes
    Never, no, never!

When shall love freely flow,
    Pure as life's river?
When shall sweet friendship glow
    Changeless forever?
Where joys celestial shrill
Where bliss each heart shall fill
And fears of parting chill
    Never, no, never!

Up to that world of light
    Take us, dear Savior;
May we all there unite,
    Happy forever!
Where kindred spirits dwell
There may our music swell,
And time our joys dispel
    Never, no, never!

Soon shall we meet again,
    Meet ne'er to sever;
Soon will Peace wreathe her chain
    Round us forever;
Our hearts will then repose
Secure from worldly woes;
Our songs of praise shall close
    Never, no, never![85]

A stillness settled over the Corps of Cadets. In that Chapel Lon and his classmates had always found peace, but what lay ahead of each of those thirty-five cadets no one knew. Lon had thought about the war. "These are glorious times in which we live," he wrote. "We will soon see some large battlefields and a war beside which our little Mexican affair and our wars with England dwindle into positive insignificance. Our present war will at least approximate if not equal or surpass in magnitude of its operations the great conflicts which desolated Europe at the beginning of the present century." It was clear to him that once he and his classmates went their separate ways into the conflict, he would never assemble with all of them again. As the months passed, every cadet in the class would remember with tenderness that little Chapel and their last Sunday at West Point.[86]

There were no graduation exercises for Lon's class; in fact, he and his classmates even had their long-awaited furloughs canceled. The First Classmen were simply relieved from duty at West Point and assigned to posts at the front. On June 24, 1861, Alonzo Hereford Cushing was commissioned a second lieutenant and a first lieutenant in the 4th United States Artillery; on June 30, Special Orders Number 120 relieved him and all his class from duty at West Point as of reveille on July 1. The new officers were ordered to report immediately to the adjutant general of the United States Army in Washington.[87]

3

"I Fancy I Did Some of the Prettiest Firing"

Alonzo Hereford Cushing, a newly commissioned first lieutenant, with other members of his West Point class, arrived at the outskirts of Washington on a scheduled Baltimore & Ohio Railroad passenger train on July 3, 1861. Just over five feet, nine inches tall, Lon weighed about 170 pounds and was fairly robust. As a cadet he had regularly worked out lifting weights in the academy gymnasium in order that he might "develop [his] physical powers." In Lon's words, he had become "a sizeable lad." He proudly wore his new blue frock coat with red shoulder straps, blue trousers, and slouch hat, clothing purchased with two hundred dollars given to him by his Uncle Albert Smith—"old Alberto," as Lon liked to call him—as a graduation present. His thick auburn hair partly covering his ears, and his round, clean-shaven face and bright blue eyes, gave him an almost girlish appearance in spite of his athletic frame.[1]

Lon was carrying an assignment to Battery A, 4th United States Artillery. Originally created by act of Congress on March 2, 1821, the 4th Artillery, on the eve of the Civil War, was composed of eleven batteries. The batteries of the regiment had seen service in the Black Hawk War, the "nullification" crises in Charleston, South Carolina, in 1832 and 1833, the Creek Indian War in Alabama, and the Seminole War in Florida in 1835 and 1836. In the war with Mexico the 4th Artillery had seen extensive action. Batteries were engaged at Corpus Christi, Palo Alto, Resaca de la Palma, Monterrey, and Independencia Hill. Battery B had won everlasting fame in the desperate engagement at Buena Vista in February 1847, where it lost a number of its guns. Batteries A, C, D, F, G, and H followed Gen. Winfield Scott in the campaign that began at Veracruz and culminated in the capture of Mexico City. At Contreras, Battery G actually recaptured the guns lost by Battery B at Buena Vista. For thirty-two days Battery A participated in the siege of Puebla. Virtually the entire regiment saw service in the fighting against the Seminole Indians in Florida in 1856. Upon the conclusion of that brief war, the War Department began sending the various batteries to the West to help protect the settlers who were pouring into the region recently won from Mexico. In 1857 the field and staff officers, regimental band, and Batteries A and I were sent to Fort Laramie, Batteries B and C to Fort Crittenden near Salt Lake, D and E to Platte Ridge, and F, H, and K to Fort Kearney, L and M to Cheyenne Pass. By the summer of 1859, Batteries E, H, I, L, and M were stationed at Fort Randall, in Dakota Territory, and F and K were at Fort Ridgely, Minnesota. Battery D, followed by Battery L, then occupied Fort Monroe, Virginia, but during John Brown's uprising in the fall of 1859, Battery G and part of Battery D were ordered to Harpers Ferry.[2] At the outbreak of the Civil War, Battery A, "Light" Battery B, and Battery C were stationed at Fort Crittenden, in Utah Territory, protecting settlers from Indian attacks. In July 1861 they were just preparing to make the long journey east.[3]

While the widely separated elements of the small regular army were trying to assemble in the East to meet the threat of full-scale war, volunteer organizations were pouring into Washington, D.C. Even though his battery was still in Utah, Lon and hundreds of other regular army officers were desperately needed in the capital city. Lon and his classmates were met at the heavily guarded Baltimore & Ohio Railroad depot at North Capitol and C streets by Lt. Douglas Ramsey of Capt. James B. Ricketts's Battery I, 1st United States Artillery. Ramsey led the eager young officers through the city in horse-drawn buses. Their destination was army headquarters and the offices of Gen. Winfield Scott.[4]

Washington had a significance to Lon beyond its importance as the nation's capital. His uncles, Commodore Joseph Smith and Albert Smith, lived there, and his oldest full brother, Milton Buckingham Cushing, Jr., had recently moved to Washington from Fitchburg, Massachusetts; he had given up becoming a pharmacist. Commodore Smith had taken Milton under his wing and given him a post as a noncommissioned officer in the Navy Department. Milton was not well; his bouts with tuberculosis had become more frequent and debilitating.[5]

Now Lon was seeing Washington for the first time. Not far from the railroad depot, on an eminence, stood the Capitol Building, still under construction. The original dome had been removed, and only the base of a new cast-iron dome, mounted by an intricate network of scaffolding, and a huge crane topped the building. Cut stones, marble columns, lumber, heaps of sand and gravel lay about the grounds. Streets leading to the Capitol were barricaded, and hundreds of armed soldiers, packed in a veritable sea of tents, protected the area. Like the nation itself, the Capitol Building was not only unfinished but presented the appearance of disorganization, even chaos. The bus turned down Pennsylvania Avenue, a cobblestone boulevard full of ruts and ditches. West of the avenue ran an old canal that connected Georgetown with the eastern branch of the Potomac River not far from the Navy Yard. Between the Capitol Building and the Treasury and State Department buildings, Pennsylvania Avenue was lined with three- to six-story federal-style brick hotels, rooming houses, and shops. Lon's bus passed the National Hotel and Brown's Hotel on opposite sides of Sixth Street, the Kirkwood on Twelfth, and the famous Willard's on the corner of Fourteenth Street. Behind Pennsylvania Avenue, in the business district, were row upon row of dingy shacks, boardinghouses, and brothels. Hogs, geese, and cattle roamed many of the streets, and peddlers and hucksters sold everything from fish and oysters to clothes and chopped wood. Refuse was everywhere, and the smell of it, combined with the heavy clouds of smoke from wood fires and the innumerable flies and mosquitoes, gave the city a most unhealthy air. Added to the dismal vistas of the city were countless soldiers—some marching, some loitering about—and endless streams of military baggage, ordnance, and commissary wagon trains. In the distance Lon could hear the tinny sounds of military bands mingled with the yells, shouts, and chatter of soldiers and civilians along the avenue. The many American flags would have added color to the scene but for the fact that most were faded or covered with soot. The bus passed the State Department Building, the enormous edifice of the Treasury Department, and the White House, which was surrounded by fruit trees only partially concealing a host of shabby outbuildings and sheds alongside the wings.[6]

The bus halted on Seventeenth Street across from the War Department and just beyond the White House. There, in what was called the Winder Building, were the offices of General Scott and the adjutant general of the United States Army. Escorted inside, Lon and his fellow classmates were greeted by "old Fuss and Feathers" himself. Scott's health, in just seven months, had declined visibly. Suffering from gout, he lay on a lounge in the center of the headquarters room while each of the new lieutenants saluted and extended his hand to the general-in-chief.[7] And then President Lincoln entered the room. The president made daily visits to the War Department and army headquarters, where he checked telegrams and conversed with his commanders about the military events of the day. Lincoln quickly put the young men at ease, taking the time to greet each new officer. Alonzo had come a long way. Born in poverty on the Wisconsin frontier, he was now greeted by the president of the United States. Unknown to either was the fact that Lincoln's great-great-great-great-great-grandfather, Samuel Lincoln, had been the boyhood friend of Lon's great-great-great-great-great-great-grandfather, Daniel Cushing, in Hingham, England, and in early Hingham, Massachusetts. Both had been members of the Parish of Hingham in Norfolk County, England, and both were baptized by Robert Peck, the pastor whose banishment from the Anglican Church for his Puritan agitation was the catalyst for the Cushings' emigration to the New World.[8]

After the president departed, Lon and his classmates were informed of the military situation in and around Washington. Gen. Joseph King Fenno Mansfield had been named commander of the newly created Military Department of Washington, which included the District of Columbia and a portion of Maryland north of the capital. Mansfield had served as General Scott's chief engineer during the war with Mexico and had toured western army installations as a colonel in the Inspector General's Department prior to the outbreak of hostilities. As early as May 23 and 24, Mansfield had pushed his troops across the Potomac River and occupied Arlington Heights, the southern ends of the Long Bridge and the Chain Bridge, and the aqueduct that carried the Chesapeake and Ohio Canal over the Potomac River from Georgetown to Virginia. His troops also occupied the old port of Alexandria. Mansfield had overseen the construction of key defensive positions around Washington—including Forts Corcoran, Haggerty, Bennett, Runyon, and Ellsworth—on critical highways and bridges leading to and from the capital and at railroad and shipping sites in northern Virginia.[9]

The military situation in the East was critical—and changing every day. Aged Brig. Gen. Robert Patterson, leading a Union force up the Potomac River valley, had taken Harpers Ferry upon the withdrawal of a Confederate army under Gen. Joseph E. Johnston. Thus far, his command was keeping the Confederates out of Maryland and securing the strategically important Baltimore & Ohio Railroad and Chesapeake and Ohio Canal. Another force, commanded by Brig. Gen. George B. McClellan, was moving into western Virginia.[10]

The main threat was the large and growing enemy force holding what was referred to as the "Alexandria line." Its headquarters was at Manassas, the junction of the strategically critical Orange & Alexandria and Manassas Gap railroads. General Beauregard, the southern hero of Fort Sumter, commanded Confederate forces that were then holding defensive positions as close as Fairfax Court House but principally along high ground above the meandering stream called Bull Run, not far from Manassas. It was widely known that Jefferson Davis, president of the new Confederate States, was with Beauregard at Manassas. Additional Confederate armies were assembling near the mouth of Aquia Creek in Virginia as well as the lower Chesapeake. General Beauregard, a capable soldier, had nearly 25,000 troops under his command; if any of the other Confederate commands joined him at Manassas, he could mount an offensive threat against the nation's capital. Thus, the operations of

General Patterson at Harpers Ferry and General McClellan in western Virginia were necessary if for no other reason than to keep General Johnston and his army tied up in the lower Shenandoah Valley and thereby reduce the offensive threat of Beauregard in front of Washington.[11]

Arrayed against Beauregard was a growing Union force under the command of his old West Point classmate Brig. Gen. Irvin McDowell, a native of Columbus, Ohio, who had been brevetted for gallantry at the Battle of Buena Vista. With the help of an Ohio friend, new Treasury Secretary Salmon P. Chase, he had been elevated to the rank of brigadier general. Even though he had never commanded any force of men—not even a squad—in combat, McDowell had been placed in command of all Union forces south of the Potomac, known as the Department of Northeastern Virginia, on May 27. He had established his headquarters in Arlington House, the abandoned home of Mary Custis Lee, the wife of Col. Robert E. Lee, who was then the chief military adviser to Jefferson Davis. McDowell's army consisted of five divisions, commanded respectively by Brig. Gen. Daniel Tyler, Col. David Hunter, Col. Samuel P. Heintzelman, Brig. Gen. Theodore Runyon, and Col. Dixon S. Miles. In all, McDowell's Grand Army contained about 35,000 men with ten batteries of artillery and seven companies of regular cavalry.[12]

As early as June 24, McDowell proposed to advance his army toward Manassas and engage Beauregard before the enemy could be reinforced. That most of the troops in his army were new recruits, some of whose brief enlistments would soon expire, added urgency to the proposal, although as the time to move drew closer, McDowell began to urge delay because he believed that his troops were not ready for combat. Many of his division and brigade commanders were in desperate need of aides who knew military drill and instruction. Lon and the other new lieutenants would be needed to assist in quickly training raw troops and adding cohesiveness to the commands.[13]

An aide to Acting Adjutant General Lorenzo Thomas handed written orders to the new lieutenants. Lon was temporarily assigned to Lt. Oliver D. Greene's Battery G, 2d United States Artillery, then stationed at Fort Runyon below Arlington Heights, and William Harris was directed to join Lon as a section commander. Patrick O'Rorke and Joseph Audenreid were assigned as aides-de-camp on General Tyler's staff; John Edie, George Woodruff, and Francis Parker to the staff of Col. Orlando B. Willcox, a brigade commander in Colonel Heintzelman's division; Henry Noyes to Capt. Romeyn B. Ayres's Battery E, 3d United States Artillery.[14]

From army headquarters, Lon and Harris were taken in a bus back through the city of Washington to the Long Bridge. The ride took them by the Washington Monument, then just under construction, and the dark red brick, sinister-looking buildings of the new Smithsonian Institution. Crossing the heavily guarded Long Bridge over the Potomac River, the two lieutenants entered Fort Jackson—a small fort that protected the bridge on the Virginia shore—then continued west along the Washington-Alexandria Turnpike.[15]

Fort Runyon was the largest installation in the defenses of Washington at the time. It covered twelve acres of land within a perimeter of 1,484 yards. The fort stood along the bottomlands of the Potomac River, below the frowning Arlington Heights, enclosing within its parapets the junction of the Washington-Alexandria and Columbia turnpikes. The tents of the men of Greene's battery were laid out in rows with pine boughs covering them to provide protection from the hot sun. Coursing the lowlands west of the fort and cutting through the vast numbers of tents, sheds, corrals, and ordnance and commissary depots was the Alexandria extension of the great Chesapeake and Ohio Canal, busy with canalboats laden with military supplies. On the heights above the fort Lon could see Arlington House. Above the lovely mansion the Stars-and-Stripes fluttered defiantly.[16] Around Forts Jackson and Runyon, filling the Potomac bottomlands on the Virginia shore, was a maze of army camps. Smoke drifted lazily to the sky from innumerable campfires. In front of the tents countless soldiers, in small detachments and wearing all kinds of odd uniforms, were being drilled. Lon heard many of the officers yelling commands in German! The stench from the camps was beyond anything he and Harris had ever encountered. They could tell in a moment that the new volunteers were ill prepared for war. The sights—and smells—did not inspire confidence.[17]

Greene's battery formed the artillery complement of Col. Thomas A. Davies's Second Brigade of Colonel Miles's Fifth Division. The battery consisted of four ten-pound Parrott rifles, which Lon believed were "most effective weapons." Designed by West Point graduate Robert P. Parrott in 1860, their barrels were made of cast iron with a wrought iron reinforcing band around the breech. In the first (1861) model ten-pound Parrotts, the barrels had 2.9-inch rifled bores with three grooves or lands roughly equal in size. Each gun in the battery was pulled by a limber and a six-horse team. Carrying extra ammunition for each gun was a caisson and another six-horse limber. Just under one hundred horses and about ninety men made up the command; with the addition of the battery forge and the commissary and quartermaster wagons, the battery presented a formidable appearance.[18]

In addition to Greene's battery, the Second Brigade consisted of the 16th, 18th, 31st, and 32d New York Infantry regiments. Its commander, Colonel Davies, a native of St. Lawrence County, New York, had been graduated in the 1829 class at West Point with Robert E. Lee, Joseph E. Johnston, and Lon's father's cousin, Catharenus Putnam Buckingham. When Lincoln issued the call for volunteers in the spring of 1861, Davies, then a merchant in New York City, became colonel of the 16th New York, which he brought to Washington. The 18th New York was raised in Albany. The men who made up those two commands hailed from towns along the Hudson and Mohawk rivers and from New York City; most were from families that had settled New York before the Revolution. The 31st and 32d New York were organized in New York City and Staten Island. The men had mostly English names, although some Dutch names were interspersed throughout the two regiments.[19]

The First Brigade of the Fifth Division, commanded by Col. Louis Blenker and encamped nearby, was wholly unlike the Second. Composed of the 8th, 29th, and 39th New York and 27th Pennsylvania, it was almost solidly German. Lon had never seen anything like it before. Colonel Blenker (whose first name was actually Ludwig) hailed from Worms, Germany, and a principality then known as Hesse Darmstadt. An entrepreneur of sorts in the old country, Blenker, like many of those in his command, had participated in the 1848 revolutions against the monarchy. He had sought asylum in Switzerland before coming to settle in Rockland County, New York. When the war broke out, his reputation as a revolutionary aided him in recruiting the 8th New York, known as the "First German Rifles" and composed entirely of Germans from New York City. The 29th New York, or "First German Infantry," was also recruited in New York City and commanded by Col. Adolph Wilhelm August Friedrich Baron von Steinwehr, a native of Blankenburg, Duchy of Brunswick, and a graduate of the Brunswick military academy. The 39th New York was one of the most interesting regiments in the army. Known as the "Garibaldi Guard," the regiment was organized by its Viennese colonel, Frederick George D'Utassy (born Frederick Strasser). Raised from newly arrived immigrants from war-torn Europe, the regiment boasted three companies of Germans, three of Poles and Hungarians, one of Swiss, one of Italians, one of Frenchmen, and one of Spanish and Portuguese! The one non-New York regiment in Blenker's brigade was Col. Max Einstein's 27th Pennsylvania, but it was solid German as well. It had accompanied the 6th Massachusetts in Baltimore just a few weeks before when an angry mob attacked the soldiers in a highly publicized incident. Many men in Blenker's brigade carried not only their German names, language, and customs but a devout Roman Catholic faith—though some, it must be noted, were free-thinkers and anticlericals.[20]

Blenker's men were part of the flotsam pouring into New York City to which the Know-Nothings had objected so strenuously. Lon had come face to face with a new and different America. Why German immigrants volunteered to fight was not such a mystery. Indeed, they abhorred the institution of slavery and believed that it represented a threat to American guarantees of freedom as they understood them. But the presence of slavery was not their basic motivation; rather, it was the lure of pay and of proving themselves worthy in their newly adopted country, where nativism crippled them socially, economically, and politically. As an ethnic group they sought respect from nativist America. As well, to preserve the Union was to preserve a sanctuary for others from their strife-torn homeland. The immigration of more Germans—family members especially—was of paramount importance to those soldiers. Looking at Blenker's brigade, however, Lon observed only a portion of the story. Virtually every regiment and artillery battery in McDowell's Grand Army numbered not only Germans but Irishmen within its ranks. Not far up the Potomac River at Fort Corcoran, protecting the Virginia side of the Aqueduct Bridge, Col. Michael Corcoran's 69th New York State Militia in Col. William T. Sherman's brigade, Tyler's division, was solid famine Irish.[21]

The day after Lon's arrival in Washington was Independence Day. Dignitaries—cabinet members and congressmen—wandered through the camps. There were speeches and parades with regimental bands and fife-and-drum corps playing patriotic music, quicksteps, and martial airs. Throughout the day and night there was an endless exploding of fireworks and shooting of guns. Fort Runyon was located on one of Washington's best known picnic and party grounds; in fact, the horses in Lon's battery were quartered in a former tenpins alley, and the commissary had formerly been a dance hall. In spite of the presence of McDowell's Grand Army, the picnickers and revelers journeyed across the Long Bridge to celebrate among the countless encampments occupying their familiar party grounds.[22]

The long-expected move of McDowell's army was telegraphed to young Lon and the officers and men of Greene's unit when, on July 16, the battery was limbered up and, in "light marching order," directed toward the city of Alexandria with the advanced skirmishers of Colonel Davies's brigade. On the eve of the great movement, Lieutenant Greene had named Lon chief of the first (right) section of the battery, the position assigned to the most senior section commander. Moving through the intense heat of the day, the battery reached Annandale with the rest of Miles's division. That same evening Tyler's division reached Vienna, Hunter's reached the Little River Turnpike, and Heintzelman's reached Accotink. Runyon's division operated as a reserve, holding the Orange & Alexandria and the Loudoun & Hampshire railroads.[23]

The next day McDowell's army moved toward Centreville, Virginia, a small village separated from Manassas Junction by about six miles of turnpike road that ran through farmlands drained by the meandering

Bull Run. Advancing through hilly and densely wooded country dotted with small clearings and subsistence farms, Lon could tell that the land was rather poor. In an effort to slow the advance of McDowell's troops, the Confederates had blocked the roads with felled trees and barricades. Although it was constantly rumored that the enemy was in force ahead, the battery experienced only minor skirmishing with enemy pickets throughout the march. Nevertheless, along the skirmish lines in advance of the columns, Lon "could hear the balls whistling around in fine style" as guns, limbers, and caissons rumbled along the dusty roads toward their destiny at Bull Run. Some men in Miles's division were wounded in the skirmishing, but the losses along the march were relatively slight: four wounded, two fatally. On the evening of July 17 the division's advance halted near Fairfax Court House, a point of convergence for the Grand Army. Lon's battery went into camp near the abandoned earthworks and camp of the 5th Alabama, which in its hasty withdrawal had left its campfires still burning and abandoned the blankets, overcoats, and mess chests of the men—and even five sick soldiers.[24]

At Fairfax Court House, a village of about forty dwellings built around a lovely brick Georgian court building, Lon learned just how undisciplined and unruly the new volunteers in McDowell's Grand Army really were. After stripping the Confederate flag from the cupola, some soldiers attempted to burn down the old courthouse, and their own officers seemed to be powerless to stop them. Seeing the vandals in the act of trying to fire the building, Lon rode up to them, drew his sword and, in his own words, "cleared them out in a hurry." Lon recalled: "I heard them grumbling after they were out of the way about 'that damned regular having his back up.' " Like most regular army officers at the time, Lon displayed a basic contempt for the volunteers. "We shall have to shoot a few of the rascals," he wrote, "before they can learn what honorable warfare means; a crowd of them came around our wounded men . . . and their own officers could not keep them off. . . . We lack discipline among our volunteers." Indeed, the volunteers did lack discipline. It appears that mobs of them pillaged and burned houses and buildings in the village in spite of all efforts to stop them. Columns of smoke signaled the presence of the Union troops to enemy observers miles away.[25]

Lon finally retired to his blanket roll behind his guns. Sitting under the stars, he penned a note to his mother. "Before you receive this (if indeed I get an opportunity to send it)," he wrote, "we shall undoubtedly have had a battle, and probably a fierce one. I am going to gain a brevet there if we have an opportunity of using our battery with effect." But by the time Lon reached the end of his letter on that clear and extremely warm night, his thoughts turned away from the coming battle. "I will report operations from time to time," he concluded, "and be at home on Christmas to eat roast turkey with you."[26]

McDowell's army reached Centreville on the afternoon of July 18. That day Gen. Daniel Tyler's division advanced against Confederate positions along high ground opposite Mitchell's Ford and Blackburn's Ford of Bull Run. After a brief but fierce engagement, Tyler's advance was repulsed. There were less than two hundred combined casualties on both sides, but that encounter signaled more ominous movements behind the Confederate lines. In the face of the growing Union threat, General Johnston's army near Winchester, Virginia, and Gen. Theophilus Holmes's army near Aquia Creek Landing were ordered to proceed to Manassas Junction to reinforce Beauregard. Within two days, Brig. Gen. Thomas J. Jackson's brigade of Johnston's Valley Command would arrive from Piedmont Station by way of the Manassas Gap Railroad; the remainder of Johnston's force—nearly 10,000—would soon be on the trains en route to join Beauregard.[27]

Greene's battery came to a halt near Centreville on the evening of July 18. The town presented a scene of desolation to Lon. Recently abandoned by Confederate troops, its dusty streets were strewn with knapsacks, haversacks, canteens, blankets, shirts, and every kind of camp article. The houses were deserted. All around the village black men and women—slaves only hours before—watched as the Union troops poured into the village.[28]

A major engagement was imminent. McDowell waited as all the elements of his Grand Army assembled nearby. On Sunday morning, July 21, Greene's battery was aroused before sunup to prepare for battle. The day dawned bright and intensely hot. The battery was ordered to move to the head of Colonel Davies's column. Lon and his fellow cannoneers and gunners believed Miles's division was going to lead the advance against the enemy across Bull Run. The men in Greene's battery waited. Maybe Lon's thoughts for a moment turned to Little Ma, going to services in the First Baptist Church in Fredonia that morning. In a few hours the order to lead Davies's column was countermanded; Greene's battery and Capt. John C. Tidball's Battery A, 2d United States Artillery, were directed to take up positions behind embrasures along the road to Union Mills, east of Centreville, in support of Blenker's and Davies's brigades. The pioneers of Colonel D'Utassy's 39th New York and Colonel Einstein's 27th Pennsylvania, many of whom could not speak a word of English, constructed the redoubts for Greene's four Parrott rifles. As Greene's battery was preparing to occupy the embrasures alongside the 27th Pennsylvania, Davies's brigade was directed south, down the road to Blackburn's Ford to support the brigade of Col. Israel B. Richardson of Tyler's division, which had been advanced to a position along high ground above the north bank of Bull Run only about six hundred yards from the Confederate skirmishers in front of the ford. Richardson's and Davies's brigades were joined shortly thereafter by Capt. Henry J. Hunt's Battery M, 2d United States Artillery. Facing them was a Virginia brigade under the command of Brig. Gen. James Longstreet.[29]

McDowell had selected other commands to spearhead the attack that Sunday morning. He determined to flank his opponent by guiding Hunter's Second Division, Heintzelman's Third, and three brigades of Tyler's First across Bull Run at Sudley Springs. A secondary attack, using Blenker's brigade, was to be launched across the Stone Bridge on the Warrenton Turnpike. The plan, though slow to unfold, worked at first, even though the flanking movement was spotted by Confederate signal stations almost as soon as it began. No sooner had the Union assault columns crossed the Sudley Springs ford of Bull Run and engaged the enemy than heavy clouds of dust appeared on the heights above Col. Andrew Porter's and Col. Ambrose Burnside's brigades of Hunter's division, which were leading the attack. Seeing this, McDowell ordered additional troops to the front to meet the growing enemy force. As Porter's and Burnside's brigades reached the open fields above Bull Run, the enemy struck. Recalled a Rhode Island soldier in Burnside's leading brigade, "A perfect hailstorm of bullets, round shot and shell was poured upon us, tearing through our ranks and scattering death and confusion everywhere." Colonel Heintzelman's troops—the brigades of Cols. William B. Franklin, Orlando B. Willcox, and Oliver Otis Howard—arrived on the field to bolster Porter and Burnside. Then regiments of Col. William T. Sherman's and Col. Erasmus D. Keyes's brigades of Tyler's division, including Colonel Corcoran's 69th New York, crossed Bull Run and entered the fray.[30]

In the advance against the Confederate positions, three of Lon's classmates found themselves in desperate circumstances. As Willcox brought his three regiments—the 1st Michigan and the 11th and 38th New York—into the contest, he was badly wounded. Without their commander, the regiments began to lose formation until George Woodruff, Francis Parker and John Edie, "under a most galling and deadly fire from the enemy," moved out in front of the wavering regiments, beckoning them to stay in formation and continue the advance. In the dense smoke and din of battle, the three lieutenants, for all practical purposes, assumed command of the brigade, brought it into the fighting, and kept it in the engagement until the end.[31]

Added to the array of infantry moving against what McDowell thought was the Confederate left flank was a battery of Rhode Island artillery (six-pound James rifles) attached to the 2d Rhode Island Infantry regiment and two regular artillery batteries: Capt. James B. Ricketts's Battery I, 1st

United States Artillery, of Colonel Franklin's brigade, with young Lts. Edmund Kirby, William Elderkin, and Douglas Ramsey commanding two-gun sections; and Battery D, 5th United States Artillery—the old West Point Battery—of Col. Andrew Porter's brigade, commanded by Capt. Charles Griffin, in which Lon's friend Lt. Charles Hazlett commanded a two-gun section.[32]

With the initial clash of arms, the Confederates were forced back upon a hill whose name was derived from a whitewashed frame house of the widow Judith Carter Henry. Along Henry House Hill, though, the rebels made a determined stand. Augmented by reinforcements from Johnston's Valley Command—three brigades commanded by Brig. Gens. Thomas J. Jackson and Bernard Bee and Col. Francis S. Bartow, respectively—the Confederates launched a counterattack against the right flank of the advancing Union lines. The Union attack was driven back. Through the din, General Tyler was kept informed of enemy movements by his two competent staff officers, Lon's classmates Patrick O'Rorke and Joseph Audenreid. Even after O'Rorke's horse was shot down beneath him, he borrowed a mount and continued to ride across the shot-torn plain, keeping his commander apprised of the ominous developments.[33]

Shortly after Greene's battery was put in place east of Centreville, orders arrived for it to limber up and advance down the road toward Blackburn's Ford, where Richardson's and Davies's brigades and Hunt's battery were positioned. Greene's battery unlimbered in the fields adjacent to the road and just above the ford, alongside the guns of Captain Hunt. Lon was in command of the right section, Harris the left; they directed their cannoneers while mounted behind their gun sections. In minutes the four Parrott rifles were blasting shell into a Confederate infantry column and battery across Bull Run. The Confederate battery soon limbered up and withdrew. Wrote Lon to his mother, "I fancy I did some of the prettiest firing that was done that day. You ought to have seen me pour the spherical case and shell into their columns." Colonel Richardson immediately advanced skirmishers forward to feel for the presence of Confederate infantry. They were found in overwhelming numbers, and soon a Confederate infantry column, formed primarily from the 17th Virginia, broke out of the dense woods ahead of Lon's guns. The enemy column, though, "incautiously" presented its flank to Greene's battery. Lieutenant Greene, on his horse in the middle of the battery, called for canister. "We opened upon them," wrote Lon, "with such a terrible fire of canister that in a very short time nothing was to be seen of them but the tail of their retreating column." In the action, Lt. Presley H. Craig, who had attended West Point in 1853 and 1854 and who had just joined Hunt's battery, was seated on his horse alongside Lon when he was hit in the head by a musket shot and then in the chest by another ball.

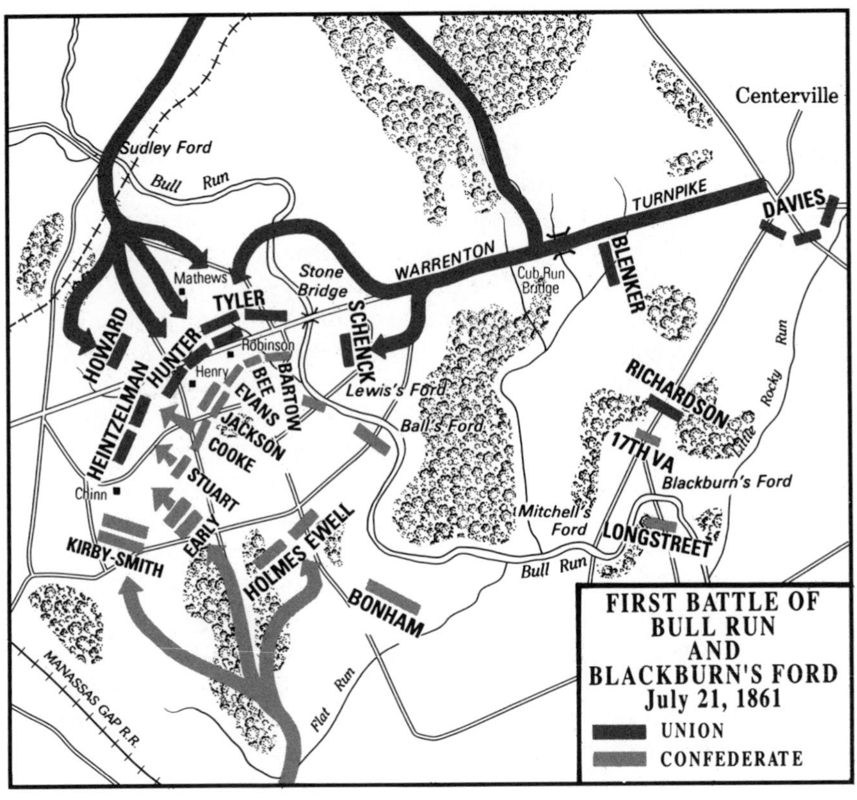
Centerville
Sudley Ford
Bull Run
TURNPIKE
DAVIES
WARRENTON
Mathews
Stone Bridge
Cub Run Bridge
BLENKER
TYLER
SCHENCK
HOWARD
HUNTER
Robinson
Henry
BEE
BARTOW
EVANS
HEINTZELMAN
JACKSON
COOKE
STUART
Chinn
Lewis's Ford
Ball's Ford
RICHARDSON
17TH VA
Little Rocky Run
Blackburn's Ford
Mitchell's Ford
LONGSTREET
Bull Run
KIRBY-SMITH
EARLY
HOLMES
EWELL
BONHAM
MANASSAS GAP R.R.
Flat Run
FIRST BATTLE OF BULL RUN AND BLACKBURN'S FORD
July 21, 1861
UNION
CONFEDERATE

He fell dead on the spot. It was Lon's first glimpse of death in combat. He would see much more.[34]

West of Blackburn's Ford, along the plain above Bull Run, McDowell's forces had begun by 4:00 P.M. to break under the enemy pressure. Little Dad Woodruff, Parker, Edie, and other officers could keep their troops in line no longer. Frantic Union soldiers began to flee in the face of the advancing Confederate lines. In an effort to save the panic-stricken army, Ricketts's and Griffin's batteries, supported for a time by two Zouave regiments (the 11th New York and 14th Brooklyn), made a determined stand along Henry House Hill. But in the terrific gunfire Lieutenant Ramsey of Ricketts's battery was killed. Then Ricketts himself was wounded and subsequently fell into the hands of the enemy. The command of the battery devolved upon young Ned Kirby, who, before he knew it, had lost twenty-seven of his cannoneers in the melee. The enemy was coming fast, and infantry supports were melting away. For all his bravery, Kirby was unable to stop the overwhelming Confederate advance. He told Lieutenant Elderkin to take the limbers and caissons to the rear as there were no cannoneers left on the field and no time to hitch up the guns. Battery I left behind on Henry House Hill all six of its guns, three of its limbers, and forty-nine of its horses; during the retreat it was forced to abandon also its six caissons, three more limbers, a battery wagon, and the forge.[35]

Like Kirby's battery, Griffin's guns were also overwhelmed. In the heat of battle the old West Point Battery had mistakenly opened up on advancing Union infantry. As confusion reigned in the Union lines, the oncoming Confederates seized the moment. Musketry became heavy, and every cannoneer of the battery fell before the murderous Confederate volleys. There were no artillerymen left on the field to help take Griffin's guns off. As it was, Griffin escaped with three of them, but two of the three were lost in the retreat. In all, Griffin lost twenty-seven men and fifty-five horses; in the end, he salvaged only a ten-pound Parrott rifle and a twelve-pound howitzer limber. After only one engagement, Battery I, 1st United States Artillery, almost ceased to exist, and the once proud West Point Battery had been utterly demolished.[36]

In the midst of the action around Ricketts's and Griffin's guns was Company G, 2d United States Cavalry. One of its platoon leaders was none other than Lt. George Armstrong Custer. Released from arrest at West Point on July 14, he had arrived in Washington on July 20 and was already commanding a platoon of cavalry on the bullet-swept plain above Bull Run.[37]

While McDowell's main threat was being overpowered along Henry House Hill, the action at Blackburn's Ford continued unabated. During the height of the action, Lt. Frederick H. Prime, an army engineer standing near Greene's battery, directed Lon's attention to a group of thirty or forty horsemen, evidently officers, on the far ridge above the creek. The distance was two to three miles—too great for the shells to reach, even at the Parrott rifles' most elevated positions. Lon turned to his drivers and ordered them to get shovels out of the battery wagons and dig holes beneath the trails of his guns. The drivers, under Lon's direction, dug holes deep enough to permit elevating the guns to about forty degrees. The trails of the Parrott rifles were set in the holes, and the shells were rammed home. At the command "Number one, fire!" the first rifle boomed, and its bolt arched nearly two and a half miles across the fields, bursting near the officer who seemed to be the center figure of the group. "Number two, fire!" The second shell ranged toward the group and exploded, sending all of the distant Confederate officers scampering. Lon and his cannoneers, with just pride in their gunnery, yelled above the din. "The best thing we did during the day," recalled Lon, "was to make Jeff Davis, Esq. travel pretty rapidly with his horse's head turned in a direction opposite from our battery."[38]

Lon's sentiments hardly told the story of Bull Run, though. McDowell's army had been whipped. Nearly 60,000 troops had seen action on that Sunday, July 21; by evening, nearly 5,000 dead and wounded were strewn across the fields above Bull Run, and McDowell's Grand Army was in full retreat. Frightened soldiers jammed the roads and dotted the fields. Members of Congress and countless civilians who had followed the army in buses, buggies, and wagons loaded with picnic baskets became panic-stricken. Their Sunday outing had turned into a nightmare. The long lines of beaten and frightened soldiers, along with terrified civilians, snaked their way along the turnpike toward Washington with Confederate artillery firing into their rear. Rifles, knapsacks, canteens, overturned wagons—equipment of every kind and description—littered the turnpike in the wake of the disaster. Almost as if to intensify the loss, the very windows of heaven opened up on July 22, and rain poured down, turning the roads into seas of mud.

As the disorganized remnants of McDowell's Grand Army fled back toward Washington, Lon remained active at the front. His number one section covered the retreat throughout the remainder of July 21 and well into the next day. Then Greene's battery, after all its infantry supports save the 18th New York had pulled back, finally withdrew up the road to Centreville. Lon's gun detachment proved to be one of the last commands to pull back toward the defenses of Washington.[39] A young Wisconsin soldier, on the evening of July 22, was trudging along the road from the Long Bridge to Bailey's Crossroads. A heavy rain was falling; the road had become a quagmire and was strewn on both sides with knapsacks, blankets, and other discarded accoutrements. Most of the soldiers walking along the road had been marching all night. The Wisconsin boy noticed Lon's section of Greene's battery move up the muddy road toward Washington as wet and weary foot soldiers scrambled to either side; years afterward, he remembered the officer in charge of the guns as Lt. Alonzo H. Cushing. Even though the events of the preceding days had been humiliating for McDowell's Grand Army, the circumstances, the soldier recalled, "had not been sufficient to take away [Alonzo's] smile."[40]

Greene's battery finally came to rest in Fort Albany on Arlington Heights, not far from Alexandria. Constructed in May by New York troops who named it in honor of their state capital, it protected the approaches to the Long Bridge as well as the Columbia Turnpike. Being on higher ground than Fort Runyon, Fort Albany became the site to which most of the Fort Runyon garrison returned, even though it had a perimeter of only 429 yards and emplacements for twelve guns. Fort Runyon was turned into a supply station.[41] Lon did not receive the recommendation for the brevet he wanted, but Lieutenant Greene had nothing but praise for his services. Lon and his fellow officers, Greene wrote in his official report of the battle, "were coolly and assiduously attentive to their duties . . . the accuracy of our fire was mainly owing to their personal supervision of each shot!"[42]

William Cushing heard the news of the disaster at Bull Run from aboard the frigate *Minnesota* in Chesapeake Bay. The loss—the carnage—that the war had already brought to the nation, and Lon's position in the heat of the fighting, frightened him. On July 31 Will penned a letter to his cousin Mary B. Edwards, daughter of former Congressman Edwards. "I don't know but I may resign before long and go into the land service," Will wrote. "I have no doubt but that I can procure a captain's berth in the volunteers. I so long to be near Allie. It seems as if I might be some protection to him in the hour of action. If the rebels should kill him I don't think that I would be a man any longer. I should become a fiend. I love that boy better than I do my own life, and I would not live without my brother." Such was the loyalty of the Cushing brothers to one another.[43]

Only days after the disaster at Bull Run, news swept through the camps surrounding Washington of the naming of a new commander of the Grand Army, Brig. Gen. George Brinton McClellan. A native of Philadelphia, McClellan had been graduated from West Point in 1846 as an army engineer and had served with General Scott in Mexico. At the outbreak of the Civil War he had been living in Cincinnati, Ohio, working as president of the Ohio & Mississippi Railroad. The soldiers had heard of McClellan's recent victories in the Rich Mountain campaign in western Virginia, and hailed him as a hero and savior of the Union.[44] At the time of McClellan's appointment, Washington was defended by a thin collection of volunteer and regular units whose capability as an army was virtually nonexistent. That collection of commands McClellan began to put into fighting shape. Using his superb organizational skills, "Little Mac," as he was called, began to instill discipline and pride in the ranks. McClellan christened his newly developing force the "Army of the Potomac." Under new calls for enlistments, men were flocking to recruiting staions all across the north, and soon new volunteer regiments and batteries were making themselves ready for service at the front. Such was McClellan's personal magnetism that in three weeks Lincoln appointed him a major general. By then, only General Scott outranked him in the regular army.[45]

Lon remained with Battery G, 2d Artillery, throughout the summer as the army settled down to drill, paper work, and boredom. Lon was directed to purchase horses and outfit a third section to be added to the battery. He busied himself at the assignment. Dull moments were often brightened by visits from his brother Milton.[46]

Then in September, while Greene's battery was in camp along Hunting Creek near Alexandria, Lon became seriously ill. For over a week a military surgeon, Dr. J.J. Woodward, attended to him. On September 18, Lon's condition was diagnosed as a "remittant fever, which is assuming a typhoid character." Woodward recommended a leave of absence, and Milton urged Lon to stay with him at his Washington quarters, a rooming house owned by two elderly ladies at 458 Twelfth Street West. Recognizing that he was too sick to carry on, Lon asked his surgeons to prepare for him his request for a leave of absence, which he signed on September 18. Permission was granted by McClellan's headquarters, and Milton took Lon to his home.[47]

In October, Will, after performing blockading duty outside of Charleston harbor and in Hampton Roads, was transferred to the blockading ship *Cambridge*, then stationed between the mouth of the Rappahannock River and Cape Henry. He heard of Lon's sickness and that he had been taken to Milton's home. While in the process of being transferred, Will hurried to Washington to visit his brothers. It must have been a joyous reunion for the three Cushing boys; they had not been together since their days in Fredonia. Will and Lon had heard that their cousin Mary Edwards had become engaged to be married. She had requested that Will serve as best man. With all three brothers present, Will believed it was a good time to write Mary a letter. Sitting at Lon's bedside he wrote of his duties at sea and asked for news from old Fredonia. He declined to serve in the wedding but sent his congratulations, and then added, "My brother, Alonzo, who is with me now, desires to add his congratulations to my own." Soon William Cushing bade his brothers farewell and sought passage to his new assignment.[48] When, in mid-November, Lon had regained enough strength to return to active duty, Will heard the news and sent a welcome note to their cousin Mary: "Alonzo is in good health."[49]

Lon received orders to proceed to Camp California near Fort Worth on the Orange & Alexandria Railroad, and to report to the commander of Batteries A and C, 4th United States Artillery. The location of Camp California was familiar to Lon; Greene's battery had occupied a site nearby just before he became ill with typhoid. Batteries A and C had arrived at Camp Duncan in the Washington defenses while Lon was on sick leave and had since been attached to the artillery brigade of a division commanded by Brig. Gen. Edwin Vose Sumner.[50]

Batteries A and C had received their orders to leave Fort Crittenden, Utah Territory, in mid-July. On July 27 they had left Salt Lake together, journeyed to Silver Creek, Utah Territory, and then just under five hundred miles to Fort Laramie, arriving there on August 29. Departing on September 2, they had journeyed nearly six hundred miles to Fort Leavenworth, Kansas, by October 6, and on October 20 they entered the defenses of Washington. Because of shortages in equipment, ordnance, and personnel, Battery A and Battery C were united upon their arrival, although they continued to maintain separate identities on muster rolls and battery returns. The combined batteries were equipped with four ten-pound Parrott rifles and caissons, eight limbers, a battery wagon, a forge, and several quartermaster wagons. Together, the batteries consisted of three officers and eighty-two enlisted men, with just over one hundred horses. By the fall of 1862, when the two batteries would be divided again, about 150 officers and enlisted men and 120 horses would be attached to Battery A alone. At the time of their arrival in Washington, the two batteries had commanders only on paper: portly and thick-bearded Capt. Francis Newman Clarke for Battery A and Capt. George Washington Hazzard for Battery C, but neither was in actual charge of the guns when they arrived in Washington. Moreover, virtually all the section commanders of both batteries had been assigned to other duties, and even their complements of noncommissioned officers were only skeletal.[51] On December 6, Lt. Evan Thomas of Battery C was temporarily named to command the combined batteries, since no more senior regular army officers were available to fill the vacancy. Thomas was probably the most well-connected young officer in the regular army. Seventeen years old at the time he had been appointed a second lieutenant in the 4th Artillery on April 9, 1861, he was the son of Gen. Lorenzo Thomas, former chief of staff to Gen. Winfield Scott and recently named adjutant general of the United States Army. That may well explain why Evan Thomas, not Alonzo Cushing, was placed in temporary command of the batteries. Born and raised in Georgetown, D.C., tall, sandy-haired, and long-faced,

Thomas bore a strong resemblance to his famous father, but unlike his father he was loose-jointed and rather unathletic-looking. His ungainly appearance, however, did not reveal the true man, for Evan Thomas was fiery and impulsive and would prove to be brave to a fault. He never flinched from using his family connections to elevate himself. In fact, obtaining rank and command through family and political connections was a practice rampant in the regular army. For professional soldiers like Lon, such use of connections by sons of prominent families made their work frustrating and difficult.[52]

One of the newly appointed section commanders assigned to Battery A was a lieutenant named Rufus King, an interesting personality, to say the least. Born in 1838 in Rome, New York, King had been raised in New York City, where his father was a lawyer; his grandfather Charles King, a noted merchant and journalist, had become president of Columbia College (now Columbia University); and his great-grandfather was the famous statesman of the federal era, Rufus King. Lieutenant King often referred to himself as "junior" in deference to yet another Rufus King, his uncle, a newly commissioned brigadier general in the Union Army whose command, made up of Wisconsin and Indiana regiments, would become known as the "Iron Brigade." When the war broke out, King had volunteered his services in the 7th New York State Militia after the unit had entered Washington, D.C. When his three-month enlistment expired, he was commissioned—undoubtedly as a result of efforts on his behalf by powerful family members—a second and first lieutenant on August 15, 1861, and assigned to Battery A. Rufus King would become a dominant personality in the combined batteries. Older than any of his senior commanders, he was a hard and excessive drinker and smoker, and he relished playing the banjo. Of large stature, King was swarthy, with his black hair and a large, full mustache; he clearly looked much older than his twenty-three years. He would become a rival of Lon's for battery command. But King was vain and overbearing; he often lacked good judgment, and his powerful political connections—although he would use them repeatedly—would never overcome Lon's position in the chain of command.[53]

Noncommissioned officers usually form the heart of any artillery battery, but Battery A had only three sergeants when it arrived in Washington. Francis Heard was serving as first sergeant. The battery carried on its rolls one newly promoted noncommissioned officer, however, who was to become the very best. Sgt. Frederick Fuger, born in Gappingen, Wurtemberg, Germany, in 1836, had emigrated to the United States during the years of famine and economic and political collapse of many German states in the early 1850s. He had worked as a bookkeeper in a New York mercantile establishment until he joined the army on August

21, 1856. Tall and powerfully built, Fuger was ideally suited for the artillery service. In September 1856 he had been assigned to Battery A, as a private. He had served in operations against the Seminole Indians in Florida in 1857 and had been with the guns at Ft. Leavenworth, Kansas, and in the expeditions in Utah, rising to the rank of corporal. He had seen hard fighting at Eagan Canyon, Nevada, in July and August 1860. On July 21, 1861, the day of the Battle of Bull Run, while his battery was still at Fort Crittenden, Fuger had reenlisted and was shortly thereafter promoted to the rank of sergeant. With sandy hair and a fair complexion, a neatly trimmed Vandyke beard and mustache, his deep German brogue, and his size and military bearing—not to mention his keen intellect—he commanded as much respect as he did attention. Although he was a German immigrant and a devout Roman Catholic, Fuger would quickly win Lon's deep respect and admiration. In a short time, he would become the soul of Battery A, 4th United States Artillery.[54]

From the date of Lon's return to active service until Christmas, the artillerymen spent their time drilling, day in and day out. Using the *Instruction for Field Artillery*, Lon drilled the cannoneers and drivers of the battery in the "School of the Piece," the "School of the Section" and the "School of the Battery." Over and over, the men trained at the Parrott rifles. They hitched the horses to the limbers and, pulling the guns and caissons, practiced "Movements in Column" and "Movements in Line." They practiced coming into battery, firing, and changing front. Marches, inspections, mock battles and parades became their constant bill of fare. Occasionally the batteries would advance closer to the Confederate positions outside Manassas to reconnoiter, but that represented all the action that took place. "I have almost given up all hope of a general engagement on the Potomac before Spring," Lon lamented.[55]

Christmas eve, 1861, was windy and rainy. Lon kept a "rousing fire" burning in his tent stove. "So long as the tents don't blow down," he wrote, "we can keep warm no matter what the weather is." Such was all the comfort Camp California could offer him that December 24. Lon's thoughts were of home—and his girlfriend. "It is almost Christmas," he wrote to his mother, "and it would afford me great pleasure to take my Christmas dinner at home but of course that is impossible." He reminded Little Ma about their parting when his furlough from West Point had come to an end exactly two years before. "You referred in your last letter to my friends having followed me to the depot for the purpose of 'seeing me off,'" he wrote. "It was a sly contrivance, but the straight part of the story you have probably not heard. One of the individuals who went to see me off—no names mentioned—refused to give me a kiss at the last moment. This was an excess of modesty which quite overcame my feelings and I was quite disconsolate. I was however in some degree comforted by the thought of having exacted two kisses from another young lady—no name mentioned—just as I was seeing her off. After reflecting upon the scriptural saying (to be found in the book of Job) that modesty is the chief beauty in woman, I gradually became satisfied with myself and all my fellow creatures and gradually fell asleep to dream about the two kisses."[56]

Lon would see his home one more time and, possibly, his girlfriend, whoever she was. And there would be one more Christmas.

4

"It Was the Grandest Sight"

For Lon, 1862 began with a visit to Milton's quarters in Washington on New Year's Day. The new year was to prove eventful from the outset. Lon had been noticed by the commander of his division and on January 21 was assigned to duty as the ordnance officer on the staff of General Sumner. Although Lon wanted to remain in the artillery service, the appointment to staff duty relieved him of the awkward situation created by the assignment of Lt. Evan Thomas as commander of Batteries A and C. He probably accepted his new assignment with some relief.[1]

From the very beginning, General Sumner and Lon developed a special relationship. It was almost inevitable that they would, for both descended from Puritans whose families had been instrumental in the development of colonial Massachusetts.[2] Moreover, Sumner's wife, the former Hanna W. Forster, and their children had been living in Syracuse, so both he and Lon called western New York their home at the time they met. During the thirteen months that Lon would know Sumner, the general would become almost a father figure to him. So close were the two men that Lon would even spend his leave with the Sumner family in Syracuse just days before the general's unexpected death in March 1863.[3]

Born in 1797, General Sumner had entered the United States Army in 1819 as a second lieutenant in the 2d United States Infantry and had served through the Black Hawk War. Promoted to the rank of major in the 2d United States Dragoons by 1846, Sumner had distinguished himself during the Mexican War at Cerro Gordo, Contreras, Churubusco, and Molino del Rey and achieved the rank of lieutenant colonel in the 1st Dragoons in 1848. By 1855 he had been elevated to the rank of colonel and had been given the command of the 1st United States Cavalry. In March 1861 he was one of the three regular army brigadier generals appointed by President Lincoln, succeeding Gen. David E. Twiggs, who had been dismissed from service after surrendering Union forces and supplies to Confederate authorities in Texas in February. Sumner arrived in the eastern theater of war after a brief stint as commander of the Department of the Pacific in San Francisco, where he had replaced Col. Albert Sidney Johnston.[4]

General Sumner was a fine-looking specimen. Of medium height and with long legs and arms, he had a clear complexion, a high forehead, and hazel eyes. His white hair and full beard gave him the appearance of a kindly grandfather. He was quick-witted, often displaying a wonderful sense of humor, but his good temper in conversation belied his bulldog tenacity under fire. He became absolutely absorbed in battle. Throwing caution—and often good judgment—to the wind, Sumner would ride into the midst of the fighting with his troops, exhorting them on by yelling and waving his hat. He had won the nickname "Bull Head" or "Old Bull" during the Mexican War when a spent musketball purportedly struck him in the head and bounced off. The nickname was fitting indeed.[5] Raised in the Presbyterian faith like all his ancestors, Sumner was fiercely Protestant and thoroughly temperate. And like other descendants of early Puritans, he was clannish; he preferred to have those of like background and religion around him. In every respect, he was a nativist. He had known many Cushings back in Massachusetts; probably attracted by what he associated with the name, he turned to Lon to serve on his staff when he learned of young Cushing's assignment to an artillery battery in his division.[6]

Lon reported to Sumner's headquarters at Camp California near Fort Worth along the tracks of the Orange & Alexandria Railroad. The general was still recovering from an injury received when he had fallen from his horse just before Christmas; nevertheless, he put his division through drills, reviews, inspections, marches, and picket duties all through the winter months. Lon quickly learned the routine of headquarters duty. He learned that as a staff officer he would be expected to serve as his commander's eyes and ears on the battlefield as well as in camp. Moreover, he would be his commander's principal means of communication with division, brigade, and regimental commanders as well as with the officers of other corps and with General McClellan on the battlefield. In all, it must have been exciting for him. At Sumner's headquarters Lon met many of the command personalities in the army, including McClellan, whom he admired from the outset. The position gave Lon a wider opportunity of seeing many of his old West Point classmates and friends such as Joseph Audenreid, who was serving on the staff of Brig. Gen. William H. Emery; Henry Noyes, on the staff of Brig. Gen. William H.T. Brooks; and last but not least, George Custer, who, although still with the 2d United States Cavalry, would be appointed to the staff of McClellan himself in the coming campaign.[7]

All through the winter months the Army of the Potomac grew in size and capability. Even though McClellan was named general-in-chief of the

Union armies upon the retirement of Winfield Scott, the administration wrangled with Little Mac over the extent of his command, the composition of the Army of the Potomac, and the direction of its movement against the enemy.[8] Richmond, the Confederate capital, was the military objective of McClellan as well as the War Department, but when the army would move and how it would get there, whether by land or by sea, were subjects of considerable discussion and political manuevering. McClellan urged a movement by water—down the Potomac River, across the Chesapeake Bay to Fort Monroe—and then an overland operation up the peninsula between the York and James Rivers to Richmond, with the Navy playing a supporting role up and down the two great rivers.[9]

The point where McClellan proposed to land the Army of the Potomac was the site of intense land and naval activity which, by early March 1862, would claim the first loss of the war in Lon's family. In Norfolk, Virginia, across Hampton Roads from Fort Monroe, Brig. Gen. Benjamin Huger commanded a sizable Confederate force; on the peninsula itself, Maj. Gen. John Bankhead Magruder, one time commander of Battery I, 1st United States Artillery, commanded another. Where the James River emptied into the great Chesapeake Bay at Hampton Roads, the shipyards of Norfolk, Newport News, Hampton (not to mention Richmond), the economic and military lifelines of Virginia and the Confederacy, were heavily protected. As part of the Anaconda Plan initiated by Gen. Winfield Scott, a Union blockading squadron of eleven frigates and gunboats under the command of Flag Officer Louis Goldsborough controlled the waters of Hampton Roads, from one of only two Union naval bases in the South at the time. Among the ships in the squadron was the screw frigate *Minnesota* (to which Midshipman William Cushing had formerly been assigned) and two sailing frigates, the *Cumberland* with twenty-four guns, and the *Congress* with fifty guns. For the previous three years the *Congress* had been commanded by Lt. Joseph B. Smith, the son of Mary Cushing's cousin Commodore Smith. Lieutenant Smith, born in 1826, had entered the Navy in 1841, the year of Lon's birth. On duty in Hampton Roads since just after Virginia's secession convention, Smith had repeatedly written to the Navy Department and his father about the dangers of an ironclad vessel the enemy was constructing in the Norfolk navy yards. Named the *Merrimack* before its alterations, the rebuilt ship had recently been rechristened the *Virginia*. Commodore Joseph Smith, although skeptical at first, had finally agreed to help persuade President Lincoln to back the construction of another ironclad, the *Monitor*, to match the *Virginia*. The arrival of the Union warship in Hampton Roads, however, proved to be just hours too late for young Joseph Smith and the *Congress*.[10]

On March 8, 1862, the *Virginia* left Norfolk accompanied by several small gunboats. Capt. Franklin Buchanan, the ironclad's commander, spotted the *Cumberland* and the *Congress* near Newport News. The *Minnesota* and the screw frigate *Roanoke* began to move to the aid of the two sailing frigates, but the *Minnesota* ran aground, and the *Roanoke* developed engine trouble. The *Virginia* delivered a terrific broadside into the *Congress* and then bore down on the *Cumberland*, ramming its starboard side and unloading round upon round of heavy shells into the wooden ship. In minutes the *Cumberland* went down. The *Virginia* then turned toward the *Congress* in company with three more Confederate warships. Lieutenant Smith put the *Congress* to sail in an attempt to escape, but even though assisted by a tug, the ship ran aground in the shallow waters. Soon the *Virginia* and its support ships opened fire, and in what was described as a "galling fire of solid shot, shell, grape and canister," the *Congress* was reduced to shambles. Lieutenant Smith was killed. His executive officer, seeing the situation was hopeless, hoisted the white flag. The ship surrendered and was burned. When Commodore Smith was informed, he bowed his head and was heard to murmur, "Then Joe's dead!" Lt. Joseph B. Smith was the first casualty of the war among Lon's close relatives.[11] The next day, the strange-looking *Monitor,* which had just arrived in Hampton Roads, engaged the *Virginia* for nearly four hours and sent the Confederate ship back to the Norfolk shipyards damaged.[12]

Back in the camps of the Army of the Potomac in front of Washington, there was a sense of anticipation. Indeed, by early spring 1862 the morale of the soldiers had improved markedly over what it had been the previous fall, in spite of the repetition of drills, and parades and the boredom of winter camp life. President Lincoln, in accordance with McClellan's reorganization efforts, established corps within the Army of the Potomac. Pursuant to General Orders Number 101, issued on March 13, 1862, the Second Army Corps was created by combining the divisions of Sumner, Blenker (though his would be detached March 21), and John Sedgwick. General Sumner that same day was named commander of the corps, and Gen. Israel B. Richardson assumed command of Sumner's division. The Second Corps, from its inception, would prove to be one of the best in the Army of the Potomac. Created as well were four other corps: the First, commanded by Brig. Gen. Irvin McDowell; the Third, commanded by Brig. Gen. Samuel P. Heintzelman; the Fourth, commanded by Brig. Gen. Erasmus D. Keyes; and the Fifth, comprising the forces on the upper Potomac. In all, McClellan, on the eve of his grand movement against Richmond, commanded an army of 130,000 men.[13]

With his elevation to Second Corps command, Sumner asked Lon to serve on his staff as an aide-de-camp, along with Lts. Lawrence Kip and Samuel Storrow Sumner (the general's son). Sumner also brought onto his staff Capt. J.H. Taylor, formerly of the 6th United States Cavalry, as acting assistant adjutant general; Capt. Francis Newman Clarke (who on the rolls of the 4th Artillery was still commander of Battery A) as chief of artillery; and surgeon J.F. Hammond as medical director of the corps.[14]

General Richardson's First Division was composed of notable personalities and units. The First Brigade of the division was commanded by Brig. Gen. Oliver Otis Howard, one of the librarians at West Point while Lon was a cadet; it was made up of such sturdy infantry units as the 61st and 64th New York, the 81st Pennsylvania and the 5th New Hampshire.[15] The Second, known as the "Irish Brigade," brought Lon, as a staff officer, face to face with the famine Irish. Its Irish-born commander, Brig. Gen. Thomas Francis Meagher, had been banished from Ireland to Tasmania for sedition and treason. He had escaped to America in 1852, and until the outbreak of the war he had been a lawyer, lecturer, and publisher in New York City. He had served as a major in Colonel Corcoran's 69th New York State Militia at First Bull Run. Commissioned a brigadier general in February 1862 for his ability to bring Irish immigrants to the Union cause, Meagher, although an honest—and somewhat outspoken—sympathizer with the southern cause, had proved his worth.[16]

Meagher's brigade was solid Irish; every one of its officers and men had been mustered from the Irish settlements in teeming New York City. It consisted of Col. John Burke's 63d New York, Col. Robert Nugent's 69th New York, and Col. Patrick Kelly's 88th New York. (Added to the brigade once the army reached the peninsula, however, would be the Yankee 29th Massachusetts.) The officers and men of the three New York regiments spoke with thick Irish brogues; they were devout and uncompromising Roman Catholics, and Catholic chaplains followed the brigade everywhere. To honor the Emerald Isle, a homeland to which they remained absolutely—in fact, romantically—devoted, the three regiments carried green silk flags with Irish emblems and Gaelic mottos. Many of those Irishmen, being exiled revolutionaries themselves, openly expressed a philosophical attachment to the southern cause. But, like Blenker's Germans, they had been socially, politically, and economically shunned by a nativist America. Although they disapproved of slavery, the institution played little or no role in their decision; its effects were too remote, too unrelated to their own desperate plight in crowded New York City. Consequently, what made them follow General Meagher to wear the Union blue was probably the simple fact that they were in desperate need not only of employment but of proving themselves worthy of a place in their new country. And, again like the Germans, the Irishmen believed that if the Union cause prevailed, America would be a sanctuary for others who sought escape from troubled Erin. Some Fenians actually felt that their military experience in America would help them someday to wrest Ireland's independence from England. As a Puritan nativist, Alonzo

Cushing probably had as great difficulty accepting the Irishmen as he had the Germans. In such feelings he was undoubtedly joined by General Sumner.[17]

The Third Brigade, commanded by Brig. Gen. William H. French, consisted of the 52d, 57th, and 66th New York and the 53d Pennsylvania. Like most Union infantry regiments from the East, they were for the most part made up of American natives plus large numbers of recent German and Irish immigrants. The 52d New York, known as the "Sigel Rifles," was almost entirely German.[18] Also attached to Richardson's division was a brigade of three artillery batteries, which included Batteries A and C, 4th United States Artillery; Capt. John D. Frank's Battery G, 1st New York Light Artillery; and Capt. Rufus D. Pettit's Battery B, 1st New York Light Artillery.[19] Pettit's battery of four ten-pound Parrott rifles would become a notable unit. Raised in Elmira and Baldwinsville by Rufus Pettit, a stoop-shouldered former carpenter and Mexican War veteran from Syracuse, its officers and enlisted men hailed for the most part from Onondaga County, New York, though a sizable number were attached from the 14th New York Independent Battery.[20] Aside from the 29th Massachusetts, Richardson's division, once it reached the peninsula, would be augmented by Col. George W. Von Schack's solid German-speaking 7th New York, known as the "Steuben Guard," and Col. Henry Wharton's 2d Delaware.[21]

General Sedgwick's Second Division of Sumner's corps was a command composed, in part, of units from the brigade of the ill-fated Brig. Gen. Charles P. Stone which had fought at the Battle of Ball's Bluff in October 1861. Like the First Division, Sedgwick's was a mixture of old-line American natives and recent German and Irish immigrants.[22] Brig. Gen. Willis A. Gorman's First Brigade—the 15th Massachusetts, 1st Minnesota, 34th and 82d New York, 1st and 2d Companies, Minnesota Sharpshooters—was composed of excellent fighting men, many of whom were native-born Americans. The commands nevertheless were liberally interspersed with Germans and Irish.[23] The Second or "Philadelphia" Brigade, commanded by Brig. Gen. William W. Burns, was virtually all Irish and German. Composed of Col. Joshua T. Owen's 69th Pennsylvania, Maj. Charles W. Smith's 71st Pennsylvania, Col. DeWitt Clinton Baxter's 72d Pennsylvania, and Col. Turner G. Morehead's 106th Pennsylvania, the brigade showed considerable promise, though it did have some command, organization, and morale problems. Morale problems or not, the soldiers of the 69th Pennsylvania proudly carried a green flag with the Irish emblems of a castle keep and wolfhound.[24] The Third Brigade, commanded by Brig. Gen. Napoleon J.T. Dana, was a strange mixture of Irish immigrants and Massachusetts natives. The men of the 19th and 20th Massachusetts, many from old-line Boston and Salem families of

Puritan lineage, formed a stark contrast to those of the 42d New York, an Irish regiment raised by the Irish Democratic political organization known as Tammany Hall. The 7th Michigan, whose men hailed from faraway Detroit and its surrounding towns, rounded out Dana's brigade.[25]

The batteries of the artillery brigade attached to Sedgwick's division were a superlative combination of volunteer and regular units. Commanded by Col. Charles H. Tompkins, the brigade consisted of Capt. John A. Tompkins's Battery A, Capt. Walter O. Bartlett's Battery B, and Capt. Charles D. Owen's Battery G, all 1st Rhode Island Light Artillery, plus Lt. Edmund Kirby's Battery I, 1st United States Artillery.[26] After Bull Run, Ned Kirby, like Lon, had become seriously ill with typhoid fever. Little Dad Woodruff had taken over command and had led the unit through the fiasco at Ball's Bluff. Having been recently equipped with six light twelve-pound Napoleons, the battery already had seen more action than any unit in the Union army. Now, to add to its luster, Ned Kirby was back in command. His section commanders were Little Dad, John Egan, and Frank S. French, son of General William H. French.[27] No finer volunteer batteries could be found in the Army of the Potomac than Battery A (with six ten-pound Parrott rifles) and Battery B (with four ten-pound Parrott rifles and two howitzers) of the 1st Rhode Island Light Artillery. Both organized at Providence, Rhode Island, they could already boast distinguished service records. Battery A had served in Burnside's brigade at Bull Run, where, in company with Ricketts's and Griffin's batteries along Henry House Hill, it had performed able service. Battery B had not been organized until August 1861, but within days it had been sent to the Virginia front. Attached to General Stone's brigade, it had seen its baptism of fire at Ball's Bluff.[28]

Although his duties called him to Sumner's headquarters, Lon often visited with the officers and men of Batteries A and C, 4th United States Artillery. In the early spring of 1862 the combined batteries were placed under the command of Capt. George Washington Hazzard, an 1847 graduate of West Point who had served in the 4th Artillery throughout his career. He had been in command of Battery C, at Fort Crittenden. Accepting a commission from his home state, however, he had become the colonel of the 37th Indiana shortly after the outbreak of the war but had resigned his volunteer commission in March 1862 and had returned to the 4th Artillery.[29]

Also in March, Batteries A and C gave up their ten-pound Parrott rifles and were issued six light, twelve-pound brass Napoleons, together with six caissons, twelve limbers, a battery wagon, forge, and four quartermaster wagons. Almost in anticipation of the increase in ordnance, Batteries A and C had sought to bolster their complements of cannoneers, drivers, and teamsters from the time they arrived in Washington. Nearly every one of the eighty-two enlisted men who accompanied the batteries into Washington had served with the two units in Utah. In the ranks of those regulars were all the noncommissioned officers and experienced cannoneers. In desperate need of manpower, the batteries had turned to the infantry regiments in General Sumner's division for help. Beginning in September 1861 and proceeding through the winter of 1862, Battery A had brought into its ranks men from the 5th New Hampshire, the 53rd and 81st Pennsylvania, and the 52d, 57th, 61st, 63d, 66th, 69th, and 88th New York, as well as the 14th New York Independent Battery. In all, fifty-one infantrymen and artillerymen from those units had been added to the rolls of Battery A alone. Battery C gained recruits similarly, among them hefty numbers of Germans and Irish. In the ethnic background of their personnel, Batteries A and C had become, by the spring of 1862, a microcosm of the Second Corps—indeed, of the Army of the Potomac.[30]

Two young lieutenants, Edward Field and Arthur Morris, joined the batteries in the early spring of 1862 as subalterns. Born in Princeton, New Jersey, in 1841, Field had enlisted in Col. William Halstead's 1st New Jersey Cavalry at the outbreak of the war; he had been commissioned a second lieutenant on August 29, 1861, and assigned to Company I. When Colonel Halstead resigned, Field had accepted a commission in the 4th Artillery. He was a young officer with great promise.[31] Morris, the son of Brig. Gen. William Walton Morris of the 4th United States Artillery, was appointed a second lieutenant in the 4th Artillery on March 24, 1862. Apparently several years younger than Lon, he was then living with his father at Fort McHenry in Baltimore.[32] Like all commissioned officers in the combined batteries, Lieutenants Field and Morris were from well-connected and thoroughly Protestant American families. Batteries A and C represented what was true throughout the regular United States Army: although enlisted personnel included many German and Irish immigrants, command was for the most part performed by old-line Protestant Americans.

McClellan's proposed advance on Richmond finally was accepted by President Lincoln. On March 17, McClellan ordered what amounted to twelve divisions to move by transports from Alexandria, Virginia, down the Potomac River and Chesapeake Bay to Fort Monroe, Virginia. The vast armada of nearly 130,000 men took three weeks to make the journey. In addition to the men, some 3,600 wagons, 700 ambulances, 300 pieces of artillery, 2,500 head of cattle, and 25,000 horses were ferried from Alexandria to Fort Monroe.[33]

The two divisions of the Second Corps were widely separated at the time McClellan's advance got under way. Richardson's division was near

Manassas; Sedgwick's was between Charles Town and Berryville, Virginia. Maintaining communications between the widely separated divisions must have been no small task for the busy aides-de-camp. Lon was in the saddle continually. Sedgwick's division, given its location near the main rail line to Washington from the Shenandoah Valley and Harpers Ferry, was the first to move. Its three brigades went north, crossed the Potomac to Point of Rocks, Maryland, and was transported by the Baltimore & Ohio Railroad to Washington. Two days later the division embarked on transports for Fort Monroe. Gen. Sumner and his staff, including Lon, accompanied Sedgwick's division.[34] Batteries A and C had been advanced to Rappahannock Station on March 10. There, where the Orange & Alexandria Railroad crosses the Rappahannock River, the batteries had engaged the enemy. After firing some 143 rounds of ammunition, they had returned to Warrenton, Virginia, on March 29. Then on April 1, Batteries A and C began their movement toward the Peninsula with Richardson's division.[35]

Arriving at the tip of the famous Peninsula, Sedgwick's division was held near Old Point Comfort until April 4, when a forward movement began. At the time of its arrival, Sedgwick's division moved under orders of General Heintzelman, commander of the Third Corps. The advance was brief; it came to a halt the very next day when it struck Confederate defense lines along the Warwick River at Yorktown. General Magruder's eighteen-mile front along the river was manned by a thin line of only 17,000 troops. But not knowing the strength of the enemy, McClellan ordered a reconnaissance of the defenses, and on April 7, even though his Army of the Potomac outnumbered its opponent by more than four to one, he resolved to place Yorktown under siege.[36] In front of Yorktown, Heintzelman's Third Corps occupied the right; General Keyes and his Fourth Corps held the left, facing the lower Warwick River. Sedgwick's division held the center of the siege lines. On April 6 McClellan placed General Sumner in command of the left wing of the army.[37]

With the growing Army of the Potomac facing Magruder, Gen. Joseph Johnston's troops of the Department of Northern Virginia near Manassas were sent to Magruder's assistance. By the end of April, Confederate strength along the Peninsula increased to nearly sixty thousand; McClellan's want of nerve had given his adversaries time to assemble their forces in his front. Behind Johnston, General McDowell's Union First Corps, which had not followed McClellan to Fort Monroe, was directed to move out of Washington to positions along the Rappahannock River near Fredericksburg in order to be in a position to protect the capital or to coordinate movements with McClellan as circumstances warranted.[38]

The war already was being fought across half a continent. Union forces had maneuvered the Confederates out of Kentucky and deep into southern Tennessee by early spring of 1862. Far away, in southwestern Tennessee, near a log meeting house called Shiloh Church, Lon's family suffered yet another loss in April 1862. There, on April 6, Confederates under Gen. Albert Sidney Johnston surprised Gen. Ulysses S. Grant's Union forces. The surprise attack rapidly exploded into a ghastly affair involving the full weight of both armies. Battery B, 1st Illinois Light Artillery, with Pvt. Howard Bass Cushing manning one of the guns, helped defend the Union right flank near Shiloh Church against one of the most desperate assaults of the battle. The left wing of Johnston's army slammed into Gen. William T. Sherman's Union division. The attack was led directly against Howard Cushing's position. One regiment in Col. John A. McDowell's brigade of Sherman's division which was brought forward to support Battery B was Col. Stephen G. Hicks's 40th Illinois; it tried to stem the tide of the determined attack, but its effort proved futile, and the regiment was decimated. Not far from Howard Cushing's guns fell his and Lon's first cousin, Pvt. Theodore P. Tupper, son of Rachel Cushing Tupper and Edward W. Tupper of Putnam, Ohio.[39]

Back along the Peninsula in Virginia, McClellan remained inactive in front of Yorktown, although his army continued to grow in size. His ability to win a decisive victory over the enemy in this theater, however, was slowly ebbing away. On May 4, just before McClellan was to begin the bombardment of Yorktown, the Confederates evacuated their Warwick River front and withdrew to the defenses encircling the city of Richmond. McClellan pursued, and a rearguard action was fought near Williamsburg on May 5. On May 9, Confederate General Huger abandoned Norfolk and withdrew up the south side of the James River toward Petersburg. McClellan's enormous army and its endless trains of wagons came to a halt at positions north of the meandering and treacherous Chickahominy River, a stream marked by vast swamps and marshlands. The army's supply base was at White House Landing on the Pamunkey River near the rail terminus of the Richmond & York River Railroad known as West Point.[40]

The Army of the Potomac continued to take shape while it pursued Johnston's withdrawal. Gen. Richardson's division along with Batteries A and C, 4th Artillery, had finally arrived on the peninsula to bolster the Second Corps. The Fifth Corps under Brig. Gen. Fitz John Porter and the Sixth Corps commanded by Brig. Gen. William B. Franklin were officially organized on May 18 after the two big commands had landed on the Peninsula. An Artillery Reserve commanded by Col. Henry J. Hunt arrived with the Fifth Corps.[41] By the end of May, Franklin's Sixth Corps lay near New Bridge with Porter's Fifth Corps in the rear, both forming the right flank of the army extending to Beaver Dam Creek, while the corps of Keyes and Heintzelman on the New Kent Road formed the left. Sumner's Second Corps held the center, occupying a grading of the Richmond & York River Railroad about three miles east of the Chickahominy River.[42]

On May 29 the left flank of the Army of the Potomac crossed the Chickahominy River: Keyes's Fourth Corps moved up the Old Williamsburg Road to within seven miles of the City of Richmond near a place called Seven Pines or Fair Oaks Station, with Heintzelman's Third Corps not far behind. The advanced flank was dangerously exposed to attack. Army engineers constructed bridges across the Chickahominy along Sumner's front to allow it to move as quickly as possible to the support of Keyes and Heintzelman. On May 30 a heavy rain fell, and soon the waters of the Chickahominy began to rise. The position of the advanced corps of General Keyes became perilous.[43]

On May 31 the Confederates seized the advantage. General Longstreet's right wing of General Johnston's army, augmented by the division of Brig. Gen. W.H.C. Whiting, was directed down Nine Mile Road to strike Keyes's right flank. Maj. Gen. Daniel Harvey Hill's division was directed to mount an assault against Keyes from the Williamsburg Road, while General Huger was ordered to move against Keyes's left flank from the Charles City Road. Heavy rains continued to fall. After a series of delays, the Confederates struck the Union advanced corps between 1:00 and 2:00 P.M.[44]

Sumner and his Second Corps heard the roar of battle ahead as Hill's division struck Keyes in what quickly grew into a vicious engagement. Immediately, Old Bull ordered his corps to move forward. Lon galloped down the long lines relaying the command. At about 2:00 P.M. the Second Corps moved down to the very edge of the Chickahominy River in anticipation of an order to enter the fight. But the bridges over the fast-rising river were in hideous condition: the corduroy logs on the approach roads had been undermined by the swollen waters and were afloat, and the spans that crossed the main channel were rising and falling and swaying back and forth under the river's raging pressure.[45] Nevertheless, at about 2:30 P.M. the order came to cross. Richardson's division was directed to what has been called "Sumner's" or "Lower" bridge, and Sedgwick's division to the famed "Grapevine" bridge. Richardson's troops ran into difficulty almost immediately. With one brigade barely across the raging stream, the bridge became so weakened that its collapse seemed imminent. Consequently, the two remaining brigades were ordered to move north to the Grapevine bridge behind Sedgwick's column. Some of the soldiers crossed the raging stream by "wading through mud and water up to their bellies," remembered Lon. The artillery had an even more difficult time. All batteries of the Second Corps became bogged down in the thick mud of the roads leading to the bridges; only one—Ned Kirby's Battery I, 1st United States Artillery—managed to get any of its guns across the swirling river. That feat was accomplished only with the help of details of infantrymen who were ordered to assist in pulling the guns by prolonges up the muddy river bank and onto the plain on the south side of the stream.[46]

General Sumner and his staff, with Lon at the general's side, galloped across the Grapevine bridge with Sedgwick's leading column in company with Kirby's guns. Ahead of the Second Corps columns, Lon could see that four regiments of Brig. Gen. Darius N. Couch's First Division of Keyes's Fourth Corps, spread out along a ridge that crossed the Williamsburg Road, were resisting heavy Confederate fire. Led by Col. Alfred Sully's 1st Minnesota of Gorman's First Brigade, Sedgwick's columns advanced down the muddy road after crossing the bridge. Seeing the dense columns of infantry moving to his support, Couch deployed his own regiments so as to form, with the Second Corps, a formidable battleline. Ahead in the fields and in the dense woods beyond, Lon could plainly see heavy lines of Confederate infantry forming for an assault.[47] There was not a moment to waste. As the head of Sedgwick's division moved into place, Ned Kirby managed to bring three of his Napoleons and one caisson to the front. There, alongside two Parrott rifles of Capt. James Brady's Battery H, 1st Pennsylvania Light Artillery, Kirby—with Lt. John Egan as his lone section commander—swung his three guns into position.[48]

As he was doing so, the Confederates advanced from the woods in force. Sedgwick's and Couch's two divisions were intermingled, straddling the road. General Sumner and Lon rode up and down behind the lines "with a perfect storm of bullets whistling around," Lon recalled, "exhorting the regiments to stand firm." Volley upon volley of musketry echoed across the plain. Kirby's guns fired rapidly, but the trail of one of them broke during a recoil after having fired only four rounds. The enemy, in places, advanced to within fifteen yards of Sumner's lines. Just then Lon's classmate Little Dad Woodruff brought out of the muddy Chickahominy two more of Kirby's Napoleons.[49]

Under the yells of Woodruff and his cannoneers and the bugle's sound of "Action front!" the mud-spattered guns were brought into battery and began shelling the Confederate lines. Behind Woodruff the last gun, under Lieutenant French, was pulled out of the muddy river bank and, under cracking whips, brought across the bullet-swept fields to its place in the battery. To Lon the sight was spectacular. Kirby ordered his guns to advance to the left to get a better fire on the Confederate lines. At that moment, General Whiting's full Confederate division advanced out of the woods toward Kirby's battery, and the fight was on in earnest.

Double charges of canister and ferocious volleys from Union infantry regiments were poured into the dense ranks of butternut and gray. As the Confederate columns wavered under the intense fire, Kirby, with the help of infantrymen from the supporting 15th Massachusetts of Sedgwick's division, attempted to push the guns farther ahead. Within minutes, though, three guns were bogged down in the mud.[50]

General Sumner seized the opportunity to mount an attack himself. Most of Sedgwick's three brigades had reached the field. Sumner ordered Sedgwick to proceed to the right flank of the lines and direct the attack from there; Couch was ordered to the left, and Sumner personally directed the regiments in the center. The enemy was just about fifty yards away in front of dense woods when Sumner gave the order to "fix bayonets." Lon rode down the lines yelling the order to the infantrymen. Then came the command, echoing down the lines: "Forward!" The long line of muddy infantrymen moved ahead. Sumner himself led the 34th and 82d New York, the 15th and 20th Massachusetts, and the 7th Michigan in the attack. The hard-charging infantry of the Second Corps crossed two fences before they struck the enemy. Four of General Whiting's Confederate brigades—Whiting's own under Col. Evander McIvor Law and those of Brig. Gens. Wade Hampton, Robert Hatton, and J. Johnston Pettigrew—collapsed. General Hatton was killed; youthful and brilliant General Pettigrew was wounded and captured as the Confederates withdrew to Fair Oaks Station. In the advance of Sumner's corps, virtually every one of Old Bull's staff officers had his horse shot down. Lon not only lost his horse; he was struck in the breast by a bullet, but his dispatch book and pistol, which were tucked in his breast pocket, took the full impact of the projectile. "It only knocked the breath out of my body," he remembered. The ferocious fighting that occurred on the evening of May 31 was "the grandest sight I ever witnessed," Lon recalled. "Just as it was getting dark—the muskets were much heated—there were two long parallel sheets of flame from the opposing lines and I can conceive of nothing more grand than the spectacle presented, nor nothing so exhilarating as that splendid bayonet charge. It was enough to almost lift one out of his boots. I never expect to witness another as beautiful a fight if I live to be as old as Methuselah."[51]

Finally darkness settled over the bloody landscape, and the fighting subsided, but there was no time for rest at corps headquarters. Lon was directed back across the Grapevine bridge to help bring forward Richardson's division. After a tedious march, Richardson's men finally emerged across the swaying bridge, and Lon directed them to their position in the lines. He worked until late at night aligning commands along the dismal field. Finally, on a wet blanket, with rain continuing to fall, Lon bedded down with the rest of the battle-weary Second Corps. "We slept with the dead and wounded all around us that night," he recalled, "but the groans did not disturb me much as I was tired."[52]

Little did the soldiers of the Second Corps know at that time that General Joseph E. Johnston, commander of the formidable Confederate army ahead of them, had been wounded and disabled in the day's action. Temporarily, Maj. Gen. Gustavus W. Smith had assumed command, but within days a new commander would take over the reins of the butternut and gray legions—none other than Gen. Robert E. Lee.[53]

Lon was aroused at 3:00 A.M. on June 1. All through the night the infantry columns, artillery batteries, and ordnance trains of the enemy could be heard moving along the muddy roads as fresh troops were being brought up to the battlefront. At about 7:00 A.M. the enemy struck Richardson's division, and the fighting quickly became desperate. To augment the Second Corps, Brig. Gen. Joseph Hooker's brigade of Heintzelman's Third Corps arrived on the field. Three Confederate brigades advanced against the Union center. Again, Lon was in the saddle, riding up and down the lines, steadying the men and carrying messages for General Sumner. In General Howard's brigade, virtually every field grade officer fell in the fighting. Howard himself was struck in his right arm and carried from the field. Lon observed the general being borne from the front on a litter "while waving his hat leading his troops on." Sumner, Lon recalled, "continually rode along the lines cheering the troops. For four hours and a half they poured in their troops, when they were finally driven back upon Richmond, the flower of their army having been whipped."[54]

In two days of bitter fighting, nearly 11,000 men were lost in the fields east and south of Fair Oaks Station. The intense battle had been far costlier than Bull Run. Gen. Gustavus Smith withdrew his Confederate forces closer to Richmond, and the Union troops—now four army corps on the south bank of the Chickahominy—moved forward to positions along Nine Mile Road, extending down to White Oak Swamp. In front of Fair Oaks Station where Sumner's corps was positioned, the dead littered the fields. "The Confederate dead," Lon said, "were heaped three deep on the field in some places and we were three days in burying them and then had to burn a great many which had become exceedingly offensive."[55] To Lon, an artilleryman, the high point of the Battle of Fair Oaks had been the work of Kirby's battery, which had covered itself with laurels. "Magruder's old battery gave 'Prince John' a very warm reception," Lon wrote to his brother Milton, "and there is no end of compliments heaped upon the three young officers—Kirby, Woodruff (of my class) and French, who worked the guns so gallantly and skilfully."[56]

After the Battle of Fair Oaks the Army of the Potomac remained strung out on both sides of the Chickahominy River. Where before the battle its left flank had been exposed to attack, after the battle Gen. Fitz John Porter's Fifth Corps, the right flank, was the only element of the army north of the river. Like Keyes's Fourth Corps only days before, Porter's Fifth Corps was isolated and invited attack; nevertheless, it held its perilous position. McClellan remained anxious that General McDowell's First Corps near Fredericksburg would soon be able to connect with the advanced right flank of his Army of the Potomac.[57] In front of Fair Oaks Station, Sumner's Second Corps began to throw up earthworks, redoubts, and embrasures "studded with artillery," all "flanked by swamps, tangled thickets and slashed timber." Although rain continued to fall, the corps slowly solidified and strengthened its foothold on Virginia soil. General Sumner turned the two-and-one-half-story Courtney house near Fair Oaks Station into his headquarters. Lon and the other staff officers pitched their tents in the yard. Behind heavy epaulements encircling the Courtney house, Battery A, 1st Rhode Island Light Artillery, and the 1st Minnesota protected the Second Corps headquarters.[58]

Like most men in the Army of the Potomac, Lon believed that the end of the war was in sight. "If their whole army was unable to whip half of ours as it stood ten days ago," wrote Lon to his brother William on June 10, "how beautifully we will be able to sweep over their whole force, intrenchments and all, when our reinforcements come." His confidence of victory—and of the conquest of the Confederate capital—was supreme. Lon's letter continued: "It rains incessantly and as our headquarters are only a few hundred yards from the enemies' batteries, and he is continually shelling us, we have to be in the saddle most of the time and are consequently pretty generally soaked. I have been wet all day and have just gotten in hungry as an earthquake. Dinner is about ready and I could not think of missing it for the world, so I must bid you an affectionate farewell, hoping that you may get a few days leave and come up to see me in Richmond when I get my quarters established there."[59]

Days passed. There was no activity except daily artillery barrages and minor skirmishes. The rain and heat seemed unending, and many soldiers became ill. Malaria, typhoid, and dysentery thinned the ranks of every Union regiment and artillery company. Among the aides-de-camp on General Sumner's staff, only Lon and Lieutenant Kip escaped illness. In Batteries A and C, Lt. Evan Thomas became seriously ill and left active duty on June 25. He would not return to the batteries until August 17.[60]

Within the Confederate lines the new commander, Gen. Robert E. Lee, worked around the clock to reorganize his army. From the Shenandoah Valley he summoned the Valley Command of Maj. Gen. Thomas J. "Stonewall" Jackson, a force renowned for its sound thrashing of Union armies in the great valley that spring. The Confederate left flank, situated on the south bank of the Chickahominy across from the little crossroads village of Mechanicsville, was poised for action. Jackson was directed to link up with Lee there.[61]

On June 26 the lull in the fighting along the peninsula came to an end. While Magruder's and Huger's Confederate divisions demonstrated along Sumner's front near Fair Oaks Station, Maj. Gen. Ambrose Powell Hill, in advance of the arrival of Jackson's delayed command, sent five of his brigades across Beaver Dam Creek in what proved to be a suicidal attack against Porter's well barricaded troops. The next day the attacks were renewed at a place called Gaines's Mill, where the main Union lines were drawn up along high ground above Boatswain's Swamp of the Chickahominy River. In spite of ferocious attacks by the divisions of Gens. A.P. Hill, D.H. Hill, and James Longstreet, the high ground held by the Union Fifth Corps above the swamp proved impenetrable.[62]

On the night of June 27, McClellan issued orders for all his corps to withdraw to the James River. McClellan had been fuming over word that the boastful Maj. Gen. John Pope, who had just been brought to Washington from the western theater, had been named commander of all troops in northeastern Virginia, including McDowell's First Corps at Fredericksburg. McClellan, deeply disturbed, believed that the War Department was actually trying to defeat him. In the wake of such news and in the wake of the terrific fighting at Gaines's Mill, McClellan lost his will. He determined he would shift his base of supply from White House Landing on the Pamunkey River to Harrison's Landing on the James River in order more easily to effect a withdrawal from the Peninsula. Such a change of base in the face of a rejuvenated enemy commanded by a general with such consummate skill as Lee was dangerous in the extreme. McClellan nevertheless directed Keyes's Fourth Corps to cross White Oak Swamp on June 28; Porter's Fifth Corps was to follow Keyes. Heintzelman's Third, Franklin's Sixth, and Sumner's Second Corps were directed to pull back on the night of June 28 and 29 and form the rearguard. The news of such a withdrawal after having come so close to Richmond left Lon, like most Union soldiers, in a state of dismay.[63]

General Sumner's Second Corps abandoned its elaborate defenseworks at Fair Oaks Station on the morning of June 29 and proceeded back across the Chickahominy River a short distance to a depot on the Richmond & York River Railroad known as Savage Station, where there were large quantities of supplies as well as a general hospital. On horseback, Lon helped coordinate the movement, directing the two divisions of the corps back across the swollen Chickahominy. Assisting Lon was his friend Fannie Custer, from General McClellan's headquarters. Arriving at Savage Station early in the morning, Sumner ordered all the military stores at the depot burned. The 15th Massachusetts was called upon to fire the stores, and soon columns of black smoke from burning crates of hardtack, barrels of pork, and sacks of coffee and sugar towered above the depot. While the 15th Massachusetts was busy destroying the commissary stores, General Meagher's Irishmen were directed to destroy ordnance supplies. Sumner then moved his corps south, across the Williamsburg Turnpike and into the fields of Allen's farm, to protect the southern approach to Savage Station.[64]

Lee observed McClellan's movements with keen perception. No sooner had the Second Corps abandoned Fair Oaks Station than Lee ordered a pursuit. Stonewall Jackson's command rebuilt the Grapevine bridge, and the divisions of Gens. Richard S. Ewell, W.H.C. Whiting, and D.H. Hill were pushed across the Chickahominy River toward White Oak Swamp. Magruder's command, meanwhile, advanced east, pursuing the Union rear, while Huger's command moved south of White Oak Swamp to pressure the Union left.[65] Magruder was right on the heels of Sumner's Second Corps. No sooner had the Second Corps entered its bivouac on Allen's farm than Magruder made contact with it at about 9:00 A.M., on June 29. Sumner called for his three best batteries: Kirby's, Pettit's, and Hazzard's, which took up positions just north of the Allen farmhouse. Only four of Hazzard's guns were placed on Allen's farm; Hazzard remained at the front with the two sections—Field's and Morris's—while Rufus King withdrew his two-gun section and all the caissons back to Savage Station, where Franklin's Corps was already preparing defensive positions. Supporting the three batteries at Allen's farm were elements of Richardson's division: Gen. William H. French's brigade, as well as the 71st Pennsylvania of the Philadelphia Brigade.[66] Using only two brigades—those of Brig. Gens. Joseph B. Kershaw and Paul J. Semmes—Magruder attacked. His brave Confederates were met by a hail of spherical case, shell, and canister from the three Second Corps batteries. Although Magruder brought his own artillery to bear on the Union guns, it was to no avail. Captain Hazzard's four brass guns fired more than a hundred rounds of ammunition, and Captain Pettit's four Parrott rifles fired some two hundred rounds before the Confederates withdrew from the field.[67]

Sumner pulled his corps back to Savage Station after he received intelligence from Gens. William B. Franklin and William F. Smith that the enemy was crossing the Chickahominy in large numbers and advancing against the railroad depot. In the saddle among the troops on Allen's farm, Lon delivered messages to the advanced units of the Second Corps as well as to Heintzelman and Franklin. Sumner directed Heintzelman to move his corps into a position to hold the Williamsburg Road. Franklin's and Sumner's corps were then aligned in position to receive the expected enemy assault. General Brooks's brigade of Franklin's corps held the left flank in a dense woods, while General Sedgwick's three brigades held the

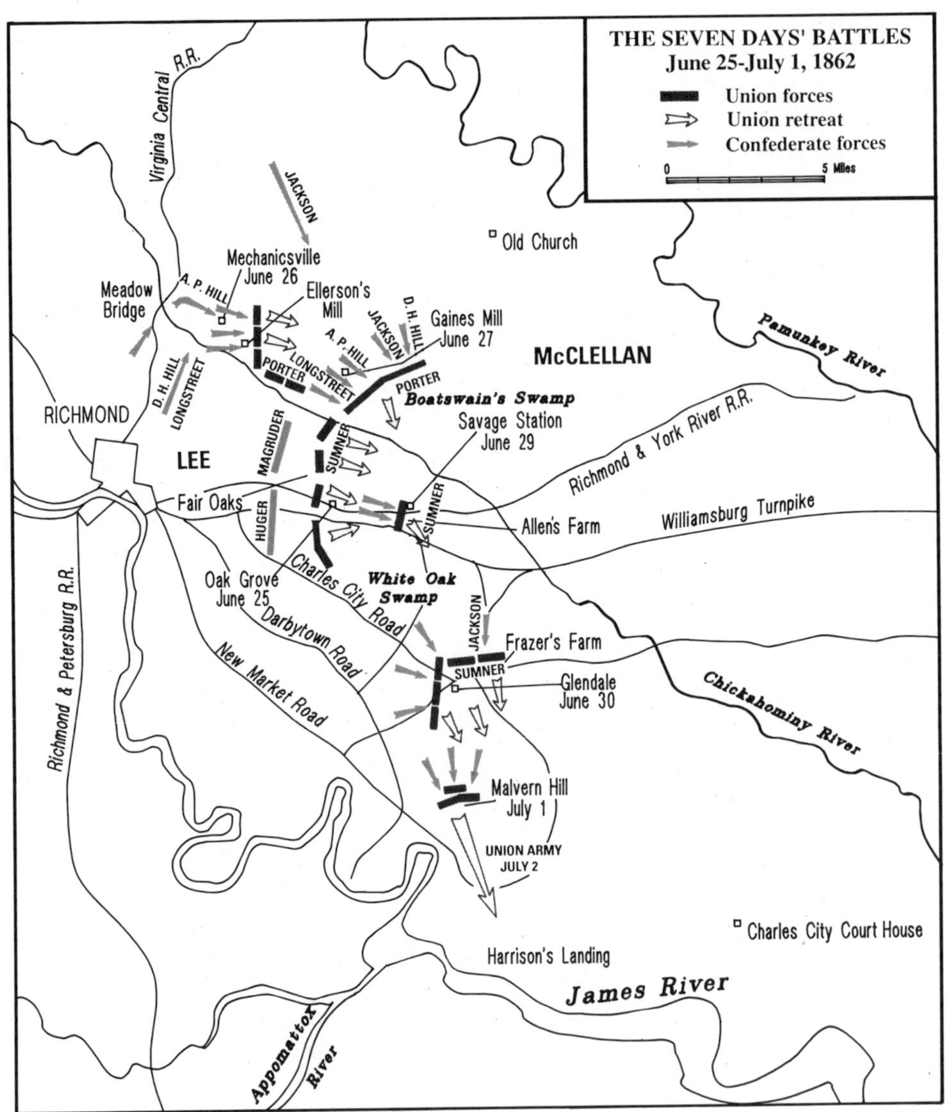
THE SEVEN DAYS' BATTLES
June 25-July 1, 1862
Union forces
Union retreat
Confederate forces
0
5 Miles
Virginia Central R.R.
JACKSON
Old Church
Mechanicsville
June 26
Meadow
Bridge
A. P. HILL
Ellerson's
Mill
JACKSON
D. H. HILL
Gaines Mill
June 27
A. P. HILL
McCLELLAN
Pamunkey River
D. H. HILL
LONGSTREET
PORTER
LONGSTREET
PORTER
Boatswain's Swamp
RICHMOND
MAGRUDER
SUMNER
Savage Station
June 29
Richmond & York River R.R.
LEE
Fair Oaks
HUGER
SUMNER
Allen's Farm
Williamsburg Turnpike
Richmond & Petersburg R.R.
Oak Grove
June 25
Charles City Road
White Oak
Swamp
JACKSON
Darbytown Road
Frazer's Farm
SUMNER
Glendale
June 30
New Market Road
Chickahominy River
Malvern Hill
July 1
UNION ARMY
JULY 2
Charles City Court House
Harrison's Landing
James River
Appomattox
River

center of the field. Lon, Lieutenant Kip, and Lon's old classmate and card-playing friend Lt. Henry Noyes, of General Brooks's staff, helped establish the new lines. Kirby's, Pettit's, and Hazzard's batteries again were positioned together along high ground west of Savage Station and in front of Richardson's division. In battery alongside Richardson's infantrymen were the guns of Capt. Tompkins's Battery A, 1st Rhode Island Light Artillery, and Capt. Thomas W. Osborn's Battery D, 1st New York Battery, along with Capt. Walter M. Bramhall's 6th New York Independent Battery of Hooker's division, Heintzelman's Third Corps.[68]

At about 4:30 P.M. Magruder attacked Savage Station with Kershaw's and Semmes's brigades, along with Brig. Gen. William Barksdale's 17th and 21st Mississippi. Although the Confederate brigades of Brig. Gens. Robert Toombs and Howell Cobb approached the battlefield to Kershaw's left, north of the railroad, they never entered the fight. Instead, the engagement turned into an fierce artillery duel which did not subside until dark. A heavy rain began to fall that night. Lon was worn out, and the cannoneers in the Second Corps batteries were completely exhausted.[69]

The soldiers of the Second Corps were aroused on June 30 by the sounds of bugles and drums as McClellan continued his withdrawal toward the James River. In a driving rain the Second Corps soldiers, led by Lon and Lieutenant Kip, left Savage Station, crossed White Oak Swamp, and concentrated on high ground behind the swamp. To Lon's disgust, the army not only withdrew in the face of the enemy but left behind a general hospital at Savage Station containing 2,500 wounded comrades and nearly 500 doctors and nurses. As General Smith's Sixth Corps division and General Richardson's Second Corps division crossed over the White Oak bridge, they made preparations to burn it in order to block further Confederate pursuit. Lon helped align the two divisions in battle order on high ground south of the swamp.[70]

The men in Captain Hazzard's battery were aroused too late to take their places in the vanguard of the corps. Once they threw off their rain-soaked blankets, though, they rushed to harness the horses to limbers and hitch up the six Napoleons and their caissons. Soon the battery was under way, followed by Battery B, 1st Rhode Island Light Artillery. Coming up fast behind them were the Confederate divisions of Stonewall Jackson and D.H. Hill. It was a close escape, but the two batteries made it to White Oak bridge at about 9:00 A.M., just as Richardson's men were preparing to fire the span. As Hazzard's six guns, caissons, baggage wagons, and forge rumbled across the bridge, the infantrymen cheered. Hazzard's men, fatigued and hungry, drove their guns to a ridge behind Richardson's division, on Nelson's farm. There Captain Hazzard was told that his battery must prevent the enemy from crossing the swamp and hold the ground at all cost.[71]

Lee continued his relentless pursuit of McClellan's weary legions. Jackson's and D.H. Hill's divisions pushed ahead through the swamp until they reached the White Oak bridge, which, by the time of their arrival, had been destroyed. There Jackson and Hill halted.[72] Holding the southern ridges overlooking White Oak Swamp to the left of Smith's and Richardson's divisions, and facing west, were elements of the Third, Fifth, and Sixth Corps. General Porter's Fifth Corps held the line at Malvern Hill, and between his commands and Smith's and Richardson's were the divisions of Brig. Gens. George A. McCall, Joseph Hooker, Philip Kearney, and Henry W. Slocum. Sedgwick's Second Corps division held a position behind McCall along the Long Bridge Road, ready to support either McCall or Richardson. With the dense swampland in front of them, the Union infantry and artillery were aligned along a series of ridges and hills in an area that proved to be a natural defensive position. To hold the hard-marching Confederates in front of White Oak Swamp would buy for McClellan the necessary time to complete the transfer of his ponderous supply trains from White House to Harrison's Landing. Lon spent his time riding between the two separate divisions of the corps, delivering messages from General Sumner and aligning the commands.[73] Meanwhile, pressing south and east, Lee directed Huger's division down the Charles City Road and Magruder's down the Darbytown Road. Gen. Theophilus Holmes's command moved up in front of Porter's strengthened position in front of Malvern Hill.[74]

At White Oak bridge and Nelson's farm, the fighting broke out in earnest at about 1:30 P.M. Stonewall Jackson, rather than advance south into the swamp, brought twenty-eight pieces of artillery to the front and, through the dense woodlands, opened fire on Smith's and Richardson's divisions. Hazzard's men had had only about two hours' rest when the heavy shelling began. Aroused, the men sprang to their guns, which were still hitched to the limbers. General Richardson rode up to Captain Hazzard and ordered him to bring his battery into position just to the left of Nelson's farmhouse. The Confederate guns continued firing. Masked by the dense woods, the cannoneers in Hazzard's battery could spot the enemy artillery only by the flame and smoke of each shot. A "perfect hail storm of artillery missiles" was hurled at Richardson's infantrymen and Hazzard's battery. In the barrage, First Sgt. Charles J. Brennan of Battery C was wounded. One shell struck the staff of the batteries' guidon, breaking it to pieces. Feeling that the batteries were too exposed, General Richardson directed four of the guns to be placed in a small gorge to the left of their first position, covering the bridge across White Oak Swamp. After only fifteen minutes, Hazzard received an order for all his guns to retire. Moving back nearly four hundred yards, he was then directed to occupy the first position to the left of Nelson's farmhouse, supported by the Irishmen of the 69th New York.[75]

With bugles sounding "Action front!" the six guns rumbled into position. In minutes—with King, Field, and Morris each commanding a two-gun section—Batteries A and C, 4th United States Artillery, began blazing away. The fire from the enemy artillery was rapid and extremely heavy, but its range was not quite long enough; most of the shells fell about twenty feet short of Hazzard's guns. Additionally, the brow of the hill in front of the battery seemed to protect Hazzard's cannoneers, many enemy shells hitting the natural epaulement and richocheting over the heads of the artillerymen. A "perfect shower of grape," though, ripped through the battery. The men stood nobly by their pieces nevertheless. Captain Hazzard cheered them on, giving them words of encouragement when they appeared most fatigued. Men were falling rapidly under the hail of iron. Lieutenant Morris was wounded slightly. At one gun, three of the horses were struck and killed; they became entangled in the harness, and simultaneously, the drivers were struck in their legs and feet and were unable to disentangle themselves from the wreckage of the dead and mangled horses. Capt. Hazzard cut the wounded men and dead horses loose himself. He then was seen carrying ammunition to a gun where the cannoneers were entirely exhausted. At one point, Hazzard and Rufus King took turns serving as the number one cannoneer with the sponge and rammer at a gun in the right section of the batteries.[76]

Within half an hour after the fighting commenced, Captain Hazzard was struck when a shell burst in the batteries while he was standing by one of the limbers superintending the unloading of ammunition. A shell fragment hit him in the leg, breaking the bone and severely mangling the flesh. Bleeding and in terrific pain, he was carried off the field, and Lt. Rufus King took over the command. The batteries continued firing until nearly all ammunition had been exhausted. Colonel Nugent and his New York Irishmen stood by the guns ready to repel any enemy infantry advance. General Meagher, although under arrest at the time, assisted the cannoneers in running one gun forward after its recoil. Upon being told by King that the batteries were just about out of ammunition, Meagher volunteered to inform General Richardson. But before additional ammunition could reach the guns, King pulled them back into a hollow. Meagher had stood alongside the batteries throughout the engagement, assisting the weary cannoneers.[77] The batteries had suffered severely. Besides Captain Hazzard, they had lost two sergeants and six privates from Battery A, and the first sergeant, two corporals, and four privates from Battery C. One sergeant was wounded while trying to carry

Hazzard to the rear. Hazzard's wound proved fatal; he would die on August 14, 1862.[78]

At about 4:30 P.M. the Confederate divisions of A.P. Hill and James Longstreet attacked McCall's Fifth Corps division and Hooker's and Kearney's Third Corps divisions southwest of White Oak bridge and Nelson's farm at a place called Fraser's farm. After the brigade of Col. Micah Jenkins struck the Union lines, Longstreet's full division launched its attack. Taking the brunt of the assault, the 12th Pennsylvania of McCall's division broke. Rallied by their colonel, the survivors of the regiment fell in with Hooker's division. The 69th Pennsylvania of Sedgwick's division was sent forward to bolster the wavering defenses. McCall's two "German" batteries—Capt. Otto Diederichs' Battery A and Capt. John Knieriem's Battery C, both of the 1st New York—were forced back, but the Confederate penetration was finally stopped by fire from the batteries from Col. Henry Hunt's Artillery Reserve.[79] As the Confederates along Fraser's farm were stopped, Hooker's division—led by the 1st Massachusetts, 2d New Hampshire, and 26th Pennsylvania, with the 71st and 72d Pennsylvania and the 19th and 20th Massachusetts of Sedgwick's division—counterattacked. The assault forced the Confederate legions back.[80]

Finding the going rough in front of Sedgwick's division, the Confederates increased the pressure farther up the line against Kearney's division and Brig. Gen. George Gordon Meade's brigade of Pennsylvania Reserves of McCall's division. As the Confederates reached Capt. George E. Randolph's Battery E, 1st Rhode Island Light Artillery, the fighting became hand to hand. General Meade was wounded, General McCall was captured, and the division command devolved upon former West Point commandant Brig. Gen. John Fulton Reynolds, who until then had commanded the First Brigade in McCall's division. Soon, though, Reynolds was captured too. On Sumner's orders, Lon rode to General Richardson, asking him to detach Gen. John C. Caldwell's First Brigade. As Meade's and Kearney's commands were reeling back, Caldwell's brigade arrived. Led by the 61st New York, the 81st Pennsylvania, and the 5th New Hampshire, the Second Corps brigade slammed ahead, beating back the Confederate assault. In an effort to encourage his muddy, wet, and tired soldiers, General Sumner grabbed a captured Confederate battle flag. With Lon looking on, Sumner yelled to his men and then dragged the captured battleflag through the mud, often walking on it to inspire his soldiers. With additional reinforcements from the Sixth Corps approaching the bloody field, the Confederate assaults against Fraser's farm finally ceased.[81]

Nightfall ended the fighting along White Oak Swamp. Behind Sumner's corps, Porter's Fifth Corps continued to prepare defensive positions along Malvern Hill. Colonel Hunt placed the guns from his Artillery Reserve all along the hill, protecting all its approaches. General Porter placed Brig. Gen. George W. Morell's division on the left of the hill with its left touching a small stream known as Turkey Run. Brig. Gen. George Sykes's Fifth Corps division supported Morell. To the right of Morell and Sykes was the Fourth Corps division of General Couch. Having marched through the darkness, Kearney's and Hooker's Third Corps divisions were positioned in reserve.[82]

Lon worked all through the night helping to pull the two Second Corps divisions together from Fraser's farm and Nelson's farm. Keeping the battle-weary and fatigued soldiers in line and on the march was exhausting work. Down the muddy roads the weary Second Corps soldiers tramped in the darkness until they arrived at a position behind the Third Corps along Malvern Hill. When the Second Corps finally came into view, the weary men were met by cheers and the playing of numerous regimental bands. The joyous sound was heartening to the wet and weary Lt. Alonzo Cushing.[83]

Having failed to deliver a knockout blow during the previous five days, Lee sought one final attempt to destroy McClellan's army, believing it had been badly damaged. Stonewall Jackson's command—his own division, together with Whiting's, Ewell's, and D. H. Hill's—advanced toward Malvern Hill on the Quaker Road. Magruder's division followed and was directed to form on Jackson's right below Malvern Hill; Magruder was misinformed by messengers, however, and actually marched away from the position he was instructed to take. Brig. Gens. Lewis Armistead's and Ambrose R. Wright's brigades of Huger's division arrived to form the right flank. Gen. D.H. Hill's division formed the center of the Confederate assault force astride the Quaker Road. General Whiting's division formed the left flank.[84]

At 1:00 P.M. on July 1, Colonel Hunt ordered his artillery to open fire on the Confederate lines. The Confederate artillery had difficulty organizing its response. Without effective artillery support, General Armistead advanced his brigade against the Union skirmishers who had worked their way down Malvern Hill. Magruder's division finally arrived, and Lee ordered it to follow Armistead's advance. D.H. Hill, hearing Magruder enter the fighting, believed it to be the signal for a general advance and moved forward. The attack proved to be suicidal: in the face of horrendous artillery fire from well-placed guns, the Confederate formations were decimated. Darkness brought the slaughter to an end.[85]

That night the Army of the Potomac withdrew in great confusion to Harrison's Landing on the James River, where McClellan ordered his army to throw up entrenchments and prepare gun emplacements to protect its precarious position. The returns of the two armies later revealed losses of nearly 36,000 men over seven days.[86] It must have seemed to Lon that it had all been for nothing. He had learned some valuable lessons, though. Not only had he participated in moving vast numbers of men into positions on hotly contested battlefields; he had paid close attention to the work of the artillery. The fighting on the peninsula had illustrated to him, as no textbook or tactics class lecture ever did, the value of the artillery arm. Though clumsy as an offensive weapon on the battlefield, an artillery battery was the key to holding any position. In the formation of lines to be defended, the artillery commanded the field. The effective placement of guns and their efficient service meant life or death to an army. Lon soon would take those lessons and put them to use himself.

On July 4, Edwin Vose Sumner was elevated to the rank of major general, and Richardson and Sedgwick were commissioned major generals of volunteers. With the wounding of Captain Hazzard, Batteries A and C desperately needed another experienced officer. On the same day, Lon was temporarily assigned to his old batteries to fill the vacancy. His classmate Joseph C. Audenreid was assigned to take his place on Sumner's staff. Named quartermaster at Second Corps headquarters was Capt. A.W. Putnam, an officer who, as his name implied, had deep roots in Puritan Massachusetts. Surgeon J.L. Liddell became the new medical director.[87]

Midshipman William Cushing, after having sailed to Cape Hatteras to seek out the Confederate blockade-runner *Nashville* earlier in the spring, had returned to the Chesapeake Bay seriously ill. Once again, the effects of tuberculosis had left him virtually incapacitated. Weak and frail, Will rested near Washington for nearly six weeks, then returned to the *Minnesota*. But after the capture of Norfolk and the destruction of the *Virginia*, he sailed up the James River in support of McClellan's peninsula operation on the staff of Flag Officer Goldsborough.[88] On July 5, without getting specific authorization from Goldsborough, Will left his vessel and headed toward the camps of the Army of the Potomac at Harrison's Landing in search of his brother. He found Lon still with General Sumner but preparing to take up his new duties with the artillery. The two boys spent several days together. Lon told and retold stories of his adventures in battle, and Will was enchanted with each and every tale. "When we met I was so fired by his story of the Seven Days battle," Will later recollected, "that I could not resist the temptation, in defiance of discipline, of going on the same in order to participate in the next affair."[89]

President Lincoln visited the army while it was at Harrison's Landing, trying to secure from McClellan some plan for putting the Army of the Potomac into action. Instead, he got a lecture from Little Mac on the political objectives of the war. Disheartened, the president did stay long enough to review the army. Accompanying General Sumner, Will and Lon helped escort Lincoln during his inspection of the Army of the Potomac. President Lincoln left the peninsula resolved to take matters into his own hands.[90]

When William returned to Norfolk, he was immediately placed under suspension for leaving his commander. He took the discipline with a boyish air of nonchalance. "But as a midshipman is hardly considered a responsible being," he said, "[I] was soon released—and not only released but promoted!" On July 16, William Barker Cushing was elevated to the rank of lieutenant, jumping thereby the ranks of master and ensign. In spite of his boyish pranks, Will was rising in the Navy.[91]

Although Lon was not recommended for a brevet for his services on the Peninsula, he did receive a glowing commendation from General Sumner after Fair Oaks. Lon's services, the general said, were "valuable." To Old Bull, Lon was "at all times ready, willing and able," and during the Seven Days, Sumner asserted, he was "indefatigable in the discharge of [his] duties."[92]

For all its efforts, though, the Army of the Potomac—that strange mixture of men—had not taken Richmond but had ended its campaign bottled up along the banks of the James River with its commander reduced in authority and the enemy on the move toward Washington.

5

"My God! We Must Get Out of This!"

While McClellan's Army of the Potomac was locked in its struggle for existence on the Peninsula, Maj. Gen. John Pope had been building a sizable force, the Army of Virginia, outside of Washington. One corps in Pope's new command consisted of nearly all German regiments, many of which had seen action in the Shenandoah Valley. They were now commanded by Maj. Gen. Franz Sigel, a German revolutionary who had been born in Sinsheim in the Grand Duchy of Baden. "I fights mit Sigel" became a rallying cry for those German immigrant soldiers in his corps, many of whom idolized him. Politician-turned-soldier Maj. Gen. Nathaniel P. Banks commanded another of Pope's corps, while Maj. Gen. Irvin McDowell was brought back to Washington to command a third corps.[1]

Pope advanced out of Washington in an effort to protect the nation's capital and threaten central Virginia. The movement was designed to draw elements of Lee's army from the Peninsula and thereby relieve the pressure on McClellan.[2] With McClellan's Army of the Potomac ahead of him and Pope's army threatening his rear, Lee detached Stonewall Jackson's command and directed it toward Gordonsville, Virginia, to confront Pope. Using the trains of the Virginia Central Railroad, Jackson transported 12,000 troops to Gordonsville, detrained there, and marched north toward Culpeper. On August 9, 1862, Jackson met General Banks's corps at Cedar Mountain and crushed it.[3]

After sitting behind trenchworks and gun emplacements at Harrison's Landing for nearly a month, the Army of the Potomac, under orders from the War Department, finally began its evacuation of the Peninsula during the week of Banks's disaster at Cedar Mountain. Heintzelman's Third Corps and Porter's Fifth Corps were the first to leave. They were both rushed north to join the Army of Virginia.[4] Observing the remnants of the Army of the Potomac withdraw down the James River, Lee struck north with the main body of his army. Pope turned his forces around and withdrew north; he sought to concentrate his forces at Gainesville, Virginia, not far from the old Bull Run battlefield. But before Pope knew it, Jackson reached Manassas Junction and destroyed his stockpiles of supplies and provisions on August 26.[5]

With Jackson at Manassas, there was genuine fear that the nation's capital was in danger. Sumner's Second Corps, after arriving at Aquia Creek Landing on the Potomac River, was ordered to move to the Rappahannock to support Pope's advance. When General Sumner received news of the rout of Banks at Cedar Mountain and of Jackson's raid at Manassas Junction, the Second Corps was turned around and directed to Alexandria. For Lon and his fellow artillerymen, the movements and counter-movements must have been as confusing as they were exhausting. From Alexandria the Second Corps finally moved to a position in front of the Chain Bridge, one of the key approaches to the city of Washington.[6]

The next few days proved disastrous for the braggart Pope. He struck Jackson at Groveton, Virginia, on August 28; Jackson's Confederates withdrew and then assembled along an unfinished railroad grading not far from the Bull Run battlefield. Pope attacked on August 29, using Sigel's and McDowell's corps, but the assault failed to break the Confederate lines. The next day Pope struck again, this time using Porter's Fifth Corps. The assaults were repulsed with heavy losses. Lee then counterattacked. By the late afternoon, the Union Army of Virginia was crushed. Ironically, Pope's army finished the battle holding Henry House Hill above the meandering Bull Run, the very site of the destruction of Ricketts's and Griffin's batteries just one year before.[7] Lee immediately set out on an encircling movement toward Fairfax Court House, and Jackson struck Union forces at Chantilly on September 1. In the end, Pope withdrew his broken and battered commands back inside the Washington defenses. The Second Bull Run campaign was over; it had cost the Union over 16,000 casualties.[8] In the wake of the disaster and to meet Lee's new threat, McClellan was again placed in command of Union forces in Washington on September 5. He set about assembling the broken and scattered elements of his Army of the Potomac and what was left of Pope's Army of Virginia outside the capital city.[9]

What McClellan was given to reformulate a new Army of the Potomac proved to be one of the largest and most imposing collections of manpower of the war. Little Mac was placed in command of the better part of seven army corps. McDowell had been relieved of command; the new First Corps of the Army of the Potomac, a capable fighting force, was commanded by Maj. Gen. Joseph Hooker, who on the Peninsula had won the sobriquet "Fighting Joe." Hooker's First Corps was composed of three divisions commanded by Brig. Gens. Rufus King, James B. Ricketts and George Meade. Maj. Gen. Fitz John Porter, a strong political and military ally of McClellan's, remained in command of the Fifth Corps; its three divisions were led by Maj. Gen. George W. Morell, Brig. Gen. George Sykes, and Brig. Gen. Andrew Humphreys. Maj. Gen. William B. Franklin commanded the Sixth Corps of two divisions, one under the command of Maj. Gen. Henry W. Slocum and the other under Maj. Gen. William F. Smith. Attached to Franklin's Sixth Corps was a division, designated the Fourth Corps, commanded by Maj. Gen. Darius N. Couch. Two new corps were added to McClellan's great army. Brought from the North Carolina coast under Maj. Gen. Ambrose E. Burnside was the Ninth Corps, composed of divisions commanded by Brig. Gens. Orlando B. Willcox and Samuel Sturgis, as well as a division brought east from the western Virginia mountains and commanded by Brig. Gen. Jacob D. Cox. The Twelfth Corps, formerly Gen. Nathaniel P. Banks's command in the Army of Virginia, was now commanded by aged Maj. Gen. Joseph King Fenno Mansfield. Its two divisions, one led by Brig. Gen. Alpheus Williams and the other by Brig. Gen. George S. Greene, included large numbers of newly recruited regiments as well as units that had seen service in the disastrous Shenandoah Valley campaign.[10]

The Second Corps remained under the command of General Sumner, and the divisions of Maj. Gens. Israel B. Richardson and John Sedgwick were intact for the most part. In Richardson's division, the First Brigade was still under the command of Brig. Gen. John C. Caldwell. Brig. Gen. Thomas Francis Meagher continued to lead the Irish Brigade, while Col. John R. Brooke took over command of the Third Brigade from Brig. Gen. William H. French, who was given the assignment of commanding a new division in the corps.

Sedgwick's division was less affected by the reorganization: the First Brigade was still commanded by Brig. Gen. Willis A. Gorman; the Second (Philadelphia) Brigade was given to Brig. Gen. Oliver Otis Howard, who had suffered the amputation of his right arm after the Battle of Fair Oaks but had recuperated enough to return to the field; Brig. Gen. Napoleon J.T. Dana continued in command of the Third Brigade. The three brigades of French's new Third Division of the Second Corps consisted entirely of newly recruited regiments, virtually all of which had arrived in Washington in late August and early September; this division would not actually reach the Army of the Potomac until September 15, 1862. To round out his own staff, General Sumner turned to yet another young man of solid Puritan ancestry, Lt. Col. Paul J. Revere of Boston, the grandson of the famous Revolutionary War hero. Revere had been serving in the 20th Massachusetts Infantry in Dana's brigade. As with the Cushings, Old Bull was acquainted with many of the members of Colonel Revere's family.[11]

Healthy again, Lt. Evan Thomas was back in command of Batteries A and C, 4th United States Artillery, which were assigned to Richardson's division, along with Capt. Rufus Pettit's Battery B, 1st New York Light Artillery. Capt. John A. Tompkins's Battery A, 1st Rhode Island Light Artillery, and Lt. Ned Kirby's Battery I, 1st United States Artillery, made up the artillery complement of Sedgwick's division. Kirby was suffering from a recurrence of typhoid fever in the wake of the Peninsula campaign. In his place, Little Dad Woodruff commanded Battery I. Three unattached batteries were also assigned to the Second Corps: Capt. John D. Frank's Battery G, 1st New York Light Artillery; Capt. John G. Hazard's Battery B, 1st Rhode Island Light Artillery; and Capt. Charles D. Owen's Battery G, 1st Rhode Island Light Artillery.[12]

Having served before and now serving with an artillery battery in the field, Lon had learned to rely upon the ordnance officer at division headquarters to keep his caissons and limber chests filled with ammunition and the guns supplied with the necessary hardware. Lon knew the duties of an ordnance officer after having briefly served in that capacity for Sumner. When the Second Corps was created and General Richardson took over as commander of Sumner's division, Richardson brought onto his staff as his ordnance officer a young immigrant, Lt. James McKay Rorty. A twenty-three-year-old native of Donegal, Ireland, Rorty had come to America in 1857. He was riddled with infirmities, not the least of which was a neurological disorder as a result of which he suffered frequent panic attacks. He had lived in squalid circumstances in New York City and worked as a book canvasser in hopes of earning enough money to bring his parents and eight brothers and sisters to America. When the war broke out, he joined Colonel Corcoran's 69th New York State Militia. At First Bull Run he was captured with Corcoran and a host of other soldiers during the chaotic retreat. After having been held in a warehouse prison in Richmond, Rorty and two other members of his unit had escaped. After returning to New York, Rorty, against his parents' wishes, had accepted a lieutenancy in the 14th New York Independent Battery.[13]

In a letter to his father, Rorty summed up his strong feelings about fighting for the Union. Like other Fenians, he thought his training as a soldier might enable him to return to Ireland someday and help free it from English domination once and for all. Down deep, though, Rorty had other feelings. "Let me reassure you of my firm conviction," he wrote, "that the separation of this Union into North and South would not only be fatal to the progress of constitutional freedom but would put impossible barriers in the way of future immigration. It would close forever the wide portals through which the pilgrims of liberty from every European clime have sought and found it. Why? Because at the North the prejudices springing from the hateful and dominant spirit of Puritanism, and at the

South, the haughty exclusiveness of an oligarchy would be equally repulsive, intolerant and despotic. Our only guarantee is the Constitution, our only safety is the Union, one and indivisible." Lt. Edward Field once described Rorty as "probably the most highly educated and accomplished young [Irishman] in the Second Corps." Although Lon's background represented everything Rorty found objectionable about the North, the two young men quickly became close companions.[14]

Lee, taking advantage of his startling victories at Cedar Mountain, Second Bull Run, and Chantilly, moved his Army of Northern Virginia across the Potomac River into Maryland. Splitting his forces into two commands on September 9, he sent General Jackson and six divisions to capture Harpers Ferry. General Longstreet, with the remaining elements of the army, moved north toward Hagerstown, Maryland.[15] McClellan's Army of the Potomac followed Lee's advance into Maryland. From Washington the army had moved to Buckeyestown by September 5; some elements went as far as Middletown. On September 9 the Second Corps entered Clarksburg, Maryland, and by September 13 it had reached Frederick, its point of concentration.[16]

Jackson struck the Union garrison at Harpers Ferry on September 14. Union Gen. Dixon S. Miles, Lon's division commander at First Bull Run, was mortally wounded, and his command surrendered Harpers Ferry to Jackson the next day. Miles would die on September 16. Having obtained a copy of Lee's orders for the campaign, McClellan was in a position to crush Lee's divided army. Readily apparent to McClellan was the fact that the passes in the South Mountain range could be crossed to confront Jackson and bring relief to Gen. Miles's command. McClellan thus directed Franklin's corps to force its way through Crampton's Gap; Hooker's and Burnside's corps were directed to force the passage of Fox's and Turner's Gaps, six miles north of Campton's. The gaps in the South Mountain range, the gateways to the Pleasant Valley, were held by the sturdy, battle-hardened veterans of the division of Confederate Gen. D.H. Hill. On September 14 and 15, from his battery park near Frederick, Lon could hear the distant roar and rumble of gunfire along South Mountain. The First and Ninth Corps broke through Turner's Gap along the National Road after bloody and determined fighting.[17]

Early on the morning of September 15 Richardson's division, with the Irish Brigade leading the way, was directed ahead to chase the retreating Confederates. Not having his own artillery within supporting distance, Richardson called upon Lt. John C. Tidball's Battery A, 2d United States Artillery, along with the 8th Illinois Cavalry, already operating in the vicinity, to accompany him. Behind Richardson, however, his two fine artillery batteries were harnessed up and soon rumbled out of Frederick to catch up with the infantry.[18] Lt. Alonzo Cushing was on his way to meet the enemy as an artilleryman. Thomas's six brass guns, with caissons, battery wagons, forge, and quartermaster wagons following, moved up the National Road along with Pettit's battery and the ordnance train, hurrying to catch up with Richardson. Lieutenant Rorty rode alongside. As Lon galloped into Turner's Gap, he could see through the early morning mist the dead Confederates piled on either side of the road, many covered with Union-issue blankets. All along the road were soldiers from the veteran Ninth Corps who had halted for a much-needed rest. In the distance Lon could hear the rumble of gunfire as Richardson's division, with the Illinois cavalrymen and Tidball's regular horse artillery battery, continued to make contact with Lee's rear. He had heard that sound for two days.[19]

After a brief halt near a hostelry called the Mountain House, the two batteries began the winding descent toward the village of Boonsboro, passing through row upon row of dusty soldiers. Ninth Corps infantry and artillery crowded the narrow passage. Marching ahead of the guns and massed along the roadway was Sykes's division—mostly United States regulars—of Porter's Fifth Corps. Ahead as well was Hooker's First Corps, fresh from its fight along South Mountain. Large numbers of Confederate prisoners, being led back toward Frederick, passed Thomas's fast-moving battery. They were an ill-fed, dirty, and tattered-looking lot.[20]

At the foot of the western slope of Turner's Gap the small, shady village of Boonsboro extended about half a mile on either side of the National Road. Among its two-story stone dwellings, Boonsboro had as many public houses as any town its size Lon had ever seen. Working his way through Sykes's dusty columns, Lon noticed that virtually every house, church, and public building had been turned into a hospital. Wounded Confederates were everywhere, some in makeshift shelters, others alongside the roadway. Many residents of the village had fled; their food, livestock, fences, bedding, and furnishings had been destroyed. Those who remained behind reported the enemy in wild and confused retreat. Debris—and, in some areas, Confederate dead—littered the streets. Lon could see the effects of the Union artillery fire from the previous day; many of the dwellings were badly shell-pocked. Apropos, a sign over one public house read, "Accommodations for man and beast." Here and there, a national flag hung from a house, evidence of the strong Union sentiment in Pleasant Valley.[21]

Lon and the two hard-riding batteries turned west and raced down the road toward Sharpsburg, passing General Porter and his staff and the leading elements of Sykes's infantrymen. Rumbling through the quaint village of Keedysville, already bedecked with American flags, the batteries turned off the road near an old tollgate just in front of the picturesque stone Antietam bridge. It was about 11:00 A.M.[22] When they arrived on a ridge about one and a half miles west of Keedysville and north of the Boonsboro Road along the east bank of Antietam Creek, which Tidball's battery had occupied for several hours, his cannoneers and horses were exhausted. Upon the approach of the two Second Corps batteries, Tidball's guns were limbered up and withdrawn to the rear. The positions Thomas's and Pettit's batteries were about to assume were along the rolling pastureland of farmer Philip Pry, Jr., whose impressive two-story brick farm home, with its barns and numerous outbuildings, stood along high ground to the northeast.[23]

With the advanced cavalry, horse artillery, and infantry, Lon saw cavalry chief Brig. Gen. Alfred Pleasonton. Accompanying General Pleasonton and the officers of the 8th Illinois Cavalry was Lon's West Point classmate Fannie Custer, on temporary assignment with Pleasonton from McClellan's headquarters. He looked every inch the horse soldier he yearned to be, sporting muttonchop whiskers, a high-crowned slouch hat, tall boots, and a saber. Somehow, it seemed, Custer always managed to get himself in the midst of the action.[24]

The foliage alongside the creek was dense and obscured the visibility of the sluggish stream. In the woods and slashings along the east bank of the creek, the 5th New Hampshire formed a skirmish line. The long ridge above the west bank of Antietam Creek was virtually clear of trees; the fields had been used for grazing livestock. Below the ridge on the west bank, just up from the stream, was a white frame farmhouse, barn, and outbuildings as well as an orchard. To Lon's left, along the Boonsboro Road, he could see the impressive barn, houses, and mill of farmer Joshua Newcomer.[25] General Meagher's Irish Brigade was aligned on either side of the Boonsboro Road—the 88th and 63d New York on the left, the 69th New York and the Yankee 29th Massachusetts on the right—supported by General Caldwell's and Colonel Brooke's brigades, the men lying on their stomachs along the eastern face of the eminence to avoid the enemy shellfire. All around him Lon could hear the distinctive Irish accents of the tired and dusty officers and soldiers of Meagher's famous brigade and from his own cannoneers and drivers, many of whom hailed from Meagher's regiments.[26] Lon never recorded his feelings at the time, but he must have felt the anxiety and apprehension so many soldiers—even veterans—feel as they enter a fight. Yet like his classmate Fannie Custer, Lon had yearned for field service ever since First Bull Run. Now he was about to enter an engagement "behind the guns," where he wanted to be.

As the guns of the two batteries were brought across the ridge, they came under heavy fire from at least four Confederate batteries of Gen. Stephen D. Lee's artillery battalion and "a considerable body of infantry" in Gen. D.H. Hill's division situated on the high ground along the west bank of the creek, protecting the approaches to the town of Sharpsburg by way of the Boonsboro Road.[27]

"Action front!" yelled Thomas. The buglers sounded the call.

The brass guns were brought to a halt, unlimbered and rolled into position. The cannoneers took their posts alongside the pieces. Lieutenant Morris took charge of the caissons. Mounted on his horse, Lon, commanding the right section, waited for the commands. Field and King commanded the center and left sections respectively. Thomas ordered the cannoneers to fire shell. Distances were quickly calculated and fuses were cut.

"Load!" shouted Thomas.

"Ready!" replied Lon and his fellow section chiefs.

"Number one, fire! Number two, fire! Number three, fire!"

The guns boomed, one by one. Thomas's six brass twelve-pounders, joined by Pettit's four Parrott rifles, roared and echoed up and down the Antietam. Dense, sulfurous smoke enveloped the landscape. On and off, for almost seven hours, the ten Union guns pounded the Confederate rear guard.[28]

General Porter moved the leading elements of his corps ahead; he and his staff rode forward to the positions of Thomas's and Pettit's batteries. After conferring with General Richardson, Porter agreed that Antietam Creek was generally too deep to ford from his vantage point, and the enemy would likely try to destroy the stone bridge in an effort to prevent the passage of the Army of the Potomac. Porter sent a staff officer back with orders to hurry Sykes's division forward, and in a short time its blue columns approached the advanced positions by way of the Boonsboro Road. Porter ordered Sykes to place his regulars in position along the high ground east of Antietam Creek, to the left of Richardson and south of the Boonsboro Road. Sykes directed the 3d United States Infantry to form the skirmish line along the creek on either side of the Antietam bridge, connecting its right flank with the left of the 5th New Hampshire.[29] The remaining two divisions of the Second Corps—Sedgwick's and French's—passed through Turner's Gap, where Burnside's weary troops still remained alongside the road resting and drinking coffee, and entered the streets of Boonsboro just as Thomas's and Pettit's batteries opened fire six miles to the west. The Twelfth Corps was well behind the Second, under urgent orders to close the gap. The remaining elements of the Fifth Corps and the army's Reserve Artillery were also moving toward Turner's Gap.[30]

According to McClellan's early morning orders, if Sumner found Lee to be in retreat and withdrawing as precipitately as Hooker had reported, he was to press the enemy, doing all the injury possible, but avoid bringing on any general engagement until the commanding general reached the front. As he entered Boonsboro, Sumner heard the same reports from the civilians in and around the town that Hooker had heard. Ahead he heard the artillery fire from Pettit's and Thomas's guns. Old Bull pushed his two big divisions forward, continually sending aides back to the head of the Twelfth Corps columns with appeals to press forward. Behind a cavalry screen, with skirmishers thrown out in front and large flanking parties moving in lines parallel to the main columns, he turned Sedgwick's and French's divisions down the road toward Sharpsburg. In the vanguard of the corps, Woodruff's, Tompkins's, Hazard's, Frank's and Owen's batteries rumbled along the dusty road.[31]

As the Second Corps columns marched toward Sharpsburg, cheering began to the rear. From Boonsboro to Keedysville—for nearly four miles—soldiers fell out of marching ranks and formed on either side of the roadway to make room for General McClellan and his staff and escorts as they galloped toward the front. Little Mac waved his cap to loud and sustained hurrahs. Hats were thrown into the air by cheering soldiers. Never, according to one Second Corps artilleryman, did the troops cheer as loud and with as much enthusiasm as they did that afternoon for McClellan.[32] The pompous little army commander and his enormous entourage rode toward the sound of gunfire, army headquarters flag flapping in the wind. Arriving at Lon's position, McClellan conferred with Porter, Sykes, and Richardson for a brief time. Sykes and Richardson soon left to join their commands, and McClellan and Porter and their staffs rode up to the spacious Pry house, where the army commander established his headquarters. In the meantime, army engineers and cavalry, along with some of McClellan's staff, including Custer, were ordered to reconnoiter the Antietam to determine where other bridges and fords might be located as well as the location of the enemy and its flanks.[33]

Passing through Keedysville, Sedgwick's and French's Second Corps divisions came to a halt in the fields on either side of the Boonsboro Road where they waited in readiness behind Richardson's and Sykes's divisions and Thomas's and Pettit's blazing guns. As directed by army headquarters, Sumner sent forward his own reconnaissance parties to locate the positions of the enemy across and up the Antietam. Behind Sumner's Second Corps were the long columns of Mansfield's Twelfth Corps. Within a few hours, the remainder of Porter's corps, along with the Reserve Artillery—after getting untangled from the log jam at Turner's Gap—and Hooker's First Corps arrived in the vicinity of Keedysville.[34]

Afternoon turned into evening, and the troops went into bivouac. Until nearly 9:00 P.M., though, the advanced artillery maintained a brisk fire along the heights overlooking Antietam Creek. Below Lon's guns, the

3d United States Infantry fought its way across the stone bridge, securing both banks of Antietam creek by the end of the day. The 5th New Hampshire was drawn back to Caldwell's lines at dark, but the division remained in its advanced position east of the creek. To the right of Richardson, near the Pry house, Sedgwick's division went into bivouac; south of the Boonsboro Road, French's division set up camp, and Sykes's troops remained in position, withdrawing its 3d Infantry to the east bank of the creek after dark.[35]

In the wee hours of September 16, the artillery opened up again along Antietam Creek. The enemy had brought into the fray the rifled guns of Parker's Virginia Battery, the Brooks South Carolina Battery, and the Bedford (Virginia) Artillery. Thomas's and Pettit's batteries came under a "galling fire" for over four hours. Sighting the guns in the inky darkness by watching for the bursts of flame from the enemy guns, Lon and his cannoneers returned the fire. Antietam had already become an artillery hell for the two batteries of Richardson's division. To assist them, General Sykes ordered Capt. Stephen H. Weed's Battery I and Lt. William E. Van Reed's Battery K, both 5th United States Artillery, into action from positions along the extension of the high ground above the creek, south of the Boonsboro Road.[36]

It seems that the discipline within one newly recruited, nine-month regiment—the 132d Pennsylvania—in Brig. Gen. Nathan Kimball's brigade, French's Second Corps division, was rather lacking. Toward dawn, the "greenhorns," as they were called by the veterans of the corps, wanted to get a closer look at the artillery duel; most of these new soldiers had never seen artillery in action. In large numbers—including even an officer of the regiment, Maj. Frederick L. Hitchcock—they crept away from their bivouac sites and climbed to the brow of the hill behind Weed's, Van Reed's, Thomas's and Pettit's batteries to watch the engagement. Hitchcock could faintly see columns of Confederate infantry moving across the fields west of the Antietam. The four Union batteries sent shell after shell into Hill's butternut lines. As the projectiles exploded in the ranks of enemy soldiers, killing, maiming, or scattering them, the young officer noted that his fellow greenhorns would cheer and yell. The fire from the four batteries was clearly well directed and effective. "We enjoyed ourselves immensely," wrote the Pennsylvania officer, "until presently some additional puffs of smoke appeared from their side, followed immediately by a series of very ugly hissing, whizzing sounds, and the dropping of shells amongst our troops which changed the whole aspect of things."[37]

Within the Second Corps bivouac sites on the Pry farm and south of the Boonsboro Road, the Confederate shells from Lee's artillery batteries were doing some damage. Lon's West Point friend Tully McCrea—who had been assigned to Little Dad's Battery I after his graduation from the academy in July 1862, and who had joined the battery while it was at Harrison's Landing—asked his commander if he could go up to the summit of the ridge ahead to observe the positions of the enemy guns. Woodruff agreed. Just as McCrea reached a point in front of Richardson's infantrymen and behind Lon's guns, however, the Confederate batteries opened up simultaneously. He observed one shell pass through an unsuspecting infantryman in Richardson's division, mangling him horribly; another shell removed a soldier's foot; a third struck the ground about ten feet in front of McCrea while a fourth bounded over his head; and a fifth shell then landed among the infantrymen just behind him. McCrea's curiosity had been totally satisfied.[38]

Thomas's and Pettit's batteries were in great danger; Thomas's smooth-bore guns were no match for the rifled guns the enemy brought into action. South of the Boonsboro Road, the Confederate shellfire was most effective. French's division and Col. Gouverneur K. Warren's tiny Fifth Corps brigade were terribly exposed to the fire. Sykes quickly ordered Warren's two regiments, along with Lt. Alanson M. Randol's Batteries E and G, 1st United States Artillery, to move farther to the left, out of range.[39]

Finally relief came for Thomas's and Pettit's weary commands. At about 5:00 A.M., September 16, the two batteries were relieved by four batteries of twenty-pound Parrott rifles from the Artillery Reserve: Capt. Elijah Taft's 5th New York Light Battery, Lt. Bernhard Wever's Battery A, Lt. Alfred von Kleiser's Battery B, and Lt. Robert Langner's Battery C, 1st Battalion, New York Light Artillery. The reserve batteries took up positions along the ridge from south of the Boonsboro Road to just in front of the Pry house. The two weary Second Corps batteries withdrew back through Keedysville to a bivouac site in a meadow to the rear of Richardson's and Sedgwick's divisions, along a road to Smoketown, where they joined the remaining batteries of the corps. Thomas's and Pettit's batteries had each expended about four hundred rounds of ammunition in the action along Antietam Creek. They reported only minor casualties. The guns were parked, and Lon spread his blanket along the ground to try to get some rest.[40]

The soldiers in Richardson's, Sedgwick's, and French's Second Corps divisions had been awake since the cannonading began; no bugles sounded or drums rolled that morning, and as one soldier wrote, "No breakfast [was] in sight or in prospect." Veterans like Lon knew a battle was in the offing. The armies were too close; the persistent fighting between Union advance units and the Confederate rear guard and the constant movement of troops toward the front gave evidence of a terrible struggle ahead. On either side of the Boonsboro Road the fields swarmed with soldiers, horses, wagons, and artillery from four army corps, all awaiting orders for the battle to begin. Artillery boomed, and picket firing resounded up and down the valley. Many of the raw soldiers in the Second Corps were visibly shaken by the prospect of the impending clash. Even veterans were nervous. Lon was no exception, although he had had his baptism of fire.[41]

McClellan determined relatively early on September 16 to strike Lee's left flank, which reconnaissance parties had located across Antietam Creek about a mile and a half west of a mill owned by Samuel Pry. Army engineers and cavalry scouts reported the location of an upper stone bridge and suitable fords along the Antietam just beyond the mill.[42] Between 1:00 and 2:00 P.M., General Hooker was informed by the commanding general that his troops could easily cross the Antietam and that he should move his First Corps north and cross the creek by way of the fords and the upper stone bridge. Further, he was given the authority to call upon the Twelfth and Second Corps if he should need them.[43] At about the same time, Second Corps artillery chief Capt. Francis N. Clarke rode to Woodruff's, Tompkins's, Pettit's, and Owen's batteries and ordered them to follow the First Corps up the road to Smoketown. At about 1:30 P.M. the long column of guns, caissons, and battery wagons moved onto the narrow Smoketown Road, falling in line behind the First Corps.[44]

As his corps neared the Antietam, Hooker directed Meade's and Ricketts's divisions across the stream by way of the stone bridge; the division of Gen. Abner Doubleday—who had assumed the unit's command in the wake of Gen. Rufus King's departure and Gen. John P. Hatch's wounding at South Mountain—was directed to ford the Antietam below the bridge, not far from Pry's mill. Just behind Meade's and Ricketts's troops, the First Corps artillery and the four Second Corps artillery batteries rumbled across the upper bridge and up the Smoketown Road. Tompkins's battery moved off the road and went into bivouac on the farm of John Hoffman on the west bank of the Antietam, just south of the Smoketown crossroads. Pettit's battery was sent ahead to a position along high ground just east of a large woods—known forever after as the East Woods—where it unlimbered and came into battery. Owen's battery rumbled through the crossroads and went into bivouac just west of the village. Little Dad and his regulars remained along the Smoketown Road overlooking Antietam Creek, just above the upper bridge.[45]

Although now overrun by two great armies, the countryside in the Antietam valley was beautiful. Lovely, undulating pasturelands were interspersed with acreages of tall corn. Great zigzag split-rail fences bordered the Smoketown Road. The setting sun cast a soft yellow glow over the landscape at dusk on September 16 as Hooker's three veteran divisions arrived at their advanced positions along the farm of Joseph Poffenberger, just under one and a half miles west of the Hoffman farm. The gently rolling terrain ahead of Fighting Joe presented a picture of peace and abundance. Looking south from the Poffenberger farm he could see the turnpike that connected the village of Sharpsburg with Hagerstown. Flanking both sides of the turnpike below the Poffenberger house were stone fences. One-half mile in front of Hooker was the farm of D.R. Miller. The Miller house, a white, two-story frame structure, stood on the east side of the Hagerstown Turnpike; the Miller barn and numerous haystacks on the west side. On either side of the turnpike, south of the Miller house, were sturdy post-and-rail fences, six rails high. Beyond the Miller house and barns the ground dipped into a long depression, and beyond the depression was a forty-acre cornfield extending east from the turnpike to the East Woods. The vast cornfield was particularly noticeable because the crop, nearing harvest maturity, was nearly seven feet tall.

The commanding point of the landscape appeared just beyond Miller's cornfield. There, on the west side of the turnpike, was a small, whitewashed brick church erected by German Brethren known as Dunkards. The little church stood out in stark contrast to the dark foliage of the dense woods behind it, since known as the West Woods, which filled a hollow that ran parallel to the turnpike. What faced Hooker in the cornfield ahead and along the undulating fields behind it, he clearly knew, was the left flank of the Army of Northern Virginia. Cavalry chief Alfred Pleasonton's and Hooker's own reconnaissances during the day had confirmed the presence of Lee's army there.[46] Hooker quickly determined that if Lee made a stand along those fields, the high ground around that little church would likely be the key point of the battlefield.

Lee had observed the movement of McClellan's army, and with the troops at hand, had formed positions to meet the advance of Hooker's corps. The troops that Hooker's men faced that evening were those of the division of Brig. Gen. John Bell Hood of Longstreet's command. Those weary Confederates had not been fed for nearly three days, and that night Hood appealed to Lee for relief for his men. At about 10:00 P.M., Hood's gallant division pulled back out of the cornfield and went into bivouac below the Dunkard Church. Into the front evacuated by Hood just south of Miller's cornfield—under cover of brisk artillery fire—came the veteran division of Brig. Gen. Richard S. Ewell of Jackson's command, led since the wounding of Ewell at Groveton by Brig. Gen. Alfred L. Lawton. Supporting Lawton's division on its left was Jackson's old division under the command of Brig. Gen. John R. Jones. Lawton's troops faced east and northeast from their lines in front of the East Woods and along the east end of the cornfield, while Jones's division faced north.[47]

Extending the Confederate lines farther south, D.H. Hill placed two of his brigades—mostly North Carolinians, Georgians, and Alabamians—in a sunken farm lane that turned off the Hagerstown Turnpike about one-third of a mile south of the Dunkard Church, extended about five hundred yards east, and then bent south about the same distance until it took on a markedly crooked course all the way to the Boonsboro Road.

On both sides of the contending lines the massing of artillery was awesome. Union batteries—thirty-six guns in all—were planted in positions east of the Hagerstown Turnpike, extending along a depression all across the First Corps front into the East Woods. Hooker also relied on the support of those twenty-four twenty-pound Parrott rifles from the Artillery Reserve batteries situated on the high ground west of Antietam Creek. Although Taft's battery had been removed, Battery D, 5th United States Artillery from the Fifth Corps, commanded by Lon's West Point friend Lt. Charles E. Hazlett, had taken its place along the Pry farm. Confederate batteries were massed in front of the Dunkard Church and west through the West Woods to a critical height known as Nicodemus Hill, from which any Union advance toward the church would be enfiladed. If an advance made any headway against the Confederate infantry and artillery located south of the cornfield, it would face, in front of the Dunkard Church, Col. Stephen D. Lee's six batteries, behind which was Hood's infantry with at least three batteries from the artillery battalion of Jones's division.[48]

As Hood's men left the cornfield and Lawton's troops took up their advanced positions connecting with D.H. Hill's commands, General Mansfield's Union Twelfth Corps was ordered to move from its bivouac site on the Pry farm, near the Smoketown Road behind Sumner's corps, to the support of Hooker. With a gentle rain falling, the Twelfth Corps marched up the Smoketown road, crossed the upper stone bridge, and proceeded to the hamlet of Smoketown. The men were ordered not to speak above a whisper and not to allow their canteens to rattle. In the darkness, with scattered picket firing in the distance, the silent, almost ghostly, columns passed Little Dad's battery above the upper bridge and came to a halt near the bivouac site of Owen's and Tompkins's batteries. Brig. Gen. Alpheus Williams, commanding the First Division in Mansfield's corps, remembered the night. "It was so dark," he recalled, "so obscure, so mysterious, so uncertain; with occasional rapid volleys of pickets and outposts, the low solemn sound of the commands as troops came into position, and with all so sleepy that there was a half-dreamy sensation about it all."[49]

Within Batteries A and C, along the Smoketown Road near Keedysville, the night was equally somber and disquieting. All around Lon's campsite, on either side of the Boonsboro Road, were the three divisions of the Second Corps. South of the Boonsboro Road were the bivouac sites of Porter's Fifth Corps divisions. The spirits of the men in the batteries had been heightened by the sight of the huge Ninth Corps as it had passed down the Boonsboro Road toward Sharpsburg and took up positions to the left of the Fifth Corps in the late afternoon of the previous day.[50]

Dawn came slowly. There was no long roll from the drummers to awaken the soldiers from their fitful sleep. There were no bugles. Lon was awake at dawn tending to the needs of his battery section. Sergeants and corporals quietly aroused those who remained under the damp blankets. A dense, foggy mist hung above the fields. The rain had stopped, but a heavy overcast sky revealed itself in the first glimmer of daylight. Sunrise on September 17, 1862, was recorded at 5:43 A.M. The temperature was about sixty-five degrees; the winds were gentle, about two miles per hour.[51]

Across Antietam Creek, along the Joseph Poffenberger farm, the order, "Fall in," passed down the Union First Corps lines between 5:30 and 6:00 A.M.. Regiments formed in columns by division. Hooker's First Corps, with the powerful, veteran divisions of Doubleday, Ricketts, and Meade, formed the right flank of the Army of the Potomac. Doubleday's division formed the right flank of the First Corps, partly straddling the Hagerstown Turnpike. To Doubleday's left were the three brigades of Meade's division of Pennsylvania Reserves. To Meade's rear was Ricketts's division. With the notable exception of Gen. John Gibbon's brigade of westerners in Doubleday's division, the First Corps was largely made up of New York and Pennsylvania regiments, although there were regiments from Massachusetts, Indiana, West Virginia, Connecticut, Minnesota, and Maryland.[52]

Hooker directed his three divisions to advance, using the white-washed Dunkard Church, a thousand yards south, as a guide. The attack was preceded by an intense artillery barrage from the long-range rifles of the Artillery Reserve, two and a half miles distant, as well as from the massed guns of the First Corps. Ahead, Lawton's Georgians were literally blown out of their ranks by the heavy rounds of canister, grape, and shell. Confederate guns from Lee's battalion in front of the Dunkard Church returned the fire. The noise was absolutely deafening; the smoke quickly became dense. The artillerymen of the advanced Second Corps batteries, as well as the infantrymen in Mansfield's corps nearby—and Lon and his cannoneers back along the Keedysville-Smoketown Road—felt the reverberations of the bombardment.[53]

All along the First Corps lines rang the shrill commands, "Forward, guide center." Enemy shells pierced the air, exploded overhead, and plowed the earth all around the massed blue columns as they moved into the smoke-engulfed fields. In Doubleday's front the lines moved quickly. The Confederates posted in the cornfield ahead fired murderous volleys at the attackers. The artillery and rifle fire that exploded in the faces of Doubleday's veterans was indescribable. In the tall corn the Union brigades quickly began to lose formation.[54]

To Doubleday's left, Meade's and Ricketts's divisions at first advanced in line with the right flank division, but in their approach to and through the East Woods, the columns faced an intense artillery barrage. Recalled one soldier, "It appeared to the blue masses in that advancing host as if all the devils infernal had been incarnated and assembled on that horrible field, with power to make the most terrible noises that were ever heard." In the face of the ghastly artillery fire, the columns began to lose formation and mass together, and the compressed lines crashed into what remained of Lawton's Georgia regiments. The tall corn concealed Lawton's men from the advancing Union soldiers until the Georgians actually opened fire. With Lawton's opening volleys, the Union thrust near the East Woods and in front of the cornfield came to a staggering, bloody halt. The house and barns of Samuel Mumma south of the Smoketown Road along Lawton's right were torched by Confederates to keep the attackers from using them as vantage points from which to fire into the Confederate flank. The two angry lines, largely Pennsylvanians against Georgians, faced each other and poured volley after volley into each other's ranks for over an hour and a half until ammunition on both sides was virtually exhausted. The roar of gunfire became deafening; the dense, sulfurous smoke hanging over the dismal cornfield badly reduced visibility. In about thirty minutes the 97th New York lost half of its men. "The dead of the regiment," wrote a soldier in the 12th Massachusetts, "lay in piles, and the wounded kept thinning the ranks, yet on Ricketts's [division] fought." The Union right near the turnpike faced a murderous fire from front and flanks and suffered terribly. "Men, I cannot say fell," recalled Maj. Rufus Dawes of the 6th Wisconsin, "they were knocked out of the ranks by the dozens. But we jumped over the fence, and pushed on, loading, firing, and shouting as we advanced."[55]

In the smoke and confusion, the Confederates had rapidly extended their left flank under cover of the dense West Woods in the face of Doubleday's potent thrust. Doubleday's troops, bolstered by Meade's advancing brigades, advanced headlong into the Confederate left wing. The Confederate line met the onslaught, but recoiled; many were killed and wounded as they ran for shelter in the woods.[56] In front of the East Woods and along the eastern end of the cornfield the two lines continued to pour murderous volleys into each other's faces. Reserve Confederate brigades were urgently called into the fray. The Confederate commands were being destroyed. Already—it was not quite 7:00 A.M.—one-half of

Lawton's men had been killed or wounded, and Jones's division within and in front of the West Woods had been reduced to just six hundred men.[57]

At about 7:00 A.M., Mansfield's Twelfth Corps approached the East Woods. As in the Second Corps, some of the Twelfth Corps troops were recent, nine-month volunteers; this would be their baptism of fire. The Confederate lines near the Dunkard Church continued to feel the pressure of Doubleday's renewed attack down the Hagerstown Turnpike and Meade's and Ricketts's thrusts through the cornfield. Lawton's and Jones's divisions, outnumbered from the beginning, were being slowly overpowered. When General Jones was wounded, Brig. Gen. William E. Starke assumed command; then he was killed, and Col. A.J. Grigsby assumed command of the battered veterans of Stonewall Jackson's old division. With the assaults of the First Corps gaining momentum and the Twelfth Corps fast approaching the battlefield, a Union victory appeared near at hand.[58]

What stood between Fighting Joe Hooker and victory, however, was the battle-hardened division of Gen. John Bell Hood below the Dunkard Church. Like Lawton's and Jones's men, Hood's soldiers were half clad and many were barefooted. They had not been fed for three days, and what rations they had tried to prepare that morning were hastily consumed or discarded upon the opening of the horrendous clash of arms in their front. Now, having stood in line of battle for over an hour, these veterans responded to Jackson's urgent summons to halt the Union advance. Yelling above the din, they struck Doubleday, Meade, and Ricketts with devastating force. Hood's two brigades, with near demoniacal fury, slammed ahead through the cornfield, now shattered and shot-torn and littered with dead and wounded. The smoke was so dense that soldiers on both sides lost sight of everything in front of and around them. Behind Hood's yelling legions, at least three more Confederate brigades advanced into the fight from their positions along the sunken road. The Confederate counterattack pressed forward until the Union infantry fell back upon its artillery support. Only in front of the massed Union First Corps batteries were Hood's division and its support brigades halted in what became a punishing contest of human flesh and searing iron. Hood's attack had driven Hooker's Corps back some six to eight hundred yards. Still, the bloodied Union First Corps troops, encouraged by the arrival of Mansfield's corps, held the ground around their artillery batteries. Hood's Confederates were exhausted and bleeding; their ammunition was seriously depleted, but they had advanced to within thirty yards of the Union lines![59]

As the heavy blue columns of Mansfield's two divisions moved rapidly toward the East Woods, the battered Confederates braced themselves in the cornfield for an even more ghastly contest. To Lee, the situation on his left wing had become critical, but McClellan had not made any serious thrusts against his center or his right flank. Thus, the Confederate commander felt free to summon troops from otherwise quiet sectors of the field to bolster the terribly weakened left wing. The brigades of Col. Van H. Manning and Brig. Gen. Robert Ransom, Jr., of Gen. John G. Walker's division were summoned to the Dunkard Church from positions in front of Sharpsburg. Brig. Gen. Jubal A. Early's brigade of Lawton's division was set in motion to the front from its position on the far left flank. The divisions of Gens. Lafayette McLaws and Richard H. Anderson, both of Longstreet's command, were on a forced march from Harpers Ferry, but they were still two hours from the battlefield.[60]

It was now 7:30 A.M. In reponse to Hooker's urgent appeal, the Twelfth Corps was moving on the double-quick. As General Mansfield was aligning his corps along the farmland of Samuel Poffenberger, preparatory to launching the second Union assault of the morning, he fell, mortally wounded by a shell burst, and the command of the corps devolved upon Gen. Alpheus S. Williams. Brig. Gen. Samuel Crawford assumed command of Williams's division. Then, as Williams was receiving instructions for the planned assault from General Hooker in the Joseph Poffenberger farmyard, Fighting Joe went down, wounded in the foot by a shell fragment. General Meade, who assumed command of the First Corps upon the wounding of Hooker, withdrew the battered corps back to the Poffenberger farm from which it had stepped off on the early morning attack.[61]

The Twelfth Corps attacked in a southwesterly direction, oblique to that of the First Corps. Crawford's division formed on the right. Lt. Col. Hector Tyndale's and Col. Henry J. Stainrook's brigades of Greene's division formed the left flank of the attack formation which, when fully extended, reached from just east of the Hagerstown Turnpike all the way to beyond the East Woods.[62] The assault was pressed hard. Hood's depleted ranks, together with the survivors of Lawton's and Jones' divisions, were pushed to the limit of endurance in their determined resistance. Crawford's and Greene's relentless advance forced the Confederates back out of the cornfield and beyond the Smoketown Road; they slowly withdrew into the West Woods in the rear of the Dunkard Church. As the two Twelfth Corps divisions battled across the Hagerstown Turnpike and into the West Woods, they faced determined resistance from the thinned Confederate ranks opposing them. Volley upon volley was fired into the attacking columns. The Twelfth Corps, so close to taking the heights around the Dunkard Church, could not sustain the attack in the face of such murderous fire; it slowly fell back through the shattered cornfield and into the East Woods.[63]

After finally receiving word from McClellan, Sumner ordered Sedgwick's division forward in three columns, followed by French's division. Sumner left instructions for Richardson's division to move in the same direction about one hour later. Fannie Custer, astride his horse just below Pry's mill, directed the Second Corps infantry to the ford across the Antietam.[64] Leaving their forge, baggage wagons, and camp gear behind, Thomas's batteries and the remaining two batteries of the Second Corps moved up the Smoketown Road from Keedysville toward Pry's mill. With Lon riding ahead of his leading section, Batteries A and C rumbled over the upper stone bridge and across the fields to Samuel Poffenberger's farm, where it came to a halt. Dense smoke covered the landscape ahead. Streams of wounded and skulking soldiers dotted the fields; ambulance wagons passed Lon, heading for hospitals near Smoketown, the Hoffman farm, Pry's mill, and farther to the rear.[65]

In anticipation of Sumner's approach—and to cover the Twelfth Corps withdrawal—Pettit's and Owen's guns were moved into the fields to the right of the Smoketown Road ahead of the East Woods. Just after Lon had crossed the upper stone bridge, orders were relayed to Captain Tompkins to report to the front. His six Parrott rifles raced ahead toward the East Woods, and there, with Sumner's huge columns coming up behind him, Tompkins was directed to bring his guns into battery between the Smoketown Road and the burning Mumma house and barns to the left. Little Dad's battery moved to a position near the Hoffman house to be ready to answer any summons.[66]

The Confederate left wing was in shambles, and the Union First and Twelfth Corps had been badly mauled. Casualties had been appalling on both sides: in just about three hours, more than 8,000 men had been killed and wounded. The First Corps alone had lost nearly 2,600 and the Twelfth Corps some 1,800. The dead lay everywhere, in some places in rows, in others literally in heaps. Through the dense smoke, litter-bearers worked feverishly; the East Woods, it might well be said, was crawling with wounded Union and Confederate soldiers. In the cornfield and along the Hagerstown Turnpike—no-man's-land—the wounded were helpless; stretcher-bearers on both sides could not reach those areas for fear of being shot down. The whole battlefield seemed to groan in agony.[67]

Thomas's, Frank's, and Hazard's batteries waited for the Second Corps infantry to pass through the fields. Grimly, Lon observed the events unfolding before him. He saw General Sumner ride ahead with his staff to find Hooker. Sumner found that Hooker had been wounded and his corps repulsed. Mansfield too, Sumner discovered, had been seriously wounded and his corps hurled back. Undaunted, Sumner pushed his two powerful divisions forward. Lon watched Sedgwick's division as it led the advance across the Samuel Poffenberger farm in three columns. French's division followed well behind. It was just about 9:00 A.M. when the head of Sedgwick's division reached the East Woods.[68]

Sedgwick quickly led his division northwest out of the East Woods, and then faced to the left and reformed his ranks in column of brigades, each brigade seventy yards apart. General Gorman's brigade (from right to left, the 1st Minnesota, 82d New York, 15th Massachusetts, and 34th New York) led the advance, followed by the brigades of General Dana (the 19th and 20th Massachusetts, 59th and 42d New York, and 7th Michigan) and Gen. Howard (the 71st, 72d, 106th, and 69th Pennsylvania), all heroes of Fair Oaks and the Seven Days. Through the dense smoke Lon could see Sedgwick as he directed his three brigades across the fields below the cornfield toward the Dunkard Church and the West Woods.[69]

The remnants of Greene's Twelfth Corps division—Tyndale's and Stainrook's brigades—and the 125th Pennsylvania of the brigade now commanded by Col. Joseph F. Knipe (formerly Crawford's) of General Crawford's Twelfth Corps division joined Sedgwick on the left. The ground east of the turnpike was contested by those weary Confederates who remained. When the Union soldiers reached the tall rail fence along the pike, the Confederates unleashed terrific volleys of rifle fire. Men fell in great numbers.[70]

In the West Woods the remnants of Jones's shattered Confederate division, numbering only two or three hundred men, held the line north of the Dunkard Church. Below the little church, Hood's division—or what was left of it—was held in readiness. General Early's brigade finally arrived from the left. As the Union columns neared the turnpike, so did the Confederate brigade of Col. George T. Anderson. Behind Anderson, the long columns of the division of General McLaws were moving toward the Dunkard Church from the southeast. As well, elements of Ransom's North Carolina and Manning's Arkansas, North Carolina, and Virginia brigades were advancing toward the West Woods. Sedgwick was marching into a trap![71]

As Sedgwick's division crossed the Hagerstown Turnpike and entered the West Woods just north of the Dunkard Church, its left flank lost contact with Greene's units. The veteran Second Corps soldiers were totally unaware of the presence of heavy Confederate reinforcements moving toward the West Woods from the south and west. First, Kershaw's South Carolina brigade of McLaws's division, along with Early's Virginians, slammed into Greene's two brigades in the fields east of the church. Greene's troops were stunned but doggedly faced the approaching columns and returned the heavy fire, assisted by well-directed artillery fire from Captain Tompkins's Rhode Island battery in the Mumma farmlands.[72] To meet the heavy flank fire, some of Sedgwick's regiments faced left. Notably, the 34th New York of Dana's brigade joined the battling 125th Pennsylvania just north of Dunkard Church as it confronted Kershaw's and Early's onslaught. While the fighting was growing heavier and heavier east and north of the church, the three Second Corps brigades slowly advanced deeper into the West Woods—halting, firing, advancing, and halting again.[73]

Sedgwick's division was slowed under pressure from the remnants of Jones's division, mostly from the Stonewall brigade, and the remnants of Hood's division in the eastern edge of the West Woods. As resistance mounted, Sedgwick's front column fired volley after volley into the tattered and grimy but determined Confederates; some forty to fifty rounds were fired by each soldier in Sedgwick's leading brigade during the halting advance through the dense woods. In the two brigades that followed, particularly among the Philadelphians in rear, the men were not able to get off any shots at all because of Gorman's dense mass of troops ahead of them. The officers and men halted instead; some even began to light up cigars and pipes as they waited for the leading brigade to clear the way ahead.[74]

One by one, Confederate brigades approaching the smoke-engulfed West Woods were committed to the action. Semmes's Georgians of McLaws's division and Ransom's North Carolinians moved alongside Grigsby's heroic veterans and crashed headlong into Sedgwick's leading brigade. Colonel Anderson's Georgians, followed by Barksdale's Mississippians of McLaws's division, joined Early's hard-fighting veterans and slammed into Gorman's surprised soldiers and the tottering remnants of the 125th Pennsylvania and 34th New York north of the Dunkard Church. The whole West Woods erupted in a volcano of gunfire so heavy that the color-bearer of the 34th New York was hit five times in rapid succession before he toppled to the ground. The attack of Sedgwick's division had turned into a crimson nightmare. Men were falling everywhere.[75] As the gap widened between Greene's Twelfth Corps brigades and Sedgwick's left, the situation became critical. Early's and Anderson's Confederate brigades, along with Barksdale's Mississippians, surged around the church, up the Hagerstown Turnpike and into the fields in the rear of Sedgwick's hapless division.[76]

Sumner, following closely behind his advancing First Division, was directed by Lt. Col. John W. Kimball of the 15th Massachusetts to observe the threatening columns of Confederates to his rear through the dense smoke and roar of gunfire. "My God! We must get out of this!" Sumner exclaimed. He called for the rear column, the Philadelphia Brigade, to about-face in order to meet the growing threat to the rear of the division. It was too late! The confusion, noise, and dense smoke made it impossible even to convey the desperate orders. Men were falling rapidly all around; the air was alive with missiles. "The enemy is behind us!" shouted soldiers in the three columns, all now massed together in the woods. The Philadelphia Brigade began to break.[77]

As General Sumner tried to correct the alignment of the Philadelphians, General Sedgwick raced to the rear to locate the Second Corps artillery batteries. He found Major Clarke and ordered him to find some guns and hurry them to the front. Clarke rode toward the East Woods and yelled for Little Dad Woodruff to bring his battery forward. He pointed down the Smoketown Road and told Woodruff that General Sedgwick would meet him in the fields ahead.[78]

From behind the East Woods, Lon watched his classmate move his battery ahead. Battery I, 1st Artillery, rumbled out of the woods and down the Smoketown Road toward the Dunkard Church, now obscured by dense banks of smoke. Seeing Sedgwick in the fields to the right, the drivers turned the battery off the road. There, the general personally ordered Little Dad to bring his pieces into battery in the open fields about 360 yards north of the Smoketown Road and 300 yards east of the West Woods. Over the horrendous noise, Sedgwick instructed Woodruff to fire into the ranks of the enemy that were moving into the rear of his division. The six guns were swung around, unhitched from the limbers, and rolled into position facing the Confederate masses who were rapidly gaining Sedgwick's rear. Lieutenants French, Egan, and McCrea commanded the battery sections. Little Dad ordered spherical case shot to be used. But, frightened and wounded Union soldiers from Sedgwick's three brigades as well as from the 125th Pennsylvania were running back toward Little Dad's guns seeking safety. They were in the line of fire! The artillerymen yelled for the fleeing soldiers to get out of the way. It was no use. Behind the stampeding soldiers were solid masses of Confederates from Early's and Colonel Anderson's brigades racing to seize the newly positioned guns. Woodruff gave the command to fire. The guns boomed, sending their death-dealing charges, behind a wall of flame and smoke, into the faces of friends and foes alike. The blasts from the six guns became methodical. Spherical case and then canister were unleashed into Early's and Anderson's butternut-clad veterans and a small body of Confederate cavalry that surged toward Woodruff. In minutes, the wreckage of men and horses in front of the twelve-pound Napoleons told of the effectiveness of the fire.[79]

Inside the West Woods ahead of Woodruff, the situation was becoming more and more desperate. In the face of the ferocious frontal and flank assault, Sedgwick's two leading brigades became confused. The whole division was trapped. "It was helpless," wrote a soldier from the 19th Massachusetts, "and a third of its number were cut down in a few minutes." To change front was impossible; the columns were being attacked from three sides![80]

The third line of the advance, the Philadelphia Brigade, broke apart completely. General Sumner, his white hair streaming in the wind, rode among the confused and frightened soldiers: "Back boys, for God's sake move back; you are in a bad fix!" Gorman's front troops tried to fire ahead but could not do so with any coordination. Many in Dana's middle brigade—particularly the 20th Massachusetts—actually turned completely around and began firing at Early's, Colonel Anderson's, and Barksdale's screaming Confederates, who were closing in on the rear of the division. Within Sedgwick's division "nearly two thousand men were disabled in a moment," wrote a Massachusetts veteran. One of those who fell from a flesh wound was Paul J. Revere of Sumner's staff. Not as lucky was his brother Edward H.R. Revere, surgeon of the 20th Massachusetts, who was killed while attending the wounded of his command during the hottest part of the engagement. Another Sumner aide-de-camp who was wounded in the melee was Lon's classmate Joseph C. Audenreid. Behind Little Dad's battery, General Sedgwick fell with three wounds and was carried unconscious from the field. The general's brother, one of his staff officers, was killed nearby. The only avenue of escape for Sedgwick's men was north toward the Miller farm and Hooker's First Corps. They began withdrawing up the Hagerstown Turnpike, but not without heavy losses.[81]

The situation was deteriorating with the passing of every second. In the clearing east of the Hagerstown Turnpike and north of the Smoketown Road, Little Dad could see that ahead of him Sedgwick's columns were being torn to pieces by the Confederate attack, though Woodruff poured round after round of case shot and canister into the surging butternut ranks that were enveloping the rear of Sedgwick's three brigades.[82]

It was about 10:00 A.M. North of the Dunkard Church the fields were a whirlpool of thunderous noise, smoke, and confusion. Sedgwick's columns had been shattered. By the end of the fighting, his division reported losses of more than 2,200 officers and men. "They have poured out their blood like water," remarked a penitent Gen. Oliver Otis Howard, then commanding the remnants of the division. Old Bull Sumner had advanced too far to the front with Sedgwick's columns and was hopelessly out of touch with the rest of his corps. French's and Richardson's divisions were about to enter the fighting without any direction from their corps commander at all.[83]

South of the Dunkard Church a portion of Manning's brigade—the 46th and 48th North Carolina and the 30th Virginia—which had just gotten into line, together with the remnants of Kershaw's brigade, burst out of the dense woods on either side of the church. The yelling Confederates charged headlong into the hard-fighting remnants of Tyndale's and Stainrook's Twelfth Corps brigades still holding the ground east of the Hagerstown Turnpike. The firing intensified along the turnpike and in the fields east of the church. To augment the two Union infantry brigades, the 13th New Jersey of the brigade commanded by Brig. Gen. George H. Gordon of Crawford's division, and the Purnell (Maryland) Legion of Col. William B. Goodrich's brigade of Greene's division raced down the Smoketown Road and across the fields.[84]

Little Dad ordered his guns limbered up. They were withdrawn from their initial position and were brought into battery along higher ground about 360 yards south to meet the new threat. The left gun of the battery was rolled into position on the Smoketown Road near the Mumma farm lane. Woodruff's battery now faced southwest toward the Dunkard Church. Woodruff soon was joined on his right by the six ten-pound Parrott rifles of Capt. George W. Cothran's Battery M, 1st New York Light Artillery, along with six more ten-pound Parrott rifles of Capt. Joseph M. Knap's Independent Battery E, Pennsylvania Light Artillery.[85]

Little Dad called for Major Clarke and appealed urgently to the Second Corps artillery chief for more assistance. There were no guns along the ridge to Woodruff's left, and he was fearful of being overwhelmed from that direction. Clarke galloped back to the East Woods. Finding Lieutenant Thomas, he ordered him to detach a section of his batteries and send it forward to help Woodruff. Thomas called to Cushing, his senior section commander, to move his two guns forward. Lon now had his chance! "Forward!" he yelled to his cannoneers, gunners, and drivers. Buglers blew the shrill call for the advance. Down the Smoketown Road rumbled Lon's two guns until he brought them into position on the left of the road, just west of the Mumma farm lane and to the left of his classmate George Woodruff and his blazing Napoleons. Behind Lon the farm lane, with its broken-down zigzag fences, was littered with dead and wounded. At the southern end of the lane the Mumma house was enveloped in flame and smoke.[86]

As Lon's two guns arrived at their position, he observed the heavy Confederate columns moving across the Hagerstown Turnpike. Ahead of his guns, along lower-lying land, were Tyndale's and Stainrook's brigades together with Tompkins's six Parrott rifles. "Action front!" shouted Lon, as the two guns swung into position. The bugler blew the signal. Lon remained in the saddle behind his guns, giving orders for the cannoneers to open fire on the advancing enemy with solid shot and spherical case shot.[87] In the faces of the hard-charging Confederates, Tyndale's and Stainrook's regiments, along with the 13th New Jersey Infantry, the Purnell Legion, and Tompkins's battery, supported by

Woodruff's and Cushing's guns, let forth a torrent of gunfire. The fighting was furious. Confederates fell by the score; many sought refuge back in the West Woods. Colonel Manning rode among his men, pleading with them not to run but to carry the attack ahead. Suddenly, a bullet struck him in the left arm, then another in the chest; the brave colonel toppled from his horse to the hard surface of the turnpike.[88] The Confederate attack along the Mumma swale began to falter. As Tyndale's and Stainrook's regiments felt the pressure begin to release, they assumed the offensive, driving ahead toward the Dunkard Church, while Little Dad and Lon fired round upon round of shell.[89]

Col. John R. Cooke of the 27th North Carolina of Manning's brigade had advanced his regiment along with the 3d Arkansas to near the Dunkard Church, but when his brigade commander fell, he ordered his own regiment and the other broken commands of the brigade to fall back to a position along a ridge below the church. There, with concentrated volleys, Cooke was able to halt the Union advance.[90] Only scattered elements of Manning's fine brigade were able to regroup. Along a lane south of the Dunkard Church, the 48th North Carolina collected only about 150 men; the 2d South Carolina nearby could find only about fifty.[91]

Fresh units were being brought into the Union lines. In farmer Mumma's fields ahead, Tompkins's battery was finally relieved by Owen's Battery G, 1st Rhode Island Light Artillery.[92] The ammunition in Woodruff's battery was exhausted. Six of Little Dad's men had been wounded, and four of his horses had been killed—both Egan's and French's horses had been shot down beneath them—but miraculously, that was all the damage to Battery I. Major Clarke summoned Thomas to bring forward the rest of his guns to take Woodruff's place. From near the East Woods the remaining four guns of Batteries A and C rolled down the Smoketown Road toward the advanced section of the battery. As they approached the Mumma lane, Woodruff was directed by Clarke to withdraw his pieces. Seeing Thomas's remaining guns arriving along the high ground to his left, Little Dad called to his cannoneers to limber up the six Napoleons and withdraw to the rear.[93]

"Action front!" shouted Thomas as the four guns swung into position alongside Lon's two advance pieces on the ridge in front of the Mumma lane. There was no infantry to support Thomas's batteries at all, and the field had been cleared of most other batteries. Cothran's remained in position to Thomas's right but considerably to his rear. After withdrawing up the Smoketown Road, Captain Knap sent back a two-gun section of his battery, which came into position on the right of Thomas's guns, and another two-gun section to support Tyndale's Ohio infantrymen in the fields ahead near the Dunkard Church.[94]

In front of Lon's guns there were open plowed and clover fields.

From the crest of the ridge the land gently fell and then rose again toward the Hagerstown Turnpike and the Dunkard Church. To the southwest, the ground sloped gently downward, rose again, and then fell in a long swale broken by rock outcroppings and divided by low-lying stone fences. Samuel Mumma had not been growing food crops along the swale; rather, he had used the land to raise hay for his livestock, and a large number of haystacks stood in the swale near the turnpike.[95] Once in place, Thomas's six brass guns, with Knap's guns to the right and Owen's six Napoleons far to the left, shelled the tattered remnants of Manning's and Kershaw's brigades unmercifully. Capt. James A. Graham of the 27th North Carolina recalled that it was the worst shelling he had experienced in the war to date.[96]

The battle was drifting to the south in earnest. French's Second Corps division had approached the battlefield behind Sedgwick's columns. With General Sumner still well out in front and not present to coordinate movements, French pushed his brigades southwest, a direction he had understood would proceed along Sedgwick's left flank but not interfere with the Twelfth Corps troops—principally Greene's division—in the fields ahead. Advancing across the fields of farmer William Roulette, French's columns ran into enemy skirmishers near Roulette's house. The Confederate skirmish lines were overwhelmed, and French moved forward, following up what he believed to be a successful advance.[97]

Richardson's First Division, although it had left its encampment about one hour behind the columns of Sedgwick and French, had marched fast. It had forded the Antietam just below the upper stone bridge near Samuel Pry's mill and crossed the open farm fields trying to catch up with the Second and Third Divisions of the corps. Richardson's division had caught up with French's division as French was moving toward the Roulette farm.[98] French's and Richardson's divisions approached the Confederate center. They marched through corn, clover, and then freshly plowed acreage. Three Confederate brigades—those of Col. A.H. Colquitt and Brig. Gens. Robert E. Rodes and George B. Anderson—held the sunken road and a portion of the fields in front of it. Principally Rodes's and Anderson's brigades—mostly Georgia and North Carolina troops—had turned the sunken road into a long rifle pit by piling up fence rails in front of its approaches.[99]

After a spirited engagement in Roulette's fields to the far left of Lon, the two Second Corps divisions directed their attack to the sunken road. Richardson, with Meagher's Irish Brigade on the right, Caldwell's brigade on the left, and Brooke's brigade in reserve, led his division into the action on foot. French's attack, spearheaded by the brigade of Brig. Gen. Max Weber—another German exile from the 1848 revolutions—was directed toward the Confederates holding the northern and angular seg-

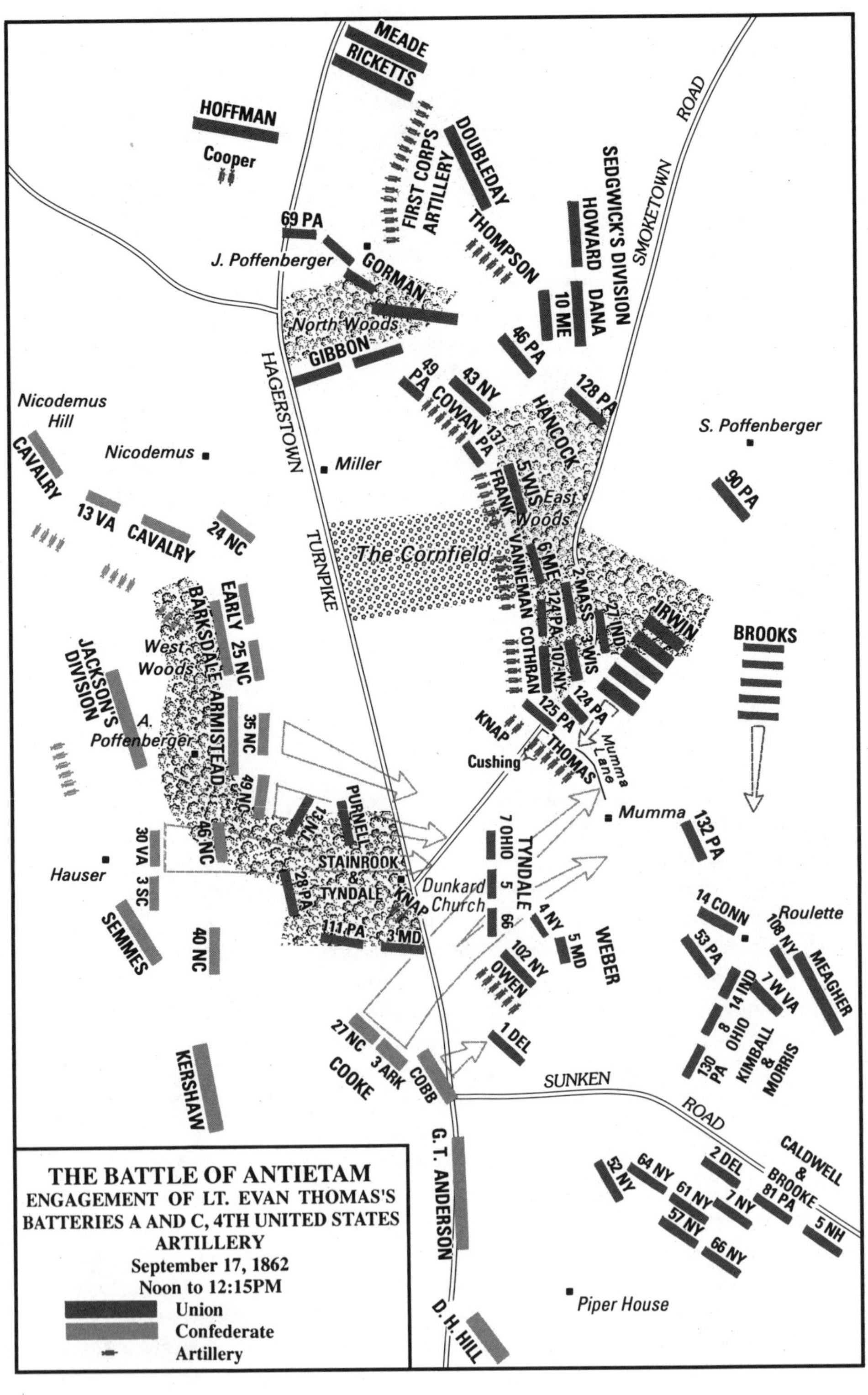

MEADE
RICKETTS
HOFFMAN
Cooper
FIRST CORPS ARTILLERY
DOUBLEDAY
THOMPSON
SEDGWICK'S DIVISION
HOWARD
DANA
SMOKETOWN ROAD
69 PA
J. Poffenberger
GORMAN
North Woods
GIBBON
10 ME
46 PA
HAGERSTOWN TURNPIKE
49 PA
43 NY
COWAN
137 PA
HANCOCK
128 PA
S. Poffenberger
Nicodemus Hill
Nicodemus
Miller
CAVALRY
13 VA
CAVALRY
24 NC
5 WIS
FRANK
East Woods
90 PA
The Cornfield
VANNEMAN
6 ME
2 MASS
124 PA
27 IND
IRWIN
BROOKS
EARLY
BARKSDALE
25 NC
West Woods
JACKSON'S DIVISION
COTHRAN
107 NY
3 WIS
124 PA
125 PA
KNAP
A. Poffenberger
ARMISTEAD
35 NC
49 NC
Cushing
THOMAS
Mumma Lane
Mumma
132 PA
13 NJ
PURNELL
7 OHIO
5
66
TYNDALE
30 VA
3 SC
46 NC
Hauser
STAINROOK & TYNDALE
28 PA
KNAP
Dunkard Church
4 NY
5 MD
WEBER
14 CONN
Roulette
53 PA
108 NY
MEAGHER
SEMMES
40 NC
111 PA
3 MD
102 NY
OWEN
14 IND
8 OHIO
7 W VA
130 PA
KIMBALL & MORRIS
27 NC
COOKE
3 ARK
COBB
1 DEL
KERSHAW
SUNKEN ROAD
G.T. ANDERSON
CALDWELL & BROOKE
2 DEL
52 NY
64 NY
61 NY
7 NY
81 PA
57 NY
66 NY
5 NH
Piper House
D.H. HILL
THE BATTLE OF ANTIETAM
ENGAGEMENT OF LT. EVAN THOMAS'S BATTERIES A AND C, 4TH UNITED STATES ARTILLERY
September 17, 1862
Noon to 12:15PM
Union
Confederate
Artillery

ments of the sunken road. French's soldiers became veterans in minutes, and the rifle and artillery fire into which the terribly exposed Irishmen and their Yankee companions marched was indescribably savage. Rodes's and Anderson's Confederate veterans behind the piled fence rails, and their artillery batteries west of the road, poured a murderous fire into the faces of the advancing Union legions. As the Irish Brigade reached the crest overlooking the Samuel Piper farm, General Meagher, whose frock-coat was already rent with bullet holes, was knocked senseless when his horse was shot out from under him. The contending lines exchanged volleys just thirty yards from one another. The green flag of the 69th New York with its emblems of Erin, riddled with bullets within minutes, went down eight times before its staff was shot in two. In less than one-half hour, Father William Corby, chaplain of the 88th New York, counted 504 men killed and wounded from the Irish Brigade alone. The shattered brigade soon was replaced in line by Caldwell's regiments, the Irishmen having exhausted all their ammunition and the brigade having been reduced to only about five hundred officers and men. It had been the most terrible hour of the war for those immigrants and exiles from Ireland.[100]

Lacking artillery support, Richardson called for help, and some guns from Pleasonton's cavalry division and a battery from the Artillery Reserve—all brass smooth-bores—came into battery and opened fire. But they were no match for the enemy's rifled guns, and they quickly retired.[101] Richardson's division, with Caldwell's and Brooke's brigade abreast, hit and enveloped Anderson's North Carolina brigade along the sunken road. Richardson fell mortally wounded under a torrent of gunfire. French's division struck the sunken road to the right of Richardson's. The fighting became ferocious. The dead and maimed in the road lay so thick that soldiers uniformly proclaimed that one could have walked the entire length of the road without ever stepping on ground.[102]

As French's and Richardson's divisions battled along the sunken road, the Confederates in front of Lon made one final thrust to reclaim the fields east of the Dunkard Church. Colonel Cooke led his own 27th North Carolina along with the 3d Arkansas and the scattered remnants of the rest of Manning's regiments—the 46th and 48th North Carolina and the 30th Virginia—out from their positions along the Dunkard Church ridge toward the remnants of the eight regiments in the line formed by Colonel Tyndale, supported by the two-gun section of Knap's battery that had been advanced to the front in the fields east and south of the Dunkard Church ahead of Thomas's guns. Joining Cooke's attack on his right was the tough little brigade of General Cobb—all Georgians—which had held the intersection of the sunken road with the Hagerstown Turnpike.[103]

The attack struck the advanced Union regiments with incredible surprise. The men in the three Ohio regiments on Tyndale's right at first thought the Confederates moving on their right flank were surrendering. By the time they realized it was a full-scale assault, it was too late. Lon observed Tyndale's lines as they melted away in the dense smoke ahead of him. Large numbers of Tyndale's men were captured.[104]

"Spherical case!" shouted Thomas.

The cannoneers feverishly cut the fuses and loaded the six brass guns.

"Ready," responded Cushing and King and Field. Manning's North Carolinians, Arkansans, and Virginians swarmed across the turnpike and into the fields ahead.

"Number one, fire! Number two, fire! Number three, fire!" commanded Thomas.

The six brass guns sent their shells exploding into the midst of the charging butternut and gray attackers.

The remnants of Tyndale's broken regiments fled back toward Thomas's batteries. Knap's advanced detachments near the Dunkard Church abandoned one Parrott rifle, but withdrew the other, leaving behind six cannoneers dead or wounded. The 27th North Carolina and 3d Arkansas directed their attack through Tyndale's fleeing commands toward Batteries A and C, 4th United States Artillery. In the fields ahead of Lon were countless numbers of frightened Union soldiers, some from Tyndale's regiments, others from the 1st Delaware, 5th Maryland, and 4th New York of Weber's brigade, which had struck the sunken road but had been repulsed. Well over two hundred Union soldiers had taken refuge behind the haystacks; some had even placed white handkerchiefs on their bayonets in an effort to survive the last onslaught. The hard-charging Confederates poured across the fields toward Thomas's guns. Lon, Evan Thomas, Rufus King, Edward Field, and all the gunners and cannoneers waved and yelled for the confused and frightened Union soldiers ahead to get out of their way. It was to no avail.[105]

"Canister!" commanded Lt. Thomas.

"Ready," yelled the section chiefs. They knew the deadly hail would hit their own men; there was nothing else they could do. The lanyards were stretched.

"Number one, fire! Number two, fire! Number three, fire!"

The six brass guns blasted forth their death-dealing shot, plowing through the knots of frightened Union soldiers ahead and tearing gaps in the fast-approaching Confederate lines.

"Commence firing!"

The guns were swabbed, loaded, and fired again and again. The cannoneers' actions became methodical. The Mumma farm swale was enveloped in dense smoke and fire.

After Tyndale's regiments broke, Stainrook's line fell back, and Thomas's guns were in danger of being overrun. With no organized Union infantry or artillery in the fields ahead of them, the gunners worked feverishly. Round upon round of grape and canister poured into the approaching ranks of yelling and screaming Confederates. The situation became desperate. Thomas and Lon shouted above the din for the cannoneers to prepare to remove the pieces by prolonge.[106]

But behind Thomas's guns another Union command—the Sixth Corps brigade of Col. William H. Irwin—was fast approaching! Its timing in this bloody, piecemeal battle could not have been more perfect. Irwin brought his command into battle formation with the 7th Maine on the left and the 20th, 49th, 77th, and 33d New York in line to the right as he advanced through the Mumma's fields toward the approaching Confederates.[107]

The five regiments coming to the relief of Thomas's beleaguered batteries were a curious mix, to say the least. Besides the big logging men from Maine, two of the New York regiments were most interesting. The 49th New York Infantry contained two companies from Erie County, one from Niagara County, and four—A, G, I, and K—from none other than Chautauqua County, New York. No one in the ranks of the 49th knew it, but they were about to save an artilleryman who would become one of their county's most famous war heroes. The 20th New York, commanded by Col. Ernest von Vegesack, was solid German. As the 20th moved through Thomas's guns, the artillerymen could hear the regimental and company commanders steadying their men in German. With visibility almost nonexistent, the sounds must have beckoned thoughts of Austerlitz or Waterloo, where some of those soldiers' Prussian ancestors would have fought.[108]

Once past Thomas's brass guns Irwin's regiments moved toward the Dunkard Church, fighting virtually every step of the way. The charging Confederates, unable to withstand the onslaught of yet another fresh Union brigade, slowly withdrew to the safety of the West Woods. The arrival of Irwin's Sixth Corps brigade on the field saved Batteries A and C from being overrun.[109] South of the Mumma farm, in the sunken road, French's and Richardson's Second Corps divisions broke through D.H. Hill's defenses. Again, however, Lee was not to be undone by the crisis. The timely arrival of the division of Maj. Gen. Richard H. Anderson bolstered the disintegrating Confederate lines in the Samuel Piper farm fields behind the sunken road, and the two Second Corps divisions were finally halted.[110]

Batteries A and C, 4th United States Artillery, had suffered only three casualties in the fighting. Pvt. James Murphy and Pvt. Michael MacDonald had received slight leg wounds; Cpl. Charles Au, however, had sustained a severe wound in the neck. The batteries had lost seventeen horses, though. Still, the losses were light indeed.[111] Thomas's batteries later were ordered to a position in the fields near the Roulette house to support the remnants of Richardson's and French's divisions, but at that location they saw no serious action.[112]

South of the Boonsboro Turnpike, General Burnside's Ninth Corps had struggled for hours to advance across the Antietam. By midafternoon, units of the corps had forded the creek, while others charged across the lower stone bridge toward the heights occupied by General Longstreet's command of the Army of Northern Virginia. The whole Ninth Corps threatened Lee's right flank, which had been anchored along the high ground in front and south of the town of Sharpsburg. As the sun was going down that seemingly endless and grisly day, Gen. A.P. Hill, with his Light Division, arrived from Harpers Ferry to force back Burnside's advance.[113]

The day finally ended. Along the fields west of Antietam Creek, nearly 27,500 men had fallen in less than twelve hours of terrible combat. For McClellan, despite his superiority in numbers, little tactical advantage had been gained—hardly sufficient to atone for the horrid losses. Never had Lon seen such carnage, such suffering. For all his youth and his excitement for war, Lon was glad to see the sun set on September 17, 1862.

6

"The Army Is Extremely Disgusted"

The rising sun on September 18 found Batteries A and C, 4th United States Artillery, and the tattered Second Corps occupying much of the ground over which they had so desperately fought the day before. Brig. Gen. Andrew Humphreys's Fifth Corps division arrived on the field near the Second Corps around midmorning. Thousands of dead, dying, and terribly wounded men lay strewn across the shot-torn cornfields, woodlots, and pasturelands ahead. All through the day litter-bearers worked in the bloody fields removing the wounded, while burial teams hastily buried the dead who lay within a safe distance. Much of Miller's cornfield, the Mumma swale, and the area in front of the Dunkard Church remained no-man's-land as Confederate snipers fired upon those who ventured too far. On and off throughout the day, "unofficial" truces were arranged by junior officers in order to retrieve the dead and wounded from under the enemy guns. It was a grim task. The cries and groans were hideous, and they continued unabated throughout the day. The smell of death hung like a pall over the Antietam valley. Everyone expected an attack at any time. Late in the evening, General Couch's Fourth Corps division arrived alongside the Second Corps to bolster the lines in the event the attack came.[1]

After a restless, heartrending night amid the carnage, the soldiers of the Army of the Potomac awoke expecting more bloodshed. McClellan had issued orders for the army to begin a general advance on September 19, but again, Little Mac was too late. It was soon discovered that Lee had withdrawn that day to the Virginia side of the Potomac River. The campaign was over.[2]

For the next several weeks, elements of the Army of the Potomac would remain on the Antietam battlefield. The Second Corps occupied the famed East Woods and the cornfield area for just under a week, its men having been assigned the horrid duty of burying the vast numbers of dead in the area. Lt. Alonzo H. Cushing and the other officers and men of Thomas's batteries parked their guns and bivouacked in the East Woods.[3]

On September 21, Lon learned that the adjutant general of the United States Army had recommended that he be transferred to the Topographical Engineers. It would mean that he would be attached to the headquarters of the Army of the Potomac. Clearly, so long as Lieutenant Thomas was still commanding the combined batteries, there was little hope that Lon would be anything more than a subaltern. From his tent in the East Woods, he wrote a note accepting the transfer. That same day Lon and his fellow officers of Batteries A and C were photographed at their bivouac site by Alexander Gardner. To Lon it must have seemed a fitting way to celebrate his new assignment. He would remain with his battery until October 19, when his new duties would begin at the headquarters of Gen. George B. McClellan. There he would serve with his old classmate Fannie Custer.[4]

Beginning on September 22—and over the course of several days thereafter—elements of the Second Corps, followed by the Twelfth Corps, began moving toward Harpers Ferry. One division at a time moved out of its bivouac site and marched down the winding road toward the great Potomac River. Once the corps reached Harpers Ferry, it would be able to rest, reequip, and, most important, replenish its manpower. Early on the morning of September 24, 1862, Thomas ordered his batteries limbered up. On that morning Lon left the dismal East Woods and the sights of the cornfield and the battered Dunkard Church forever. By that evening the batteries arrived along Bolivar Heights above Harpers Ferry, where the Second Corps had established its camp. General Sumner's headquarters was in the administration building of the United States Arsenal in Harpers Ferry.[5]

In early October, Sumner was granted a leave of absence to visit his family in Syracuse, but not until after President Lincoln had paid him a visit on his way to confer with McClellan. Lincoln stayed overnight at Sumner's headquarters, giving Lon another glimpse of the tall, careworn president he had met just before the First Battle of Bull Run.[6] Named in Sumner's place as commander of the Second Corps was Darius N. Couch, who was elevated to the rank of major general of volunteers and whose own division was transferred to the Sixth Corps. General Couch hailed from Putnam County, New York. He had been graduated from West Point in the class of 1846 along with George McClellan and Stonewall Jackson. Brevetted for gallantry in the Mexican War, he had resigned his commission in 1855 to enter the copper fabricating business of his wife's family in Massachusetts. At the outbreak of this war, he had been commissioned colonel of the 7th Massachusetts Infantry. With the meteoric rise of his close friend McClellan, Couch had been promoted to brigadier general of volunteers on August 9, 1861. He had served through the Peninsula campaign with great distinction, commanding a division in Gen. Erasmus Keyes's Fourth Corps. Couch was a man of slight build and very quiet demeanor; he shied away from any form of display. His conservative command outlook resulted in his having a small staff, only enough to do the necessary work. In all, Couch was an exceptionally capable soldier who administered to the needs of his men as well as bravely leading them in combat.[7]

Shortly after they arrived at Bolivar Heights, Lon learned that Batteries A and C were going to be divided again, and the command of Battery A was offered to him if he wanted it. Lon reassessed his acceptance of the position in the Topographical Engineers and wrote to the adjutant general on October 11, asking that his acceptance of the engineering post be withdrawn. "I have the honor to respectfully report," he wrote, "that at the time I gave my consent to be transferred to the Topographical Engineers, I was serving as a subaltern in a light battery. I can now have command of a battery in the 4th Arty., and under existing circumstances would consider it much more to my advantage to remain in the regiment." Lon's request was endorsed not only by the chief of artillery of the Second Corps but by Gen. Henry Hunt, chief of Reserve Artillery in the Army of the Potomac, and by McClellan himself. Already, Lon had become well recognized as a brave and capable young officer.[8]

Only once while the Second Corps was at Harpers Ferry and Bolivar Heights did any serious action occur. On October 16, in response to reports of enemy forces near Charles Town, Virginia (soon to be West Virginia), just under three miles away, the First Division—led, since the mortal wounding of General Richardson, by Brig. Gen. Winfield S. Hancock—was directed out to confront the enemy. Batteries A and C, along with Pettit's Battery B, 1st New York Light Artillery, accompanied the division. Cooperating with Hancock's movement was General Humphreys's Sixth Corps division, which started out toward Charles Town from its bivouac site near Shepherdstown. Humphrey's division ran into Confederate cavalry at Kearneysville; Hancock met the 6th, 7th, and 12th Virginia Cavalry of Col. Thomas T. Munford's brigade, together with one gun from Capt. Roger Preston Chew's battery of horse artillery and three guns from Capt. William Smith's Richmond Howitzer Battalion. A fiercely contested engagement ensued for several hours. Darkness halted the firing, though, and when the Confederates slowly withdrew from the field, Hancock marched his division back to Bolivar Heights. The combined batteries had fought their last engagement together.[9]

Almost from the moment of their arrival at Bolivar Heights, the officers of the batteries went about the task of separating the two commands. Lt. Evan Thomas was left in command of Battery C, which was given all of the ordnance. Battery A was at last given its wartime birth, even though it had no guns at all. On its rolls, Lts. Alonzo H. Cushing, Rufus King, and Arthur Morris were listed as the commissioned officers; Frederick Fuger was named first sergeant. Obtaining thirty-nine men from the 4th Ohio Infantry, which had just joined Gen. Nathan Kimball's brigade after lengthy duty in the Virginia mountains and the Shenandoah Valley, the fully assembled battery contained 147 enlisted men, including many of the recruits (from the 5th New Hampshire; 53d and 81st Pennsylvania; 52d, 57th, 61st, 63d, 66th, 69th, and 88th New York; 1st Company, Minnesota Sharpshooters; and 14th New York Independent Battery) who had enlisted in the battery when General Sumner was assembling and training his original division at Camp California in the fall of 1861.[10]

Lon, it seems, commanded Battery A on the day of its separation from Battery C. His tenure, of course, was short-lived, because his request to cancel his acceptance of the position in the Topographical Engineers would take weeks to process. As Lon was ordered to report to McClellan's headquarters on October 19, he turned the battery over to its most senior commissioned officer, Lt. Rufus King, that day. The next day its officers and enlisted men left Bolivar Heights for Washington, by way of the Baltimore & Ohio Railroad, to secure ordnance and equipment.[11]

In Washington, Battery A was equipped with six three-inch Ordnance rifles. The Ordnance rifle had its origin in 1854 with a New York-born inventor by the name of John Griffen, who, in a Pennsylvania iron foundry, had developed an artillery manufacturing process whereby strips of wrought iron were wrapped by a lathe around an iron core. Five such layers were laid in alternate spirals until the gun tube met the needed thickness and strength. The iron core was then removed, the breach was closed with an iron plug, and the metal brought to welding heat and rolled out from five to seven feet. Trunions were welded to the tube, and the bore was reamed out. The process produced a rifle that immediately caught the interest of the United States Ordnance Board, which, upon inspection, recommended that all such guns be rifled and manufactured with bores no greater than 3.35 inches. Because of the involvement of the Ordnance Board in the manufacturing process, the gun became known as the Ordnance rifle, one of the most accurate and highly valued artillery pieces in the war.[12]

To fill the vacancy created by Lon's departure, the War Department assigned a young artilleryman named Lt. Samuel Canby to Battery A. Canby had been born in Wilmington, Delaware, in 1837. After attending Haverford Boarding School (now Haverford College) in Pennsylvania, he had been graduated from Delaware College with a degree in civil engineering and worked as an engineer in the construction of a railroad in western New Jersey. When the war broke out, Canby enlisted in the 4th

New Jersey Infantry, a three-month unit; subsequently, he volunteered to serve in the 2d Delaware. Commissioned a second lieutenant in the regular army on October 21, 1861, Canby had been transferred to Capt. John Mendenhall's Batteries H and M, 4th United States Artillery, and had fought in the Battle of Shiloh, where he was awarded the brevet rank of first lieutenant. Thereafter, he had served through the siege of Corinth, Mississippi. On August 5, 1862, Canby was promoted to the rank of first lieutenant and ordered to the eastern theater.[13]

As Lee fell back deeper into Virginia, McClellan finally determined to give chase. The Army of the Potomac had been concentrating at Harpers Ferry. Lee, on the other hand, had divided his army again. Stonewall Jackson's command withdrew to the lower Shenandoah Valley not far from Winchester, while Longstreet's command marched all the way to Culpeper. In response, McClellan determined that the Army of the Potomac would move south toward Warrenton, Virginia, on a line parallel with the Blue Ridge Mountains, to confront Longstreet. To protect its flank and rear from any movements Jackson might make, the army would seize each pass in the mountains. McClellan's base of supply would continue to be Harpers Ferry and Berlin (now Brunswick), Maryland, until he passed Piedmont Station on the Manassas Gap Railroad, and then that rail line and the connecting Orange & Alexandria Railroad would serve as the supply line for the army.[14]

After a pontoon bridge was constructed across the Potomac River at Berlin on October 26, the Army of the Potomac began its movement south. Between October 26 and November 2 the First, Sixth, and Ninth Corps, along with the cavalry and reserve artillery, crossed the Potomac River at Berlin. The Second and Fifth Corps crossed the Shenandoah River at Harpers Ferry and marched around Loudon Heights between October 29 and November 1. Heavy rains fell, delaying the movement considerably. It seems the rains were so heavy, the First and Sixth Corps were forced to halt for at least a day at the Berlin crossing in order to allow supply trains to keep pace through the mud.[15] On November 6 the First Corps arrived at Warrenton. The Fifth Corps left Snicker's Gap that same day and moved toward White Plains, while the Ninth Corps moved toward Waterloo on the Rappahannock River. The Second Corps, having held Asby's Gap, commenced its movement toward Warrenton, arriving at Rectortown.[16] Battery A, 4th United States Artillery, now equipped with its six three-inch Ordnance rifles, twelve limbers, six caissons, a battery wagon, forge, and three quartermaster wagons as well as 120 horses, pulled out of Washington and headed to Clarksburg, Maryland, during the last week of October. Assigned to rejoin the Second Corps, the battery left Clarksburg on November 1; it would take nine days to arrive in Warrenton.[17]

General McClellan, with Lon in his entourage, arrived at Rectortown, Virginia, in a heavy snowstorm on November 6; there Little Mac established his headquarters. That same day General Sumner returned to the army from his leave of absence but did not take back the command of the Second Corps; by then, McClellan had conceived of the idea of forming three "Grand Divisions," and Sumner was a candidate to assume command of one of them.[18] In the meantime, Gen. McClellan had given Lon the task of crafting plans for the development of a Topographical Engineer command at army headquarters. On November 7 Lon formally requested the chief of the Bureau of Topographical Engineers in Washington to forward the necessary enlistment blanks for recruiting the new command.[19]

While Lon was busy preparing that request, a locomotive was chugging up the tracks of the Manassas Gap Railroad toward Salem (now Marshall), Virginia. Unscheduled and not pulling any cars, the fast-moving engine presented a curious sight to casual onlookers. In the cab beside the engineer and fireman was none other than white-haired Catharenus Putnam Buckingham, cousin and former partner of Lon's father, Milton Buckingham Cushing, in the dry goods business back in Putnam, Ohio. Now wearing the shoulder straps of a brigadier general of volunteers, Buckingham was on a special mission for the War Department.[20]

Buckingham had come a long way since the day he left Putnam. After teaching mathematics at Kenyon College and operating an ironworks in Knox County, Ohio, he had been called by his native state to assist in the war effort. He had served successively as assistant adjutant general, commissary general, and adjutant general of the state of Ohio after the outbreak of the war. While aiding in the recruitment of troops, Buckingham had been appointed brigadier general of volunteers upon the recommendation of Secretary of War Edwin Stanton, an 1832 graduate of Kenyon College, who had come to know and like Buckingham during the Ohioan's numerous visits to the War Department. Assigned to the adjutant general's office in Washington, General Buckingham had performed mostly clerical duties until he was assigned in the late summer of 1862 to travel to New York, Massachusetts, Ohio, Indiana, and Illinois with Secretary of State William Seward and Gens. John C. Frémont and James Shields in order to induce the governors of those states to raise more troops. Among those whom Buckingham and his companions, particularly General Shields, had encouraged the states to recruit with special enthusiasm were the Irish—for the old Puritan Buckingham, a particularly odd assignment.[21]

In early November, after returning to Washington, Catharenus P. Buckingham had visited an old West Point friend, Col. W.R. Lee, who was seriously ill. Back at his lodging that evening, his servant handed him a message summoning him to the War Department. Buckingham dashed across town and found the secretary of war in his office with his assistant secretary and Gens. Henry W. Halleck and James Wadsworth. Stanton informed the Ohioan that he wanted him to go over to Virginia on an important mission. He ushered Buckingham into an adjoining room, showed him a map of Virginia and the location of McClellan's army, and handed him two envelopes. One was addressed to General McClellan, the other to Gen. Ambrose Burnside. Buckingham recalled: "[It] occurred to me that it was a singular proceeding to make a mere messenger of a brig[adier] gen[eral] when a corporal would have done just as well." The envelopes were unsealed; he was told by the assistant secretary that he could read the messages but must seal them thereafter. Buckingham found that they were orders from the president and the War Department relieving McClellan from command of the Army of the Potomac and replacing him with Burnside![22]

On the morning of November 6, General Buckingham visited with Stanton at the secretary's home, where Stanton handed the general the necessary passes to enable him to proceed through all the sentinels and picket posts. The secretary said he feared Burnside would not take the position; Buckingham must use his best efforts to persuade Burnside to accept. Likewise, Stanton told Buckingham, he feared McClellan would not relinquish command but would insist on an order directly from the president and passed through military channels.[23]

Buckingham traveled to Alexandria, Virginia, by ferry and secured passage aboard the lone locomotive (all that was available in the United States Military Railroad yards) that took him down the tracks of the Orange & Alexandria Railroad to Manassas Junction and then proceeded up the Manassas Gap Railroad toward Salem.[24] Under a full head of steam, stopping only to collect wood to fire the locomotive (after losing its supply in a near-accident when the engineer tried to avoid hitting ties left along the tracks by Union soldiers, probably from Burnside's Ninth Corps, looking for firewood), the lone engine finally reached Salem at sundown. Buckingham discovered that Burnside's corps had passed through the area that day on its way to the Rappahannock River. The general stayed in Salem overnight, and the next morning he secured a horse from an army teamster and rode toward Burnside's encampment in the company of a couple of cavalrymen.[25]

On the evening of November 7, Buckingham found Ninth Corps headquarters in a small frame house near a crossroads called Wellington, Virginia. General Burnside was alone in an upstairs room. As expected, when informed of the appointment, the portly corps commander refused it. He told Buckingham that "he did not feel competent to command [the army] and that he was under very great personal obligations to McClellan." Buckingham explained that whether he accepted the position or not, the president would still relieve McClellan; if Burnside refused, Gen. Joseph Hooker would be named commander of the Army of the Potomac. Clearly feeling superior to Hooker, Burnside then agreed to accept the appointment.[26]

Now General Buckingham had the even more difficult task of informing McClellan. Riding in an ambulance with an officer from the British army who had been observing the operations of the Army of the Potomac, Buckingham started back to Salem. Alongside the ambulance rode Burnside and two of his aides on horseback. A light snow began to fall. Almost as if to foreshadow coming events, the entourage got lost. They found themselves in the foothills of the Blue Ridge Mountains before they determined to turn around and follow the tracks of the ambulance back toward Wellington. They did not reach Salem until 9:00 P.M.[27] After a hasty supper, Buckingham, Burnside and the troopers crowded into the cab of the lone locomotive. The engine was fired up and, belching smoke and steam, backed down the tracks for nearly five miles. Heavy snow continued to fall. The group finally arrived at Gen. McClellan's headquarters.[28]

Just before midnight, November 7, Buckingham and Burnside entered McClellan's tent, not far from Lon's quarters. Lon probably was fast asleep. The commanding general was busy looking over maps. He received Buckingham and Burnside cordially, inviting them to seats and cigars. "General," Buckingham said, "I might as well tell you at once what my business is." He handed Little Mac the envelopes. McClellan read the papers and then looked at Burnside. "General," said McClellan to Buckingham, "if you would permit Burnside and myself to consult together I will turn over the command to him." Buckingham retired from the tent. In a few minutes McClellan requested Buckingham to return and asked if he could accompany Burnside the next day so that he could make him aware of the details of the army's command and of his own plans. Buckingham thought there would be no objection.[29] His task accomplished, Catharenus Putnam Buckingham returned to the railroad with General Burnside and climbed back aboard the cab of the locomotive, accompanied by the British officer, for the return trip to Washington. He had performed a historic mission.[30] Unknown to Lt. Alonzo H. Cushing at the time, his father's cousin had just delivered the orders and secured the orderly transfer of command of the Army of Potomac from Gen. George B. McClellan to Gen. Ambrose Burnside.

News of the change in command soon swept through the army, and in only a few days a seriously adverse reaction to the change became evident. Officers tendered their resignations in great numbers, and the morale of the army—already at a low ebb—sank even lower. Lon, like most officers and enlisted men, admired General McClellan; that Little Mac had been relieved of command deeply disturbed him. "Of course, the army is extremely disgusted not to say disaffected by the change of commanders," Lon wrote. "Everybody has high respect for Gen. Burnside, but they have not the same affection for and confidence in him that they had for General McClellan—many resignations have been tendered, and if they are accepted the Army will be to some extent disorganized. Every body in the Army has felt since the change as if a funeral of some dear friend had just taken place."[31]

Indeed, officers and enlisted men alike expressed significant displeasure; there was even talk of a mutiny. The replacement of McClellan was the cause of most of the unrest, but the choice of Burnside to replace Little Mac caused a crisis in confidence among the troops. Burnside himself believed that he was not fit to command the army and openly and repeatedly expressed that sentiment.[32]

Ambrose Everett Burnside—born in 1824 at Liberty, Indiana, and graduated from West Point in the class of 1847—had served briefly in the Mexican War and on the southwestern frontier fighting Indians. Having invented a breech-loading carbine, he resigned his commission in 1853, in order to manufacture it in Bristol, Rhode Island. At the outbreak of war, as a major general in the Rhode Island militia, he had organized the 1st Rhode Island Infantry, a three-month unit, which was one of the first regiments to arrive in the defenses of Washington. Thereafter, Burnside commanded a brigade of largely Rhode Island troops that fought at the First Battle of Bull Run. A friend of McClellan's and something of a favorite in the White House, Burnside was then placed in command of what turned out to be a most successful expedition against the coast of North Carolina. From there he was promoted to the rank of major general of volunteers, and much of his command, designated the Ninth Corps, was ordered to join the Army of the Potomac, but his performance at the Battle of Antietam had been uneven at best. Although affable and likable, Burnside did not inspire confidence. He genuinely cared for his men but was never able to delegate responsibility. There was nothing about him to excite the army, and his own feelings of unfitness for command would become a self-fulfilling prophecy.[33]

The Army of the Potomac, moving cautiously south, was nearing a position from which it could take advantage of the enemy's separated commands and defeat them in detail. Under McClellan's final orders, the First and Fifth Corps and Reserve Artillery, along with army headquarters, moved to Warrenton on November 9; the Ninth Corps moved into position along the Rappahannock River near Waterloo, and the Sixth Corps moved to New Baltimore. By the end of that day virtually the entire

Army of the Potomac was massed at or near Warrenton, Virginia.[34] The Second Corps too, after a long, tiring march, reached Warrenton on November 9. As Gen. Sumner rode through the troops entering the outskirts of the village, the soldiers opened a passageway, forming on opposite sides of the road. Regiment after regiment let forth "three cheers for General Sumner" as he passed. The general, acknowledging his men's respect and admiration, raised his hat as he galloped by.[35]

Clearly, Sumner had Lon on his mind when he arrived at Warrenton. Knowing he was in line for the command of a Grand Division, he asked General Burnside if Lon could be transferred to his headquarters as his topographical engineer; according to Lon, Sumner made an "urgent application" for the transfer, and Burnside reluctantly granted the request. Besides Lon, Sumner's staff consisted of many of those who had been with Old Bull from the beginning. There was Lt. Col. J.H. Taylor, chief of staff; Lt. Col. Paul J. Revere, inspector general; Lt. Col. C.G. Sawtelle, chief quartermaster; Surgeon Alexander N. Dougherty, medical director; Maj. Lawrence Kip and Capts. Joseph C. Audenreid (Lon's classmate) and Samuel S. Sumner, as well as Lts. W.G. Jones and Ranald S. Mackenzie (Lon's friend from the West Point class of 1862), all personal aides. One new addition was Sumner's son-in-law from Syracuse, Lt. Col. William W. Teall, who would serve as commissary of subsistence for the new Grand Division. Lon knew all the officers except Teall, but Sumner's son-in-law was an affable man, and the two quickly became close. Virtually all the members of the staff came from old New England families.[36]

General Sumner and his staff, upon entering Warrenton, set up headquarters in the Warren Green Hotel on Main Street, but spent only one night there, then moved into a house occupied by Catherine Hooe Middleton Semmes, the widowed mother of none other than Confederate Navy Commander Raphael Semmes. "We are in Warrenton, Virginia," Lon wrote to Will on November 12, "occupying most elegant quarters and having a comparatively comfortable time." Teall penned a note to his wife about the friendliness and hospitality of Mrs. Semmes, but then added, as though it was important to note, that "she is a Catholic." By November 12 there was still no word as to the formation of the Grand Divisions of the Army. "We will move," Lon wrote to Will, "as soon as the new organization of the army—into Grand divisions—is effected."[37]

Lon's brother William was becoming something of a celebrity. After his accelerated promotion in mid-July, he had been assigned to duty off the North Carolina coast as executive officer aboard the *Commodore Perry*. Heralded for his bravery in close-order fighting on the Blackwater River, Will was given command of the gunboat *Ellis*—a captured hundred-ton iron vessel mounting an eighty-pound rifle on its forward deck and a twelve-pound rifle howitzer aft—and assigned the task of observing Bouge Inlet, thirty miles south of Beaufort, South Carolina, for enemy shipping. But finding nothing there, Will, without orders, sailed the *Ellis* up to New Topsail Inlet, twelve miles south of Wilmington, North Carolina, and there captured the schooner *Adelaide*, which was carrying $100,000 worth of cotton and turpentine bound for Bermuda. Newspapers reported the event widely. From that point forward, Will was permitted to sail whatever inlets he chose![38]

Not so newsworthy had been the action of Pvt. Howard B. Cushing. Terribly ill with dysentery after Shiloh, Howard had caught up with Battery B, 1st Illinois Light Artillery, at Corinth, Mississippi, in the late spring and had been involved in the siege of that critical railroad junction. Afterward, he returned to Memphis, Tennessee. Then, as part of General Grant's central Mississippi campaign, Howard and his battery moved southward in early November in an effort to seize fortress Vicksburg. Lon had heard nothing from Howard himself since the spring. He could only guess from newspaper accounts where his older brother was.[39]

Lon went to Washington to visit the Bureau of Topographical Engineers just after the Second Corps arrived in Warrenton. While in Washington he had visited with his brother Milton, who had informed him of William's adventures off the Carolina coasts. Lon returned to Warrenton deeply impressed with Will's advancement and his record of service. He wrote to his young brother, encouraging him as always: "Accept my hearty congratulations on your success and your promotion. You have undergone more transformations since we met than myself, and finally you being up in command of a U.S. Gunboat . . . Old Pounce was doing nothing but collect[ing] papers containing an account of the capture of the *Adelaide*, and was continually publishing them to the Farquhars and Mr. Hobbs, while old Albertus [Uncle Albert Smith] proudly claims you as his? gallant young protige [*sic*]. He always knew from the time you were a small boy that you were bound to do yourself—him and your country credit. A great old humbug he is . . . If we go to Fredericksburg as I think we shall, I shall expect to see you there. I have had some faint expectations of seeing you here during the last two or three days. I shall not be surprised to see you at any time. You always turn up where I am. In the meantime just go ahead, capture *Adelaides* in abundance and in another year you will command a squadron."[40]

In accordance with McClellan's original plans, General Burnside finally issued the orders reorganizing the Army of the Potomac into three Grand Divisions. Sumner was given command of the Right Grand Division, consisting of the Second Corps under General Couch and the Ninth Corps, then under the command of Brig. Gen. Orlando B. Willcox.

General Hooker, although still lame and using a cane as a result of his Antietam wound, was assigned to command the Center Grand Division, consisting of the new Third Corps, commanded by Brig. Gen. George Stoneman, and the Fifth Corps, commanded by Brig. Gen. Daniel Butterfield, who succeeded Fitz John Porter. Command of the Left Grand Division was given to Gen. William B. Franklin. It consisted of the Sixth Corps under Gen. William F. Smith, and the First Corps, commanded by Gen. John Fulton Reynolds.[41]

The Second Corps remained virtually intact, with only a few regiments added and some commanders changed. Gen. Winfield Scott Hancock remained in command of the First Division. Gen. Oliver Otis Howard was given command of Sedgwick's old Second Division, as General Sedgwick was still recuperating from his Antietam wounds. The Third Division remained under the command of Gen. William H. French.[42]

Burnside put his army on the march toward Fredericksburg on November 15. By marching east, Burnside abandoned any opportunity of striking Lee's divided forces. The columns of the Second Corps with all its baggage trains, seven miles in length, marched to Warrenton Junction, and then to a location west of Fredericksburg called Spotted Tavern on November 16. There Sumner and his staff bedded down in an old house by the roadside; the general, his son, and his son-in-law slept on the floor of one room, and Lon and the rest of the staff on the floor of another. The men of the Second Corps bivouacked in the fields on either side of the road. The next day—November 17—the corps reached Falmouth. There Sumner set up his headquarters in the Phillips house, a lovely mansion east of Stafford Heights. Lon busied himself reconnoitering the area and preparing maps to be used by his commander. General Burnside readjusted his supply lines to the new base at Aquia Creek Landing on the Potomac River.[43]

Lee rapidly withdrew Longstreet's command across the swollen Rappahannock River to the heights behind the city of Fredericksburg. No sooner had Longstreet's command entered Fredericksburg than it set about the task of entrenching itself and preparing gun emplacements along high ground, known locally as Marye's Heights, behind the city. Jackson's command was urgently summoned to rejoin the army on the south bank of the river. With each passing day Lee's position became stronger and stronger.[44] On November 30 Jackson arrived with his command and took up positions in Lee's defense lines south of Fredericksburg along the high ground called Prospect Heights. Burnside's enemy, by then, was in an impregnable position.[45]

General Sumner had attempted to secure the surrender of the city of Fredericksburg on November 21 but was unsuccessful, as Longstreet's corps began to enter the outskirts of the city that day. The two armies since then had been gathering on either side of the river. Finally, on December 9, General Burnside called his commanders to a council of war, at which Lon was present. It was determined then that the army on December 12 would cross the Rappahannock on pontoon bridges and seize Fredericksburg, covered by the fire of some 150 artillery pieces. Sumner's Right Grand Division and Hooker's Center Grand Division were to cross on three bridges in front of the city. The attack would be spearheaded by the Second Corps. Franklin's Left Grand Division would cross a little more than one mile below the town on two bridges.[46]

On the evening of December 10, Gen. Henry Hunt placed a vast array of artillery in position along Stafford Heights opposite Fredericksburg, commanding the town's northern and southern approaches. Lt. Rufus King's Battery A, 4th United States Artillery, was positioned along the right flank of the enormous concentration, together with seven others that included two from the Second Corps: Owen's Battery G, 1st Rhode Island Light Artillery, and Pettit's Battery B, 1st New York Light Artillery. The remaining artillery batteries of the Second Corps were held in readiness to support the infantry. Battery D, 5th United States Artillery, under the command of Lt. Charles E. Hazlett, was also stationed near King's guns. Hunt arrayed thirty-one batteries—151 guns in all, including five batteries of twenty-pound Parrott rifles—in four distinct commands (the Right, the Right Center, the Left Center, and the Left) up and down Stafford Heights preparatory to the bombardment of the city.[47]

The Second Corps regiments designated to spearhead the assault through the streets of the city concentrated in the vicinity of the Phillips house. There, in the bitter cold, the regiments waited for the construction of the pontoon bridges across the Rappahannock, directly below the William Lacy house, by the engineers of the 50th New York in Brig. Gen. Daniel P. Woodbury's Engineer Brigade.[48] Lon observed the engineers as, under cover of darkness, they hauled the pontoons and trestle work to the designated positions along the north bank of the river during the wee hours of December 11. To protect the engineers, the 57th and 66th New York were ordered to take up supporting positions along the north bank at the rope ferry; Sumner ordered Col. Norman J. Hall's brigade of General Howard's Second Division, Second Corps, into position near the Lacy house to provide additional support; and the 89th New York was directed to a position across from the steamboat landing. Through the terribly cold and dark night, the engineers anchored the bridges and completed all three to the river's midpoint.[49]

Gen. William Barksdale's Mississippians, along with companies from two Florida regiments and one Georgia regiment, were posted behind barricades and in the windows of abandoned buildings and houses that stood on Fredericksburg's riverfront. From such vantage points, those battle-hardened Confederates listened in the cold darkness to the construction process, firing only occasional shots at the engineers. But when the bridges were nearly two-thirds completed—within rifle range of the city—the Confederates opened fire in earnest. Sheets of flame erupted from behind barricades and from windows of buildings all along the riverfront. The engineers were literally swept from the bridges by the concentrated gunfire. To protect them, General Hunt quickly ordered the massed batteries along Stafford Heights to open fire on the city. Amid the roll of gunfire the river, the city, and Stafford Heights became wrapped in smoke. The rain of shells hurled at the venerable city was devastating. Soldiers watched as houses and buildings were demolished piecemeal by the torrent of explosive shells or collapsed in flame and smoke after having been set on fire by the shell bursts. The echoes of the artillery fire and bursting shells rolled back and forth between the heights commanding the great Rappahannock, adding to the fury of the moment. Work on the bridges ceased altogether. The engineers sought cover, and the infantry supports along the riverbank were withdrawn to positions of safety.[50]

The firing soon subsided, and the engineers scurried back across the bridges to the work of completing the structures. The Confederates, still occupying barricades and shell-pocked buildings, opened fire again. Federal artillery then opened up on the town once more. As General Hunt's guns again entered the fray, the engineers once more tried to complete the bridges but were stopped by the heavy small arms fire. Nine different times between dawn and midafternoon, recalled a Mississippi colonel, the Union engineers tried to complete the bridges across the river, and each time they were stopped by Confederate rifle fire. The engineers and their infantry supports suffered terribly. Construction had come to a complete standstill. The empty pontoons used in the bridge construction bobbed in the water alongside the partially completed bridges and lined the north bank of the river.[51]

Colonel Hall's brigade had been lying close to the bluff near the Lacy house, awaiting the completion of the bridges and the order to advance. Now General Hunt and Colonel Woodbury, viewing the impossible situation below, called for Hall. Pointing to the pontoons, Hunt asked the colonel whether his brigade could use them as boats, cross the river, and clear the town of the enemy sharpshooters. Doing so would enable the bridges to be completed and would secure a foothold for the rest of the army on the south bank of the river. Assuring the artillery chief that his brigade would try, Hall called for volunteers for the hazardous duty. The commanders of his own 7th Michigan and the 19th Massachusetts immediately offered the services of their commands.[52]

Preparatory to the perilous operation, Gen. Hunt ordered the massed artillery on Stafford Heights to open fire on the city in order to give the two brave regiments cover as they ran down the bank to the boats on the shore and alongside the bridges. Lon was directed to the vicinity of the Lacy house to provide assistance to the Second Corps assault forces. Lt. Col. Henry Baxter led an advance party—two companies of the 7th Michigan, on the run down the bank and onto the partially-constructed bridges below the Lacy house. The advance party was followed by the rest of the Michigan men and the Bay Staters. The river valley rumbled and rolled with the terrific artillery barrages; the river became enveloped in smoke. Across the Rappahannock the waterfront exploded in rifle fire as Baxter's soldiers clambered into the empty pontoons alongside the bridges and rowed through the cold and swift river current toward the city of Fredericksburg. With bullets zipping through the air all about them, the 50th New York engineers scrambled across the partially completed bridges to renew their perilous work. The two advance companies cleared the ends of the unfinished bridges through a hail of gunfire and in moments—which must have seemed to the soldiers like hours—reached the south bank. There they formed ranks. At the high-pitched command of their brave lieutenant colonel, the Michiganders stormed up Fauquier Street, driving the rebel sharpshooters out of their positions and securing the city riverfront. Baxter was struck by a shell fragment just as his little command stepped off on its attack up the streets of the city. The advance companies of the 19th Massachusetts, including the color company, reached the south shore, formed ranks, and then stormed ahead to the right of Baxter's two Michigan companies. The remainder of the 19th Massachusetts and the 7th Michigan completed the crossing of the frigid river in pontoons only moments behind the leading companies of the two regiments.[53]

Below Lon's vantage point, the 20th Massachusetts formed along the north bank of the river. It had been directed to storm across the bridge as soon as the last plank was laid, but thanks to garbled orders, the regiment instead scrambled into the remaining pontoons along the shoreline and rowed across the river. As the engineers placed the last planks into position on the bridges, the 59th and 42d New York and 127th Pennsylvania charged across them and into the lower streets of Fredericksburg.[54] The 20th Massachusetts, ordered to clear the street directly ahead of the pontoon bridges through to the center of town, formed its battleline across the riverfront, supported by the 59th New York. The 42d New York formed in the street to the left of the 59th. Moving by the flank in columns of four, the 20th Massachusetts entered Fauquier Street and immediately came under ferocious gunfire from Barksdale's infantrymen, who had withdrawn to positions in buildings fronting the streets ahead. Breaking up into platoons, the 20th Massachusetts drove ahead into Confederate strongholds along Water and Caroline Streets. The rifle fire intensified. In a space no greater than fifty yards, wrote Colonel Hall, ninety-seven officers and men of the splendid Massachusetts regiment were killed or wounded. As darkness fell, though, the 20th Massachusetts cleared the city of Fredericksburg of Barksdale's stubborn fighters.[55] Under Lon's direction, all of General Howard's division streamed across the bridges and into Fredericksburg, along with Col. Rush Hawkins's brigade from the Ninth Corps and Brig. Gen. Charles Devens's Sixth Corps brigade of Franklin's Left Grand Division. Fredericksburg was at last in Union hands.[56]

General Couch, accompanied by Lon, entered the city on the morning of December 12, along with Hancock's and French's divisions. The remainder of General Willcox's Ninth Corps crossed downstream and occupied the lower part of the city. The Second Corps bivouacked in the streets. Though the night was terribly cold, the men were instructed not to light any campfires, lest they draw enemy artillery fire. Campfires dotted the streets anyway. Many soldiers climbed into the cellars of houses and buildings in the city, where they built fires and sought protection from the falling temperature.[57]

Burnside was in a quandary. Many of his troops were across the river, and he, like General Sumner, had been under the impression that Lee, if attacked, would not hold his positions behind the town. But Lee remained. Clearly, the Union troops could not be left in the city indefinitely; they were terribly exposed to enemy artillery fire and forced to sleep without the benefit of campfires. As night turned to morning, Burnside finally determined to launch a frontal assault against the heights behind the town. At 6:00 A.M. he forwarded orders to Gen. Sumner to "push a column of a division or more along the Plank and Telegraph Roads, with a view to seizing the heights in rear of town."[58] The freezing temperatures of the days past had given way to a thaw. With the temperature change on the morning of December 13 came a dense fog that blanketed the river bottom and countryside, enveloping the city. Only the church spires were faintly visible in the fog, giving the center stage of the coming battle an eerie appearance.[59]

General Sumner, upon receiving Burnside's early morning directive, called his staff together. He examined Lon's maps of the city and the heights beyond it. According to Burnside's order, the assault would be directed up two roads: the Plank Road, which ran through Fredericksburg west toward Chancellorsville; and the Telegraph Road, which ran roughly parallel with the Plank Road until it reached the heights behind the town and then south until it reached an unfinished railroad grading, where it turned west again. Where the Telegraph Road ran along the heights, it was below ground level, forming a long, natural entrenchment. Any assault force would not only have to advance against a heavily fortified enemy situated along high ground; it would also have to contend with a waste water canal or mill race, fifteen feet wide and four to six feet deep, which ran through the western suburbs of Fredericksburg and coursed the very fields over which the attack must be made. General Couch warned Burnside of the problem such an obstacle would present in any attack; committed to the operation, Burnside was unmoved. About 150 yards from the stone wall alongside the Telegraph Road stood a large, square brick house and a cluster of small houses and outbuildings. In the muddy fields between the canal and the brick house were plank fences that would have to be cleared before an attack could reach the advance line of the enemy. Where the Telegraph Road ran along Marye's Heights, a stout stone wall formed the border of the sunken road.[60]

Behind the stone wall Gen. James Longstreet had placed the 18th and 24th Georgia, Phillips's Georgia Legion of Brig. Gen. Thomas R.R. Cobb's brigade, Gen. Lafayette McLaws's division; and the 24th North Carolina of Brig. Gen. Robert Ransom's brigade, Gen. John Bell Hood's division. All along the heights, Longstreet's command was situated in compressed lines, supported by well-positioned batteries of artillery. Maj. Gen. Richard H. Anderson's division anchored the left of the line along the northern slopes of Marye's Heights, while McLaws, with Ransom's brigade and Gen. George Pickett's and General Hood's divisions, extended the lines from Marye's Heights to the left flank of General Jackson's command. In spite of the enemy's imposing positions, Burnside and Sumner still harbored doubts that the Confederates would hold the heights in the face of a determined assault.[61]

Even though Burnside placed nine divisions under Sumner's control that morning—three from the Second Corps, two from the Ninth Corps, three from the Fifth Corps, and one from the Third Corps—no orders were ever issued by the commanding general for any cooperation of the Ninth Corps with the Second Corps, and the Fifth Corps remained on the north bank of the Rappahannock River. Of all those divisions, only one was directed by Sumner to attack the heights behind the town, and it was to be supported by just one other. These two divisions, both from the Second Corps, were to assault the fortified heights held by Longstreet's entire command![62]

His own staff being small and needing the assistance of a stout-hearted aide, particularly one conversant with the roads and land features of the area, General Couch, upon receiving his final instructions from General Sumner, asked if he could use Lon's services during the day. Couch must have recalled Lon's gallantry at Fair Oaks and the Seven Days, and he had observed him in action over the past two days. Sumner

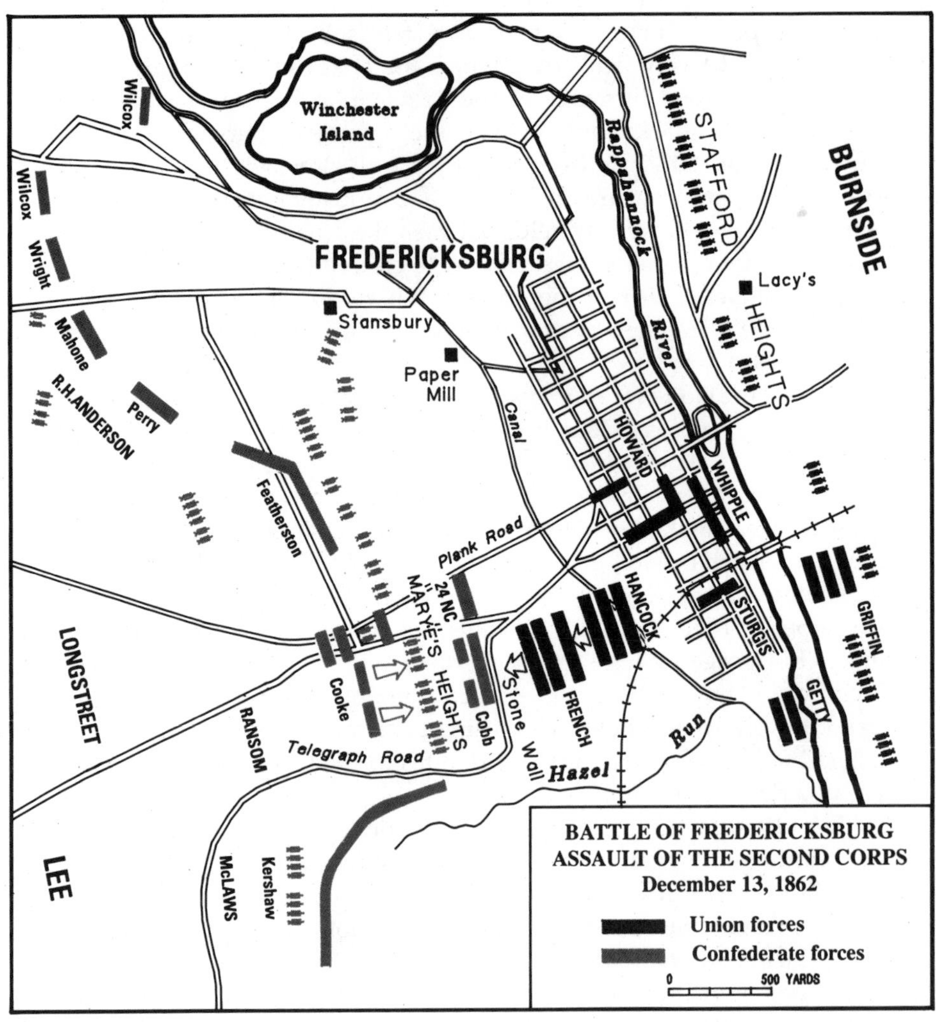
Winchester Island
FREDERICKSBURG
Rappahannock River
STAFFORD HEIGHTS
BURNSIDE
Lacy's
Stansbury
Paper Mill
Canal
Wilcox
Wilcox
Wright
Mahone
R.H.ANDERSON
Perry
Featherston
Plank Road
24 NC
MARYE'S HEIGHTS
HOWARD
WHIPPLE
HANCOCK
STURGIS
FRENCH
Stone Wall
Cobb
Cooke
RANSOM
Telegraph Road
Hazel Run
GRIFFIN
GETTY
LONGSTREET
LEE
McLAWS
Kershaw
BATTLE OF FREDERICKSBURG
ASSAULT OF THE SECOND CORPS
December 13, 1862
Union forces
Confederate forces
0
500 YARDS

quickly agreed, and thus Lon was directed to accompany General Couch on the battlefield.[63]

In conformity with the orders from his commanding general, Couch ordered General French to form his Third Division in column of brigades in the streets of Fredericksburg with intervals between brigades of two hundred yards. Hancock's First Division was directed to support French. General Howard's division was ordered to hold the northern approaches to the town to protect the Second Corps against any enemy movement from that sector. Lon rode up and down the lines giving commanders General Couch's orders and helping to steady the men.[64]

The dense fog began to lift. At 10:00 A.M., Couch informed Sumner that French was in position and was waiting for the order to advance. Already, General Couch had heard the guns from the far left flank. Gen. Franklin's Left Grand Division, spearheaded by the First Corps divisions of Brig. Gen. John Gibbon and Maj. Gen. George Meade, had rushed across the pontoon bridges south of Fredericksburg and were assaulting the Prospect Heights defenses of Stonewall Jackson. At about 11:00 A.M. a courier from Sumner's headquarters galloped up to Gen. Couch with instructions to open the attack. Lon relayed the orders down the long columns of Second Corps infantrymen.[65]

Sumner and his staff vacated the Phillips house and took over the Lacy house as the new headquarters for the Right Grand Division. The Lacy house, also known as Chatham, stood on the heights directly opposite the city of Fredericksburg, closer to the field of action. From there Sumner could more easily direct the movements of his Grand Division.[66]

Behind a "cloud of skirmishers" from his own 4th and 8th Ohio, along with the 1st Delaware of Col. John W. Andrews's Third Brigade, General Kimball ordered forward the 14th Indiana, 24th and 28th New Jersey, and 7th West Virginia by way of Hanover, Princess Ann, and Caroline Streets shortly after noon. The dense mass of Union soldiers, wearing their powder blue greatcoats, their muskets at "right shoulder shift," moved ahead. The fog was still so dense that the Confederates could not see the approaching columns; they could only hear the tread of thousands of feet and the yells of officers as the columns advanced. Lon, along with General Couch, helped direct the regiments as they moved out of the city. The columns were within range of the enemy guns on the heights, and the Confederates, listening intently to the sounds of the approaching enemy, opened up an intense artillery barrage upon the hapless Union soldiers. To negotiate the canal, Kimball's brigade crossed the Hanover Street bridge, most of the planks of which had been removed, and then marched forward, by the left flank, across the shot-swept fields in columns of fours. Behind the advance, General Hunt ordered the massed artillery along Stafford Heights to open up on the distant Confederate positions. Section by section, Capt. William A. Arnold's Battery A, 1st Rhode Island Light Artillery, rumbled through the streets of Fredericksburg following the advance of French's division. Arnold's battery unlimbered on the outskirts of town and opened fire from behind the advancing infantry. Soon Fredericksburg, already dim with the lifting fog, was enveloped in smoke and the roar of artillery and bursting shells.[67]

General Couch could not follow the fighting from his position in the streets. He and Lon rode to the courthouse, where they were met by General Howard. Couch and his Second Division commander, along with Lon, climbed up into the steeple of the courthouse and from there observed the clash of arms west of town.[68] What Lon could see from the steeple was horrible. All that saved Kimball's men from annihilation was the ridge just west of the canal; the brigade was able to get into the fields almost intact. But as Kimball ordered his men over the ridge toward the entrenched Confederate lines, they came under blistering small arms and artillery fire without any cover whatsoever. Men fell by the score. General Kimball was wounded, as were the regimental commanders of the 7th West Virginia, 28th New Jersey, and 4th Ohio in the futile effort.[69]

Following closely behind Kimball's brigade was Andrews's Third Brigade of French's division—then composed of the 4th and 10th New York and 132d Pennsylvania—and then Col. Oliver H. Palmer's Second Brigade, which included the 14th Connecticut, 108th New York, and 130th Pennsylvania. Following the same path as Kimball's men, the Third and Second Brigades crowded together in their attempt to get over and beyond the ridge west of the canal. Men were knocked out of the ranks by the dozens. The commander of the 130th Pennsylvania was killed just as his regiment entered the fight; the colonel of the 14th Connecticut was struck down moments later. The massed columns, moving out into the open fields in a fruitless attempt to seize the heights, were torn apart by heavy gunfire. One Connecticut soldier recalled: "The belching forth of two hundred pieces of artillery seemed to lift the earth from its foundation. Shells screeched and burst in the air among the men as if possessed with demons and were seeking revenge, the shot from tens of thousands of musketry fell like rain drops in a summer shower, brother saw brother writhing in agony of mortal wounds and could offer no aid, comrade saw comrade with whom he had marched shoulder to shoulder in the wearisome marches or shared the meagre food in their cheerless bivouac, still in death. Men fell like pins in an alley before the well aimed ball of a skillful bowler." The attack staggered to a bloody halt. All up and down the lines, the living fell to the still-frozen ground among the dead and wounded in an effort to save themselves, fearful of moving one way or another. Lon observed that some soldiers managed to crawl to within forty feet of the stone wall, only to be stopped by the terrible gunfire. General French's attack had ended in minutes.[70]

From his vantage point in the courthouse steeple, General Couch watched the gruesome panorama. "I remember," he wrote, "the whole plain was covered with men, prostrate and dropping, the live men running here and there, and in front closing upon each other, and the wounded coming back. The commands seemed to be mixed up. I had never before seen fighting like that, nothing approaching it in terrible uproar and destruction. There was no cheering on the part of the men, but a stubborn determination to obey orders and do their duty." Seeing his commands being decimated, Couch immediately ordered Howard to bring forward two of his brigades to flank the entrenched enemy from the right. Couch and Lon scurried back down to their horses, and the two rode toward the front.[71]

As French's division was repulsed, fresh regiments poured into the Confederate lines. The 46th North Carolina rushed down to the stone wall just ahead of French's helpless attackers and added its gunfire to the scorching and merciless fusilades of the 27th North Carolina, already there.[72] Behind French's broken brigades moved the division of General Hancock. As Hancock's legions massed toward the Confederate positions, the 25th North Carolina rushed down the hill and joined the 24th North Carolina behind the stone wall. General Kershaw threw forward the 2d and 8th South Carolina. Then the 16th Georgia arrived to reinforce its comrades in Cobb's brigade. From the sunken road, ten Confederate regiments poured volley upon volley into the ranks of Hancock's brave legions. On the heights above the stone wall and sunken road, the remaining regiments of Kershaw's, Cooke's and Ransom's Confederate brigades unleashed a volcano of gunfire.[73]

Through the din, Lon could see Hancock's veteran division as it moved quickly to bolster and support French's ill-fated soldiers. The six light twelve-pounders of Capt. John G. Hazard's Battery B, 1st Rhode Island Light Artillery, moved through the streets to support Hancock's men. The first of Hancock's troops to emerge into the fields were those of Col. Samuel K. Zook: the 2d Delaware, 27th Connecticut, 52d, 57th, and 66th New York, and 53d Pennsylvania. Zook advanced over fields littered with the dead and wounded of French's division. Many lying on the ground were unhurt but too terrified to move either forward or rearward. Yet at the approach of Zook's men, large numbers of French's soldiers courageously got up and joined the assault. Like French's division, though, Zook's brigade came under a blistering fire from the heights which terribly thinned its ranks. Zook himself was wounded. Then, from behind Zook came the Irish Brigade—the 63d, 69th, and 88th New York, 28th Massachusetts, and 116th Pennsylvania. With green sprigs in their bummer's caps to honor the land of their birth, the Irishmen surged up the street toward the dismal battlefield. What they encountered was awful; dead and wounded were everywhere. Many of the Irishmen remembered seeing a German soldier from a New York regiment in French's division lying in a wheelbarrow with a tourniquet on one leg; his foot had been shot off, and blood dripped from his stump onto the icy ground. The old German, likely in a state of shock, was calmly puffing on a meerschaum pipe. "Ach," he would utter, "make right!" In the fields covered with dense smoke, General Meagher turned to his men and shouted: "Irish Brigade, advance! Forward, double-quick, guide center!" Beneath flapping green banners, the Irishmen negotiated the canal, and then, to Lon's horror, they too were struck by the horrendous gunfire and knocked out of their ranks by the score. As the brave soldiers of Hancock's brigades, raked by enemy gunfire, tried to clear the plank fences in front of the Confederate lines, the dead and wounded literally began to pile up below the heights. Within minutes, over five hundred of the 1,200 members of the Irish Brigade were lost. What more could those Irishmen prove to their newly adopted country?[74]

Riding across the shot-torn fields, General Hancock ordered Gen. John C. Caldwell's brigade forward for one last effort to breach the Confederate defenses. Caldwell's brigade—the 5th New Hampshire, 7th, 61st, and 64th New York, and the 81st and 145th Pennsylvania—entered the fighting from behind the decimated ranks of the Irish Brigade. Lon helped direct the men into place. Some stouthearted men in Hancock's division actually crept forward far enough to seize gaps in the stone wall ahead, and others clung to positions along the board fences and around the cluster of brick and frame houses below the Confederate positions.[75] But the whole Second Corps line was soon halted by the terrific gunfire: 994 men in Caldwell's brigade were killed or wounded in a matter of minutes.[76]

Couch told Lon that he feared a counterattack. Fortunately, two divisions of the Ninth Corps advanced across the fields to the left of the Second Corps and engaged the enemy just as Caldwell's regiments were halted. In the meantime, General Howard's division arrived through the streets of Fredericksburg to bolster what was left of the Second Corps attackers. Brig. Gen. Amiel W. Whipple's Third Corps division of Hooker's Center Grand Division had taken up the positions vacated by Howard's division along the northern approaches of the city.

The leading brigade of Howard's division was that of Col. Joshua Owen: the 69th, 72d, and 106th Pennsylvania (the 71st Pennsylvania was on picket duty). Led by the 127th Pennsylvania Infantry of Col. Norman J. Hall's Third Brigade, it crossed the bridge over the canal and deployed in the fields to the left of the Telegraph Road. Moving forward toward the brick house where many of French's and Hancock's men were lying down among the dead and wounded to avoid the heavy shellfire, Owen's brigade was subjected to brutal fusillades from enemy infantry and artillery. The heroic brigade of Colonel Hall—19th and 20th Massachusetts, 7th Michigan, and 42d and 59th New York—moved out of Fredericksburg abreast of Owen's. General Couch resolved to lead the two brigades in person; Lon rode alongside his commander. Hall was ordered to deploy on the right of the Telegraph Road. Then, the two brigades moved ahead together against the Confederate works on Marye's Heights. "Shells and canister," wrote one soldier in the 19th Massachusetts, "poured down upon [the two brigades] like rain." No sooner had the command, "Forward," been given than the 19th Massachusetts began to lose color-bearers in rapid succession: between the streets of Fredericksburg and the canal, two fell; then, from the canal bank forward, at least eleven more bearers of the regimental and national colors were shot down. Finally, a lieutenant from Company I grabbed the flags, both badly rent by bullets and torn by artillery fire, and rushed to the board fences with the men of the regiment following him. There they lay down and began to return the fire of the enemy. Behind Colonel Hall, Brig. Gen. Alfred Sulley's brigade—the 1st Minnesota, 19th Maine, 15th Massachusetts, 34th and 82d New York, the 1st Company of Massachusetts Sharpshooters, and the 2d Company of Minnesota Sharpshooters—moved into a position of support. From the wounded and dying soldiers who littered the frozen ground all around came the heart-rending cries: "Water"; "Give us some water"; "For God's sake, take me out of this."[77]

Portions of Hooker's Center Grand Division—two Fifth Corps divisions—had moved into Fredericksburg. Although Hooker had had orders to send General Butterfield's Fifth Corps in support of Couch, when he consulted with the Second Corps commander at about 2:00 P.M., Couch discouraged the advance, feeling it was a waste of life. After having sent some of his units, notably the Third Corps, to the left to support Franklin's Left Grand Division, Hooker next sought out General Burnside to ask him to suspend further attacks, but Burnside refused to call off the assault. Before Hooker returned from his futile mission, General Couch and Lon at about 4:00 P.M. directed Gens. Andrew A. Humphreys's and George Sykes's Fifth Corps divisions in line to the left of the remnants of the Second Corps.[78]

In Sykes's division of "regulars" was one brigade of volunteer troops commanded by Brig. Gen. Gouverneur K. Warren. Only three infantry regiments made up the little brigade: the 5th, 140th, and 146th New York. Commanding the 140th New York, a Zouave regiment, was none other than Col. Patrick Henry O'Rorke of Lon's West Point class. After the First Battle of Bull Run, O'Rorke had been assigned to duty as an assistant engineer in the defenses at Washington; he had served successively as an engineer at Fort Monroe, Port Royal, and Fort Pulaski, rising to the rank of brevet captain. While on leave in the summer of 1862, O'Rorke had married Clara Wadsworth Bishop in his hometown of Rochester, New York. Learning of the formation of the 140th New York, he had requested a volunteer commission in his "hometown" regiment, and on September 8, 1862, he had been commissioned colonel of the 140th. Unlike the days when he and Lon were young subalterns at First Bull Run, Paddy O'Rorke now sported large black sideburns and a mustache, much like General Burnside. O'Rorke was the first member of the West Point class of June 1861 to command a regiment. For the 140th New York, this ghastly affair at Fredericksburg would be its baptism of fire.[79]

To Couch's left, the Ninth Corps was being decimated. At about 4:15 P.M. Couch called for Hazard's Battery B to move forward. As he gave the command, Col. Charles H. Morgan, the corps artillery chief, remarked, "General, a battery can't live there." Couch sternly replied, "Then it must die there!" Capt. John Hazard ordered his six light twelve-pounders over the canal bridge, and they came into action to the left of the road, directly in front of the Confederate works. Under heavy gunfire, the battery unlimbered in the midst of infantrymen who were pinned down along the ice-cold fields, and opened fire on the Confederate lines to the left of the Marye house. The right piece of the battery was pushed even farther ahead, but every one of its horses was soon shot down, and one by one the cannoneers of the advanced piece were killed or wounded until none were left to serve it. The battery had advanced to within three hundred yards of the enemy works. Capt. John D. Frank's Battery G, 1st New York Light Artillery, joined Hazard on the left, and to Frank's left Lt. Evan Thomas unlimbered the six light twelve-pound guns of his Battery C. Never before had artillery been advanced so far to the front! Held back to act as circumstances warranted, Lt. Edmund Kirby's Battery I unlimbered by sections near the outskirts of town and opened fire.[80]

Couch, along with Lon, Col. Francis A. Walker, and an orderly, galloped ahead, up the Telegraph Road. The little Second Corps commander paused to confer with the officers of Hazard's battery, then trotted ahead to speak with the men serving the most advanced gun. Lon, as an artilleryman, was deeply impressed with the bravery of Hazard's cannoneers. Couch, thinking he was alone, then galloped across the bullet-swept fields to the area where the remnants of French's and Hancock's brave regiments, partly sheltered by the houses and outbuildings, held the most advanced position of the army. Lon would not leave his commander; he dug his spurs into the sides of his horse and, with Couch's orderly and Colonel Walker, followed the general across the fields. "The smoke," recalled Couch years later, "was so thick that we could not see the enemy, and I think they could not see us, but we were aware of the fact that somebody in our front was doing a great deal of shooting." The artillery batteries on both sides kept up a merciless fire, and shells flew across the fields, smashing into buildings and bursting overhead. Near the brick house, Couch surveyed the field and conferred with Col. John R. Brooke of the 53d Pennsylvania. Every soldier and every officer was lying on the cold, muddy ground to avoid the gunfire. Many of the men found shelter behind the brick house, its outbuildings, and a nearby blacksmith shop. "I found the brick house packed with men," Couch recalled, "and behind it the dead and the living were as thick as they could be crowded together. The dead were rolled out for shelter, and the dead horses were used for breastworks." General Couch, Colonel Walker, Lon, and the orderly sought shelter from the gunfire behind the brick house, but the crowd of living and dead soldiers was so vast they could not find room. Couch and his little staff, consequently, continued their ride, reviewing the lines of the Second Corps.[81]

General Hooker returned to the field and called Humphreys's division of Pennsylvanians, Sykes's division, and Lt. Alanson M. Randol's Batteries E and G, 1st United States Artillery, to advance across the fields littered with the dead and maimed of Couch's Second Corps. The mass of Second Corps soldiers who were still clinging to the muddy ground partly hampered the movement; many Second Corps soldiers called for the men of Humphreys's leading division to turn around, as the attack was fruitless. It proved to be just that. Confederate gunfire was poured into the faces of the Fifth Corps infantrymen, thinning their ranks. The columns were halted, then reformed and advanced again, only to be stopped once more by horrendous gunfire. It was no use. The battle was lost. On the far left, the army fared no better. Franklin's Left Grand Division had been similarly repulsed after repeated attempts to breach Jackson's stout defense lines along Prospect Heights.[82]

With darkness falling, Fighting Joe Hooker rode up to General Couch and suggested that Sykes's division be sent forward to relieve the battered remnants of the Second Corps brigades at the front. Couch's great pride in his men burst forth. "No!" he said. "No men shall take the place of the Second Corps unless General Sumner gives the orders. It has fought and gained that ground and it shall hold it!" Only under a direct order from Sumner at 11:00 P.M. did the remnants of the Second Corps withdraw from the frozen, bloody heights behind Fredericksburg.[83]

It had been an extraordinarily sad day for Lon as he watched his old corps being torn to shreds by enemy fire, never even effectively getting into a position to fire back. Just under 13,000 Union soldiers had fallen in the assaults against the heights west of Fredericksburg, well over 4,000 of them from the Second Corps alone.[84] It must have seemed as though the war was just about lost; there had been no real victories, and Fredericksburg had been the worst experience yet. Of solace to Lon was his own performance that terrible day. General Couch singled him out in his report of the bloody engagement: "Lieutenant Cushing, topographical engineers, staff of Major General Sumner, was with me throughout the battle, and acted with his well-known gallantry." In the end, Lon would be awarded the brevet rank of captain for his services at Fredericksburg and would soon be known throughout the Army of the Potomac as Captain Cushing.[85]

7

"The Elements Are at War with the Army"

The Second Corps, its ranks bloodied and horribly thinned, was finally called back from its advanced positions in front of Marye's Heights late on the night of December 13. Lon was in the saddle until the wee hours of December 14, directing the cold and weary soldiers back to positions in the streets of Fredericksburg and along the desolate riverbank. General Sykes's Fifth Corps division formed the front lines out near the brick house, just below the frowning heights.[1]

After having been moved into park near the Lacy house, the batteries of Rufus King and Charles Owen had been ordered across the Rappahannock River at about 9:00 P.M., December 13, to replace Capt. Charles Kusserow's Battery D, First New York Light Artillery, just west of the center of town along a slight ridge. It was nearly 11:30 P.M.—while the Second Corps infantry was pulling back from the front—when King's and Owen's Ordnance rifles took up their positions on the edge of town.[2] To protect the approaches to Fredericksburg, artillery battery sections were positioned at each cross street. Every house and building in the city had been turned into a hospital. All during the day and night of December 14, ambulances in seemingly endless lines streamed through the streets and over the three pontoon bridges, as medical teams frantically attempted to get as many of the wounded across the river as possible.[3]

On the evening of December 14, General Howard was ordered to relieve a portion of General Sykes's regulars. Under falling darkness, Col. George H. Morgan of the 1st Minnesota, with five of Howard's regiments, moved back out of the city and into the bloody fields ahead. There, once again, those Second Corps veterans were subjected to heavy gunfire from the well-positioned Confederates along Marye's Heights. Rufus King's and Charles Owen's batteries near the edge of town came under a terrific bombardment of "fuse shell, solid shot and spherical case, [the enemy] using rifled and smooth-bore guns." One cannoneer in King's battery, a Pvt. John Sheridan, was severely wounded in the head. King's and

Owen's cannoneers replied to the enemy fire, King's battery alone firing over fifty rounds from its six Ordnance rifles. With darkness, though, the firing subsided, and at about 9:00 P.M. that same night the advanced Second Corps regiments were ordered back into the city.[4] By dawn, December 15, a "careworn" General Burnside had given up any idea of striking Lee behind Fredericksburg again. Despondent, he confided to General Sumner that he likely would resign from command of the army.[5]

The tattered and exhausted Second Corps was ordered back across the Rappahannock River some time after 7:00 P.M. on December 15. Elements of Hooker's Center Grand Division covered the withdrawal. Such a vast movement in the darkness was dangerous. If Lee attacked the retreating Union troops, it could prove disastrous. Therefore, campfires were started throughout Fredericksburg in an effort to deceive the enemy into believing the army was still in the city. Wearily, through the dark, windy night, beneath a spectacular but eerie aurora borealis lighting the black skies, the soldiers of the Second Corps marched back across the pontoon bridges, which had been covered with heavy beds of straw in order to muffle the noise of the large movement. "What an anxious moment for our officers as well as our entire army," wrote Colonel William Teall. "Should a panic occur none can tell the extent of the disaster which would unavoidably occur." Lt. Alonzo H. Cushing was among the last men of the Second Corps to recross the Rappahannock that night.[6]

Behind the long columns of the Second Corps lay the dead and wounded along the fields west of Fredericksburg. "What a cosmopolitan crowd [those] dead and wounded [of the Second Corps] were," Col. St. Clair Mulholland of the Irish 116th Pennsylvania wrote, "Americans from the Atlantic coast and the Pacific states, from the prairies, from the great valleys of the Mississippi and Ohio; Irishmen from the banks of the Shannon and Germans from the Rhine and the blue Danube; Frenchmen from the Seine and Italians from the classic Tiber mingled their blood and went down in death together that the cause of the Union might live."[7] As the last of the men, guns, and wagons reached the northern bank of the river, the engineers cut the pontoon bridges loose. The currents of the frigid waters carried the bridges back toward Fredericksburg. "The battle was over," wrote Colonel Mulholland, "the result, a grave yard."[8]

The wind picked up during the wee hours of the morning. By 5:30 A.M., December 16, a heavy rain began to fall, drenching the weary men. The thunder, recalled one soldier in the 8th Ohio, was almost as loud and continuous as the cannonade heard two days before.[9] With daylight, Teall observed the enemy through a telescope from the Phillips house. Two columns of Confederate infantry approached the city. Soon the fields over which the battle had been fought were "covered with them," he wrote. Teall watched the Confederates as they took from the Union dead and wounded all the overcoats, clothing, shoes, and weapons they could find. In "a short time," Teall recalled, "they looked like federal soldiers. Oh what a scene!"[10]

On the afternoon of December 16, under a flag of truce, Lee agreed to permit Union burial teams to cross the river and enter the fields west of Fredericksburg to bury the dead. Most had been stripped of clothes and valuables by the needy Confederates; many were completely naked. Lt. Col. Enos Brooks, who had succeeded to the command of the 61st and 64th New York after Col. Nelson A. Miles was wounded by a gunshot in the throat on December 13, was ordered to collect a burial detail of three officers and one hundred men. As Brooks and his little command started back across the river under flapping white flags of truce, all firing ceased. By that evening, Brooks's detail had buried some 620 soldiers in the fields below Marye's Heights. He returned to the Phillips house well after dark, reporting that he had brought back the bodies of four officers and that there were still more than four hundred soldiers to bury. The next day Brooks completed his grim task.[11]

By the time General Couch and the Second Corps had returned to Stafford Heights, Sumner had reestablished his headquarters in the Phillips house. There, Lon returned to his room on the second floor, just off the main hall. Also at the Phillips house Lon's cousin Capt. Samuel Tobey Cushing, then serving as acting chief signal officer of the Army of the Potomac, had established his headquarters and principal signal station. Nearby, Prof. Thaddeus Lowe had observed the operations on the previous days from the balloon *Eagle*.[12]

Most soldiers believed that Burnside was finished; many had heard that the army was about to withdraw to the defenses of Washington. The first sign that there would be no change of front came with orders just before Christmas to construct winter quarters. All through the army, the soldiers began felling trees and building log and mud huts. The countryside around Falmouth, Virginia, was soon denuded of forests. In days, row upon row of log huts covered the north bank of the Rappahannock River, standing along the barren grounds, amidst the countless tree stumps. Only the snow that began to fall covered the ugliness of the scene.[13]

No sooner had Lon become settled in the Phillips house than he received a telegram from the Bureau of Topographical Engineers, inquiring whether it was still his wish to cancel his transfer. On December 19 Lon scribbled a note to Maj. I.C. Woodruff, the bureau's chief. "It is still my earnest wish that the transfer should be cancelled," he wrote. "If you can have it cancelled I shall be gratefully obliged to you." Lon had observed some of the most heroic artillery fighting of the war in front of

Marye's Heights just five days before. He earnestly desired to command a battery.[14]

At 11:00 A.M. on the day before Christmas, Lon accompanied General Sumner on an inspection of the three Second Corps divisions. General Burnside joined Old Bull during the inspection of General Hancock's division. As Sumner approached, the men of the Irish Brigade let forth a loud and sustained cheer, but when Burnside rode by, the cheering stopped. Sumner noticed the rebuff. He rode over to each regimental commander—Puritan to Irishman—and instructed them to order their regiments to cheer General Burnside. To Sumner's satisfaction, the regiments responded with enthusiasm.[15] In all, Sumner seemed pleased with the old corps. In spite of its terrible losses and privations—and very low morale—it still maintained a rather trim appearance. Most of the officers and men, even before the Battle of Fredericksburg, had despaired of ever winning the war. After the fighting at Fredericksburg, they had become despondent. Sumner's corps, like all elements of the Army of the Potomac, was having a serious problem with desertions. Still, those who remained in the ranks could justifiably boast that they were a part of the best fighting corps in the Army of the Potomac.[16]

Duties completed for the day, Sumner and his staff returned to the Phillips house at 5:00 P.M. Like those of all soldiers along the Rappahannock River that evening, Lon's thoughts were of home. He recalled those wonderful but simple Christmases with his brothers and sister and, of course, Little Ma back in Fredonia. How Lon loved Christmas. Colonel Taylor brightened up Christmas Eve by giving General Sumner three partridges. The partridges would make good eating, and that was something to cheer about indeed, since most of the army was having trouble getting supplied with food at all—hunger would accompany most soldiers in the Second Corps on Christmas Day. At 9:30 P.M., to Lon's great surprise, Capt. Samuel S. Sumner returned from Aquia Creek Landing with a real Christmas dinner for the staff: a large turkey with celery, cranberries, mince pies, and all the trimmings. Lon's eyes brightened at the prospect of such a feast. The sight of the food, coupled with the snow that blanketed the countryside, brought him some spirit of Christmas, in spite of the otherwise depressing circumstances.[17] No sooner had Captain Sumner arrived than Gen. John Sedgwick, having recovered from his Antietam wound, rode up to Sumner's headquarters. With hearty greetings, Sedgwick embraced Old Bull and shook hands with all the staff officers; he was then given a bed in Taylor's room. "Uncle John" Sedgwick would be Sumner's Christmas guest.[18]

On Christmas Day, Sumner and Sedgwick and all of the staff enjoyed their turkey feast together. Lon savored every morsel. Bottles of sherry were opened and passed around to the merriment of all except, of course, the temperate General Sumner. When the meal was finished, cigars and pipes were lighted. Lon lighted the meerschaum pipe Will had given him while he was at West Point. But soon the festivities were over, and the young officers dispersed to make their rounds among the troops. It was Lon's last Christmas.

The soldiers in the ranks made the best of their blighted situation. Within the camp of the Irish Brigade, the men had erected a large Christmas tree, and, "to peals of laughter," had decorated it with "tin cups, hard tack, pieces of pork and other odd articles." Canteens of whiskey were passed from soldier to soldier in front of blazing campfires and dancing sparks. Lingering in the minds of all were the loved ones so far away, and of those whose husbands, fathers, or sons had fallen in front of Marye's Heights just twelve days before.[19]

The next day General Burnside ordered the army to prepare three days' rations. Troops were resupplied with ammunition; horses were watered and fed. Burnside had determined to move the army to Banks's and United States fords on the Rappahannock, twenty-five miles north of Falmouth, in order to direct it across the river and strike Lee from the flank and rear. Brig. Gen. William W. Averell, commanding the First Cavalry Brigade in Hooker's Center Grand Division, had been conducting reconnaissance and raiding operations in the area throughout December. He was ordered by Burnside to get his command in readiness to move north, ford the Rappahannock River and then strike south toward Richmond and Petersburg, destroying railroad bridges and telegraph wires along the way. Knowing that Lon was familiar with the roads in the area, Burnside ordered him to accompany Averell. Thus, on December 29, Lon left General Sumner's headquarters and reported to General Averell. He carried a large cache of explosives along with him.[20]

After receiving a communication from the president, however, General Burnside countermanded the order for the flanking movement. Lon returned to Sumner's headquarters, and Burnside raced to Washington to confer with Lincoln. He learned that a number of his high-ranking officers had informed the White House that the army was in no shape for another movement. Despite what Burnside regarded as disloyalty within his high command, he returned to Falmouth convinced that he could strike a blow at Lee. Even with the slumping morale of the Army of the Potomac, Burnside determined to attempt the operation he had previously planned.[21]

Early on the morning of January 20, 1863, the great movement began. Burnside put all three of his Grand Divisions on the move by midmorning. He directed General Sumner to place Couch's Second Corps on the road ahead of the Ninth Corps to lead the Right Grand Division. "Mr. Cushing, of your staff," Burnside wrote, "is conversant with the roads."[22]

With the leading Second Corps directed by Lon, the Army of the Potomac snaked its way toward the fords all through the day. In the evening a violent rainstorm broke; rain fell in blinding sheets, and soon the roads became utterly impassable. Artillery and wagon trains bogged down in mud so thick and so deep that even the infantrymen could not move.[23] By the morning of January 21 the army had come to a complete halt. After herculean efforts to push the army forward, Burnside gave up. At 11:00 P.M. he concluded that "it is most likely we will have to change the plan." The operation was stopped, and the disheartened soldiers of the Army of the Potomac sullenly trudged back to Falmouth through the drenching rain and thick mud. It was General Burnside's last attempt at command in the Army of the Potomac.[24]

Upon returning to Falmouth, Generals Burnside and Sumner asked to be relieved of command. On January 25 Burnside was relieved of command of the Army of the Potomac; that same day, Maj. Gens. Edwin V. Sumner and William B. Franklin were relieved of command of their Grand Divisions and ordered to report to the adjutant general's office in Washington. Sumner left immediately. Before he departed, though, he informed Lon that he would be returning to Syracuse before proceeding to any new assignment, and that if Lon obtained a leave of absence, he would welcome him at his home. Lon assured the general that he would stop by for a visit if he could obtain a leave to go back to Fredonia.[25]

To replace Burnside, Maj. Gen. Joseph Hooker was named commander of the Army of the Potomac. Hooker was born in 1814 in Hedley, Massachusetts. An 1837 graduate of West Point, he had served with distinction in both Zachary Taylor's and Winfield Scott's armies in Mexico. From the end of hostilities in Mexico until the outbreak of the Civil War, he had served in garrisons in Oregon and California. Hooker's record in the war to date was fairly impressive. Commissioned a brigadier general of volunteers on August 6, 1861, he served through the fighting on the Peninsula as a division commander in Heintzelman's Third Corps. At the Battle of Antietam he commanded the First Corps, and at Fredericksburg he commanded the Center Grand Division.[26] But what Hooker achieved on the battlefield seemed to have been more than offset by a generally low perception of his military and personal character among the officers of the Army of the Potomac. Lt. Tully McCrea of Ned Kirby's battery probably best summed up the opinion of Hooker held by most officers in the army. "A feeling of despondency hangs over the whole Army," wrote McCrea. "Burnside was liked, although none had much confidence in his ability to command this large army. General Franklin, who is regarded as the most able of the generals with the army, has been ordered to Washington like General Sumner, and Joe Hooker takes command. Dear me! This army is fast going to ruin. It is hard indeed after all the hardships, gallant fighting, and long service that it has seen that it should at last be disgraced."[27]

After Sumner was relieved, all his staff officers were reassigned. Lt. Col. Paul J. Revere, on sick leave at the time, would return to the 20th Massachusetts. Lon did not yet know whether he would be reassigned to the Topographical Engineers or return to the 4th Artillery.[28] Rather than wait in Falmouth for news, Lon, like all of Sumner's staff officers except Lt. Ranald Mackenzie, asked the new commanding general for a thirty-day leave of absence. On January 26, 1863, he scribbled a note to Col. J.H. Taylor, assistant adjutant general and chief of staff of Sumner's Right Grand Division, initiating his request for the leave. Lon's request was granted by army headquarters the same day.[29]

After visiting with all the officers of Battery A, 4th United States Artillery, as well as with his friends Ned Kirby, Little Dad Woodruff, and Tully McCrea of Battery I, 1st United States Artillery, a tired and disheartened Lt. Alonzo H. Cushing journeyed to Aquia Creek Landing and took a steamer to Washington. He then headed north by train to New York City, where he was entertained by the mother of one of Will's classmates at Annapolis. From there he traveled up the Hudson River, past West Point, to Albany. A New York Central train took him through the beautiful Mohawk River Valley, where snow blanketed the landscape; ponds and lakes were frozen solid; and the countryside seemed elegant compared to war-torn Virginia.[30]

At Syracuse, Lon stopped to visit Sumner and his family, as he had promised. Sumner welcomed his young aide with open arms. At the time, he and his family were living in a sturdy old frame mansion on Fayette Park, owned by his son-in-law, Lieutenant Colonel Teall, who was also on leave. Lon "passed a few days there very pleasantly," he wrote. "On the first night, I was hustled off on a big sleigh ride, and packed in a sleigh which held twenty-four. I was between a couple of feminines both of whom were as 'pretty as spotted purps.' We had an elegant ride and supper and dance and returned to Syracuse on Sunday morning." The next day Lon "went skating with the charming feminines." But since he could not skate very well, he chose a clever course of action: "I put myself between a couple of Syracuse girls and got along splendidly."[31] After a few days Lon bid the Sumner family farewell, little realizing that it was the last time he would see Old Bull. The general would be reassigned to service in the Department of the West on March 9, but twelve days later he would die after a very short illness.[32]

Lon traveled on to Fredonia by train and coach. His reunion with his mother was joyous. Tears must have freely flowed; it was the first time Mary had seen her son since his furlough from West Point in 1859. Mary had continued to depend on Lon. He had dutifully forwarded to his mother at least twenty dollars of his army pay each month in order that she and Mary Isabel might live more comfortably.[33] Aside from the wonderful reunion with his mother, however, Lon's experience in Fredonia was neither relaxing nor pleasant. To a young man who had seen almost continuous action at the front, Fredonia was a "slow, dull old town." Everyone—cousins, uncles, aunts, and family friends—bombarded him with requests for stories of the war or bored him by conversation that tested his patience. "It is decidedly the dullest place in America," he wrote. "Old women bored me to death while I was there, by inviting me to dine with them, and slow old uncles and aunts bored me by their conversation. I escaped a great deal of persecution by being entirely in civ[ilian] clothes and by telling them point blank that I was not going to talk war. While I was a civ[ilian] and in order to be as unmilitary as possible I borrowed Pouncer's cane, bought an umbrella and a pair of rubbers. I had never carried a cane, never worn rubbers and had not carried an umbrella in six years. The consequence was that I lost them all the first day."[34] If Lon visited with the young lady who had captured his attention nearly four years before, he left no record of it. As he does not appear to have been the sort of person to write freely of such things, what occurred remains anyone's guess.

Mary wanted to be near her sisters back in Chelsea, Massachusetts, and Lon readily agreed to accompany his mother there; he had never met most of his mother's family. After a week or so, he was ready to leave Fredonia anyway, so he packed up his and Mary's bags, and the two of them set out for Chelsea. Lon would never see Fredonia again.[35] On their way to Massachusetts, Lon and Little Ma stopped briefly at Canandaigua, New York, to visit Mary Isabel, who was then attending boarding school. Lon found Sis "looking splendidly and . . . improving in music and French." While there, they also were visited by Miss Ellen Douglas Grosvenor, the daughter of Judge Thomas P. Grosvenor of Buffalo, New York, and a young lady in whom Lon's brother Milton had been showing considerable interest.[36] Continuing their journey east by train and coach, the two weary travelers reached Chelsea. Lon was now back where his own immigrant ancestors had first set foot on the land they claimed as their New Zion. From that sandy soil his grandfather had moved to western New York. Lon was only six years old when he had last visited Chelsea. It was then, he must have remembered, that his mother received word of the death of his father.

Living in Chelsea were Little Ma's five sisters, Margaret, Elizabeth, Jane, Cordelia, and Sara. Margaret Sprague Smith Loring and her husband, Joshua, had had seven children, but only two of them were living. Joshua was a rising officer in the Blackstone National Bank and was the superintendent of the Sunday School for the Charles Street Baptist

Church. Lon and Mary stayed in Margaret's and Joshua's home. Elizabeth's husband, John Pillsbury, had died in 1858, leaving her with four children ranging in age from sixteen to seven. Cordelia and her husband, William Robert Pearmain, had seven children, two born in Delafield, Wisconsin. Cordelia had been pregnant with her second child, Elizabeth Bass—twenty-two years old in 1863—at the time she had stood by Mary when Lon was born. The Pearmains' youngest child, named Sumner Bass, was only four years old. Mr. Pearmain had become a prominent citizen of Chelsea. He was president of the Tradesman's Bank, a corporation he had organized in 1850, a director of at least two railroad companies and active in local political affairs. Jane and her husband, Dr. John Henry Batchelder, had had six children, but only two were living. Dr. Batchelder was still practicing dentistry.[37]

Lon visited with all his aunts, uncles, and cousins. The Pillsburys, Pearmains, and Batchelders must have talked with him about days gone by, of the happy and sad times in Ohio and on the Wisconsin frontier. They likely spoke of Lon's father, Milton, too. Lon had come face to face with his own roots and much of his own history. "I had a delightful time," he wrote to Will of his visit to Chelsea."I was there exactly a week. I went to Salem one day, and I believe I made the acquaintance of all relations . . . I think we have a decidedly agreeable lot of cousins there."[38]

Lon at last said farewell to Mary and all his relatives and headed back to the army. "I left mother enjoying herself very much in Chelsea," he wrote to William. "She is at Aunt Margaret's. The only thing required to make her perfectly happy is to hear from you and How[ard]. Aunt Margaret is going to have her fat in a month and is then going to send me her photograph with a little explanatory note informing me who the handsome young lady is whose photograph she sends. Mother will stay till May or June."[39]

As Lon passed through Washington, he visited with his brother Milton, and his cousin Houghton Wheeler, from Fredonia, who had been given a post with Milton in the Navy Department by Commodore Joseph Smith. But soon Lon secured passage aboard a steamer for Aquia Creek Landing. On board he found David Parker, his and Will's boyhood friend from home, who was then serving as superintendent of mails for the Army of the Potomac and was making his regular run. Apparently, Parker and William Cushing had seen each other often during Will's journeys in and out of the capital city and the Washington Navy Yards. From Washington to Aquia Creek Landing, Lon and Parker must have talked and laughed about the mischievous "Bill Coon" and his "Muss Company" and about their days as boys in old Fredonia.[40]

By February 22 Lon was back with the army. He learned that at last his request to cancel his transfer to the Topographical Engineers had been granted, and that he was assigned to command Battery A, 4th United States Artillery! Lon's appearance had changed somewhat: clean shaven during his year and a half in the army, he had now started growing a reddish-colored Vandyke beard and mustache. They were to Lon a symbol of maturity, and now a symbol of his position of command.[41]

Lon took over command of Battery A on February 24, 1863. To man its six Ordnance rifles took a sizable number of men. Lon obtained a count of the officers and enlisted men of the battery on February 28 when he prepared his first muster roll as a battery commander. On the rolls were only two other commissioned officers: Lts. Rufus King, Jr., and Samuel Canby. Lt. Arthur Morris had left Battery A on January 12 after being reassigned to the staff of his father, Brig. Gen. William W. Morris, at Fort McHenry in Baltimore. Among the noncommissioned officers, Frederick Fuger was the first sergeant; Louis Blockinger, Owen Keating, and Francis Abraham were gun detachment commanders. All had served on the Utah frontier. Cpls. Charles Au and Thomas Whetston were German- and probably Irish-born respectively; like the sergeants, the corporals commanded gun detachments and were both veterans of the Utah frontier service. The battery boasted a fine bugler, Albert Keyser, who had also been with Battery A since its days in Utah. A second bugler, James H. Patterson, was a volunteer from the 4th Ohio Infantry. The artificers, Daniel Wallace and Edward Hickey, were regular army enlistees and had served with the battery in Utah. And although he does not appear on the muster rolls, Lon had a black servant and cook at his headquarters by the name of Henry. How long he had been with the battery is not known.[42]

Lon counted 147 enlisted men in the battery. Most were from volunteer infantry regiments in the Second Corps, although the battery retained on its rolls about twenty "regulars" who had served in Utah. Thirty-nine of the enlisted men were veterans of the 4th Ohio, a mixture of German, Irish, and native-born soldiers who hailed from such Ohio towns as Mt. Vernon, Delaware, Kenton, Wooster, Canton, and Marion.[43]

Exemplary of those volunteers from the 4th Ohio was Pvt. Thomas Moon. Twenty-six years of age when he joined Battery A, Moon was born in 1836 in Allegheny County, Pennsylvania. His father, Solomon Moon, hailed from Cattaraugus County, New York; his mother had been born in Switzerland. Moon's parents had moved to Frankfort, Kentucky, the year after his birth, and there he grew into young adulthood on a parcel of land near Lock Number 4 on the Kentucky River. His father died in 1840, and Thomas had been raised by a kindly stepfather, native Kentuckian Andrew Sharp. In 1852 Moon moved to Marion, Ohio. Having escaped the cholera epidemic that decimated the town in 1854, he became a butcher in a local grocery. Upon the outbreak of war, he joined Company K, 4th Ohio. After serving through the rough campaigns in the western Virginia mountains and the Shenandoah Valley, Moon came to the conclusion, like many of his compatriots, that he "did not like walking & carrying a gun and knapsack." Thus it was that Moon and thirty-eight of his companions volunteered for service in Battery A, 4th United States Artillery, at Harpers Ferry on October 17, 1862. Moon would soon be elevated to the rank of corporal and would command the battery's caissons.[44]

Some of the enlisted men of the battery had fought in the Irish Brigade; others had seen service in heavily German New York regiments. One cannoneer who exemplified those hearty New York volunteers was Pvt. Christopher Smith. Nicknamed "Christy," Private Smith was born in Baden, Germany—the same locality as Sergeant Fuger—in 1845. He had come to the United States on the eve of the war, settled in Buffalo, and worked as a clerk in a dry goods store. With the outbreak of war, Smith had volunteered in Company K, 61st New York, the regiment initially commanded by Brig. Gen. Francis Barlow. His service record in that regiment had been exemplary. He had been wounded in the right eye at the Battle of Fair Oaks and in the forehead in the attack on the sunken road at the Battle of Antietam. Like Thomas Moon, Smith had had enough of the infantry by the fall of 1862, and on October 17 of that year, while at Harpers Ferry, he had volunteered for the artillery. Smith spoke only broken English, but like Sergeant Fuger, he was deeply patriotic and committed to the Union cause.[45]

While Lon had been on leave, Fighting Joe Hooker had been busy reorganizing the Army of the Potomac. He had scrapped the three Grand Divisions; the Ninth Corps had been reassigned to duty in the West; and the seven remaining corps were being refitted and reorganized. Maj. Gen. John Fulton Reynolds retained command of the First Corps, and Maj. Gen. Daniel E. Sickles of the Third. Command of the Fifth Corps was given to Maj. Gen. George Gordon Meade after General Butterfield was named chief of staff to Hooker. Maj. Gen. John Sedgwick assumed command of the large Sixth Corps. Maj. Gen. Henry Warren Slocum's Twelfth Corps had joined the army just before Christmas 1862, and Slocum remained in command of it.[46]

Also added to the Army of the Potomac before Christmas was the newly designated Eleventh Corps, then under the command of the former German revolutionary Maj. Gen. Franz Sigel. About half of the regiments in the Eleventh Corps were composed of German-speaking soldiers. Sigel was soon relieved of command of the Eleventh Corps, and named in his place on March 31 was the Puritanical, one-armed Maj. Gen. Oliver Otis Howard, formerly commander of the Second Division of the Second Corps. Howard, who hailed from Leeds, Maine, and had been graduated from West Point in the class of 1854, was not a very popular choice among the Germans in the corps. A descendant of Puritans who had settled in Duxbury and Bridgewater, Massachusetts, as early as 1643, he was very religious and temperate and his Bible-preaching and puritanical ways angered many of the German soldiers in the Eleventh Corps from the very beginning.[47]

The roll of German regiments in the Eleventh Corps was astounding. In Brig. Gen. Charles Devens's First Division was a brigade, commanded by German-born Col. Leopold von Gilsa, which included Maj. Detleo von Einsiedel's 41st New York, Col. George von Amsburg's 45th New York, and Col. Charles Glanz's 153d Pennsylvania. The Second Division of the Eleventh Corps was commanded by the Brunswickian revolutionary Brig. Gen. Adolph Wilhelm August Friedrich, Baron von Steinwehr, whom Lon remembered from the First Bull Run campaign. Steinwehr's division consisted of Col. Adolphus Buschbeck's First and Brig. Gen. Francis Barlow's Second Brigade. A number of regiments in these two brigades were solid German-speaking. Notable among them were Col. Louis Hartmann's 29th New York and Lt. Col. Lorenz Cantador's 27th Pennsylvania, which had both been part of Gen. Louis Blenker's brigade of General Miles's division at First Bull Run. German revolutionary Maj. Gen. Carl Schurz commanded the Third Division, which likewise had its share of German-speaking regiments. Brig. Gen. Alexander Schimmelfennig commanded the First Brigade of the Third Division, which included Col. Frederick Hecker's 82d Illinois, Col. Gotthilf Bourry's 68th New York, and Lt. Col. Adolph von Hartung's 74th Pennsylvania, among others. Col. Wilhelm Krzyzanowski commanded the Second Brigade, which boasted such German-speaking regiments as Capt. Frederick Braun's 58th New York, Col. Elias Reissner's 119th New York, and Col. Francis Mahler's 75th Pennsylvania. The artillery batteries of the Eleventh Corps, as German as many of the infantry regiments, were commanded by such German volunteer captains as Julius Dieckmann, Michael Wiedrich, Hubert Dilger, and Hermann Jahn.[48]

The composition of the Eleventh Corps illustrated how many Germans had emigrated to America and how readily some had volunteered to fight for the Union. Although most regiments and artillery batteries in other corps had large numbers of Germans in their ranks, the Eleventh Corps, being so heavily German-speaking, became the target of the animus against foreigners and Catholics among many of the native-born soldiers. Know-Nothingism as a political movement was dead and gone, but the ethnic and religious hatred so rampant in the nation prior to the war continued in the ranks of the Army of the Potomac.[49]

Maj. Gen. Darius N. Couch retained command of the old Second Corps. Maj. Gen. Winfield Scott Hancock remained in command of the

First Division. As at Fredericksburg, the four brigades of Hancock's division were commanded by Brig. Gens. John C. Caldwell, Thomas Francis Meagher, Samuel K. Zook, and Col. John R. Brooke. In place of General Howard, command of the Second Division of the corps was given to native North Carolinian Brig. Gen. John Gibbon; command of its three brigades remained with Brig. Gens. Alfred Sully and Joshua Owen and Col. Norman J. Hall. The Third Division remained under the command of Maj. Gen. William H. French. French's First Brigade was commanded by Col. Samuel S. Carroll (General Kimball having been wounded at Fredericksburg), the Second by Brig. Gen. William Hays (Col. Oliver Palmer also having been wounded at Fredericksburg), and the Third by Col. John D. MacGregor. The enlistments of most of the soldiers in MacGregor's brigade would expire by the end of the spring.[50]

To add esprit to the Army of the Potomac, General Hooker on March 27 issued a circular assigning to each of his seven corps an identifying badge to be worn on each soldier's cap. To the First Corps was assigned a sphere, the Second a trefoil, the Third a diamond, the Fifth a Maltese cross, the Sixth a Greek cross, the Eleventh a crescent, and the Twelfth a five-pointed star. Divisions of the various corps would be designated by the color of the corps insignia: the first division of each corps would wear a red corps badge; the second division, white; and the third, blue. Headquarters flags and division and brigade pennants were designed to incorporate the new insignia.[51]

With the morale of the Army of the Potomac on the rise by early spring, General Hooker set about devising an operation to draw Lee out of his impregnable positions along the heights behind Fredericksburg. Mimicking the route mapped out by General Burnside only three months before, Hooker determined to make a wide movement by way of Kelly's Ford on the Rappahannock River in an effort to get onto Lee's left flank. For that movement, Hooker selected Howard's Eleventh Corps, Slocum's Twelfth Corps, and Meade's Fifth Corps. Brig. Gen. George Stoneman, with 10,000 troopers of his Cavalry Corps, would ride up the Rappahannock, move behind Lee, and place his horsemen between Fredericksburg and Richmond. Sedgwick's Sixth Corps was directed to move across the Rappahannock and directly attack Marye's Heights in a diversionary move. Gen. Abner Doubleday's division of the First Corps was to be sent to Port Conway, twenty miles below Fredericksburg, as a further diversion.[52]

With a portion of Gen. James Longstreet's Confederate command—led by Longstreet himself—on a foraging expedition in Suffolk, Virginia, Lee was again in a precarious situation at the time Hooker resolved to make his flanking movement. His army was ill equipped and poorly fed. In the face of any movement, he would be forced to maintain a position that would protect the approaches to Richmond, yet also meet the advances of the enemy.

As the two armies were bracing themselves for the spring campaign, Lon's brother Will was once again on his way back to Washington, D.C. He had just assumed command of the gunship *Commodore Barney*. William stayed for twelve days in the capital city. "Mud and contractors were thick in the streets," he recalled, "and it was impossible to keep from soiling my hands, clothes, etc., by contact with one another." With Milton back in Boston attending a family wedding, Will helped himself to his brother's quarters and visited with his cousin Houghton Wheeler.[53] Upon Milton's return to Washington, he and Will "commenced to be as jolly as circumstances would permit." Among other things, they attended the theaters. "I patronized them extensively," William wrote, "laughing at the farces and comedians, and looking grave, sometimes, at the tragedies. Sometimes, I say, for that brother of mine was almost sure to set me off into convulsing laughter by some absurd remark just in a thrilling part, much to the amazement, and sometimes indignation of the surrounding multitude."[54]

Will wanted to visit Lon at Falmouth; it was the "thing I had most set my heart on," he wrote. So one night in early April he secured a pass to proceed through the lines and filled a carpetbag with "sherry, cigars and other promoters of happiness, that were to have been consumed in the tent of Alonzo, 'The Indian,' who dwells in the camp in Falmouth." His trip turned into a nightmare. "The hackmen were disposed to cheat me," he wrote, "so I got on my feet and determined to walk." Will tramped up Sixth Street toward the Navy Yards in order to take the boat to Aquia Creek Landing. He had determined that from there he could get to Falmouth by railroad. "The farther I went," he continued, "the deeper became the mud, but I swam along without much trouble until I reached the wharf. I struck bottom four times on the way, or rather I ran into that number of sunken hacks, and I no longer wondered at the extravagant charges of the jehus in front of Kirkwood's [Hotel]. The provost marshal had told me the name of a boat that was to run that morning, so I went on board and made it my first business to get rested, but I had not been seated long, when I was informed that if I proposed to go to the tents of the wicked at Falmouth, I would have to make tracks for the next wharf, as I was on the wrong boat, and the right one was there. Off I started in a great hurry, and off started the object of my search in a greater hurry." Will arrived "just one minute too late." The boat had pulled away from the wharf. "On my way to the wharf, the carpetbag, though heavy, was lightened by the thought that a jolly good time was ahead, but think what must have been its weight in the three miles back. When I got back to my quarters my hands were covered with blisters, and my clothes soaked with mud." William would never have the opportunity to see his brother Lon again.[55]

At Falmouth, Lon knew by April 12 that the army was about to move. Hospitals were being cleared of the wounded and sick, and arms were being inspected. In Lon's battery all of the horses were ordered to be shod and ammunition replenished.[56] The next day Lon mustered his battery. It was payday, which often enabled many of the cannoneers and drivers to obtain cheap liquor. Writing to Will the next morning, Lon remarked, "My men were all paid yesterday, and as a matter of course out of a company of one hundred and sixty, some half dozen must be drunk on such occasion. I have them all in the Guard House now where I shall let them remain till they get sober, and tomorrow I shall make 'Spread Eagles' of them all by tying them up to the various wheels in the battery."[57]

Snowdrifts remained until early April, and thereafter rain fell almost continuously. Any movements against the enemy were put on hold. Lon, like most of the officers and men, was deeply disturbed by the delays. "The Army of the Potomac is again ready for a move," Lon wrote to William on April 14, "and in fact a move of considerable importance has already taken place. A terrible rain storm has however come on. It has been pouring down in torrents all day, and the movement of the main body of the A[rmy of the] P[otomac] will I am afraid be delayed for two or three days. It is very strange that the elements are always against us. The Army of the Potomac was never before in the superb condition which it is in at present. When we start this time we are bound to whip anything and everything in the shape of a Reb Army which comes in our way. I know one battery of the 4th Arty. which is ready to engage in any heavy work which may be cut out for it."[58]

The rain continued to fall mercilessly. The roads turned to quagmires. "The elements are at war with the army," Lon wrote, "and will not allow it to move." As the heavy spring rains fell, he set about obtaining provisions for his battery and making the best of difficult and trying times. "I have made myself very comfortable now," he wrote to William. Indeed, Lon had appointed a sutler and had sent him to Baltimore for "officers' mess stores." "I expect him back with a superb lot of wines, cigars and mess stores today," Lon noted.[59] As he had done at West Point, Lon continued his interest in body-building. It is likely that all the family sickness convinced him that by working out vigorously he might keep himself from falling victim to the maladies of his brothers. Thus, Lon "set all of his artificers and carpenters at work constructing a gymnasium" on April 22. He ordered his blacksmith to "manufacture" dumbbells; by that afternoon the job was finished. "I commenced exercising," Lon wrote to Will on April 23, "and continued my calisthenical performances for too long, as I discovered when I attempted to get out of bed this morning. Every muscle in my body is sore and I feel very aged. It was not till half past ten that I could muster sufficient energy to make the requisite effort to set me on my feet."[60]

Hooker was immobilized by the rain. "I wonder what the Rebs propose doing now," Lon wrote. "They have made nothing either at Suffolk or Newburn and are said to be retreating from both places. I wish we could have moved as we wanted to do while they were attacking both places and [Capt. Stephen F.] Dupont was keeping them busy at Charleston. Whether this army moves sooner or later, it is bound to be successful."[61]

With clearing skies, General Hooker began his long-awaited movement on April 27. After having been turned back once by heavy rain, General Stoneman finally departed Falmouth on his long circuitous raid. The next day, Howard's Eleventh Corps and Slocum's Twelfth Corps would begin their march toward Kelly's Ford, followed by Meade's Fifth Corps. Couch's Second Corps was ordered to be ready to move. As the plan was designed, two divisions of the Second Corps—the First and Third, together with Kirby's, Thomas's, Arnold's, Pettit's, and Cushing's batteries—would move up the Rappahannock River to Banks's Ford on April 28. There they would cross the river and form a junction with Meade's left flank. To confuse Lee, the First, Third, and Sixth Corps with their artillery brigades and General Gibbon's Second Division of the Second Corps, along with Capt. George W. Adams's Battery G, and Capt. John G. Hazard's Battery B, 1st Rhode Island Light Artillery—all under the command of General Sedgwick—were ordered to assemble at Franklin's Crossing and Pollock's Mill, about three miles below Fredericksburg, before daylight on April 29. They would construct pontoon bridges across the river and hold them preparatory to an advance directly against Confederate positions along the heights west of Fredericksburg.[62]

From his camp at Falmouth, Lon sat down on April 27 to write to his mother. "I write you a few lines on the eve of the long expected 'Onward to Richmond' move," he wrote. "It is now eleven P.M. and I have to be up at three A.M. tomorrow so my letter must necessarily be short. In the course of the next week you may look for news that the Reb Army in Virginia is very badly whipped—We are going now to inflict such punishment on the Confederate troops as they have never received before. I shall write to you immediately after the Reb Army is annihilated. There was a superb review of the 3rd Army Corps today. Secretary [of State William] Seward and nearly all the foreign ministers were present. The troops looked remarkably well and 'Fighting Joe' appeared radiant. The Confederates from the heights on the opposite side of the river had a very fine view of the display. They must have been intensely gratified. I shall try the voices of my guns tomorrow or the next day and see what effect they have on the Confederates. The guns will say Run—Rebs!—Run! which the Rebs will accordingly do."[63]

On April 28, General Meagher's Irish Brigade was ordered to Banks's Ford and United States Ford on the Rappahannock River to guard those crossings. Col. Patrick Kelly, with his own 88th New York and the 63d New York, would hold Banks's Ford, while the balance of the brigade—the 69th New York, 28th Massachusetts, and 116th Pennsylvania—would protect United States Ford.[64]

That same morning General Hancock's First Division and General French's Third Division of the Second Corps, with the five batteries in the vanguard—moved before sunrise in the direction of Banks's Ford, where they bivouacked for the night. Colonel Carroll's brigade, along with Capt. Nelson Ames's Battery G, 1st New York Light Artillery, was sent forward to join the Irishmen at United States Ford. The Fifth, Eleventh, and Twelfth Corps reached Kelly's Ford that night. Throughout the night and the wee hours of the morning of April 29, the three advanced corps of the Army of the Potomac crossed the Rappahannock River. They continued their march, crossing the Rapidan River (which enters into the Rappahannock River from the west below Kelly's Ford) at Germana and Ely's fords. The three corps pushed on toward Chancellorsville, a crossroads along the road to Fredericksburg, literally in the rear of Lee's army.[65]

On the morning of April 30, Hancock's and French's Second Corps divisions marched up the Rappahannock River toward United States Ford. At 3:30 P.M., after the completion of a pontoon bridge, the two divisions began crossing the river. They bivouacked under beautiful moonlight about one mile from Chancellorsville. General Couch established his headquarters in the nearby Chandler house.[66] Fighting Joe Hooker, after riding along the marching Second Corps troops, stopped to confer with Couch at about 9:00 P.M. He appeared to be in great spirits. With almost no losses at all, he had placed his right wing, consisting of three full corps and two divisions—nearly 50,000 troops—in a position threatening Lee's left flank and rear. His left wing, consisting of three full corps and one division, had by then, effected a virtually bloodless crossing of the Rappahannock below Fredericksburg.[67] Once the crossroads of Chancellorsville had been occupied by the right wing, Hooker sent for General Sickles's Third Corps. Sickles got his men on the move quickly, and by May 1 they too had crossed the Rappahannock River at United States Ford and were within a few miles of Chancellorsville.[68]

The ground around Chancellorsville was low and densely wooded. Three roads led directly to Fredericksburg from the positions taken up by Hooker's right wing. Along those three roads, Fighting Joe pushed his advanced units ahead toward the Confederate flank and rear on May 1. Brig. Gens. Charles Griffin's and Andrew A. Humphreys's Fifth Corps divisions were directed down the River Road toward Fredericksburg. The other two roads, known as the Orange Turnpike and the Plank Road, forked near Chancellorsville, then ran east in an almost parallel course from one-half to one mile apart until they united again just beyond Tabernacle Church, halfway to Fredericksburg. Hooker directed General Sykes's regulars of the Fifth Corps down the Orange Turnpike toward Fredericksburg. General Hancock's Second Corps division followed. With Hancock rode General Couch himself. General Slocum's Twelfth Corps was directed down the Plank Road toward Fredericksburg. The heavy Union columns halted along high ground about a mile east of Chancellorsville, and there they began to construct entrenchments.[69]

Inexplicably, at 2:00 P.M., General Hooker ordered his advanced commands to abandon the high ground they had just occupied and fall back to the low, heavily wooded grounds around the Chancellor house. General Couch was furious. He was so upset about the order to withdraw that he delayed moving Hancock's division back until he could communicate with Hooker. By the time his courier reached Fighting Joe, however, it was too late. Although Hooker agreed to allow Hancock's division to remain on the Orange Turnpike, with Gen. Slocum's Twelfth Corps holding the position to Couch's right, until 5:00 P.M., most of the troops of the three advanced corps were already moving back when Hooker's communication arrived at the front. Slocum, by then, had completely withdrawn, and Couch's men were on the road marching west.[70]

In the meantime, Lee had directed Gens. Richard H. Anderson's and Lafayette McLaws's divisions of Longstreet's command to evacuate their lines behind Fredericksburg, advance west, and apply as much pressure as possible against Hooker's troops along the Orange Turnpike and Plank Road. The two big, hard-fighting divisions took up positions facing west along either side of the Plank Road. As the Twelfth Corps and Hancock's division were pulling back, the Confederates pressed them. Heavy fighting erupted all along Hancock's front. The roads leading back to the Chancellor house soon were filled with Union troops. To meet the emergency ahead—and to protect his withdrawing infantry commands—Couch called for elements of his own escort artillery batteries, a section of Cushing's battery and Arnold's battery. Back galloped Couch's aide to the artillery park near the Chancellor house where Kirby's, Cushing's, Arnold's, Thomas's and a portion of Pettit's batteries waited for orders to move. Hearing the order, Lon yelled for Lieutenant King to move his right section forward with Arnold's guns. Couch met the eight guns on the turnpike as infantrymen gave way, opening a corridor through which the guns and caissons could pass. The little general rode ahead with the artillery, boldly exposing himself to the enemy gunfire. Sykes's division was brought up to Hancock's assistance. In Sykes's division, Brig.

Gen. Gouverneur K. Warren's brigade was then under the temporary command of none other than Col. Patrick H. O'Rorke, Warren having been named acting chief topographical engineer for the Army of the Potomac.[71]

With King's and Arnold's guns firing salvos into the approaching enemy columns, Hancock safely withdrew his division from its forward position and took up a line of defense about one-half mile east of Chancellorsville, alongside the Fifth Corps. General French's Second Corps division, which had been advanced to Todd's Tavern, west of Chancellorsville, was likewise withdrawn to the Chancellor house. Casualties that day were rather light, but Couch lost his adjutant general, Francis A. Walker, who was seriously wounded by a shell burst.[72]

During the night of May 1 and the morning of May 2, Hooker placed his army in positions around the Chancellor house. The left flank was held by Meade's Fifth Corps, east of Chancellorsville as far north as Scott's Dam on the Rappahannock River. Couch's two Second Corps divisions took up positions along Meade's right, French's division to the left and Hancock's extending across the Orange Turnpike on the right, connecting with Brig. Gen. John W. Geary's Twelfth Corps division not far from the Plank Road. To the right of Geary was Brig. Gen. Alpheus S. Williams's division of the Twelfth Corps. Holding the center of the line, and facing south, was Sickles's newly arrived Third Corps. To the right of Sickles, and facing generally south, was Howard's Eleventh Corps with all its Germans, its right flank completely "in the air" along the Orange Turnpike. Lon and his battery, along with most of the Second Corps batteries, were parked in the clearing in front of the Chancellor house, ready to respond to any emergency.[73]

Hancock's and French's divisions constructed heavy breastworks and slashed the woods in front of the entrenchments to provide a clear field of fire. In the main trench within Hancock's lines, Col. Edward Cross—with his own 5th New Hampshire, the 81st Pennsylvania, and the Irish 88th New York—held the right. General Caldwell—with the 66th New York, 148th Pennsylvania, and 61st New York—held the line to Cross's left. Colonel Brooke—with the 2d Delaware, 145th Pennsylvania, 27th Connecticut, 64th New York, and 53d Pennsylvania, along with the 57th and 52d New York—was aligned on the left. General Meagher and the Irish 63d and 69th New York, 28th Massachusetts, and 116th Pennsylvania, along with one section of Pettit's battery, remained behind on duty along the road to Banks's Ford.[74]

Lee was not about to attack Hooker's left flank, which stretched across the wooded terrain ahead of him. Instead, he resolved to make a diversionary attack against that flank and then send Stonewall Jackson's command—the divisions of Maj. Gen. A.P. Hill, Brig. Gen. Robert E.

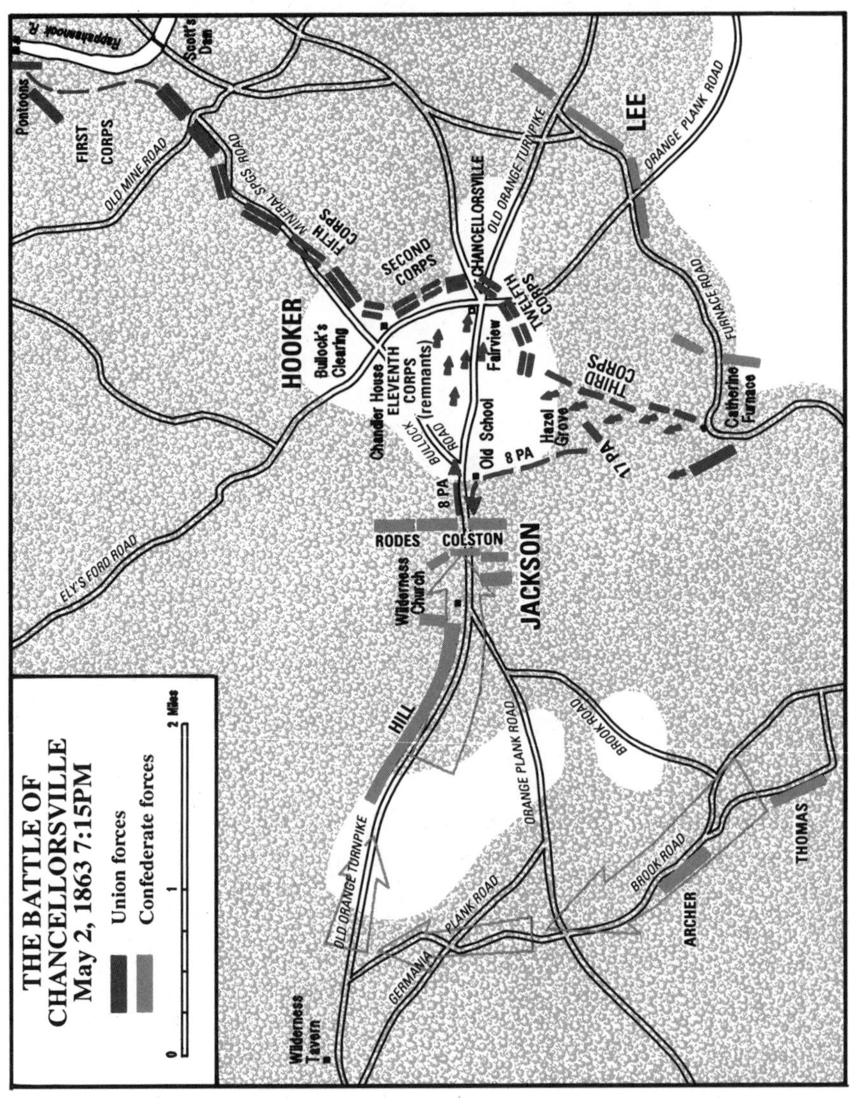
THE BATTLE OF CHANCELLORSVILLE
May 2, 1863 7:15PM
Union forces
Confederate forces
0
1
2 Miles
Rappahannock R.
Scott's Dam
Pontoons
FIRST CORPS
OLD MINE ROAD
FIFTH CORPS
MINERAL SPGS ROAD
SECOND CORPS
HOOKER
Bullock's Clearing
Chandler House
ELEVENTH CORPS (remnants)
BULLOCK ROAD
CHANCELLORSVILLE
OLD ORANGE TURNPIKE
TWELFTH CORPS
Fairview
Old School
8 PA
8 PA
Hazel Grove
17 PA
THIRD CORPS
LEE
ORANGE PLANK ROAD
FURNACE ROAD
Catherine Furnace
RODES
COLSTON
JACKSON
Wilderness Church
ELY'S FORD ROAD
HILL
OLD ORANGE TURNPIKE
ORANGE PLANK ROAD
BROOK ROAD
BROOK ROAD
THOMAS
ARCHER
GERMANIA PLANK ROAD
Wilderness Tavern

Rodes, and Brig. Gen. Raleigh E. Colston—on a wide, flanking march completely around Hooker's army, to a position from which he could strike what his reconnaissance reported was the unprotected Union right.[75] Early on the morning of May 2, Lee opened a cannonade against Hooker's left. The artillery fire was followed by heavy infantry demonstrations. Soon Stonewall Jackson's command moved out on the Gordonsville Road in an effort to reach Hooker's right flank. Spotted by Union signal stations, the Confederate movement was viewed by General Hooker as evidence that Lee was withdrawing into central Virginia. When Couch appeared at the Chancellor house at 2:00 P.M., he was greeted by Fighting Joe Hooker, who exclaimed, "Lee is in full retreat toward Gordonsville, and I have sent out Sickles to capture his artillery."[76] Sickles advanced through the woods and thickets against what was believed to be the retreating column. Fighting erupted along Sickles's front, but it failed to escalate. Only several hundred prisoners were taken.[77]

After his long, circuitous march through the paths of the dense wilderness of Spotsylvania County, the head of Jackson's column of over 25,000 veteran troops moved up on the right flank of the Army of the Potomac near Wilderness Tavern at about 5:30 P.M. In front of Jackson was Howard's Eleventh Corps, its right flank completely unprotected.[78]

Most of Howard's soldiers had no idea of the presence of the enemy until a heavy volley of musketry announced the opening of the attack at 6:00 P.M. Many officers, including General Schurz, Colonel von Gilsa and even Capt. Hubert Dilger of Battery I, 1st Ohio Light Artillery, had tried to warn General Howard of the approach of the enemy, but to no avail. The opening volley was followed by a ferocious and relentless advance, which rolled up all that was in front of it. The weight of numbers in favor of the Confederates was overwhelming. Although there were pockets of resistance and significant bravery displayed by Schurz, Dilger and his cannoneers, and others, the Eleventh Corps virtually dissolved into a stampede of men, horses, mules, artillery, wagons, and ambulances. The stampede was made even more chaotic by the fact that Gen. Howard had brought up behind his corps all its cattle and provision wagons. Recalled Col. Charles H. Morgan of Gen. Couch's staff: "The stampede of the Eleventh Corps was something curious and wonderful to behold. I have seen horses and cattle stampeded on the plains, blinded, apparently, by fright, rush over wagons, rocks, streams, any obstacle in the way; but never before or since, saw I thousands of men actuated seemingly by the same unreasoning fear that takes possession of a herd of animals. As the crowd of fugitives swept by the Chancellor house, the greatest efforts were made to check them; but those only stopped who were knocked down by the swords of staff officers or the sponge staffs of Kirby's battery, which was drawn up across the road leading to the ford. Many of them ran right on down the turnpike toward Fredericksburg, through our line of battle and picket line, and into the enemy's line! The only reply one could get to argument or entreaty was, 'all is veloren; vere is der pontoon?' "[79]

The roar of the battle on the right flank was deafening. Great clouds of smoke rose into the sky as artillery and small arms fire rolled through and shattered the dense thickets. Fleeing soldiers from the Eleventh Corps were everywhere. In places the thickets caught on fire, adding to the frightening situation. The enemy, in overwhelming numbers, was rapidly coming up on the rear of the Second Corps. Here, it seems, General Couch again turned to Lon for assistance. His own staff reduced and the situation appearing desperate, Couch apparently ordered Lon to turn over his battery—then still in park in front of the Chancellor house—to its most senior officer, Lieutenant King, and temporarily serve as a staff officer as he had done at Fredericksburg. Although no contemporaneous writings or memoirs confirm this, the evidence is significant. Although Battery A would enter the fighting during the late hours of May 2, its services would not be extraordinary, and it would suffer no casualties; in addition, Lon filed no report of the battery's services at Chancellorsville. Yet he would be brevetted to the rank of major for gallantry on May 2 at Chancellorsville. Couch liked Lon, who had served him well at Fredericksburg. With his battery parked in front of the Chancellor house waiting for orders at the time, Lon was readily available to the general.[80]

Col. Nelson Miles, with the 57th, 64th, and 65th New York, detachments of the 52d New York, the 2d Delaware, and 148th Pennsylvania, and probably with Lon's assistance, turned his commands around and moved them across the smoke-laden clearing into a position facing west. There the brave colonel and his stouthearted soldiers helped beat back the attacks of Jackson's troops, aided by elements of the Third Corps and a small number of Gen. Alfred Pleasonton's cavalrymen.[81]

At about 9:00 P.M., under the direction of Capt. Cyrus B. Comstock of the U.S. Engineers, Battery A, 4th United States Artillery, was brought into position on the right of the Plank Road, not far from the Chancellor house, facing east and supporting General Geary's lines. On the same side of the road was placed Ned Kirby's battery, joined by three pieces of Thomas's battery, commanded by Lieutenant Thomas himself. The remaining pieces of Thomas's battery, under Lts. William O'Donahue and Edward Field, were directed to support General Hancock's line. Later, two sections of Pettit's battery joined the line of Second Corps guns after having been engaged along the Orange Turnpike. Lon likely helped Captain Comstock select the sites for the guns and direct them into their positions.[82]

The fighting subsided with falling darkness. The day had been a smashing success for Lee's army. The Confederates had beaten back the entire right flank of the Army of the Potomac, which now crowded around the low, wooded lands and clearings in front of the Chancellor house. Great portions of the woods and thickets were on fire, and the flames consumed the dead and wounded alike. Although Lee had taken heavy losses in the attacks, no loss was greater to him and his army's future than the wounding that night of Stonewall Jackson, who was accidentally shot by his own men.[83]

In preparation for the battle on May 3, Fighting Joe Hooker contracted his lines around the Chancellor house. Hancock's division remained in its position across the turnpike facing east and southeast. On Hancock's left were placed the remnants of Howard's Eleventh Corps. Slocum's Twelfth Corps, with a portion of Sickles's Third Corps, held the center of the army, facing east and south, while French's Second Corps division, with the remainder of the Third Corps, fronted west to meet the renewed attacks of Jackson's command, now under the direction of Lee's cavalry chieftain, Maj. Gen. J.E.B. Stuart. To the right and rear of the Army of the Potomac, covering the road to Ely's Ford, lay Reynolds's First Corps, which had finished a twenty-four mile march the previous day. Meade's Fifth Corps was moved from the left to a position near the road from Chancellorsville to United States Ford, ready to go into action on the Union right with Reynolds's corps or on the left with the remnants of Howard's corps as circumstances warranted. Army engineers had constructed a new defense line, three-quarters of a mile to the rear, crossing the road to United States Ford at Bullock's clearing in the event it was needed to protect the army's withdrawal. With the positions established, General Couch directed Lon to return to his battery.[84]

General Hooker, overwhelmed at the prospect of the army's being destroyed, began to concentrate his efforts at protecting his line of retreat. Thus, at 3:00 A.M. on May 3, all the artillery units of the Second Corps, except Pettit's battery and three pieces of Thomas's battery, were ordered to limber up and return to United States Ford! Pettit's and Thomas's guns changed front to rear and came into battery facing west. Lon, Ned Kirby, and William Arnold ordered their cannoneers to hitch up the guns, and then, with bugles blaring, the three batteries rumbled up the road to United States Ford, where the guns were placed in park.[85]

As the Third Corps was withdrawing from the high ground at Hazel Grove, south of Chancellorsville, early on the morning of May 3, Lee attacked again. Stuart fell upon Sickles's line with a vengeance. Gens. Charles K. Graham's and Hobart Ward's brigades of Gen. David B. Birney's Third Corps division became locked in a desperate struggle. Then the hard-charging Confederates slammed into Gen. Hiram Berry's division of Sickles's Third Corps, on the right of the road near Dowdall's Tavern, and Gen. William Hays's brigade of French's Second Corps division. Colonel Carroll's Second Corps brigade was moved up to support Hays. Stuart then brought up Confederate reserves. Gens. Francis T. Nicholls's and Alfred Iverson's gray brigades of Rodes's and Colston's divisions were thrown into the fight. French was reinforced by a brigade of General Humphrey's Fifth Corps division. Stuart then brought forward Gen. Alfred H. Colquitt's brigade of Rodes's division to check French's advance.[86]

Among the Union batteries holding the Third Corps lines against the Confederate advance was Lt. Justin E. Dimick's Battery H, 1st United States Artillery. Dimick, Lon's West Point classmate and close friend, poured shell and canister into the enemy for well over an hour. All through that time his battery received a galling fire from the heavy concentration of enemy guns. Dimick's horse was shot down beneath him. His men were falling rapidly. As the infantry crowded back through his guns, he was ordered to limber up his battery and fall back. As he was carrying out the command, some of the battery horses became entangled in their harness; Dimick tried to free them and while doing so was wounded in the foot. Keeping his wound hidden from his men, Dimick continued his efforts to extricate his battery. Then a second bullet entered his spine, hurling him to the ground for good. The brave lieutenant would die two days later.[87]

By 8:30 A.M. the headquarters flags of the Third and Twelfth Corps became visible in the clearing near Chancellorsville, startling evidence of the fact that the two corps had given up significant ground. A Confederate shell struck a pillar of the Chancellor house against which General Hooker was leaning, momentarily knocking him senseless. Hooker retired from the field, leaving Couch to patch together the defense of Chancellorsville.[88] With only portions of Pettit's and Thomas's batteries providing artillery support to the Second Corps infantrymen, Couch recognized the horrible error of sending the Second Corps batteries to the rear and took it upon himself to order Kirby's, Cushing's, and Arnold's batteries back to the Chancellor house at about 10:00 A.M. At United States Ford, bugles sounded, and the three batteries moved out in a matter of minutes. Lon directed his battery, led by Ned Kirby's guns, back up the road toward the sound of gunfire.[89]

The conflict continued along the center of Hooker's line, where General Whipple's Third Corps division and General Geary's Twelfth Corps division were assailed by Rodes's and Colston's divisions, elements of which forced their way to the very Union trench lines in front of the Chancellor clearing.[90] On the left, in front of Hancock's division, Lee threw forward the three brigades of McLaws's division, while Anderson's division slammed into Geary's and Williams's Twelfth Corps divisions. Repeatedly, the Confederates sent forth "clouds of skirmishers" against the Union rifle pits along Hooker's left flank. In the melee, the brave Colonel Miles was badly wounded and carried from the field to a hospital site just above the Chancellor house.[91]

Hooker's forces were pressured on all fronts. From every quarter, Confederate artillery opened up on the Union lines; then the two flanks of Lee's army made a simultaneous advance. McLaws and Anderson pushed ahead against Hancock and Geary. Hill, Rodes and Colston renewed their attacks on Williams, Sickles, and French. Brought into position in support of the lines held by Generals Williams and Berry south of the Plank Road—in line with what was left of Dimick's guns—were four additional batteries of artillery, including young Lt. Franklin B. Crosby's Battery F, 4th United States Artillery.[92] French's commands were thrown back upon the left of Meade's Fifth Corps. Gen. Hiram Berry's division of Sickles's Third Corps was assailed on both flanks; Berry was killed, and Brig. Gen. Gershom Mott, who succeeded him in command, fell wounded. Gen. Joseph W. Revere of New Jersey succeeded to command and ordered a withdrawal. Sickles dashed forward to prevent the disaster. The brigades of Whipple's and Birney's divisions, supporting Berry, were thrown back. Crosby was struck in the heart and killed as he was directing the fire of his guns. The Union line was soon overwhelmed.[93]

While the right and center of the Union line was being driven back, General Anderson's Confederate division, after repeated efforts, finally dislodged the Twelfth Corps division of General Geary, whose men had been subjected to terrible artillery fire all morning. In the center, Sickles managed to hold his broken commands together even in retreat, but the field was all but lost. Only Hancock's and Geary's divisions remained on the left, and both commands had been terribly reduced in numbers. Caldwell, with the 61st, 52d, and 57th New York and four companies of the 148th Pennsylvania, had been sent to the United States Ford with a view to help block an anticipated breakthrough on the right. With General Meagher's brigade still absent, Hancock had only eleven of his eighteen regiments left on the field. The situation was desperate.[94]

Colonel Cross changed his front to assist General Geary, who was slowly withdrawing his division. Hancock's division, in two lines of battle—one fronting west toward Gordonsville, the other facing east toward Fredericksburg—held its ground. Four of Captain Pettit's Parrott rifles, along with three light twelve-pound Napoleons of Thomas's battery, under O'Donahue and Field, were directed to fire east, up the Orange Turnpike. Capt. George F. Leppien's 5th Maine Battery from the First Corps was brought up and placed in a peach orchard behind the Chancellor house to assist Thomas. Geary's division held the approach from the south along the Plank Road. It was all that remained of the Army of the Potomac at Chancellorsville. Even though Reynolds's First Corps and Meade's Fifth Corps were just north of the Chancellor house, neither was committed to the fighting.[95]

In spite of their small numbers, the brave Union commands around the Chancellor house held the advancing enemy in check, but they paid a hideous price. The Confederate artillery fire, which had concentrated on the collapsing Union defense lines, was unmerciful. In Thomas's battery, Lieutenant O'Donahue was mortally wounded and Lieutenant Field assumed command of the three-gun section. Captain Leppien's 5th Maine Battery in the peach orchard was cut to pieces: every officer was wounded, twenty-five of its cannoneers were killed or wounded, and forty-three horses were killed. Captain Leppien's wound proved to be mortal. General Couch, observing the crisis within the Maine battery, called upon the approaching Ned Kirby to leave his guns and take command of what was left of the 5th Maine Battery. Lon observed the heroic fight as he was leading his guns forward. Kirby turned the command of his battery over to Little Dad and galloped to the front. Hardly had he arrived at the peach orchard than his horse was killed beneath him. A few minutes later, as he was relaying the command for the battery to limber up and pull out, he was desperately wounded in the thigh by two balls from an exploding spherical case shot. As the Maine men were trying to remove Kirby from the field, the gallant lieutenant pointed to one of the guns still remaining behind. "No!" he exclaimed, "take off that gun first." The gun was removed, and Kirby was finally placed in an ambulance and taken to the rear. Lt. George Woodruff was left in command of Battery I.[96]

Heavy butternut and gray infantry columns fell upon Geary's front. Stubbornly, the Union soldiers resisted the attack but fell back nevertheless to Bullock's clearing, north of the Chancellor house.[97] Couch attempted to reform his commands. Hancock rode by and lent his assistance until his horse was killed. The Chancellorsville clearing was a "hell of fire," and the Chancellor house was in flames. Hancock's division alone stood in two lines, back to back, east and west, while fourteen guns held the enemy back on the south.[98]

At last Hancock's division was ordered to withdraw. General Hancock came upon General Meagher's brigade, which was placed in the rear of the Chancellor peach orchard. General Caldwell's absent regiments returned and were posted in support of Meagher. The wreckage of the 5th Maine Battery was finally drawn off the field by the men of the 53d, 116th, and 140th Pennsylvania. The wounded were recovered from the burning Chancellor house by a detail from the 2d Delaware. Then the heroic rear guard fell back to the Chancellor house. The withdrawal of the Second Corps was completed by 11:00 A.M.[99]

Lee did not renew the attacks. He halted the pursuit after learning that General Sedgwick, with General Gibbon's Second Corps division, had broken through Gen. Jubal A. Early's and Gen. William Barksdale's defense lines along Marye's Heights. Lee ordered Gens. William Mahone's, William T. Wofford's, Joseph B. Kershaw's and Paul J. Semmes's brigades of McLaws's division to about-face and reinforce Gen. Cadmus Wilcox's brigade of Anderson's division, which had taken up a position blocking the Union advance at Salem Church. Sedgwick, after renewed attacks by the reinforced Confederate lines on May 4, was stopped, and he withdrew back across the Rappahannock River at Banks's Ford.[100]

The Battle of Chancellorsville was over. It had been a nightmare. Of some 30,000 men who had fallen in the dense and burning thickets around Chancellorsville and between Fredericksburg and Salem Church, more than 17,000 were Union soldiers. The Second Corps alone suffered nearly 2,000 casualties.[101]

On May 5 the armies around Chancellorsville remained still; there was neither advance nor withdrawal. Picket firing, though, was heard in every direction, and the suspense of not knowing what was going to happen next began to tell on officers and enlisted men alike. "This continued suspense is worse than the greatest danger," wrote Colonel O'Rorke. Then, at 5:00 P.M., the skies darkened. Soon, with flashing lightning and peal upon peal of thunder, a heavy rain began to fall. By 7:00 P.M. the Army of the Potomac was under arms, but still there was no movement.[102] Not until about 2:00 A.M. on May 6, did the Army of the Potomac begin its march through the drenching rain toward United States Ford. All through that dark, rainy day the men trudged through the deep mud, recrossed the Rappahannock, and, over the next day, slowly returned to their encampments at Falmouth. Assigned to protect the approaches to United States Ford, Lon's battery was one of the last units in the Second Corps to recross the river.[103]

From his camp near Falmouth on May 7, Lon penned a note to his brother Will. "I am well and all my guns are safe," he wrote. "The fighting has been terrific but as usual void of results. Jo [Joseph Hooker] is not the man. He did not fight the army as it ought to have been fought. I will write again in a day or two. I am tired now having marched in a drenching rain and deep mud a large portion of last night. [Lt. Justin E.] Dimmick [*sic*] of my class I believe you knew. Poor Dimmick was killed while gallantly fighting his battery. [Franklin B.] Crosby who commanded Battery F of my regt. do [ditto]. He was superb gallant fellow such as we regret to lose from the regt. We are under orders to be in readiness to resume the offensive immediately."[104]

While Lon was writing to Will, the Union war effort was gaining momentum half a continent away. Pvt. Howard B. Cushing's Battery B, 1st Illinois Light Artillery, in Maj. Gen. William T. Sherman's Fifteenth Army Corps of Ulysses S. Grant's Army of the Tennessee, had closed in on Vicksburg.[105] On May 19, Battery B took up a position within Sherman's lines along the Graveyard Road, facing the northernmost extension of Gen. John C. Pemberton's Confederate defenses, a bastion known as Stockade Redan. Once his three corps were in position, Grant ordered an assault. Private Cushing's battery was said to have fired the opening artillery rounds of the attack. Although some advanced positions were gained, the assaults of May 19 failed to dislodge the enemy. On May 22 Grant ordered a second wave, with Gen. James B. McPherson's Seventeenth Army Corps spearheading the attacks, but they too met with no success. By day's end Grant determined to lay siege to the city.[106]

Inside the city of Vicksburg lived Lon and Howard's cousin, Judge Lawrence Sterne Houghton, and his wife, Jane Billings Houghton, and their eight children: Theodosia Fredonia, Sara Lavina, Harriet Antoinette, Kate Irene, Douglass, Almira Olivia, Frances Ayer, and Laura Winona, who ranged in age from nineteen to three years—and Jane at the time, was four months pregnant. The Houghtons' oldest daughter had attended Fredonia Academy just after Lon had been graduated.[107]

The artillery shelling of the city began on May 22; it would continue unabated for forty-seven days. Within hours after the bombardment began, the Houghtons abandoned their lovely home on Locust and Randolph Streets—where Howard's father, Milton Buckingham Cushing, had gone to "take the cure" in 1846—and secured cramped quarters in a cave inside the city. The city was sealed off: no food or ammunition could get in, and no one could get out. Day and night, the sky rained exploding shells from Grant's batteries and from Union gunboats on the Mississippi. Some of those shells were from the artillery piece manned by Howard Cushing, the son of Judge Houghton's uncle and former employer in the dry goods store of Cushing & Buckingham in old Putnam, Ohio, over thirty years before.[108] News of the siege of Vicksburg was greeted in the camps of the weary Army of the Potomac with cheers and elation. What was occurring in the West lifted the hearts of those Union soldiers on the Virginia front who had experienced only frustration and defeat.

Within the Second Corps a significant change had occurred on May 13. Artillery brigades had been created for all seven army corps, and Capt. John Gardner Hazard had been named by General Couch to command the Second Corps Artillery Brigade, which had been trimmed down. By

May 13 it consisted of Cushing's Battery A, 4th United States Artillery, Lt. George A. Woodruff's Battery I, 1st United States Artillery, Capt. William A. Arnold's Battery A, 1st Rhode Island Light Artillery, and Lt. T. Fred Brown's Battery B, 1st Rhode Island Light Artillery. Lt. Evan Thomas's Battery C, 4th United States Artillery, Capt. Nelson Ames's Battery G, 1st New York Light Artillery, and Capt. Rufus Pettit's Battery B, 1st New York Light Artillery, had been reassigned to the Artillery Reserve; and Capt. George W. Adams's Battery G, 1st Rhode Island Light Artillery, had been assigned to the Sixth Corps Artillery Brigade. Captain Hazard was an able artillery officer. Having been commissioned a first lieutenant on August 25, 1861, he had served in Battery A as well as Battery C, 1st Rhode Island Light Artillery, before assuming command of Battery B on the eve of the Peninsula campaign. Probably few officers in the volunteer service were more admired by Lon. Hazard was brave and had proved himself capable of such a large command.[109] One of Lon's first formal requests of his new brigade commander was a rather mundane one, however. On May 24 he requested that his men be permitted to water the battery horses and further, that they be allowed to wash their clothes and bathe in the Rappahannock River.[110]

Three days later the inevitable finally occurred. Lt. Rufus King, Jr., unhappy with his position in Cushing's battery, requested a leave of absence. His application was predicated on illness, but it is known that he immediately left the Army of the Potomac and became an aide-de-camp to Gen. William F. Smith in the Department of the Susquehanna. Even though Lon was already short of commissioned officers, he immediately approved King's application, as did Hazard—evidence that both men were more than willing to let the hard-drinking and boastful King leave.[111] With Lieutenants Morris and King gone, Lon was left with Lt. Samuel Canby as the only other commissioned officer in the battery and therefore formally requested that two commissioned officers be assigned to his battery.[112]

Horses and equipment needed replacing as well, and the men needed new clothing, shoes, and accoutrements. Between May 26 and May 30, Lon filed four requisitions for horses and equipment. On May 27 he filed a requisition for six forage caps, ten artillery uniform jackets, eight flannel sack coats, twelve pairs of mounted pants, nine shirts, nine pairs of drawers, nine pairs of boots, one pair of booties, thirteen pairs of stockings, one blanket and fifty crossed cannons. On May 30 he filed a requisition for nine battery horses to replace those that had been condemned. Illustrative of how quickly equipment was lost or damaged during campaigning and how much equipment was needed to keep a six-gun battery in the field, he forwarded a requisition that same day, for "articles lost, condemned and expended in repairs," including "five hundred pounds of coal [for the battery forge], one hundred pounds of horse shoes (No. 3, fore), one hundred pounds of horse shoes (No. 3, hind), one hundred pounds of horse shoes (No. 5, hind), fifty pounds of horseshoe nails, forty-eight nosebags, eighteen curry combs, twenty-seven horse brushes, five head halters and straps, eight sabre belts and plates, two scarlet blankets, twenty pair of spurs and straps, eight watering buckets, fifteen whips, one felling axe, one long-handled shovel, one can of lacker, and one complete saddle."[113]

While Lon was busy refitting his battery, the wounded from the Battle of Chancellorsville who filled the hospitals at Falmouth were being moved to Aquia Creek Landing as fast as medical teams could take them, so that they could be transported to hospitals in Washington. Ned Kirby reached Aquia Creek Landing several days after the Battle of Chancellorsville. Awaiting Kirby's arrival were Lts. John Edie and Morris Schaff, old West Point friends who carried Kirby to their quarters, where the three talked of old times and made plans for the leave they would spend together in Washington.[114]

The next morning Kirby was taken by steamer to Washington and sent to the Ebbitt House Hotel, which had been converted into an army hospital. When Gen. James B. Ricketts, Kirby's commander at First Bull Run, and his wife, Fanny, heard of Kirby's wound and of his presence at the Ebbitt House, they quickly had him removed to their home at 242 Ninth Street. An army surgeon who examined Kirby's wound determined that the leg was broken and must be removed. Two balls had shattered the bone, and blood poisoning had set in.[115] After the leg was amputated complications occurred. Although he was nursed around the clock by Fanny Ricketts and her husband, Kirby was dying. His West Point classmate, newly commissioned Brig. Gen. Adelbert Ames, came by to visit and comfort him.[116]

Over the course of the war, Kirby had refused a number of field promotions in order to remain with his battery. Now, facing death, he knew his widowed mother would have been eligible for a much larger pension if he had only accepted the promotions. An admiring General Ricketts drew up a recommendation for Kirby's elevation to the rank of brigadier general. Signed by Gen. William F. Barry and Ricketts himself, and endorsed by General-in-Chief Henry W. Halleck, the request reached President Lincoln's desk on May 28, 1863. Lincoln signed Kirby's commission that day, then traveled to the Ricketts home and delivered it to the brave young officer in person. Later that same night, newly commissioned Brig. Gen. Edmund Kirby died.[117]

Lon had lost another West Point friend and comrade-in-arms. The war seemed far from resolution, and the humiliations of the most recent battle made the deaths of the noble Dimick and Kirby difficult to accept.

Cushing's loyal and brave first sergeant, Frederick H. Fuger. National Archives.

Above: Blackburn's Ford at Bull Run, looking toward the high ground occupied by General Longstreet's brigade on July 21, 1861. *Below:* The Grapevine Bridge across the Chickahominy River, June 1862, with construction crews from the 5th New Hampshire and 64th New York. Both from Library of Congress.

Above left: Gen. Edwin Vose Sumner, commander of the Second Corps until October 2, 1862, and of the Right Grand Division at Fredericksburg. He was like a father to Alonzo Cushing. *Above right:* Gen. George Brinton McClellan, commander of the Army of the Potomac during the Peninsula and Antietam campaigns. *Below:* General Sumner and staff, May 1862, just before the Battle of Fair Oaks. Left to right: Lt. Alonzo Cushing, Maj. A.M. Clark, Capt. Francis Newman Clarke, Lt. Col. Joseph H. Taylor, General Sumner, Capt. Samuel S. Sumner, Lt. Col. J.F. Hammond, and Lt. Lawrence Kipp. All from Library of Congress.

Above: A sketch by artist Arthur Lumley of the action at Savage Station, June 29, 1862. Stores and ammunition are being destroyed as the Confederates open fire on the distant Union skirmishers. In the foreground, a shell explodes near General Sumner and his staff. *Below:* A wash illustration, by artist Alfred R. Waud, showing what probably are Batteries A and C, 4th U.S. Artillery, under fire from Jackson's artillery at White Oak Swamp. Both from Library of Congress.

The Mumma farm lane and burning Mumma house and barn, Antietam, September 17, 1862. Shown moving up the lane is Tompkins's Rhode Island battery. Cushing brought his battery section into place just to the right (west) of the Mumma lane, followed later by the remaining sections of Batteries A and C, 4th U.S. Artillery. The drawing was made during the Battle of Antietam by an artist for Frank Leslie's newspaper. New York Public Library.

Dunkard Church at Antietam. Thomas's and Cushing's guns were positioned several hundred yards to the right, along the Mumma lane and near the Smoketown Road. Library of Congress.

Above: Officers of Batteries A and C, 4th U.S. Artillery, at East Woods, Antietam Battlefield, September 21, 1862. Seated left to right: Lt. Evan Thomas, Lt. Rufus King, Jr., and (it is believed) Lt. James McKay Rorty. Standing: Lt. Arthur Morris, Lt. Alonzo Cushing, and Lt. Edward Field. The photograph was taken on the day Cushing accepted an assignment to the Topographical Engineers. Library of Congress.
Right: Gen. Darius N. Couch, commander of the Second Corps at Fredericksburg and Chancellorsville. He recommended Cushing for two brevets. National Archives.

Above: General Sumner and staff, November 1862, at the Semmes house in Warrenton, Virginia. Left to right: Capt. W.G. Jones, Maj. Lawrence Kipp, Lt. Col. Joseph H. Taylor, General Sumner, Capt. John Garland, Capt. Samuel S. Sumner (with hands on hips), Lt. Alonzo Cushing, and Lt. Col. William W. Teall. Note Cushing's meerschaum pipe, a gift from his brother William. *Below left:* Gen. Catharenus Putnam Buckingham, a cousin and business partner of Alonzo's father in Putnam, Ohio. He delivered the orders relieving General McClellan of command and replacing him with General Burnside. *Below right:* Gen. Ambrose Everett Burnside, commander of the Army of the Potomac at Fredericksburg. All from Library of Congress.

Above: The attack of the Second Corps against Marye's Heights, Fredericksburg, December 13, 1862. Library of Congress. *Below:* Telegraph Road west of Fredericksburg, with Marye's Heights in the distance. Taken from the ridge west of the canal, the scene shows the fields over which the Second Corps assaulted Marye's Heights. National Archives.

The Phillips house near Stafford Heights, Virginia, Sumner's headquarters during the Fredericksburg campaign, shown burning in February 1863. Alonzo Cushing spent his last Christmas there. Francis T. Miller, *Photographic History of the Civil War,* 2:100.

The Mud March, January 20-21, 1863. Drawing by Alfred R. Waud. Library of Congress.

Left: Gen. Joseph Hooker, commander of the Army of the Potomac from January 26 to June 28, 1863. *Right:* Gen. Henry Hunt, Chief of Artillery, Army of the Potomac, at Gettysburg. Library of Congress.

Left: Gen. John Gibbon, commander of the Second Division, Second Corps, at Gettysburg. *Right:* Gen. Winfield Scott Hancock, commander of the Second Corps at Gettysburg. Library of Congress.

Above: Gen. George Gordon Meade, commander of the Army of the Potomac at Gettysburg. Library of Congress. *Below:* A seven-man crew of cannoneers and a gunner at an Ordnance rifle and limber. The gun and crew are believed to have served in Capt. Andrew Cowan's First New York Independent Battery at Gettysburg. Francis T. Miller, *Photographic History of the Civil War*, 9:217.

The Leister house and the Taneytown Road, Gettysburg. On the morning of July 2, Cushing's battery turned left off the road to the farm lane (open gate). During the bombardment on July 3, his caissons were driven back to the Taneytown Road via the same farm lane and later crossed the road and moved up the Granite School House Road to the right.

Below and opposite: Cushing's battery position at the angle on Cemetery Ridge. Taken in 1882 for artist Paul Philippoteaux, these photographs show the area occupied by Companies A and B of the 71st Pennsylvania. *Below:* The low stone wall is visible in the center of the picture, as are the Codori house and barn along the Emmitsburg Road. The distant treeline marks Seminary Ridge. Cushing fell alongside his number four gun, near where the figure stands at the fenceline. *Opposite:* To the right of Cushing's battery was the perpendicular fenceline, behind which the 71st poured an enfilading fire into General Pickett's troops as they swarmed through Cushing's silent guns. Gettysburg National Military Park.

Above left: Lt. Joseph S. Milne. *Above right:* Capt. and Bvt. Brig. Gen. John G. Hazard, commander of the Artillery Brigade of the Second Corps at Gettysburg. Both from John S. Rhodes, *The History of Battery B., First Rhode Island Light Artillery.*

Gen. Alexander Stewart Webb, commander of the Philadelphia Brigade at Gettysburg. Library of Congress.

The high water mark of the Confederacy at the angle, Gettysburg. At left, the 72d Pennsylvania surges toward the angle. Cushing's guns have been abandoned. The left sections of Woodruff's Battery and Arnold's Battery pour an enfilading fire into the angle as General Pickett's division makes a momentary breakthrough. Library of Congress.

Death of Brevet Lieut. Colonel Alonzo Hereford Cushing, 1st Lieut., commanding Battery A, 4th U.S. Artillery, at Gettysburg, July 3, 1863, by Henry Edwin Brown (Braun). Sergeant Fuger comes to Cushing's assistance as General Webb brings forward the 72d Pennsylvania. Richard Grosclose Collections, Hartland, Wisconsin.

Wrecked limbers and caisson with dead horses at the angle, Gettysburg. Drawn by Edwin Forbes immediately after the fighting. Library of Congress.

Cushing's battery memorial at Gettysburg. National Archives.

8

"Forward into Battery!"

At Guinea Station, Virginia, tragedy struck Lee and his Army of Northern Virginia in the wake of the spectacular victory at Chancellorsville. There, on May 10, the wounded Stonewall Jackson died. For days thereafter Union army telegraphers were busy tapping out the news.[1]

With the loss of Jackson, Lee reorganized his army into three powerful corps. Lt. Gen. James Longstreet, recalled from Suffolk, was given the command of the First Corps, Lt. Gen. Richard S. Ewell the Second Corps, and Lt. Gen. Ambrose Powell Hill the Third Corps. Maj. Gen. J.E.B. Stuart resumed command of a cavalry corps of six brigades as well as a large battalion of horse artillery. In all, Lee's Army of Northern Virginia boasted over 60,000 officers and men.[2]

Despite Lee's victories in Virginia, the Confederate cause was facing the cold specter of defeat. The Confederacy west of the Virginia mountains and south to the Gulf of Mexico was simply too large a territory to defend with the region's limited manpower and resources. That fact had become apparent from the outset of the bloody conflict. Months before the Battle of Shiloh in April 1862, Confederate forces had abandoned all of Kentucky and Tennessee. From there on the war in the West had become one of desperation. Gens. Braxton Bragg's and E. Kirby Smith's Confederate armies had invaded Kentucky in the summer and fall of 1862, but with no success. And after bitter fighting along Stone's River near Murfreesboro, Tennessee, in December 1862 and January 1863, Bragg had withdrawn his Army of Tennessee to the highlands of southeast Tennessee at Tullahoma. There Bragg remained in May 1863, facing a powerful Union army commanded by Gen. William S. Rosecrans. Farther west it was even worse. The Union freshwater navy, by the end of May 1863, controlled the Mississippi River from Vicksburg north and, save for Port Hudson, south from Vicksburg all the way to New Orleans. General Grant and his Army of the Tennessee was besieging fortress Vicksburg, one of two remaining Confederate strongholds along the great river.[3]

There was a sense of desperation within the Confederate government as well as Lee's closest councils. To afford relief to the dwindling western armies, there had been talk of sending elements of the Army of Northern Virginia to Vicksburg or Tullahoma or even the eastern Tennessee mountains. In spite of its air of invincibility, Lee's army faced chronic shortages of food, clothing, equipment, and munitions. Vast numbers of Lee's soldiers were barefooted. Hard campaigning over the past year had worn the army to tatters.[4]

To forage his army, possibly to bring about a political end to the war, and most surely to prevent elements of his forces from being detached and sent to the western theater of war, Lee determined to move out of wartorn Virginia and invade Maryland and Pennsylvania. On June 3, without ever notifying President Davis or his War Department in advance, Lee commenced to withdraw portions of his army from the vicinity of Fredericksburg. Led by the divisions of Maj. Gens. Lafayette McLaws and John Bell Hood of Longstreet's corps, which previously had advanced to the Rapidan River, the movement was followed by Ewell's corps on June 4 and 5. The immediate destination of the Confederate advance was Culpeper Court House. Hill's corps remained at Fredericksburg in front of the Army of the Potomac.[5]

General Hooker became aware of the Confederate advance almost immediately and ordered Union cavalry to move toward Culpeper to ascertain the enemy's intentions. General Sedgwick's Sixth Corps Artillery Brigade—the largest of any of the corps artillery brigades in the army—was ordered to open fire on the enemy from its positions along the Rappahannock River. That same day the Sixth Corps was sent across the Rappahannock on pontoon bridges in an effort to "feel the enemy's presence" in the positions at Deep Run, south of Fredericksburg.[6]

Hooker seemed adrift as to what to do in the face of the Confederate movements. He did put his army in a state of preparedness for a major shift of position, however. Orders were issued to transfer all sick and wounded to hospitals in Washington. Stores not needed for immediate use were secured on board transports at Aquia Creek Landing for passage to the capital city, and all unnecessary materiel was ordered destroyed. Officers and enlisted men were directed to remain close to their camps.[7] To Lt. Alonzo H. Cushing and his men, the first sign of Hooker's intention to abandon the Fredericksburg-Falmouth front came in the form of a telegram received at Second Corps headquarters on June 6, which directed that the soldiers of the corps have three days' rations in their haversacks, and that all wagons be loaded with stores and the trains put in readiness for any order to move. The order, the telegram stated, "may possibly be given to move early tomorrow."[8]

Lon's request for additional officers for his battery finally met with success that same day. Reporting to Lon's headquarters tent at Falmouth was a second lieutenant by the name of Joseph A. Milne from Lt. T. Fred Brown's Battery B, 1st Rhode Island Light Artillery, who handed Cushing an order from Captain Hazard that temporarily relieved him from duty with Brown's battery and assigned him to Cushing's.[9]

Milne was a dark-haired, rather patrician-looking young man who, in his brief stint with Battery A, would for some unknown reason become disliked by many of the regular army and volunteer enlisted men alike. Milne was born in Bollow, New York, in 1843. After working for his father's Baptist newspaper in Glens Falls, New York, he had moved to Fall River, Rhode Island, where he worked as a compositor for the *Fall River Daily News*. Two years later he found a position with the *Providence Daily Post* and was living in Tiverton, Rhode Island, when the war broke out. At Governor William Sprague's call for recruits for a battalion of Rhode Island artillery in August 1861, Joseph Milne, then but eighteen years of age, volunteered for service in Battery E, 1st Rhode Island Light Artillery. Battery commander Capt. George E. Randolph had appointed him sergeant of the number five gun detachment on September 30, 1861, and in that capacity Milne had served with distinction through the Peninsula campaign.[10]

After he was commissioned a second lieutenant and transferred to Battery B, 1st Rhode Island Light Artillery, on November 11, 1862, Milne's first assignment was as chief of caissons. During the assault on Marye's Heights at Fredericksburg, Milne acted with conspicuous gallantry while commanding the caissons during the battery's heroic advance alongside the brave Second Corps infantry. He was later placed in command of the battery's left gun section, and his last assignment before being transferred to Cushing's battery had been to take his two guns down to the Rappahannock River by the "old church" in Falmouth to perform picket duty near the "fishing ground."[11]

In the midst of all the commotion caused by the enemy movements, the internal political machinations between the high command of the Army of Potomac and the Lincoln administration ground inexorably onward. General Couch, after unsuccessfully advocating Hooker's removal from command, requested a leave of absence. It was refused. He then asked to be relieved of command of the Second Corps. That request was granted (officially, on June 10), and he was immediately assigned to command the Department of the Susquehanna in Harrisburg, Pennsylvania. Lon undoubtedly hated to see General Couch go. He was a brave and highly valued officer; Lon truly liked him, and the general had developed a sincere fondness for Lon. It was Couch, after all, who had recommended Lon for two brevets.[12]

In Couch's place, Maj. Gen. Winfield Scott Hancock was named commander of the Second Corps on June 9. Born near Norristown,

Pennsylvania, in 1824, Hancock had been graduated from West Point in the class of 1844. He had served through the Seminole and Mexican Wars with distinction, and accompanied Gen. William S. Harney in the Mormon expedition in Utah. Like an ever dwindling number of general officers in the Army of the Potomac at that time, Hancock's appointment as brigadier general of volunteers had been secured by none other than Gen. George B. McClellan in the fall of 1861. Since the Battle of Antietam he had served as commander of the First Division of the Second Corps, leading it against Marye's Heights at Fredericksburg and through the wilderness thickets of Chancellorsville. He was brave and well liked by both officers and enlisted men. Among the generals in the Army of the Potomac, Hancock's presence and personal magnetism were the most profound. In him the men of the Second Corps placed immediate confidence.[13]

Replacing Hancock as commander of the First Division of the Second Corps was Brig. Gen. John C. Caldwell. Col. Edward Cross of the famed 5th New Hampshire took over as commander of Caldwell's former brigade. Brig. Gen. Samuel K. Zook remained in command of the Third Brigade and Col. John R. Brooke of the Fourth. Brig. Gen. Thomas Francis Meagher had resigned as commander of the Irish Brigade and returned home to New York City. He was replaced by Col. Patrick Kelly, formerly the commander of the Irish 88th New York.[14] In Brig. Gen. John Gibbon's Second Division, Brig. Gen. William Harrow assumed command of the First Brigade. Brig. Gen. Joshua T. Owen remained with the Second Brigade, and Col. Norman J. Hall with the Third.[15] Still in command of an undersized Third Division of only two brigades was Maj. Gen. William H. French. His First Brigade continued under the command of the gallant Col. Samuel S. Carroll; the Second Brigade had been taken over by Col. Thomas A. Smyth, commander of the 1st Delaware, after Brig. Gen. William Hays was captured at Chancellorsville. Expiring enlistments after Chancellorsville had eliminated the Third Brigade altogether.[16]

The Army of Northern Virginia was moving rapidly. By June 10, Ewell's corps was on the march from Culpeper to Cedarville, a small village north of Front Royal. At Cedarville, it would be joined by Brig. Gen. Albert G. Jenkins's cavalry brigade. By June 13, Ewell's corps would appear in the lower Shenandoah Valley just south of Winchester. Two days later Longstreet's corps would be moving toward the Bull Run mountains.[17] Lee's movements were becoming clearer to Hooker. Certainly, they represented no simple flanking operation across the Rappahannock River. Whatever Lee was doing, it was presenting a decided threat to the nation's capital and other northern population centers. After considerable prodding from the president and the War Department,

Hooker finally resolved to move his army north to keep it interposed between Lee's forces and Washington.[18]

The movement of the Army of the Potomac began on the morning of June 11, led by the Third Corps, followed by the First, then the Eleventh and finally the Fifth Corps, the four commands collectively referred to then as the right wing of the army, commanded by Maj. Gen. John Fulton Reynolds.[19] Rumors as to the army's destination abounded. In the midst of all the speculation, news arrived on June 12 of the worsting of Gen. J.E.B. Stuart's Confederate horsemen by Union cavalry at Brandy Station just three days before.[20]

For the Second Corps, the waiting finally ended on June 13, when General Hancock issued marching orders in anticipation of a forward movement. The next day reveille was sounded in Cushing's battery at sunrise. The day promised to be cool; the skies were overcast. Sick call was sounded an hour earlier than usual. The air was alive with excitement and expectation.[21] At about midday, Lon was handed the artillery brigade's marching orders by an orderly from Captain Hazard's headquarters.[22] The orders were detailed and included highly significant duties for Lon.

Headquarters Artillery Brigade
2nd Army Corps
June 14, 1863

Special Orders
No. 21

1. A detail of one (1) man from Lt. Co. "I", 1st U.S. Arty. is hereby ordered to report to 1st Lieutenant G.L. Dwight, Ordnance officer, Artillery Brigade, 2nd Army Corps, in place of Acting Ordnance Sergeant William E. Smith, relieved.

2. One Section of Battery "A", 4th U.S. Artillery is hereby ordered to report at headquarters, 2nd Army Corps, at once.

3. The remaining two sections of Battery "A", 4th U.S. Art., will report to General Gibbon at dark.

4. One section of Lt. Co. "I", 1st U.S. Art., will report to General Gibbon at dark. The remainder of the battery will be formed on the Telegraph Road, the head of the column resting a few hundred yards beyond the junction of the Telegraph Road and the road leading to General Hancock's Headquarters, at dark.

5. Battery "A", 1st R.I. Lt. Art., will be withdrawn from its present position at dark, and will be formed on the Telegraph Road, the head of the column resting a

few hundred yards beyond the junction of the Telegraph Road, and the road leading to General Hancock's Headquarters, in rear of Lt. Co. "I" 1st U.S. Art.

6. Battery "B", 1st R.I. Lt. Art., will be formed in rear of Battery "A" on the Telegraph Road, the head of the column resting a few hundred yards beyond the junction of the Telegraph Road and the road leading to General Hancock's headquarters, at dark.

By order of
Jno. G. Hazard

One section of Cushing's battery would accompany Gen. Hancock. Although no records indicate where Lon himself traveled in the order of march, he undoubtedly accompanied the section attached to Second Corps headquarters. In fact, his long-time duty as a Second Corps staff officer must have played a role in Hancock's request that a section of Cushing's battery accompany his headquarters. Having served as a staff officer in the Second Corps, Lon was familiar with its division, brigade, and regimental commanders and their respective staffs; they, in turn, were familiar with him. Newly assigned to corps command, Hancock needed all the staff assistance he could find. Lon would serve Hancock as a temporary aide-de-camp.

Lon's men were issued three days' rations, consisting of pork, hardtack, coffee, and sugar. "Stable call" followed, and the battery horses were watered, fed, and groomed. Then the buglers blew "assembly call." The artillerymen packed up their gear, harnessed the horses to the limbers and battery wagons, and hitched up the guns and caissons. One by one, Lon's guns, caissons, and battery wagons pulled out of the breastworks at Falmouth and onto the Telegraph Road. One two-gun section, with its caissons and baggage wagons—and with Lon probably accompanying it—moved to Hancock's headquarters at the head of the Second Corps, where it parked and waited for orders to begin the long march. The remaining two battery sections, under the command of Lt. Samuel Canby, moved to the headquarters of General Gibbon, whose Second Division formed the rear of the Second Corps column.[23]

At 8:00 P.M. the command was given: "Forward, march!" Lon and Canby shouted to their respective battery sections: "Battery at-ten-tion! Drivers—prepare to mount—mount—first piece—forward into line—march!" With the crack of whips, the snorts and neighs of the horses, and the creaking and groaning of the wagons, limbers, caissons, and guns, Battery A, 4th United States Artillery—one section at the front and the other two near the rear of the Second Corps line—began the northward movement out of Falmouth that would lead it to immortality in the fields south of a little crossroads town in Pennsylvania named Gettysburg.[24]

All through the night Lon's guns rumbled up the Telegraph Road with what seemed to be endless columns of dusty infantry. A short distance to the left of the road, a line of flankers or skirmishers filed through the fields and brush and woods. The soldiers could also see Union cavalry forming an even more distant screen to protect the columns from a surprise attack. All along the marching lines one could spot the brilliant Second Corps division and brigade pennants bearing red, white, or blue trefoils set in contrasting backgrounds. Accompanying Captain Hazard's Second Corps Artillery Brigade headquarters was a bright red pennant bearing a white trefoil. The trefoil emblem already had become a symbol of immense pride to the officers and men of the Second Corps.[25] The Second Corps formed the rear guard of the army; as a consequence, frequent halts were called for felling trees and destroying bridges behind the columns in order to retard any enemy pursuit. In front of the Second Corps marched the Sixth and the Twelfth Corps and the Reserve Artillery. This "second wing" of the army covered the evacuation of supplies and equipment from Aquia Creek Landing and other depots until it passed Dumfries. The operations of the wing thereafter would be dictated by the movements of the enemy.[26]

The bold objective of Lee began to unfold. On June 14 and 15, General Ewell's corps crushed Maj. Gen. Robert H. Milroy's Union garrison at Winchester. Ewell pressed on to Martinsburg, capturing vast amounts of supplies. By June 16, Ewell's corps would be across the Potomac River. General Longstreet's corps had moved into the mountains in front of Berryville, while General Hill's corps, after waiting for the last of Hooker's army to leave Falmouth, evacuated Fredericksburg, moved north to Culpeper Court House, and raced toward the Bull Run mountains to catch up with Longstreet.[27]

Near dawn on June 15 the Second Corps entered Stafford Court House, a small village built up around a courthouse and jail. Most of the public buildings and private dwellings had been burned by the recently evacuated Confederate forces, and many were still on fire as Lon's battery sections moved through the dismal village.[28] At Stafford Court House the Second Corps rested during the early morning of June 15. At 10:00 A.M., though, Cushing and Canby ordered their men to hitch up the guns and move out again. At about 1:00 P.M. the corps reached Aquia Creek, and after fording the stream, the men rested once more. "The day," wrote one cannoneer with Brown's battery, "had been intensely hot, and the march, through the dusty roads, proved most fatiguing to the men, hundreds of whom fell out of the infantry columns." It had been nearly a month since the last rainstorm. Vast numbers of soldiers suffered from exhaustion and heatstroke. The situation became so bad that corps ambulances were brought into service at the rear of the long, dusty columns, bringing forward those who had fallen out of the ranks. The columns finally came to a halt at midnight.[29]

Reveille sounded at 2:30 A.M. on June 16, and soon the Second Corps columns were marching again. Around 7:00 A.M. the corps arrived at Dumfries. The town apparently presented a rather poor presence to Lon and his fellow soldiers; one Second Corps artilleryman noted disgustedly that the village must have been "inhabited by poor white trash." A halt was called in the line of march, and the men were given time to prepare their meager breakfasts and to water the horses. In addition, three more days' rations were issued. Within two hours, however, the Second Corps —including Lon's battery—was back on the road.[30]

As on the day before, the heat was intense, and the wagons of the ambulance corps continued to follow the columns, picking up soldiers who had fallen out of the ranks with heat exhaustion, sunstroke, and fatigue. One soldier in the 15th Massachusetts in Gibbon's division recalled seeing men lying by the side of the road who had died under the combined effects of heat and exhaustion. "A few more such days," wrote a cannoneer in Arnold's battery, "would have stayed the progress of the whole army. It was an up and down-hill road, and the dust was suffocating." By evening the columns reached Occoquan Creek and forded the stream at Wolf Run Shoals. There, at 8:00 P.M., the troops halted and went into bivouac. "It was the warmest night I ever experienced," recorded one infantryman.[31] To give the men needed rest, reveille was not sounded on the morning of June 17 until well after sunrise. The soldiers had time to bathe in Occoquan Creek, "a luxury," wrote one Rhode Island cannoneer, "not always obtainable."[32] By 1:00 P.M., the drivers had harnessed the horses, the guns had been hitched to the limbers, and the Second Corps was on the march again. At about 6:00 P.M., the corps reached Sangster's Station on the Orange & Alexandria Railroad, and there it went into bivouac.[33]

June 18 proved to be a day of rest for Lon and his men. Light marching orders were issued, and the wagons used to carry officers' baggage as well as the brigade and battery ambulances were sent to the ambulance corps in order to speed the movement of the vanguard of the corps. Soothing to all the troops at last was the cool air brought by the rain showers that fell on and off throughout the day.[34] At 1:00 P.M. on June 19 the march was resumed. Again, frequent showers fell. The day's march brought the column to Centreville, where the corps bivouacked behind the fortifications that had been constructed outside the town during the First Bull Run campaign.[35]

The Second Corps was awakened at 5:00 A.M. on June 20, and the march was resumed. The troops passed over the old Bull Run battlegrounds, where they saw the skeletal remains of soldiers who had died in those two previous battles. Many shallow graves had eroded away. One soldier recalled seeing two skulls kicked around the roadside by the passing troops. "[I] saw the hands and feet of those half buried," he remembered, "and the whole ground was completely strewn with the bones of the dead." Young Lt. Tully McCrea of Woodruff's battery later recalled that sad and memorable day. "Never have I seen such a horribly disgusting sight," he wrote. "Our dead had never been buried, nor had any pretensions been made to do it. Our soldiers remained where they fell, nothing left but the bare skeletons and the tattered rags around them. It was estimated by some that there were two hundred skeletons in one small piece of woods. I saw a few lying by the side of the road and was satisfied with that, having no curiosity to search further." Lon remembered those fields from the days of July 1861. The gruesome sights brought back to him memories of Greene's battery and those first, exciting days of war.[36]

Lon's battery sections crossed the famous Stone Bridge and, in company with the Second Corps columns, left the Warrenton Turnpike and headed north. At about 9:00 P.M. the march was halted, and the corps went into bivouac between Gainesville and Haymarket. The Philadelphia Brigade pushed on as far as Thoroughfare Gap in the Bull Run mountains.[37] Between June 21 and June 24 the Second Corps remained in the Bull Run mountains. The men spent the time washing their clothes and bathing. The corps supply wagons arrived, and the men were again issued rations and received a mail delivery as well—the first in days.[38]

The soldiers of the Second Corps were aroused at sunrise on June 25. The day was pleasant and warm. Ahead, they heard gunfire. Lon's battery sections were limbered up and set in motion along with the rest of the corps. As the columns headed toward Haymarket, the rear of the Gibbon's division came under fire from Confederate cavalrymen and a battery of artillery situated along a ridge to the right of the road.[39]

Gibbon ordered Canby's two battery sections into action, the four guns were brought into position and they commenced firing at the Confederate battery. Soon, from the very rear of the long Second Division lines, came Brown's battery, which unlimbered to the right of Canby's guns. By that time, Canby had obtained a "raking fire" upon the Confederates; his guns had succeeded in dismounting one of the enemy's fieldpieces. Union infantry columns appeared in support of the artillery, and General Gibbon advanced a long skirmish line toward the Confederate vantage point. By then, however, the effective fire from Battery A had forced the Confederate cannoneers to abandon their position. Twenty-eight rounds of ammunition had been fired by Canby's four guns in the brief encounter.[40] His cannoneers hitched the guns to the limbers and moved back into their position in the marching columns. Luckily, neither men nor horses had been wounded. Brown's battery was less fortunate: two Rhode Island artillerymen were wounded, and two of the battery's horses wounded and one killed. Enemy artillery fire had found its mark within the passing infantry regiments as well, wounding a number of men.[41]

Farther ahead, Confederate cavalry had engaged General Zook's brigade of the First Division and managed briefly to sever it from the rest of the corps. The Confederate attack there, however, finally had been beaten back.[42] Soon the long columns of the Second Corps were on the march again; they reached Gum Springs in a drenching rain about 10:00 P.M. The ranks filed off the road and into the open fields, where the weary soldiers bivouacked for the night.[43]

At Gum Springs the undersized Third Division of the Second Corps was augmented by the arrival of Brig. Gen. Alexander Hays's brigade, consisting of Maj. Hugo Hildebrandt's 39th New York (the famed Garibaldi Guards from the days of First Bull Run), Col. Clinton D. McDougall's 111th New York; Col. George L. Willard's 125th New York; and Col. Eliakim Sherrill's 126th New York. General French was relieved of command of the Third Division and assigned to command the garrison at Harpers Ferry. Under orders from General Hancock, General Hays, a close friend and West Point classmate of the new corps commander, assumed command of the Third Division. Colonel Willard took over Hays's New York brigade.[44]

The soldiers were up at 5:30 A.M. on June 26. The day was warm, and drenching rains continued to fall. After a breakfast of coffee, fried or broiled pork, and hardtack, Lon's divided battery was inspected. Rolls were taken, and equipment, accoutrements and arms were examined.[45]

At 10:00 A.M. the Second Corps moved out of Gum Springs and, marched for six hours to just south of the Potomac River. The soldiers had marched virtually the entire distance in ankle-deep mud. Many of them, by day's end, were barefooted. After a brief rest, the columns started north again at 7:00 P.M. Long delays occurred as the corps trains were moved across the river on the two pontoon bridges at Edward's Ferry. By midnight, all of Lon's battery sections had crossed. Once the whole corps was across the river, a halt to the march was called, and the wet and muddy soldiers bedded down for the night along the rain-soaked but verdant farmlands south of Poolsville, Maryland.[46]

All of Lee's army was across the Potomac River by June 26. Ewell's divided corps was threatening points as far east in Pennsylvania as Wrightsville on the Susquehanna River and as far north as Carlisle. Longstreet's and Hill's corps were moving up the Cumberland Valley toward Chambersburg. Three brigades of Stuart's cavalry command were operating between the Army of the Potomac and Washington, D.C. The situation was growing more ominous and threatening with the passing of every day.[47]

The morning of June 27 was a time of rest for the Second Corps. Just past midmorning, the order officially appointing General Hancock to command of the corps was read to the men. By noon, the corps was again in motion. Marching through Poolsville, the troops took the road to Barnesville, where a halt was ordered at 7:00 P.M.[48] At sunrise on Sunday, June 28, the buglers blew reveille. Lon's and Canby's men prepared their spartan breakfasts and then harnessed the horses and limbered up the caissons and guns. By 7:00 A.M. the battery was on the move again. The men of the Second Corps marched all through the day, halting only briefly for much-needed periods of rest.[49]

During the day another major command change took place in the corps. Brig. Gen. Alexander Stewart Webb arrived at corps headquarters. He had sought a field assignment in the campaign. General Hancock knew and liked him. One brigade in the corps, the Philadelphia Brigade—the 69th, 71st, 72d, and 106th Pennsylvania—had been suffering serious discipline and morale problems. The brigade was composed of men of sturdy stock who had served well at Yorktown, Fair Oaks, Savage Station, White Oak Swamp, Glendale, Malvern Hill, Antietam, and Fredericksburg. Yet recently the sick rolls had been unduly lengthy, and there had been a noticeable increase in charges of insubordination among officers and enlisted men alike. Large numbers of the men were either under arrest or absent without leave. There had even been a shooting incident between two company commanders in the 69th and 71st Pennsylvania. The brigade leadership of General Owen, it seems, had been ineffective. Owen was relieved of command. In his place, Hancock assigned Gen. Webb.[50]

No finer officer could have been selected to command the Philadelphia Brigade than twenty-eight-year-old General Webb. A native of New York City, he was an 1855 graduate of West Point. He had fought the Seminole Indians; he had seen action at First Bull Run and as a staff assistant to Maj. Gen. William F. Barry, artillery chief of the Army of the Potomac, during the peninsula campaign. Only recently he had served as a staff officer in the Fifth Corps. Webb was a tough disciplinarian and would prove to be a hard fighter. No sooner had the change in command been announced to the men of the Philadelphia Brigade than Webb set about letting the men know, in no uncertain terms, that he was in control.[51]

At sunset, the Second Corps halted at Monocacy Junction, a thriving little town located on a branch of the Baltimore & Ohio Railroad just south of Frederick, Maryland. There the corps went into bivouac.[52]

Fighting Joe Hooker's response to Lee's bold movements had been

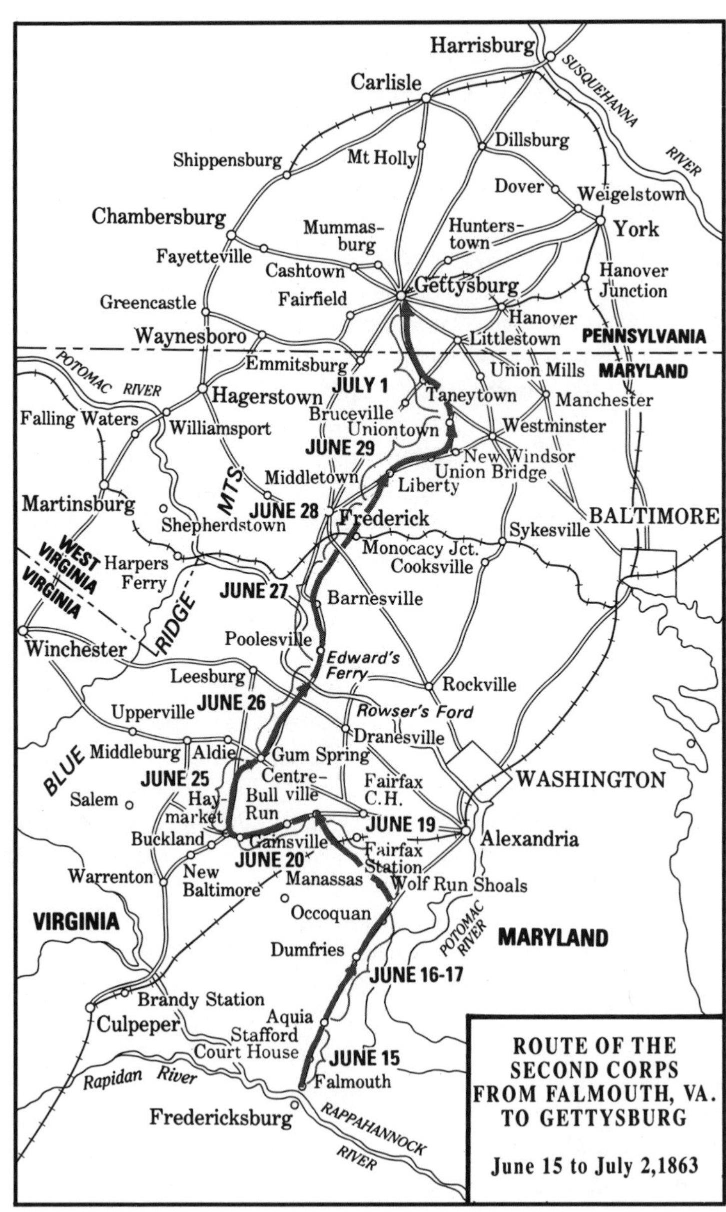
ROUTE OF THE
SECOND CORPS
FROM FALMOUTH, VA.
TO GETTYSBURG
June 15 to July 2,1863
Harrisburg
Carlisle
SUSQUEHANNA
RIVER
Dillsburg
Shippensburg
Mt Holly
Dover
Weigelstown
Chambersburg
Mummas-
burg
Hunters-
town
York
Fayetteville
Cashtown
Hanover
Junction
Greencastle
Fairfield
Gettysburg
Hanover
Waynesboro
Littlestown
PENNSYLVANIA
MARYLAND
Emmitsburg
Union Mills
POTOMAC RIVER
JULY 1
Hagerstown
Taneytown
Manchester
Falling Waters
Bruceville
Williamsport
Uniontown
Westminster
JUNE 29
New Windsor
Union Bridge
MTS.
Middletown
Liberty
Martinsburg
JUNE 28
Frederick
BALTIMORE
Shepherdstown
Sykesville
WEST VIRGINIA
VIRGINIA
Harpers
Ferry
Monocacy Jct.
Cooksville
JUNE 27
Barnesville
RIDGE
Poolesville
Winchester
Edward's
Ferry
Leesburg
Rockville
JUNE 26
Upperville
Rowser's Ford
Dranesville
BLUE
Middleburg
Aldie
Gum Spring
WASHINGTON
JUNE 25
Centre-
ville
Fairfax
C.H.
Salem
Hay-
market
Bull
Run
JUNE 19
Buckland
Gainsville
Alexandria
Fairfax
Station
JUNE 20
Warrenton
New
Baltimore
Manassas
Wolf Run Shoals
Occoquan
VIRGINIA
POTOMAC
RIVER
MARYLAND
Dumfries
JUNE 16-17
Brandy Station
Aquia
Culpeper
Stafford
Court House
JUNE 15
Rapidan River
Falmouth
Fredericksburg
RAPPAHANNOCK
RIVER

skillful. He had moved the Army of the Potomac into positions that not only protected the approaches to Washington and Baltimore but were within striking distance of the enemy. Yet despite of Hooker's rapid and well-conceived movements, he did not have the confidence of his army. More important, he had completely lost confidence in himself. He became preoccupied with trying to get General Halleck and the War Department to augment his army with General French's garrison at Harpers Ferry. His requests were refused. Then, as if he had intended it all along, Hooker resigned from command of the Army of the Potomac.[53] In his place, the White House named Maj. Gen. George Gordon Meade. He was notified of his elevation in command early on the morning of June 28 while his Fifth Corps was bivouacked near Frederick. He now commanded an army of seven corps and just under 120,000 officers and enlisted men.[54]

Born in 1815 while his mother and merchant father were living in Cadiz, Spain, Meade was of Irish and Roman Catholic descent. Raised near Philadelphia, he had been graduated from West Point in the class of 1835. After a brief service, he resigned from the army in 1836 to become a civil engineer. Returning to the army in 1842, he was assigned to the Topographical Engineers and served through the Mexican War. Meade had risen to the rank of captain by 1861, and that same year he was elevated to the rank of brigadier general of volunteers at the insistence of Gov. Andrew Curtin of Pennsylvania. As the commander of a brigade in the Pennsylvania Reserve Corps, he served through the Seven Days' fighting and at the Second Battle of Bull Run. He then led General Reynolds's division through the Battle of South Mountain and at Antietam and commanded the Third Division in Reynolds's First Corps at Fredericksburg. Thereafter, he was named commander of the Fifth Corps, which he led at Chancellorsville. General McClellan thought Meade "an excellent officer; cool, brave and intelligent." Meade was a solid front-line officer who, though cautious, would prove to be a capable army administrator.[55]

On Monday, June 29, the Second Corps was aroused at daybreak, and by 8:00 A.M. the soldiers were on the march again. Lon's battery sections passed through Mount Pleasant and Liberty early in the day. "We are marching through one of the attractive garden spots of the world . . . a veritable paradise," wrote one Massachusetts soldier. "Crops of every kind and variety [are] hastening forward to maturity, and from open barns [comes] the sweet smell of the newly gathered hay."[56]

As the long, dirty columns of soldiers, wagons, and artillery snaked their way through Johnsville and Union Bridge, ladies stood along the roadside and handed out drinking water and milk. Some townspeople offered pieces of pie and bread and butter. The loyalty of the people of the beautiful towns in central Maryland gave the soldiers a spiritual lift. They were out of hostile, wartorn Virginia and in a lush region visibly loyal to the Union. The troops became so enspirited that many began singing "The Battle Cry of Freedom" and other familiar patriotic songs as they marched along. General Gibbon asked the "Glee Club" of the 19th Massachusetts to start singing, and it soon broke into the melodious "Marching along, we are marching along." "The effect," wrote a soldier, "was magical. The division fell into step and the chorus could be heard ringing along the entire line." The heat and humidity was intense but the singing seemed to make the miles pass with less pain. The long march continued through the heat of the day and well into evening. "We called up all our determination," recalled one soldier, "and hurried on through the shadows . . . There was little heard in the ranks, but the tread of feet, the clanking of arms and equipment, and an occasional oath or grumble from some tired mortal." As darkness fell, the march took on an eerie quality. "The sun sank below the horizon," the soldier continued. "Evening breezes took the place of its hot breath, bushes by the wayside grew shadowy, and finally faded into dark, irregular masses, taking on fantastic and weird forms as the night settled over the land. The stars came out one by one in a moonless sky, but there was still the incessant tramp, tramp, tramp, tramp as the line moved forward without a halt."[57]

Finally, in the darkness, the corps reached Uniontown, Maryland. All the way down the long, dusty columns of infantry and artillery rang the shrill command, "Column halt, break ranks." The Second Corps that day had marched thirty-two miles through country marked by rolling hills and deep valleys. Up to that time in the war, it was the longest one-day march made by any unit in the Army of the Potomac.[58] The head of the Second Corps—Hancock's headquarters with Lon and his battery section, along with the First Division—went into bivouac two miles beyond Uniontown on the Westminster Road at about 10:00 P.M. The Third Division and the rear-guard Second Division bivouacked along what was known as the Babylon farm just outside of Uniontown. That night General Hancock issued a congratulatory circular to his soldiers.[59]

Uniontown was a tiny hamlet nestled in one of Maryland's loveliest farming regions. There, in the open, rolling fields near the beautiful little village, the soldiers of the Second Corps officially were made aware of the resignation of Maj. Gen. Joseph Hooker as commander of the army and his replacement by Maj. Gen. George Gordon Meade. The men universally welcomed the change in command; they were, at least, pleased to know that Hooker had resigned. Tully McCrea summed up the attitude of the soldiers. "We were all delighted with the news that General Hooker had been relieved and General Meade assigned to the command of the army," he wrote. "This is universally popular and received with great glee . . . His blundering was so apparent that when we returned to Falmouth the army had lost all confidence in him. Hence, the general rejoicing at his removal and the total absence of sympathy over his downfall."[60]

On June 30, after the troops were inspected, a much more pleasant task was accomplished: since it was the last day of the month, the soldiers were paid! Then they rested during the day while their corps commander awaited orders from General Meade.[61] The Army of the Potomac had moved deep into Maryland. The First and Eleventh Corps had reached Emmitsburg. The Third Corps had arrived at Taneytown, and the Sixth Corps had moved to New Windsor. The Twelfth Corps was at Bruceville, and the Fifth Corps had reached Liberty. The enemy seemed to be concentrating along the South Mountain range between Chambersburg and a village named Cashtown. The two wings of Ewell's corps, by month's end, were marching westward from the Susquehanna River and southward from Carlisle toward the area of concentration of Lee's army.[62]

On July 1 the drummers beat "the general" at sunrise. Hancock received an order from Meade, then at Taneytown, to move the Second Corps there at once. Three days' rations of salt pork, hardtack, sugar, and coffee were issued to each man, and at about 7:00 A.M. the order was given to pack up. Cushing's battery sections hitched the guns and caissons to their limbers. At 8:00 A.M. the Second Corps moved out of the fields around Uniontown and onto the road to Taneytown.[63] After a grueling march, the head of the Second Corps columns arrived at Taneytown late in the morning. There the order "Break ranks" was barked out by weary officers, and the troops set about building fires for much-needed coffee. In the distance, all could hear the dull thunder of cannonading toward Gettysburg. What was occurring there, the men could only guess.[64]

West of the crossroads town of Gettysburg, less than ten miles ahead, the two armies had finally met. Early that morning, Maj. Gen. Henry Heth's division of Hill's Confederate Third Corps struck two brigades of Union cavalry commanded by Brig. Gen. John Buford. The Union First Corps had moved to Gettysburg early in the morning; General Reynolds led his troops onto the field, but moments after having placed an artillery battery along the Chambersburg Pike, he was killed. Howard's Eleventh Corps moved to Gettysburg from Emmitsburg as the fighting grew in intensity, and the First Corps, then under the command of Maj. Gen. Abner Doubleday, desperately held the rolling farmlands west of the town.[65] But the enemy was growing in numbers and firepower. By late morning the Third Corps division of Maj. Gen. William D. Pender was moving up behind Heth, and from the north Ewell's Second Corps was closing in on Gettysburg and the right flank of the hard-fighting Union First Corps.[66]

Back at Taneytown, General Hancock was directed to Meade's headquarters. The sound of guns toward Gettysburg seemed ominous, but Meade had as yet received no report of what was occurring there. The two generals discussed Meade's proposed Pipe Creek defense lines, and Hancock returned to his troops.[67] Just after Hancock left—about 11:30 A.M.—Meade received the message from hard-riding Capt. Stephen M. Weld of Reynolds's staff that Buford's two cavalry brigades and the First Corps had engaged the enemy west of Gettysburg and had been fighting there all morning long. At 1:00 P.M. another messenger, Maj. William Riddle, brought Meade the grievous news that General Reynolds had been killed in the morning engagement.[68]

Meade did not wait for messengers to locate Hancock and bring him to headquarters; rather, he rode to the Second Corps headquarters himself. Lon saw the army commander and his entourage ride up to Hancock's mobile command post, located on a farm owned by a Dr. Swope. Lon's two guns, with their limbers and caissons, were parked near the road that led directly to Gettysburg. The horses were still hitched to the limbers and were being watered and fed. Lon and his men were preparing coffee. Meade dismounted and was greeted by his hearty Second Corps commander. Meade told Hancock of the sad news about Reynolds; he then ordered him to transfer the command of the Second Corps to General Gibbon and to proceed immediately to Gettysburg and take command there.[69]

Hancock hesitated. He told Meade that he was outranked by two corps commanders, General Howard of the Eleventh and General Sickles of the Third Corps, whose troops were at or near Gettysburg. As well, he informed Meade that General Gibbon was not the ranking division commander in the Second Corps. Meade brushed Hancock's concerns aside, showing his Second Corps commander a letter from the Secretary of War authorizing him to make whatever changes he desired among the army's commanders. Hancock was satisfied. Meade told Hancock to proceed to the front and assume command of the corps assembled there. Meade further instructed Hancock that if he thought the ground and position at Gettysburg a good one on which to fight a battle, to send him notification and all the troops would then be ordered forward.[70] Hancock ordered General Gibbon to put the Second Corps on the march toward Gettysburg as soon as possible. Between 1:30 and 2:00 P.M. the men were on the move again.[71]

Plaguing the Second Corps commander throughout the entire campaign was the lack of adequate maps. Of the Gettysburg area he knew nothing. And, being new to corps command, Hancock was still in the process of assembling his staff. He needed all the help he could get, and it appears that he called upon Lon to go with him to the front. Lon had traveled with Hancock's entourage all the way to Taneytown from Falmouth, Virginia; he had served with great distinction on the staffs of two previous commanders of the Second Corps and on the staff of the commander of the Army of the Potomac; and much of his staff service had been performed in the field, directing the placement of troops or as a topographical engineer. His courageous staff service at Fredericksburg and Chancellorsville had been performed in the presence of General Hancock. Convincing evidence that Lon now accompanied Hancock is the fact that the brevet to the rank of lieutenant colonel posthumously awarded him as a result of the Battle of Gettysburg was given not for his service on July 3 but rather for his service on July 1! Noteworthy too is the fact that Col. Charles H. Morgan, Hancock's chief of staff, recalled that the general and his staff were accompanied to Gettysburg by "two or three other officers on duty at his headquarters." Further, the June 30, 1863, returns for Battery A, 4th United States Artillery, were never signed by Cushing; rather they were signed by Lt. Rufus King in late July, an indication that Lon was not with his battery at the time of its last muster or until it actually arrived at Gettysburg. One late nineteenth- and early twentieth-century writer of the lives of the Cushing brothers asserted, without authority save for family legend, that Lon accompanied Hancock to Gettysburg. On the whole, then, the evidence seems to place Lon in Hancock's company. Leaving Taneytown, he turned the command of his battery over to Lt. Samuel Canby.[72]

Hancock departed Taneytown in an ambulance brought to his headquarters from the rear of the Second Corps columns. On the rough road, Hancock and members of his staff studied their rather inadequate maps of the area. The ride proved slow, and only four miles into the journey the general became impatient. He ordered the ambulance stopped, stepped outside, and mounted his horse. Many of his staff officers mounted up as well. Off he galloped with his staff behind him, some on horses and others still in the rattling ambulance. Lon rode along behind the portly general. Near the crossroads called Barlow, they passed the ambulance carrying the body of General Reynolds. Hancock, Lon, and the others solemnly removed their hats at the passing of Reynolds's remains. Lon remembered Reynolds well from his days of West Point; he remembered him in the Cadet Chapel on the last Sunday before graduation. Now Reynolds was dead. From there on, the journey to Gettysburg became for Lon became a solemn one indeed.[73]

The closer they got to Gettysburg, the more the road became jammed with army trains and frightened and demoralized soldiers. General Hancock ordered all of the trains retired and the roads cleared. From his horse, Lon yelled at fleeing soldiers, exhorting them to return to their regiments at the front.[74] The entourage finally reached the Evergreen Cemetery on the heights just south of Gettysburg at about 3:30 P.M. Near the cemetery gatehouse, Hancock met General Howard and informed him of Meade's directive placing him in command of all the elements of the army in and near Gettysburg. Nearby, Hancock greeted General Buford as well as General Warren, the army's chief topographical engineer.[75]

What Hancock and Lon observed along the rolling farmlands and roads south and east of Gettysburg was an awesome spectacle of defeat. Early in the afternoon, Hill's and Ewell's two Confederate corps had renewed their assaults against the battered but brave ranks of the First Corps west of Gettysburg and two divisions of Howard's Eleventh Corps, which had been poorly positioned along rather low ground north of Gettysburg. Just as at Chancellorsville, the Eleventh Corps had been doomed from the start. In the face of Ewell's powerful thrust, the hapless corps had given way, exposing the right flank of the First Corps along the northern extension of Seminary Ridge. Unable to remain in its perilous position, the First Corps had withdrawn through the town, which had by then, become filled with fleeing soldiers of the Eleventh Corps. The victorious Confederates had pursued, capturing some 3,500 prisoners in the streets of the town. General Howard had positioned General Steinwehr's division along the foot of Cemetery Hill as a reserve when he first entered Gettysburg. The wisdom of that placement was apparent. To Steinwehr's position the remnants of the First and Eleventh Corps were fleeing for safety at the time of Hancock's arrival.[76]

Hancock's work was cut out for him. He and his staff—including Lon, who had had experience arresting fleeing soldiers at Fair Oaks, during the Seven Days' battles, and at Fredericksburg and Chancellorsville—directed the fugitives of the two broken corps to positions along Cemetery Hill and the heavily wooded eminences to the east, known locally as Culp's Hill. Hancock ordered the remnants of the First Corps under General Doubleday, with the exception of Gen. William Wadsworth's division, to be placed on the right and left of the Taneytown Road, facing west. The remnants of the Eleventh Corps were placed in a position around Steinwehr's division along Cemetery Hill, on both sides of the Baltimore Pike, facing west and north. General Wadsworth's First Corps division was directed to a position along Culp's Hill, supported by Lt. Greenleaf Stevens's 5th Maine Battery. Lon rode from unit to unit, directing the men to their positions and, at the same time, halting fleeing soldiers and directing them back to the defense lines. It was exhausting work. Approaching Gettysburg on the Baltimore Pike from Littlestown, Pennsylvania, was Gen. Henry W. Slocum's Twelfth Corps. Under orders from General Slocum, Gen. Alpheus S. Williams's division was placed along Culp's Hill to the right of Wadsworth's lines; and Gen. John W. Geary's division, under the direction of General Hancock, was moved to a position far to the south along an eminence known locally as Little Round Top, which Hancock had observed as he approached Gettysburg.[77]

Lee's exultant legions poured into Gettysburg. Ewell's corps took up positions in the town itself and along the ground below Cemetery and Culp's Hills. Hill's corps, partly occupying the town, extended the Confederate lines along the southern extension of the densely wooded Seminary Ridge south of Gettysburg. Hood's and McLaws's divisions of Longstreet's corps were marching toward Gettysburg. Lee, however, did not continue the attacks that evening.[78]

Having established the defense lines on the heights east and south of Gettysburg, Hancock sent his senior aide, Maj. W.G. Mitchell, to General Meade with an oral message that the army could hold the defensive positions along Cemetery and Culp's Hills until nightfall, and that given the superior ground the army held, he believed Gettysburg was a good place to offer Lee battle. Mitchell galloped down the Taneytown Road, passing through the dense masses of the Second Corps columns as they were marching toward the battlefield. Arriving at Meade's headquarters about 6:30 P.M., Mitchell delivered Hancock's message. Meade, trusting Hancock's judgment, sent Mitchell back to the Second Corps commander with the terse reply, "I will send up the troops!"[79]

Alonzo Cushing, his duties with General Hancock completed, was ordered to return to his battery. He met his guns as they were approaching along the Taneytown Road during the evening of July 1. For the march to Gettysburg, Lieutenant Canby had assembled the battery into one unit; his own section, with its caissons, was leading the battery, followed by Sergeant Fuger's and Lieutenant Milne's, each section commander riding just ahead of his leading drivers. Lon rode up alongside Fuger, just ahead of the center section. The guidon of the battery was carried alongside the leading horses of the first piece; near Lon were Buglers Albert Keyser and James Patterson. The battery wagons and forge rumbled along to the rear of the gun sections. The battery, in the vanguard of the hard-marching Second Corps, finally came to a halt around three miles south of Gettysburg, behind Little and Big Round Tops.[80]

Moving into park with Cushing's, Woodruff's, Arnold's, and Brown's Second Corps batteries that evening were the four Parrott rifles of Battery B, 1st New York Light Artillery. The New York battery had been ordered to join the Second Corps Artillery Brigade that day. Capt. Rufus Pettit had resigned as its commander just before it had been transferred to the Artillery Reserve in the wake of the Battle of Chancellorsville. To take his place, General Hancock had named none other than his own former ordnance officer and Lon's old Fenian friend, Capt. James McKay Rorty.[81]

The men of the Second Corps were aroused before dawn on July 2. Marching ranks were formed in the Taneytown Road preparatory to the final movement into position. Lon shouted the orders: "Battery at-tention! Drivers prepare to mount—mount—first piece—forward into line—march!" When all the guns, limbers, and caissons had reached their positions in the line of march, Lon ordered the battery forward. Bugles blared, the men and horses responded quickly, and the battery moved on up the Taneytown Road until it reached a sunken farm lane in front of the whitewashed frame house of the widow Lydia Leister. There it was directed west by Captain Hazard to a position along the summit of Cemetery Ridge near a large clump of chestnut oak trees.[82]

As Lon's battery came to a halt along the ridge, he looked over the position. To his right Capt. William A. Arnold's Battery A, 1st Rhode Island Light Artillery (six three-inch Ordnance rifles), was being brought into place, to the left, Lt. T. Fred Brown's Battery B, 1st Rhode Island Light Artillery (six twelve-pound Napoleons). About two hundred yards farther to the left was Captain Rorty's Battery B, 1st New York Light Artillery (four ten-pound Parrott rifles), while three hundred yards to the far right—beyond the whitewashed frame house and barn of a free black man named Abraham Brian, and in front of a crescent-shaped area of woods known locally as Ziegler's Grove—Little Dad Woodruff's Battery I, 1st United States Artillery was unlimbering (six twelve-pound Napoleons).[83]

In front of Lon was a low stone fence that ran chiefly north and south, defining the pasturelands of farmers Pius A. Small and Peter Frey. The fence angled east to the front and right of Lon's position, followed that course for about 125 yards back to where Lon brought his guns into position, then angled north again. Arnold's battery was positioned behind the stone wall's "inner" angle. Lon's guns were ordered to hold the space just to the left, or south, of the inner angle, in front of the section of the wall that ran south from the "outer" angle.[84]

"Forward into battery!" ordered Lon. Buglers Albert Keyser and James Patterson blew the shrill signal. Section by section, Lon brought his six Ordnance rifles into position along farmer Peter Frey's pastureland on Cemetery Ridge. Canby's leading section was the first to move into place on the right, just to the left or south of the inner angle and to the left of Arnold's battery. Fuger's center section was brought into position to the left of Canby's two guns, and Milne's section to the left of Fuger's guns and to the right of Brown's battery.[85]

Lon placed his six Ordnance rifles just under fourteen yards apart, giving ample room for the cannoneers to work. Six yards behind the handspikes of each piece were the heads of the lead horses pulling the limbers. Eleven yards behind the limbers were the heads of the lead horses pulling the caissons. Along the left flank of the battery was its guidon.[86]

Lon, mounted on his horse, took up a position just to the left of the center section of the battery. From there his commands could be heard by all his cannoneers and drivers. Albert Keyser and James Patterson stood alongside Lon, grasping their bugles. The section commanders—Canby on the right, Fuger in the center and Milne on the left—were all mounted, each positioned in the center of his section. Gunners Louis Blockinger, Thomas Whetston, Angus Brenan, James Murphy, Charles Au, Edwin Smedley, and Edward Hurley—all old army regulars who had served in Utah—commanded the gun detachments and the caissons.[87]

The gunners at the six Ordnance rifles took their positions at the end of the trailspikes; number one and two cannoneers, about two feet outside the wheels. Number three and four cannoneers lined up on either side of the knobs of the cascabels of the six guns, behind one and two. Number five cannoneers were positioned about five yards to the rear of the left wheels; number six, behind the limbers. Number seven cannoneers lined up to cover number five; number eight, the chiefs of the caissons, were positioned four yards in rear and to the left of the limbers. The drivers attended to the horses harnessed to the limbers and caissons.[88]

In front of the battery were broad, open, and undulating fields of rye, wheat, and oats. Just under one mile to the west Lon saw the long, dense strip of woods, running north and south, that defined the southern extension of Seminary Ridge. Between his position and Seminary Ridge coursed the Emmitsburg Road. On either side of the road were heavy post-and-rail fences, some of which, on the west side, had been torn down by Reynolds's First Corps when it had moved off of the road and marched across the fields to enter the fighting west of Gettysburg the day before. Along the east side of the Emmitsburg Road, to Lon's left front, stood the red brick house and red barn of farmer Nicholas Codori. Farther south, Lon could see the whitewashed house of Daniel Klingle. On the west side of the road, between the Klingle and Codori houses, stood the farmhouse of Peter Rogers, marked by its white picket fences. To Lon's right front, set back from the west side of Emmitsburg Road, was the brick house and fortresslike brick barn of farmer William Bliss.

Lon's guns formed the artillery support for General Webb's Philadelphia Brigade. In front and to the left of his battery, along the stone wall, was the 69th Pennsylvania. Upon their arrival along the ridge, the men of the 69th began clearing out the slashings and underbrush between the clump of trees and the wall. To the right of the battery, along the stone wall at the outer angle, were Companies A and B of the 71st Pennsylvania; the rest of the regiment was behind Lon's guns. Behind and to the left of Cushing's guns were the 72d and 106th Pennsylvania, of which two companies each were detailed as skirmishers in the fields out along the west side of the Emmitsburg Road.[89]

To the left of Cushing's battery and Webb's Philadelphians was the brigade of Col. Norman J. Hall, with the 59th New York, 7th Michigan, and 20th Massachusetts holding the line along the low stone fence, and the 19th Massachusetts and 42d New York forming the reserve. To Hall's rear, in reserve, was the brigade of Gen. William Harrow: the 15th Massachusets, 19th Maine, 1st Minnesota and 82d New York. To the left of Hall's and Harrow's brigades was General Caldwell's First Division of the Second Corps. Sickles's Third Corps, which had arrived on the field from Emmitsburg the evening before, formed on the left of Caldwell's division, extending the defense lines nearly all the way to the base of Little Round Top.[90]

To Lon's right, just beyond Arnold's battery, was Col. Thomas Smyth's Second Brigade of Hays's Third Division: the 14th Connecticut, 12th New Jersey, and 108th New York. Joining the companies of the 106th and 72d Pennsylvania as skirmishers along the Emmitsburg Road was the 1st Delaware of Smyth's brigade; his 10th New York was on duty at Meade's headquarters. To Smyth's right and partly in reserve was Col. George L. Willard's Third Brigade: the 39th, 111th, 125th, and 126th New York. The First Brigade of Hays's Division, commanded by Col. Samuel S. Carroll—the 14th Indiana, 4th and 8th Ohio, and 7th West Virginia—held the line to the right of Willard and to the left of the remnants of the Eleventh and First Corps along the western face of Cemetery Hill.[91]

No sooner had Lon's battery taken up its position near the center of the Second Corps lines than its cannoneers and the infantrymen in Hays's division began to be annoyed by Confederate sharpshooters from inside the Bliss barn, across the Emmitsburg Road, to the right front. With the commands "Fire to the right, forty-five degrees" and "Change front forward on the right piece," Lon brought his battery into a position facing northwest to direct its fire at the brick barn. Calling for case shot and shell, the cannoneers loaded the six Ordnance rifles.[92]

"Ready," yelled the section chiefs, one by one.

"Number one, fire!" shouted Lon. "Number two, fire! Number three, fire!"

The guns boomed, and the shells burst in and around the Bliss barn and farmyard. The shellfire soon became too hot for the Confederate snipers, and they abandoned the building. After calling to his cannoneers to "cease firing," Lon brought his battery back into its original position along the ridge, facing west.[93] By 11:00 A.M.,however, the action around the Bliss barn was renewed. Brig. Gen. Carnot Posey, commanding a brigade in Hill's corps, advanced his 19th and 48th Mississippi infantry regiments out toward the barn. Lon again called for his battery to reposition itself obliquely to the right, facing northwest, and opened fire with case shot and shell. The effect was telling; within thirty minutes the Confederate columns fell back.[94]

Lee had been active all through the morning of July 2. Hood's and McLaws's divisions of Longstreet's corps, except for Brig. Gen. Evander McIvor Law's brigade, had arrived on the battlefield the night before. Reconnaissance parties had been probing the Union flanks, particularly the Union left flank south of the round tops. By the late morning, Lee had determined to strike Meade. Upon the arrival of Law's brigade, which had hastened to Gettysburg from Chambersburg, Lee directed Hood's and McLaws's divisions from their bivouac sites along Herr Ridge, between the Chambersburg and Hagerstown Roads, on a wide march along Seminary Ridge to positions behind that ridge, south of and partly straddling the Millerstown Road. The planned attacks of Hood's and McLaws's divisions, once launched, would be followed by assaults of Anderson's and Pender's divisions of Hill's corps up the Emmitsburg Road, toward the Union lines along Cemetery Ridge. At the same time, Ewell's corps would assault Union positions along Culp's Hill and Cemetery Hill.[95]

No sooner had Hood's and McLaws's divisions stepped off on their march than the soldiers of the Second Corps were greeted by an awe-inspiring spectacle. Shortly before 1:00 P.M., Gen. Sickles moved his entire Union Third Corps out of line and headed across the open fields to positions along the Emmitsburg Road. Brig. Gen. Andrew A. Humphreys, who had been transferred from the Fifth Corps to command of the Second Division in Sickles's Corps after the Battle of Chancellorsville, brought his division to a halt out along the Emmitsburg Road, facing west, and forming a line that began just south of the Codori house and barn and proceeded all the way to the intersection of the Millerstown Road and a peach orchard owned by a farmer named John Sherfy. Connecting with and at a right angle to Humphreys's left, Sickles placed Maj. Gen. David B. Birney's First Division along high ground from the peach orchard east, all the way to an area of huge boulders below the round tops, known locally as "Devil's Den."[96]

Well in advance of the line of the Second Corps along Cemetery Ridge, Sickles's Third Corps, although occupying somewhat higher ground, was wholly unsupported, its flanks entirely unprotected. Unknown to General Sickles, two powerful Confederate divisions were moving into place directly in front of him. Lon could not believe his eyes. Seeing the movement of Sickles's corps, Gen. Henry Hunt, chief of artillery of the Army of the Potomac, rode out to the front, urgently calling forward batteries from the Artillery Reserve parked behind the round top to bolster the Third Corps lines. By midafternoon, Maj. Freeman McGilvery's and Col. Dunbar Ransom's brigades from the Artillery Reserve were on the field. One by one, the batteries were ordered into line by General Hunt. Three of McGilvery's batteries were posted along General Birney's front; directed to positions along the Emmitsburg Road, supporting General Humphreys's division, were batteries from Ransom's brigade. One battery, Lt. Evan Thomas's Battery C, 4th United States Artillery, was positioned in the fields along General Gibbon's left flank.[97]

Concerned about his own front as well as Sickles's unprotected right flank, General Gibbon ordered forward the 82d New York and the 15th Massachusetts of General Harrow's brigade to hold a line on the east side of the Emmitsburg Road, directly ahead of Lon's position. The 82d New York formed on the left—just to the right of the Codori house—and the 15th Massachusetts formed on the New Yorkers' right. The movement of Sickles's corps and the two regiments from Harrow's brigade left a yawning gap between those advanced units and the main line along Cemetery Ridge. Lon could see the danger immediately. Into that space General Hancock ordered Brown's battery. The guns were limbered up and advanced out into the Codori and Small fields in front and to the left of Lon's position. The six Napoleons were brought into position facing northwest, the left gun several hundred yards from the Codori house, to the rear of the 82d New York and the 15th Massachusetts, and the right gun about one hundred yards in front of the clump of trees and the 69th Pennsylvania. The battery was situated along a slight knoll at about a forty-five degree angle to the main Second Corps lines. Brown's Rhode Islanders became engaged with a Confederate battery along Seminary Ridge almost as soon as they had brought their guns into position.[98]

General Meade, accompanied by General Warren, rode out to Sickles's front. Meade had already despatched urgent orders for General Sykes, whose Fifth Corps had arrived at Gettysburg that morning and was positioned along the Baltimore Pike, to send his divisions to fill the gap left by Sickles's advance. While inspecting the Third Corps lines, Warren noticed that the two round tops on Sickles's left were completely unprotected. Little Round Top, an eminence at the southern extension of Meade's Cemetery Ridge defense lines, had been stripped of timber along its western and part of its southern and northern faces. It commanded the Union positions. As early as dawn, with the arrival into line of Sickles' Third Corps, General Geary's division had returned to the Twelfth Corps lines along Culp's Hill, leaving Little Round Top unoccupied save for a small number of signalmen.[99]

General Warren raced to Little Round Top with his two aides, Lt.

Washington A. Roebling and Lon's friend Lt. Ranald S. Mackenzie. Artillery firing and skirmishing had already broken out along the contending lines. Ascending the northern slope and reaching the summit, Warren met a horrifying spectacle. Looking down on Sickles's ill-placed corps, he could see that Birney's division did not cover the approaches to Little Round Top; rather, the left flank of the division was anchored along the enormous boulders of Devil's Den. From Devil's Den to the summit of Little Round Top, there was nothing to stop a Confederate advance. Ahead, Warren could see the dense masses of Confederates from General Hood's division forming for an assault. Those lines, once advanced, would completely overlap Sickles's left, and Little Round Top would be theirs for the taking![100]

General Hood's division, with Brig. Gens. Evander McIvor Law's Alabamians and Jerome B. Robertson's Texans and Arkansans, followed by Brig. Gens. George T. Anderson's and Henry L. Benning's Georgians, slammed into General Birney's lines. Law's brigade, on the right, was directed around Birney's left flank, then moved up the western slope of Big Round Top, faced north, and moved against the southern slope of Little Round Top. Robertson's brigade, on Law's left, headed straight for the Union lines along Devil's Den.[101]

With the fields below erupting in flame and smoke, and with the key to the Union position imperiled, Warren rode back down the slope of Little Round Top to find help. Approaching the battlefield was Brig. Gen. James Barnes's division of Sykes's Fifth Corps, which General Meade had ordered forward. Warren rode up to Harvard-educated Col. Strong Vincent, commander of the Third Brigade of Barnes's division, and ordered him to take his brigade to the summit of Little Round Top. Barnes's remaining two brigades, Col. William S. Tilton's and Col. Jacob B. Sweitzer's, pressed on ahead to the aid of Sickles.[102]

Time was of the essence! Colonel Vincent led his four regiments up the northern slope to the summit of Little Round Top. In minutes, they deployed and engaged General Law's Alabamians along the southern slope of the eminence. Vincent's left flank was anchored by Col. Joshua Chamberlain's 20th Maine; his own 83d Pennsylvania held the center, supported by the 44th New York, with the 16th Michigan on the right. The fighting became bitter and confused as dense smoke engulfed the hillside. "I wish that I could picture with my pen the awful details of that hour," wrote a soldier in the 20th Maine, "how rapidly the cartridges were torn from the boxes and stuffed in the smoking muzzles of the guns; how the steel rammers clashed and clanged in the heated barrels; how the men's hands and faces grew grim and black with burning powder; how our little line, baptized with fire, reeled to and fro as it advanced or was pressed back; how our officers bravely exposed themselves to the enemy's fire—a terrible medley of cries, shouts, cheers, groans, prayers, curses, bursting shells, whizzing rifle bullets and clanging steel . . . The air seemed to be alive with lead. The lines at times were so near each other that the hostile gun barrels almost touched."[103]

Moving out into the fields behind the brigades of Colonels Tilton and Sweitzer was Lt. Charles E. Hazlett's Battery D, 5th United States Artillery—the old West Point Battery. When first ordered forward, Hazlett had hesitated. During the march to Gettysburg he had received the dreaded news of the death of his brother, Capt. John C. Hazlett, who had been horribly wounded while leading Company E of the 2d Ohio at Stones River on December 31, 1862. Charles, overwhelmed by the sad news, had a premonition that he himself would die in the next engagement. Fifth Corps Artillery Brigade commander Capt. Augustus P. Martin heard Hazlett's appeal not to move forward but brushed it aside. Resolved not to give in to his fears, the brave Hazlett moved his guns to positions behind Tilton's and Sweitzer's brigades.[104] Martin told Hazlett to accompany him to the summit of Little Round Top to see whether artillery could be placed there. At the top, the two artillerymen immediately saw the need for field guns. General Warren did not believe artillery could be effective in such a position. "Never mind that," Hazlett said. "The sound of my guns will be encouraging to our troops and disheartening to the others, and my battery's of no use if this hill is lost."[105] He rode back down the hill, calling to his second-in-command, Lt. Benjamin F. Rittenhouse, to bring the battery up the northern slope. One by one the guns were pulled and pushed up the rocky slope; the number two gun in the right section came into place first, followed by the number one gun. So difficult was it to move the guns up the slope that General Warren even helped push one of the pieces.[106] Nevertheless, amid the roar of battle, Hazlett managed to bring four of his guns into battery along the summit. "He sat on his horse on the summit of the hill," recalled Warren, "with whole-souled animation encouraging our men, and pointing with his sword toward the enemy amidst the storm of bullets—a figure of intense admiration to me, even in that desperate scene . . . There stood the impersonation of valor and heroic beauty."[107]

With the cannoneers hauling ammunition to the guns by hand from the limbers and caissons at the foot of the slope, Hazlett's first four guns opened fire. As Hood's division pressed Sickles's lines back from Devil's Den, Hazlett directed his fire toward the butternut and gray masses, while cannoneers continued to push his remaining two guns up the northern slope of the hill.[108] But General Birney's left was crushed in minutes. General Robertson's Texans and Arkansans joined Law's Alabamians as they raced across the Plum Run Valley and up the slopes against Vincent's hard-fighting lines, now extended along the southern and western faces of Little Round Top. While trying to steady his men, Colonel Vincent fell; he would die on July 7 in the farmhouse of Lewis A. Bushman just behind Little Round Top. The situation was critical. More infantry was needed.[109]

Gen. Stephen Weed's brigade of Brig. Gen. Romeyn B. Ayres's Second Division of the Fifth Corps had been resting a little more than one-half mile from Little Round Top when the firing became heavy. General Weed and Lon's classmate Colonel O'Rorke had been singing the song "Some one to love, some one to cherish" when word came to move on the double in support of the Third Corps. Bugles had sounded, and the brigade had started its march to the fateful field. The Zouave 140th New York was in the lead, its men—mostly German and Irish—dressed in their baggy red pantaloons, blue monkey jackets, and red fezzes with white turbans. When the brigade reached the base of Little Round Top, General Warren, who had commanded Weed's brigade at Fredericksburg, rode to the head of the column, shouting, "Paddy, give me a regiment!" O'Rorke replied, "General, select a position." "Take your command," yelled Warren, "and secure the hill before the enemy reaches it; that position must not be lost." O'Rorke aligned his command in columns of four and ordered it to ascend the hill on the double-quick. Through the ranks of O'Rorke's infantrymen were pushed the remaining two guns of Hazlett's battery.[110]

When the 140th New York reached the summit of Little Round Top, O'Rorke dismounted, drew his sword, and shouted to his men, "Follow me, my brave boys." In front of the two leading companies of the regiment, he took the command in a southwesterly direction down the slope to within forty feet of the enemy. "Here they are, men. Commence firing," he ordered. Instantly, Paddy O'Rorke fell with a gunshot wound in the throat. He was dead within minutes. The rest of General Weed's brigade—the 91st Pennsylvania along with the 146th New York and 155th Pennsylvania, both Zouave regiments—rushed up the slope behind the 140th New York. By then the fighting had become terrific.[111]

After conferring with Sickles and Sykes, General Weed had ridden to the summit of Little Round Top. He was standing alongside Hazlett's booming guns when he was shot down. Paralyzed below the shoulders by the wound, Weed called for Lieutenant Hazlett, and Rittenhouse yelled for Hazlett to come quickly. Kneeling beside Weed and leaning over to hear his last words, Hazlett was struck in the head by a bullet and fell over the mortally wounded general. Both men were taken back to the Jacob Weikert house behind Little Round Top. Weed died there after lapsing into unconsciousness; Hazlett, who never regained consciousness, died at 8:00 P.M. that night. In a matter of minutes, two of Lon's closest West Point friends had fallen, but Little Round Top had been saved.[112]

From his position along Cemetery Ridge, Lon could see the dense smoke and could hear the deafening roar of gunfire from Little Round Top. The cannoneers and drivers and horses in his battery were tense. What success the enemy had had was unknown to Lon, but he could tell that the fighting would reach his position before long. More and more elements of the Army of the Potomac were being shifted toward the raging inferno in the fields to the south.

At about 4:30 P.M., fifty-four Confederate guns from Col. Henry C. Cabell's battalion and Col. E. Porter Alexander's artillery reserve of Longstreet's corps opened fire on Sickles's advanced lines, concentrating their firepower on the Union troops holding the peach orchard salient along the Emmitsburg Road. Stepping off in the attack was the division of General McLaws, with Brig. Gens. Joseph B. Kershaw's brigade of South Carolinians and Paul Jones Semmes's brigade of Georgians on the right and Brig. Gens. William Barksdale's brigade of Mississippians and William Wofford's brigade of Georgians on the left. Kershaw and Semmes rushed across the fields of farmer George W. Rose into Birney's staggering lines. Barksdale and Wofford struck the Union lines along the Emmitsburg Road north of the peach orchard and along the Sherfy farm. McLaws's division overwhelmed the peach orchard salient, and the right flank of his division stormed into a large wheatfield just west of Devil's Den, only to be held up by the stubborn fighting of Birney's veteran troops and the arrival of Tilton's and Sweitzer's brigades of the Fifth Corps.[113]

The fighting in the wheatfield swayed back and forth; it was often hand to hand, the contending forces using bayonets and clubbed muskets. The dead and wounded began to litter the fields and pile up in front of stone fences. The musketry was ferocious and the smoke dense. General Birney's regiments were decimated; the Fifth Corps brigades were unable to turn back the horrendous assaults. General Hancock rode up to General Caldwell on Cemetery Ridge and ordered him to send his First Division of the Second Corps across the fields and into the fight. The moment was not without its poignant scene. Shells screeched through the air, bursting all around, and the noise of the gunfire was absolutely deafening when Father William Corby, the Irish Brigade chaplain, mounted a large boulder. With the men of his brigade "prostrated . . . in humble adoration of the true God," Corby reminded them to do their duty and fear nothing; he then "absolved" them of their sins. Moving by the left flank, Caldwell's division assumed a position on the right of the Fifth Corps and the left of Birney's battered lines. Lon watched as it disappeared into the dense banks of smoke along the fields south of his position. Gibbon's division was now all that remained to anchor the left flank of the army along Cemetery Ridge. Caldwell ordered Cross's First Brigade forward into the wheatfield, already littered with dead and wounded. Advancing only a short distance, Cross was met by furious gunfire that drove him to the east end of the field; he was mortally wounded in the melee. In the meantime, Caldwell placed the Irish Brigade to the right of Cross's brigade and Zook's Third Brigade to the right of the Irishmen and sent them across the bloody, smoke-engulfed fields. Soon Zook fell with a mortal wound. As Colonel Brooke's brigade was directed to the relief of Cross's battered command, the battle reached its full fury, and the Confederates were driven back through the wheatfield. Then, as Caldwell's attack spent itself, the momentum shifted again, and the brave Second Corps soldiers fell back, leaving a carpet of dead and wounded behind.[114]

General Sickles was seriously wounded and taken to the rear. His corps was battered and broken. With Birney's lines slowly giving way in the face of Hood's and McLaws's determined assaults, General Humphreys's division was imperiled. The more ground Birney and his supports gave up, the farther into the rear of Humphreys's division the exultant Confederates drove. To add to the discomfort of Humphreys's soldiers along the Emmitsburg Road, Lee's assaults up that road continued. Brig. Gen. Cadmus Wilcox's brigade of Alabamians and Col. David Lang's brigade of Floridians (formerly led by Brig. Gen. Edward A. Perry, who had contracted typhoid fever after the Chancellorsville campaign) moved across the fields to the left of Barksdale and Wofford, striking Humphreys's division head on. "Our batteries ploughed lanes through the living masses in front of them," recalled a soldier in the 11th New Jersey near the Klingle house, "yet on [the enemy] pressed." It became a desperate struggle along the Emmitsburg Road. Union regiments changed front to meet enemy breakthroughs and then dissolved, only to have knots of survivors rally around shot-torn battleflags or sword-waving field officers in the fields to the rear. All the time, the Confederate attack pressed closer and closer to Lon's position along Cemetery Ridge; all the time the losses mounted on both sides.[115]

Hancock ordered forward Lt. Gulian Verplanck Weir's Battery C, 5th United States Artillery, of Colonel Ransom's Artillery Reserve, into the fields south of the Codori house and barn, about five hundred yards ahead of General Harrow's main brigade line, to meet the attack of Lang's Floridians. Gulian Weir, born at West Point, New York, in 1837, was well-known to Lon. His father, Robert Weir, Lon's professor of drawing at the academy, had painted the scene with the figures representing "Peace" and "War" which was mounted over the chancel in the Cadet Chapel. Lieutenant Weir did not attend the academy; rather, he joined the 7th

New York State Militia at the outbreak of the war and then obtained a commission in the 5th Artillery in May 1861. His battery, like Evan Thomas's, consisted of six light twelve-pound Napoleons. To the left and front of Weir's guns, Hancock directed the 19th Maine of Harrow's brigade.[116]

Colonel Willard's Second Corps brigade was ordered by Hancock to move to the left to bolster Sickles's collapsing front in the face of Barksdale's and Wilcox's attacks. On the double, Willard led his men behind Lon and down the ridge toward the battlefront, joined by elements of the Twelfth Corps and the newly arrived Sixth Corps. In those bloody fields just south of Lon, Colonel Willard was killed, part of his head being carried away by an artillery shell.[117] Lon could get only momentary glimpses of the terrible struggle along the Emmitsburg Road. The smoke was extraordinarily dense and the fighting confused, but through his field glasses he watched Sickles's front give way. The attacks were moving steadily and ominously toward his perilous position.

By 6:00 P.M. more Confederate columns were observed emerging from the dense woods along Seminary Ridge. Brig. Gen. Ambrose R. Wright's brigade—the 3d, 22d, and 48th Georgia regiments and 2d Georgia battalion—of Anderson's Third Corps division, forming on the left of Colonel Lang's brigade, was moving directly toward the Codori house and the two Second Corps regiments posted along the Emmitsburg Road. The Georgians let out a yell and raced toward the road. The skirmishers from the 72d Pennsylvania fled to the rear. The 82d New York and 15th Massachusetts, behind volleys of rifle fire, held their ground until they were overlapped by the charging enemy brigade. The commanders of both regiments—Lt. Col. James Huston and Col. George H. Ward, respectively—fell in the Codori fields as their units were pushed back.[118]

To the left of the Codori house and barn, Lieutenant Weir's horse was shot down beneath him, and then, he was wounded. Three of his Napoleons were left behind as he tried to extricate his battery in the face of Lang's advance against his front and Wright's advance to his right. Weir withdrew his three remaining guns to a position to the left of General Harrow's brigade along Cemetery Ridge. Only a charge of the 19th Maine recovered the abandoned guns and halted Lang's attack.[119]

To the left of Weir's battery and the 19th Maine a serious gap had been opened in the remnants of Humphreys's division. Wilcox's yelling Alabamians stormed through the breach and across the pastures toward the left flank of Gibbon's division. General Hancock, seeing the approaching infantry columns, rode up to the 1st Minnesota in General Harrow's brigade, then supporting Thomas's guns. Pointing to the enemy, Hancock yelled to Col. William Colvill, Jr., the regimental commander, "Charge those lines!" Waving his sword, Colonel Colvill—a native of Chautauqua

County, New York, and a graduate of the Fredonia Academy—advanced his brave Minnesotans across the smoke-laden fields, directly into the enemy columns. The 1st Minnesota broke up Wilcox's attack but suffered the loss of nearly 82 percent of its 262 officers and men in roughly fifteen minutes of fighting.[120]

As Wright's Georgians pressed forward against the Codori house, the skirmishers from the 106th Pennsylvania still on the west side of the Emmitsburg Road observed a heavy Confederate column moving out from Seminary Ridge toward the Bliss house and barn. It was Gen. Carnot Posey's brigade of Mississippians. Dislodging the 1st Delaware, the Mississippians threatened the skirmishers. Reinforcements were urgently needed. The brave Pennsylvanians were alone on the flank of one enemy brigade and in the rear another! They nevertheless opened fire in an effort to purchase time.[121]

General Hays, seeing the growing threat to his front, rode up to Colonel Smyth. "Have you a regiment that will drive them out?" Hays asked. "Yes sir," replied Smyth, "the 12th New Jersey will do it." Smyth called for volunteers, and the whole regiment responded. "But I don't want all of you," yelled Hays. "Send four companies."[122] Four companies were selected. They formed ranks, faced to the right in front of the stone fence, and then marched past the Abraham Brian house. Forming in columns of companies, the men gave three cheers for Colonel Smyth and three more cheers for New Jersey, then swept across the fields toward the Bliss barn "like a cyclone." Aided by the 1st Delaware and the skirmishers of the 106th Pennsylvania, the New Jersey soldiers broke the advance of the Mississippians, forcing them to withdraw.[123]

Back along the Codori and Small fields in front of Lon's guns, Lt. T. Fred Brown ordered his battery to change front to the left to meet the attack of Wright's Georgians. The Rhode Island cannoneers responded, and the left and center sections of the battery were pivoted to the left into positions facing southwest; the enemy was coming forward so rapidly that there was no time to swing the right two guns into position. Darkness was falling, and the smoke was dense. Brown ordered his cannoneers to fire case shot and shells and to cut the fuses for three seconds. The four guns were loaded and fired. The shells burst among the approaching Georgians, staggering but not halting the attack. Brown called for the fuses of the next rounds to be cut for two seconds as the enemy continued to move closer. One by one, the four Napoleons blasted forth their death-dealing fury. The enemy, closing ranks behind those killed and wounded by the artillery fire, continued to move closer. Brown ordered the shell fuses to be cut for one second! All guns were loaded. As each piece was fired, the shells appeared to burst just as it exited the muzzle of the gun. The brave lieutenant then called for double-shotted

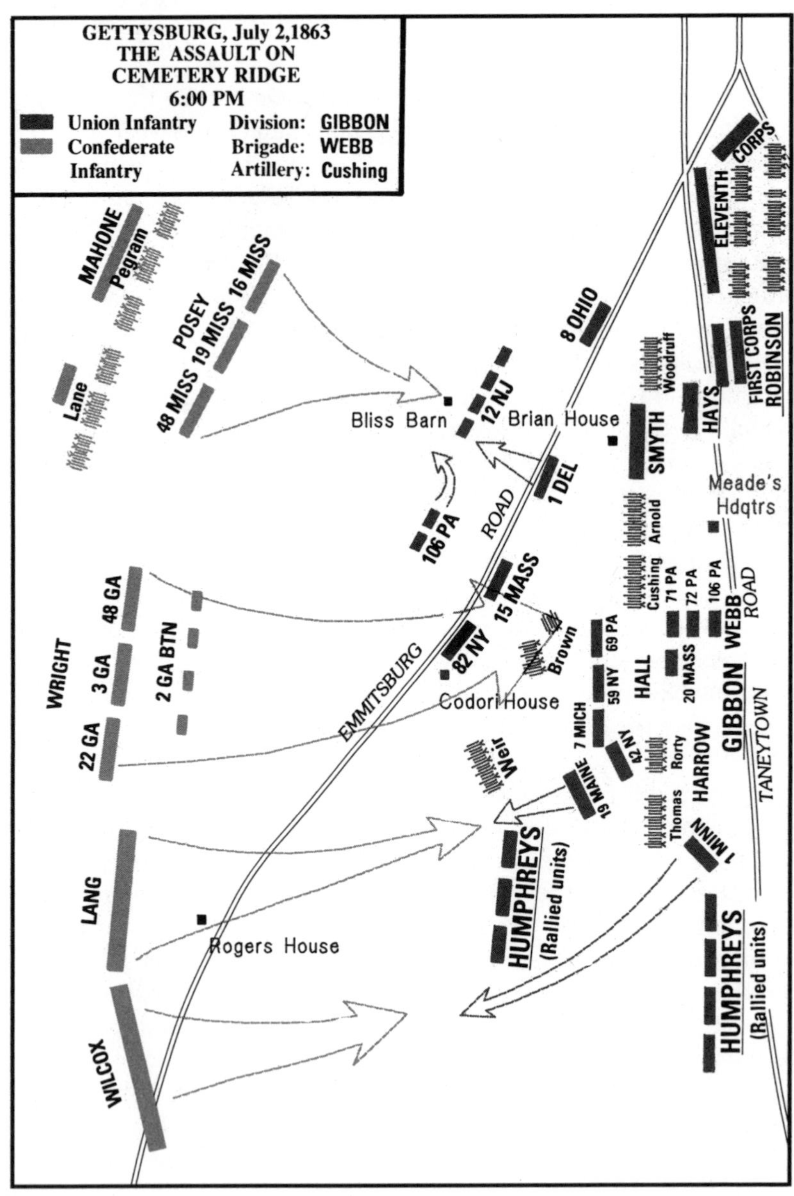
GETTYSBURG, July 2,1863
THE ASSAULT ON
CEMETERY RIDGE
6:00 PM
Union Infantry
Confederate Infantry
Division: GIBBON
Brigade: WEBB
Artillery: Cushing
MAHONE
Pegram
POSEY
16 MISS
19 MISS
48 MISS
Lane
8 OHIO
12 NJ
Bliss Barn
Brian House
1 DEL
SMYTH
Woodruff
HAYS
ELEVENTH CORPS
FIRST CORPS
ROBINSON
Meade's Hdqtrs
Arnold
106 PA
ROAD
15 MASS
82 NY
48 GA
3 GA
22 GA
2 GA BTN
WRIGHT
Brown
Codori House
EMMITSBURG
Cushing
71 PA
72 PA
106 PA
WEBB
ROAD
69 PA
59 NY
HALL
20 MASS
GIBBON
TANEYTOWN
7 MICH
42 NY
Rorty
HARROW
Weir
19 MAINE
Thomas
1 MINN
LANG
HUMPHREYS
(Rallied units)
Rogers House
WILCOX

canister, as Wright's yelling legions, their ranks bloodied and thinned, stormed up the ridge toward the Rhode Island battery.[124]

Infantrymen along Cemetery Ridge yelled to the Rhode Islanders above the din, "Get out of that, you will be killed!" Cannoneers in Lon's battery called out, "Don't give up the guns!" Brown, having run out of time, ordered his cannoneers and drivers to "limber to the rear!" The cannoneers worked feverishly to hitch the guns to the limbers. The right section was pulled back toward the main Second Corps lines, but the Confederates reached the left section before both guns could be removed. The left and center sections were then stalled by an enfilading fire poured into the cannoneers and drivers by the hard-charging Georgians, whose lines completely overlapped the Rhode Islanders. Men and horses fell in great numbers. Few along Cemetery Ridge could see what was happening in the falling darkness and heavy smoke. Brown was badly wounded in the neck, and Lt. W.S. Perrin took over command of the battery. Three of Brown's men had been killed and seventeen wounded. Nearly thirty battery horses had fallen; left on the field as a result were the numbers four and six guns of the battery, both still hitched to the limbers. The remaining guns were hauled through a gap in the stone wall, unlimbered, and brought into position again alongside Lon's battery.[125]

The center of the Second Corps line, from Lon's battery to Rorty's guns, suddenly became the objective of the Georgians. By this time Lon's three section commanders had dismounted and were directing the fire of their guns on foot. From alongside Brown's abandoned guns, the Georgians poured heavy volleys of rifle fire into Lon's cannoneers. Lieutenant Canby fell, struck in the hand, and Lon ordered him taken to the rear. Cannoneers began to fall rapidly. Pvt. Andrew Missimer was killed, as was Pvt. Sylvester Brown of the 1st Company, Minnesota Sharpshooters, attached. Pvt. John Kuntz was hit in the head, Joseph Kibler in the arm, William Schmidt in the shoulder, Frederick Ensign in the thigh; Pvts. Adam Schriner and William Grandon received leg wounds. Wounded also were Pvts. Norton L. Newbury, William Smith, and Henry Burtruff. With the loss of Canby, Lon, probably still mounted, called to Sergeant Fuger, Lieutenant Milne, and the cannoneers that the battery would be realigned, for purposes of command, into two three-gun sections; Milne would command the right three guns and Fuger the left.[126]

In the fields ahead, the Georgians seized the opportunity to make use of the guns the Rhode Islanders had left behind. Unlimbering them in the face of withering gunfire from Webb's and Hall's infantrymen, the Confederates attempted to load the guns and fire them into Cushing's battery. Into the Georgians' right flank, Rorty's four Parrott rifles and Thomas's six Napoleons poured forth a devastating fire of canister. From Milne's three and Arnold's six Ordnance rifles round upon round of canister was fired into the Georgians' left. Lon ordered the left three guns of his battery, "Fire to the left, forty-five degrees." Fuger ordered his three Ordnance rifles trained on the brave Georgians who were loading the captured guns in the fields ahead. The Ordnance rifles were loaded with single rounds of canister.

"Ready," called out Fuger. Infantrymen in the 69th Pennsylvania ahead of the guns scattered to positions of safety.

"Fire!" yelled Lon.

The three guns boomed, shattering the two Napoleons and killing and wounding large numbers of the Georgians. Milne kept up a steady fire with his three Ordnance rifles on the right. With gunfire pouring into their ranks from right and left, and with no supports on either side of them, Wright's Georgians slowly gave way.[127]

General Hancock rode up behind Colonel Hall's brigade to observe the heavy fighting. Seeing the Confederate attack waver under the heavy artillery fire, he ordered the 72d and 106th Pennsylvania forward. The 106th advanced to within sixty yards of the enemy. Standing alongside Lon's cannoneers, the infantrymen fired several volleys. Then, waving his sword, the regimental commander of the 106th, Col. W.L. Curry, ordered his men to charge the enemy. The Pennsylvanians, yelling beneath their flapping national colors, rushed over the wall and drove the Georgians all the way to the Emmitsburg Road, followed by the 82d New York.[128]

As the fighting reached its peak along Cemetery Ridge, a heavy artillery bombardment signaled the commencement of attacks along Culp's Hill and Cemetery Hill. The artillery firing in front of those positions continued unabated for nearly one hour, with the batteries from the First, Eleventh, and Twelfth Corps and the Artillery Reserve returning the fire. Then, just before dark, behind yells, shouts, and deafening rifle fire, Gen. Allegheny Johnson's Confederate division struck the Union defense lines along Culp's Hill. Soon thereafter General Early, with Brig. Gen. Harry T. Hays's Louisianians and Col. Isaac E. Avery's North Carolinians, stormed toward East Cemetery Hill. The hard-charging Confederates reached the summit in front of the cemetery gatehouse, where cannoneers beat the attackers back with sponge staffs and handspikes. Then, to the relief of the hard-pressed defenders of the hill, Hancock ordered forward Colonel Carroll's brigade from Hays's division, along with the 71st Pennsylvania and all of the weary 106th Pennsylvania except a skirmish detail along the Emmitsburg Road. With the arrival of the Second Corps regiments, the attackers were overwhelmed; they slowly withdrew back down the bloody slopes of East Cemetery Hill. Farther east, General Johnson's Confederates had by nightfall fought their way to the Union breastworks, where they precariously held on just a few hundred yards from the

Baltimore Pike and the Union rear. The 71st Pennsylvania and two companies of the 106th Pennsylvania returned to the angle at midnight.[129]

The fighting ended in the darkness. As the evening grew deeper, the moonlight cast eerie shadows over the dismal battlefield. In front of Lon lay more than thirty dead horses, some actually along the low stone wall. Wright's Georgia brigade had lost a staggering 688 killed and wounded, and many of the maimed howled and cried all through the night, though medical teams sought to clear the fields of the wounded of both sides. The dense smoke still hung close to the ground, and its noxious odor, coupled with the growing stench of the dead, filled the air.[130]

All up and down the lines, soldiers were hearing and passing rumors of movements and news of the loss of family members or those they had known. Late that night news arrived at Lon's battery of the deaths of Paddy O'Rorke and Charles Hazlett. It was a sad moment, but Lon received the news in much the same way as his classmate Little Dad Woodruff did. Woodruff remarked to Col. Francis Edwin Pierce, commander of the 108th New York, that O'Rorke's death was "a glorious termination of existence." Colonel Pierce, when he heard those words, thought that Little Dad "almost envied" O'Rorke.[131]

9

"By Hand to the Front!"

All through the night Lon and his men heard the sounds of gunfire: occasional artillery salvos, intermittent shots from skirmishers, and sudden bursts of musketry where the opposing armies' positions were separated only by a small pasture, creek, fenceline, or trench. Infantrymen from the 69th and 71st Pennsylvania roamed through the bloody fields ahead, scouring muskets and cartridges from the fallen Confederates. They believed they would need them for the next day's fighting. Within the Union lines the body of Lt. Charles E. Hazlett was buried in the garden of Jacob Weikert behind Little Round Top, and the remains of Col. Patrick H. O'Rorke in the farmyard of Lewis A. Bushman just east of Little Round Top.[1]

The scene ahead of Lon was sickening. The bodies of the fallen lay everywhere; the wounded still moaned and cried. Dead and wounded Georgians were mingled with Bay Staters, New Yorkers, Pennsylvanians, and Rhode Islanders. The cannoneers of Brown's battery had removed the shattered Napoleon guns that the Georgians had seized but had been unable to fire or take from the field. Dead artillery horses—nearly thirty of them—were sprawled along the ridge from the stone wall all the way to the Codori fields, some still harnessed to the tongues of wrecked caissons. Medical teams had worked all through the night tending the wounded, while burial squads hastily dug trenches for the dead.[2]

Twenty-two-year-old Alonzo H. Cushing stood out in the crowd of soldiers along Cemetery Ridge. His athletic five foot, nine inch frame dominated many of those around him. In his blue officer's kepi with embroidered crossed cannons bearing the numeral "4" in a red disc, Lon looked every inch the soldier he was. He wore a rain- and perspiration-soaked, twelve-button officer's shell jacket with the red and gold artillery shoulder straps of a first lieutenant. His trousers were dark blue with a red stripe down the seam; they were tucked in a pair of mud-spattered cavalry boots, complete with fenders that covered his knees. As he did while a staff officer, Lon carried a revolver and a cavalry saber. Heavy buff gauntlets covered his hands. He was often seen using field glasses. Invariably, his meerschaum pipe or, at times, a cigar protruded from his mouth and reddish Vandyke whiskers. Even from afar, one could always tell Lon; his dark complexion, round face, and toothy smile gave him away.[3]

In the predawn hours of July 3 the gunfire increased in fury, announcing a Union counterassault along the Culp's Hill trenchlines well to Lon's rear, over a mile distant. As the morning hours passed, stray shells, shell bursts, and the sounds of the distant clash of infantry provided Lon with every indication that it would be a difficult day. Up and down the roads and across the fields behind him moved dense masses of infantry and artillery to bolster the Union effort on the army's right flank. In the darkness, through the thick woodlots and along the rolling hills to the northeast, Lon observed the flashes of artillery fire and musketry.[4] The fighting spread down the lines as the first rays of sunlight appeared over the treetops on the eastern horizon. At approximately 5:00 A.M., Capt. James W. Wyatt's Albemarle (Virginia) Artillery of Maj. William T. Poague's Third Corps artillery battalion opened fire on Lon's position. On and off, the firing was kept up through the early morning hours.[5]

Confederate sharpshooters had retaken the Bliss house and barn. The attack the evening before had dislodged the Confederates, but the Union troops had not been able to hold the buildings; General Posey's Mississippians had seized them again. Four companies of the 12th New Jersey were sent across the fields to take the Bliss barn and house again, but after half an hour Confederate artillery fire forced the New Jersey soldiers to withdraw. The Bliss buildings once more fell into Confederate hands.[6]

Under Gen. Alexander Hays's orders, Colonel Smyth rode to the 14th Connecticut and ordered it to take the buildings. It was about 7:30 A.M. Four companies of the 14th Connecticut, led by a captain, marched up the Second Corps lines and then across the Emmitsburg Road toward the Bliss buildings. As the infantrymen reached the fields in front of the house and barn, they came under a withering fire from Confederates within the buildings as well as from those in Col. Abner Perrin's and Brig. Gen. Edward L. Thomas's brigades in the Long Lane to their right. The Connecticut soldiers were ordered to break ranks; each man was admonished to reach the barn as best he could.[7] The soldiers rushed forward. Heavy gunfire rang out, and the great brick barn was covered in smoke. Soon the Confederates withdrew from the barn to the Bliss house, from which they began shooting at the Connecticut soldiers.[8]

Seeing that the capture of the barn did not remedy the problem, Maj. Theodore Ellis ordered forward the rest of his 14th Connecticut. Across the fields the remaining companies marched. The Bliss farmyard erupted in gunfire. So great was the rifle fire poured into their ranks, one of the Connecticut soldiers remarked, that marching into it "was like dodging ten thousand shafts of lightening."[9] Nevertheless, by midmorning the Bliss barn and house were in the hands of the Connecticut men. Major Ellis sent back a request that he be permitted to burn the buildings as he could not hold them for long. In minutes, an aide from Colonel Smyth returned with orders from General Hays to set the buildings on fire. The barn and house were torched. Flames towered into the air, and heavy black smoke covered the fields. When the roofs of the buildings collapsed, Second Corps soldiers yelled and cheered. Slowly, Major Ellis brought his gallant 14th Connecticut back to the safety of Cemetery Ridge. The contest over the Bliss buildings had finally come to an end.[10]

At about 8:00 A.M., while the fighting raged at the Bliss barn and house, Maj. Gen. Henry Hunt, Meade's chief of artillery, came over to confer with Lon about the location of the reserve ammunition train. Cushing had known General Hunt since the First Battle of Bull Run. Sergeant Fuger joined them, and the trio discussed Meade's decision to hold his ground, a decision made with his lieutenants in the Leister house just behind Lon's position the previous night. General Webb joined the little conference, which was being held about four yards behind the limber to the number three gun in Lieutenant Milne's section. As cannoneers number six, seven, and eight at each limber were standing alongside the open limber chests ready for firing and all the drivers had dismounted, the conference took on the appearance of a mass meeting. Hunt informed Lon and Fuger that the reserve ammunition train was located along the Taneytown Road. He quickly scribbled out a map showing the location of the train behind the two round tops and handed it to Sergeant Fuger.[11]

Suddenly, from the Confederate lines along Seminary Ridge ahead of Lon, two guns were fired. The shells arched through the air and smashed into the limber to Lon's number one gun. The limber exploded; the blast shook the earth. Flames, smoke, and fragments of wood and iron flew into the air and then rained down upon the limbers to the number two and three guns, and in a moment they exploded as well, catapulting wheels, chassis, and fragments of the chests into the air and across the ground. The limbers in the left section of Arnold's battery, on Lon's right, were as close to his number one limber as those in his own center section. The concussions knocked cannoneer Thomas A. Aldrich of Arnold's battery to the ground; the riderless horses attached to the Rhode Islander's limbers turned completely around and became tangled in their harness. In Cushing's battery, horses ran wild. Some broke loose and ran toward the Confederate lines. Infantrymen along the stone wall managed to stop most of them, but some horses from limber number one, to the cheers and jeers of the distant Confederate cannoneers, ran headlong across the fields and managed to enter the rebel lines. Lon's cannoneers and drivers calmed the neighing and snorting battery horses that remained; they finally brought the situation under control. No one, miraculously, had been hurt; recalled Sergeant Fuger, "Only a few of the wheel horses had their tails singed." In the dust, smoke, and confusion, Lon's, Hunt's, and Webb's conference ended abruptly. Lon ordered the caissons for the number one, two, and three guns brought forward to take the place of the exploded limbers.[12]

At least twelve distinct times, artillery fire erupted over the fields south of Gettysburg during the morning. Lon returned the enemy fire. Each duel lasted for up to ten minutes and then died away. An intense quiet settled over the landscape after each cannonade, only to be shattered by renewed firing. Lon, it seemed, was "in his element" during such bombardments. Often dismounted during the cannonades, he stood between the number three and four guns in the battery, observing the effect of the fire through his field glasses. Between shots, with the field glasses at his eyes, he talked to his men, always reassuring and calming them. His men deeply admired him.[13]

At one point Lon observed a group of what appeared to be mounted general officers ride out into the clearing in front of the heavy Seminary Ridge woods nearly a mile across the smoke-laden fields. Turning to Pvt. Edward Drummond, who temporarily had taken over as the gunner at the number four gun, Lon said, "Sergeant, train your gun on that group." It was First Bull Run all over again! The piece was elevated to provide the proper trajectory.

"Spherical case," ordered Cushing. The gun was loaded.

"Ready," replied Drummond.

"Fire!"

The lanyard was jerked, and the gun boomed; its shell arched over the fields, crashing in the woods beyond the officers.[14] Not satisfied, Lon ordered the cannoneers at the piece to try it again. The gun was loaded.

"Ready," Drummond said. The cannoneers waited.

"Fire!"

With the jerk of the lanyard, the gun blasted forth its case shot. This time the shell burst just as it was passing over the heads of the distant Confederate officers. Pvt. Christopher "Christy" Smith, one of the cannoneers working the Ordnance rifle, recalled that the Confederate officers scattered "at a lively rate." To the absolute delight of Lon, his cannoneers let out a hearty cheer.[15]

Capt. John G. Hazard was near Cushing's battery and watched the effect of the fire with both admiration and annoyance. Although it evidenced excellent gunnery, the long-distance shot was a waste of ammunition, which was already in short supply. Riding over to Cushing as the cheers of the cannoneers were dying away, the angry brigade commander called out, "Young man, are you aware that every round you fire costs the government two dollars and sixty-seven cents?" If Cushing replied, there is no record of it. Without doubt, though, he got the message.[16]

Artillery firing ceased altogether at approximately 11:00 A.M. Lon and his men settled down. Just behind the six Ordnance rifles, the officers of the battery had dug a small pit, over which they had constructed an arch of stones. A fire was started, and soon coffee was boiling.[17] The men in the artillery brigade of the Second Corps had waited for their long-overdue rations all morning long. The Rhode Islanders of Brown's battery kept calling for the driver of their ration wagon, artilleryman Bob Niles. Soon ration wagons were seen jouncing up the ridge from the Taneytown Road, including—to the relief of Lon and his cannoneers—the ration wagon of Battery A. To the utter dismay of Brown's Rhode Islanders, however, Bob Niles was nowhere to be seen.[18] No rations had been delivered to Webb's infantrymen, either, and hungry soldiers of the Philadelphia Brigade brazenly wandered among the artillery mess, asking if they could have something to eat. One soldier from the 69th Pennsylvania begged successfully for a hatful of hardbread. Grateful, he returned to the low stone wall with his old Kossuth hat loaded with the hard crackers. There he was greeted cheerfully by his hungry fellow foot soldiers.[19]

Tired and apprehensive, Lon lit up his meerschaum pipe. Then he sat down to drink a tin of coffee and eat some pork and hardtack with the faithful Sergeant Fuger and Lieutenant Milne. It would be his last meal.[20]

Lon had come a long way for a lad of twenty-two. A son of nativists, he was fighting a war to preserve a country that was fast becoming remarkable for its ethnic diversity. For two years he had fought alongside infantry regiments and artillery batteries whose rank and file could speak only German or were solid famine Irish. Like him, they were brave men; those Germans and Irishmen had freely bled. Unlike Lon, whose ancestry went so deep into the English colonial history of the nation that he could trace a direct blood line from his mother back to John and Priscilla Alden of the *Mayflower*, these immigrants around him were fighting to preserve a country other than the one of their birth. Born and raised in indescribable hardships, crop failures, famines, and revolutions, those new citizens had answered the call of the Union which they had chosen as their home because of its promise of personal liberty, and the limited power of the state in its organic laws, and its promise, in spite of nativism and Puritanism, to be the sanctuary for others like them—in overwhelming numbers.[21]

The contrasts, consequently, within the regiments and artillery batteries of the old Second Corps along Cemetery Ridge were notable. Lon, a Baptist of Puritan descent, conversed with his first sergeant, a German-speaking, devout Roman Catholic. Both in turn spoke with cannoneers who addressed them in thick German or Irish brogues and who were, in large numbers, Roman Catholics.[22]

The Philadelphia Brigade, which Lon's guns supported, was as Irish as it was native-born. Col. Dennis O'Kane's 69th Pennsylvania, down along the wall to the left of Cushing's battery, was almost entirely Irish. Proudly, its men held upright, alongside the tattered national colors, their handsome green flag trimmed in gold, bearing the images of a wolfhound, a castle keep and a sunburst—the emblems of Ireland—given to them by the citizens of Philadelphia. Among the few non-Irishmen who followed the flag of Erin in the 69th were a number from the Society of Friends and several Jewish soldiers. Col. R. Penn Smith's 71st Pennsylvania to Lon's right, like Col. DeWitt Clinton Baxter's 72d Pennsylvania to Lon's left and rear, was composed principally of soldiers who were Irish-born. Like many regiments in the Army of the Potomac that were mustered out of the great, emerging cities of the North, the regiments that formed the Philadelphia Brigade were largely a mixture of the Irish- and German- and native-born, the devout Roman Catholic and the fiercely Protestant. Such was the new America.[23]

Farther down the line was Col. Norman J. Hall's Third Brigade of the Second Division, Second Corps. One of Hall's regiments was the 59th New York, whose officers and enlisted men of boasted old-line English and Dutch names reminiscent of New York's colonial experience. Alongside the 59th was Hall's own 7th Michigan, composed of soldiers from the city of Detroit. Beside them stood the Brahmin and native-born soldiers of the 20th Massachusetts, commanded by Lon's former compatriot at General Sumner's headquarters, Col. Paul J. Revere. What a contrast those sons of Massachusetts Puritans presented to the sons of Erin, just up the line beneath their green and gold flag. If that was not contrast enough, behind the 20th Massachusetts were the four guns of the Fenian, Capt. James McKay Rorty; and to Rorty's rear were the 19th Massachusetts—old Salem and Boston Puritans and Irish factory workers—and the 42d New York, a regiment of Irishmen raised and financed entirely by the emerging Democratic political organization known as Tammany Hall.[24]

Up the line to Lon's right, the contrasts continued. In Col. Thomas A. Smyth's Second Brigade of the Third Division, Second Corps, were the "wooden nutmegs" of the 14th Connecticut, men largely native-born. Most boasted of Puritan ancestry, or, as one officer put it: "[they are] a noble representation of the best elements of the state." There were also many Irish within the ranks of the 14th Connecticut, but an even more notable contrast in the command was that one enlisted man, named Joseph L. Pierce—complete with a pigtail that hung down his back—was the only soldier of Chinese birth in the Army of the Potomac.[25]

In the Third Brigade of the Third Division, Second Corps, which supported Little Dad's guns, were three upstate New York regiments—the 111th, 125th, and 126th—along with the most remarkable of all units along that ridge, the 39th New York. Known as the Garibaldi Guards, the 39th had marched alongside Lon during the First Bull Run campaign. Although it was originally intended that the regiment consist of Germans, Poles, Hungarians, Swiss, Italians, French, and Spanish-Portuguese, it had become heavily German, Hungarian, and Italian.

The wide variation in uniforms within the Army of the Potomac even gave it the appearance of a European army. All around Lon and his battery it was noticeable. The Italians in the Garibaldi Guards wore feathered hats reminiscent of the *bersaglieri* of their homeland, in addition to their odd green frocks and trousers. The influence of the French-Algerian armies among regiments of foreign-born soldiers was profound. Many in Baxter's Fire Zouaves, the 72d Pennsylvania, still wore their baggy, light blue pantaloons with white gaiters. The National Zouaves, the 10th New York of Smyth's brigade, back near the Leister house, wore powder blue pantaloons with white gaiters, dark blue monkey jackets trimmed in red, and red fezzes with white turbans. Before the end of the day, one of the most remarkable of all Zouave regiments in the Army of the Potomac, Col. Charles Collis's 114th Pennsylvania, would arrive at the angle along with the 99th Pennsylvania and the 3d and 4th Maine, all from the Third Corps. Collis's Zouaves wore crimson pantaloons with white gaiters, blue monkey jackets with red facings, and crimson fezzes with white turbans. The uniforms pleased the men of the regiment, many of whom were European-born. A large number were native French-Alsatians.[26]

Add to all these the infantry regiments from New Jersey, West Virginia, Maine, and Minnesota as well as from Delaware, along with artillery batteries from New York and Rhode Island and the regular army, among all of whose enlisted men the same ethnic, cultural, national, and religious mixture could be found in varying proportions, and one begins to appreciate what manner of men stood between the Union and its dissolution on that most climactic of afternoons in the history of the nation. In the midst of them all—center stage—was Lt. Alonzo Hereford Cushing, son of nativist Milton Buckingham Cushing and his wife, Mary Barker Smith Cushing, and defender of a Union that was becoming something his parents actually had feared.

But Lon, it seems, had developed a different attitude about it all. Since March 1862 he had fought alongside nearly every one of the regiments and artillery batteries in the old Second Corps aligned along Cemetery Ridge. He had led many into formation preceding bloody attacks and had followed the attacks to relay commands as a staff officer. On some fields he had manned the guns of his battery alongside the infantrymen and other artillerymen of the corps. Lon knew the men of the Second Corps well, and nearly all of its officers and men knew him. They shared a common history: the Peninsula, Antietam, Fredericksburg, Chancellorsville. Whatever their difference in religion and ethnic background, there was mutual respect and admiration, born of some of the most desperate and bloody fighting of the war.

It was nearly noon. Just in rear of the 20th Massachusetts and to the left of Lon's battery, General Gibbon had his dinner served. For a table he used his old mess chest. With him was General Hancock. Both were seated on camp stools, their staff officers on the ground. General Meade, with one of his staff, rode down the lines behind Lon and the Philadelphia Brigade and stopped at Gibbon's and Hancock's mess. General Gibbon had apparently appealed to the "worn and haggard" Meade to join him for the meal. The army commander dismounted, and an old cracker box was located for him to use as a stool. Soon Gens. John Newton, who had taken over as commander of the First Corps, and Alfred Pleasonton, the cavalry commander, with their staff officers, joined the group. Blankets were rolled out for them. Lighting cigars, they talked of the previous engagements and of their hopes for the outcome of the afternoon ahead. Meade felt that the commands assigned to provost guard duty should be returned to their regiments at the front line; they would be most needed there. Gibbon called for Capt. Wilson B. Ferrell of the 1st Minnesota to take his provost guard detachment back to its regiment. One by one the generals departed, each returning to his duties. Gibbon and his staff officers remained. Recalled Col. Frank A. Haskell of Gibbon's staff, "We dozed in the heat and lolled upon the ground with half-open eyes. Our horses were hitched to the trees munching some oats. A great lull rests upon all the field. Time ways [*sic*] heavy." From noon until just before 1:00 P.M. a deathly silence fell across the fields. The Rhode Islanders of Brown's battery finally observed Bob Niles bringing the company's ration wagon over the ridge. The men were relieved; they would eat breakfast after all.[27]

The day had dawned with the sky almost completely covered with heavy clouds and a gentle breeze out of the south-southwest. From seventy-three degrees at 7:00 A.M., however, the temperature had risen to nearly eighty-seven degrees by noon, and the sun was beating down on Cemetery Ridge. Under fire, the soldiers would suffer terribly in such heat and humidity; smoke would linger close to the ground, burning their eyes and choking them. As midday passed, many took out their canvas shelter halves and fastened them up with sticks or bayonets to provide relief from the hot sun. The routine activities of the morning had ended, and the soldiers "lulled, sweltered and waited" in the searing heat of the day. Across the Emmitsburg Road the Bliss barn and house still burned, and the smoke hung in the long, deep swales between the two contending armies. In the fields ahead the still unburied dead had begun to turn black. The heavy odor of death was sickening.[28]

Cushing's battery was still arranged in two three-gun sections, Lieutenant Milne commanding the right and Sergeant Fuger the left. The gun detachment commanders and commanders of caissons remained the same: Gunners Blockinger, Whetston, Brenan, Murphy, Au, Smedley, and Hurley. Two were Germans and five were Irish. Replacements for the cannoneers who had fallen the evening before had taken their positions at the guns and caissons.[29]

Across the fields of tall rye, oats, and wheat, one mile in front of Lon's position, Lee had conducted several councils of war with his chief lieutenants during the morning. He had determined to strike Meade's center, using the newly arrived but undersized Virginia division in Lt. Gen. James Longstreet's corps, commanded by the dapper Maj. Gen. George E. Pickett. Pickett's division had been relieved from guarding supply trains at Chambersburg just the evening before; it had seen no fighting in the campaign up to the moment of its arrival at Gettysburg. The division was composed of three fine brigades, Brig. Gens. Richard B. Garnett's (the 8th, 18th, 19th, 28th, and 56th Virginia), Lewis A. Armistead's (the 9th, 14th, 38th, 53d, and 57th Virginia), and James Lawson Kemper's (the 1st, 3d, 7th, 11th, and 24th Virginia). In all, Pickett's division numbered about 4,300 officers and men. Its soldiers had been mustered out of nearly every geographic section of the Old Dominion. Some referred to those gallant men as the "flower of Lee's army."[30]

In addition to Pickett's division, Lee determined that the attack would be made by a division and a demi-division from General Hill's Third Corps. Inexplicably, he selected General Heth's division, decimated in the fighting on July 1 and its commander wounded. Replacing Heth was the youthful Brig. Gen. J. Johnston Pettigrew of North Carolina. The division was composed of four battle-hardened brigades: Pettigrew's own, commanded on July 3 by Col. James K. Marshall (the 11th, 26th, 47th, and 52d North Carolina), Col. John M. Brockenbrough's, then under the command of Col. Robert M. Mayo (the 40th, 47th, and 55th Virginia and the 22d Virginia Battalion), Brig. Gen. James J. Archer's, commanded on July 3 by Col. Birkett Davenport Fry, because Archer had been captured on July 1 (the 13th Alabama, 5th Alabama Battalion, and 1st, 7th, and 14th Tennessee), and Brig. Gen. Joseph R. Davis's (the 2d, 11th, and 42d Mississippi and the 55th North Carolina).[31]

Supporting Pettigrew, two brigades from the Third Corps division of Maj. Gen. William Dorsey Pender were to advance in the great assault. Pender having been badly wounded the previous evening, his brigades were to be commanded by Maj. Gen. Isaac R. Trimble of Maryland. As only two of Pender's brigades were selected—Brig. Gen. James H. Lane's (the 7th, 18th, 28th, 33d, and 37th North Carolina) and Brig. Gen. Alfred Moore Scales's, commanded on July 3 by Col. William Lee J. Lowrance because Scales had been wounded on July 1 (the 13th, 16th, 22d, 34th, and 38th North Carolina)—Trimble's command may be considered a demi-division.[32]

Numbering in all nearly 6,200 officers and men, Pettigrew's and Trimble's gallant commands did indeed boast some of the best fighting men in the Confederate forces. Although badly reduced in numbers as a result of the first two days of battle at Gettysburg, these regiments had earned unsurpassed reputations on virtually every battlefield where Lee's army had been engaged. If Pickett's men were the "flower of Lee's army," Pettigrew's and Trimble's veterans were surely the "flower of the Confederacy" as they entered the last great drama of Gettysburg.[33]

In the great assault, Pickett's division was to form the right flank. Within Pickett's lines, Kemper's brigade would form the right and Garnett's the left; Armistead's brigade would form the second line behind Garnett. To the left of Pickett would form Pettigrew's division with Fry's (Archer's) brigade on the right (connecting with the left of Garnett's Virginians), Marshall's (Pettigrew's own) to the left of Fry, Davis's brigade to the left of Marshall, and Mayo's (Brockenbrough's) brigade to the extreme left. Pettigrew's men, on line with Pickett's Virginians, made up the front rank. In Pettigrew's rear, forming a second line, would be the brigades of Lane and Lowrance (Scales) of Trimble's demi-division.[34] To Pickett's right, the Alabama and Florida brigades of Brig. Gen. Cadmus M. Wilcox (the 8th, 9th, 10th, and 11th Alabama) and Col. David L. Lang (the 2d, 5th, and 8th Florida), although badly mangled in the fighting on July 2, would also advance into the fight.[35]

With the Union concentration—particularly artillery—along the Cemetery Ridge, and with the fields over which the assault was to proceed being open, it was determined that the attack would be preceded by a heavy artillery bombardment to weaken the Union defenses; the dense smoke it created would also provide sufficient cover to conceal much of the advance. As the heat and humidity were high that day, the smoke from a prolonged bombardment would linger close to the ground for a considerable time. Lee easily envisioned the effect, having observed the smoke from the morning cannonades and the burning Bliss buildings.[36]

All through the morning of July 3, Confederate artillery—just under

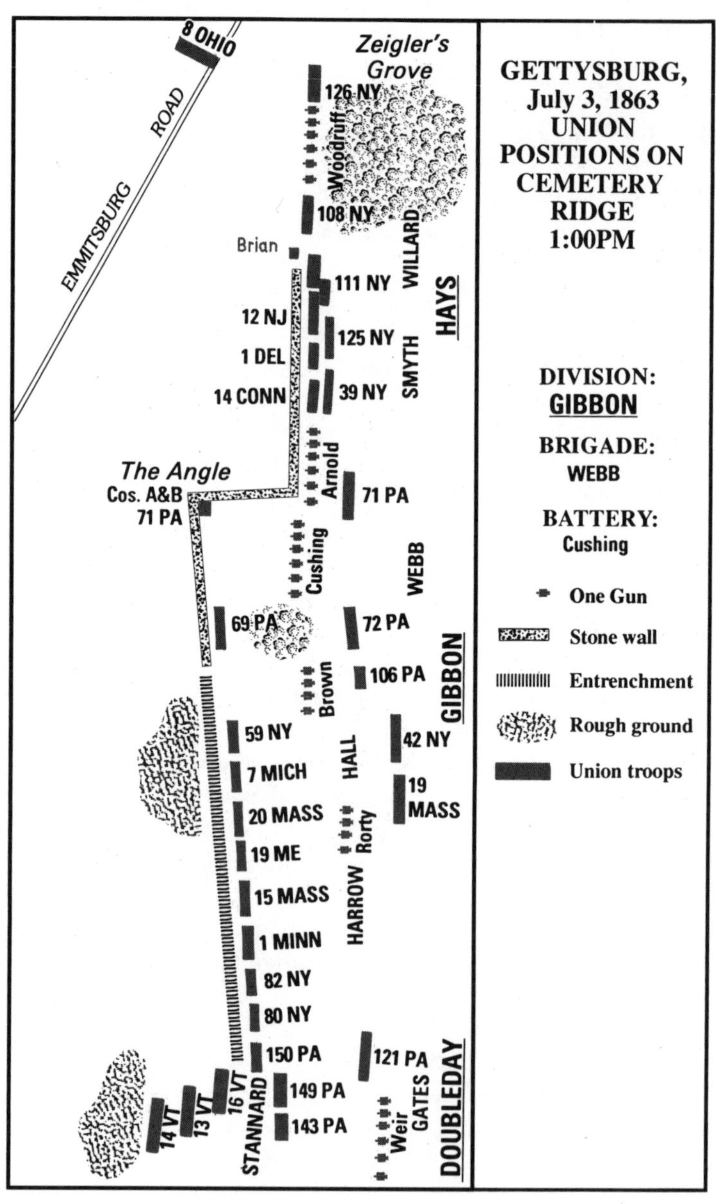
GETTYSBURG,
July 3, 1863
UNION
POSITIONS ON
CEMETERY
RIDGE
1:00PM
DIVISION:
GIBBON
BRIGADE:
WEBB
BATTERY:
Cushing
One Gun
Stone wall
Entrenchment
Rough ground
Union troops
8 OHIO
EMMITSBURG ROAD
Zeigler's Grove
126 NY
Woodruff
108 NY
WILLARD
Brian
111 NY
HAYS
12 NJ
125 NY
1 DEL
SMYTH
14 CONN
39 NY
The Angle
Cos. A&B
71 PA
Arnold
71 PA
Cushing
WEBB
69 PA
72 PA
106 PA
Brown
GIBBON
59 NY
42 NY
7 MICH
HALL
20 MASS
19
MASS
Rorty
19 ME
15 MASS
HARROW
1 MINN
82 NY
80 NY
150 PA
121 PA
16 VT
149 PA
13 VT
14 VT
143 PA
STANNARD
Weir
GATES
DOUBLEDAY

150 guns—was massed in front of and along Seminary Ridge. The alignment was plainly visible to Lon and his fellow artillerymen. General Longstreet had assigned the task of assembling the batteries for the bombardment to Col. E. Porter Alexander, commander of a reserve battalion of artillery in the First Corps. Along the line, Colonel Alexander placed the First Corps artillery battalions of Col. Henry C. Cabell, Maj. James Dearing (Lon's old classmate and whist and dancing partner at West Point), Maj. B.F. Eshleman, Lt. Col. Frank Huger (commanding Alexander's own battalion), and Maj. M.W. Henry—twenty-two batteries with seventy-five guns in all. The line of guns from Longstreet's corps artillery extended from the Sherfy peach orchard on the Emmitsburg Road all the way to the northeast corner of the Spangler Woods, directly opposite Lon's position. Col. Reuben Lindsay Walker's Third Corps artillery reserve batteries, with just under sixty guns in all, formed the line from the left of the First Corps guns all the way to the Hagerstown Road. Still farther to the left, elements of Capt. Willis J. Dance's, Lt. Col. William Nelson's, and Maj. J.W. Latimer's Second Corps battalions were included in the awesome lineup of Confederate artillery positioned to bombard the Union positions. In addition, Gen. William N. Pendleton, Lee's chief of artillery, ordered forward Lt. Col. Charles Richardson's nine twelve-pound howitzers from Lt. Col. John L. Garnett's Third Corps artillery battalion. Being short-range guns, Richardson's howitzers were directed by Colonel Alexander to find cover behind the infantry and advance with the attacking columns.[37]

Col. Frank Haskell, resting on the ground near Gibbon and Hancock and not far from the clump of trees and Lon's guns, looked at his watch. It was 12:55 P.M. Suddenly, two shots were fired by Confederate guns from Maj. B.F. Eshleman's famed Washington Artillery of New Orleans, whose four companies were positioned near the peach orchard. The shells arched across the sky, hit the earth, and bounded toward the Union lines. The first crashed into Lon's mess, overturning the coffee, scattering pots and pans, and sending officers and men running for cover. The second plowed into the rifle stacks of the 19th Massachusetts. Lt. Sherman Robinson of the 19th leaped to his feet at the sound of the guns; he was in the act of wiping his mouth with his handkerchief when the second shot struck him on the left side below the shoulder, literally tearing him to pieces. The infantrymen "hit the dirt," and all the artillerymen in the Second Corps batteries scurried to their posts. For Brown's Rhode Islanders, it was a most frustrating experience; they saw Bob Niles stop their ration wagon, turn it around, and head back down the slope toward the Taneytown Road. Everyone knew the battle was about to begin. Dozens upon dozens of quartermaster, commissary, and sutlers' wagons as well as ambulances began rumbling over Cemetery Ridge toward the Taneytown Road to get out of the line of fire. It was a mass exodus. An observer concluded that an inexperienced soul would have thought the army was in full retreat.[38]

Within seconds, the lanyards were jerked on 150 Confederate guns. The entire countryside was enveloped in smoke and the deafening roar of artillery fire. Colonel Alexander's massed artillery had opened what has since been regarded as the greatest bombardment ever unleashed on the North American continent.[39]

Recognizing that the caissons to his number four, five, and six guns were too vulnerable in their exposed positions along the crest of the ridge, Lon ordered Cpl. Thomas Moon to take them back to the Taneytown Road, along the base of the eastern slope of the ridge. There, he believed, they would be safe from the bombardment. Corporal Moon led the caissons through the storm of shells back down the sunken farm lane to a position in front of the Leister house.[40]

About ten or fifteen minutes after the Confederate guns opened fire, Lon gave the command for his artillerymen to return the fire with shell. Distances were counted, fuses were cut, and charges were hurried to the six Ordnance rifles.

"Load!" yelled Lon. The six Ordnance rifles were loaded.

"Ready," replied the detachment commanders, one by one.

"Number one, fire! Number two, fire! Number three, fire!"

The Ordnance rifles boomed and recoiled.

"Commence firing!" shouted Lon.[41]

One after another, the six Ordnance rifles blasted forth their shell behind clouds of smoke and dust. All of the Union batteries along Cemetery Ridge commenced firing. "The earth shook beneath our very feet, and the hills and woods seemed to reel like a drunken man," wrote Sergeant Fuger. Shells streaked across the sky, burst overhead, plowed into the earth, crashed into limbers, caissons, horses, trees, and farm buildings. "The splash of bursting shells and shrapnel," recalled Fuger, "and the fierce neighing of wounded artillery horses, made a picture terribly grand and sublime." Cushing's battery was low on ammunition. Lon cautioned each gun detachment that their fire must be as deliberate and effective as possible. The cannoneers worked feverishly. The smoke was so dense that virtually nothing was visible beyond arm's length. Wrote Colonel Haskell: "The thunder and lightening of these two hundred and fifty guns, and their shells, whose smoke darkens the sky, are incessant, all pervading, in the air above our heads, on the ground at our feet, remote, near, deafening, ear-piercing, astounding; and these hailstones, are massy iron charged with exploding fire. . . . the projectiles shriek long and sharp,—they hiss,—they scream,—they growl,—they sputter,—and all sounds of life and rage; and each has its different note, and all are discordant. Was ever such a chaos of sound before."[42]

The incoming shells and solid shot wreaked havoc in Cushing's battery. One of Lon's cannoneers was standing in the rear of the limber nearest to General Gibbon with the lid open showing the cartridges inside. "Suddenly with a shriek," the general recalled, "came a shell right under the limberbox, and the poor gunner went hopping to the rear on one leg, the shreds of the other dangling about as he went."[43]

Colonel Haskell observed one of the horses of General Gibbon's mess wagon struck by an incoming shell. The horses plunged, the driver lost his reins, and horses, driver, and wagon smashed into a tree. Gibbon's groom was then hit while trying to take the general's horse to him. The shell "[tore] away the groom's breast," Haskell recalled. Nearby stood two mules carrying boxes of ammunition. Another incoming shell literally knocked them "all to pieces."[44]

Lon's number six gun, near the clump of trees, was hit and disabled; then the number five gun was struck. The roar was so terrible that fear overtook the men. Men and horses were being torn to pieces. "The shot and shell," wrote one of Lon's cannoneers, "seemed to be tearing and plowing the hill to its very foundation all around us." The scene must have been terrifying. Cannoneer Christopher Smith, serving at Private Murphy's gun, recalled the sun appearing "like a great red ball" through the dense, yellowish clouds of smoke. "All around us was a great cloud of smoke," he remembered. "Below us we could occasionally get a glimpse of the green wheatfield, and the very fury of the cannonading seemed to send waves across it like gusts of wind. Peal after peal from the heavy guns all along the hill on the other side constantly thundering and roaring, and with each sound there was a red flash that made a strange effect through the smoke with the heat of the obscured sun pouring down full upon us."[45]

One incoming shell hit the number three gun, commanded by Sgt. Thomas Whetston in Lieutenant Milne's section, tearing away a wheel. In the excitement, the sergeant and his gun crew panicked and started to run. Lon, knowing that an extra wheel was always carried on the caisson and that the rifle could still be served, drew his revolver and called out amid the roar, "Sergeant Whetston, come back to your post. The first man who leaves his post again I'll blow his brains out!" Whetston was a good soldier; he called for his men to return at once. In minutes the wheel was changed, and the Ordnance rifle was blazing away. During the course of the bombardment the wheels of two more of Cushing's guns were struck by incoming shells and destroyed. Each time, the cannoneers, as if on drill, replaced the shattered wheels under fire and soon had the guns back in service.[46]

The bombardment was furious. Confederate guns appeared to have been slightly overelevated; consequently, many shells and solid shot passed over the Union front lines and crashed into the area along the Taneytown Road. The Leister house was riddled, and the three caissons Lon had sent there were more exposed to enemy fire than they would have been had they remained along Cemetery Ridge. As shells began to find their mark close to the caissons, Corporal Moon wisely ordered them moved on up the Granite School House Road.[47]

Infantrymen from the Philadelphia Brigade hugged the earth and huddled behind the low stone wall, rock outcroppings, or haversacks filled with dirt. In the 72d Pennsylvania, positioned behind the copse of trees and badly exposed to the enemy artillery fire, large numbers of men were struck by the rain of missiles. A shell exploding within the 20th Massachusetts critically wounded its commander, Lon's friend Col. Paul J. Revere. The wound would prove to be fatal.[48] All of the Second Corps batteries returned a furious fire. One cannoneer in Lt. Gulian V. Weir's battery, south of the angle, recalled how every recoil of the guns along Cemetery Ridge would send enormous flashes over the dead and wounded who lay along the ground in front of the guns, scorching them and setting their clothes and flesh on fire.[49]

Capt. James McKay Rorty's four Parrott rifles of Battery B, 1st New York Light Artillery, were within range of a sizable number of Confederate guns. As the bombardment reached its height, Rorty rapidly lost men and equipment. Incoming shells rained down upon the battery. Five horses and nearly all of the drivers at the limber to the number one gun were killed in minutes; then the gun itself was hit. Within moments the number three gun was torn from its carriage, and its caisson exploded. The infantrymen in the 19th Massachusetts, situated just behind Rorty's battery, watched in awe as the brave Irishman sought to keep his remaining two guns in action. Then the number four gun on the left received a direct hit, rendering it useless. In less than half an hour, Rorty's cannoneers had been reduced to only four manning the number two gun! Rorty unbuckled his sword, took off his coat, and threw them aside. Grabbing a rammer, he assisted his cannoneers in firing the one Parrott rifle that remained. He called to the infantrymen behind them for more water to swab the hot gun tube. A Lt. Moses Shackley of the 19th Massachusetts sprang from his prostrate position, grabbed a sponge bucket, and through the smoke and hail of shells and shell fragments ran toward the Leister house, where there was a spring. While he was filling the bucket, a solid shot landed between his feet. Startled and scared but unhurt, he returned to Rorty's gun with his bucket of water. To his cheering fellow infantrymen, he only remarked, "The water is cold enough, boys, but it's devilish hot around the spring!" When Rorty asked

Col. Arthur Devereux of the 19th Massachusetts for some men to assist him, nearly twenty-five infantrymen responded. Soon the wheels were replaced on one gun—probably the number one piece—and Rorty's battery began to reply to the bombardment with two of his four Parrott rifles.[50]

Projectiles continued to hit their mark in Cushing's battery. An explosive shell whirred through the air, plowed completely through one of the battery horses and then slammed into a second horse, exploding inside the animal. A shell crashed into another horse and exploded, disembowling the poor brute and badly mangling the driver, Pvt. Arsenal H. Griffin, who was seated in the saddle. Griffin, who began the war as a volunteer in a Michigan regiment, had been badly wounded at the Battle of Fair Oaks in May 1862; afterward, he swore should he ever be seriously wounded again, he wanted his fellow artillerymen to put him out of his misery. Now he was writhing in agony; cannoneer Christy Smith observed that the shell fragment had torn away the flesh of Griffin's abdomen, so that some of his entrails spilled out onto the ground. In intense pain, he called out for someone to shoot him. Then, as smoke and dust partly obscured the terrible scene, Griffin methodically pulled out his own revolver and put it to his head. "Good-by boys," he said, and shot himself.[51]

Guns, limbers, horses, and men were literally blown out of position. A shell exploded over one of Lon's open limber boxes, then another over a neighboring box. Both limber boxes "blew up with an explosion that shook the ground, throwing fire and splinters and shells far into the air and all around, destroying several men." Shells shrieked through the dense, sulfurous air. Fragments of rocks blasted out of the stone wall ahead of Lon's cannoneers whirred and buzzed all around. Shells burst, throwing searing hot shrapnel all across the angle. Horses neighed and fell to the dusty earth as the missiles found their marks, disemboweling some animals, dismembering others. Parts of horses' legs, mingled with their entrails and blood, were strewn about the ground. The fallen animals, still harnessed to the tongues of the limbers, received the incoming iron hail without any cover or protection. "Men and horses were being torn to pieces on all sides," remembered Christy Smith. "Every few seconds a shot or shell would strike in among our guns, but we could not stop for anything. We could not even close our eyes when death seemed to be coming." General Webb stood behind Lon's cannoneers shouting for them to be calm and not leave their posts.[52]

Lon's cannoneers continued to fire the remaining guns, but losses mounted. Private Murphy at the number four gun was killed. Sergeant Au fell, desperately wounded, as did Pvt. Andrew Eagan. Pvt. William Patton was killed. Lon's bugler, Albert Keyser, fell. "At that time," recalled Fuger, "Cushing was wounded in the right shoulder, and within a few seconds after that he was wounded in the testicles, a very severe and painful wound." Lon, his right shoulder strap nearly torn from his blood-stained shell jacket and his breeches torn and soaked with blood, became terribly ill and began vomiting. He "suffered frightfully" from intense pain and nausea, remembered Fuger, but quickly, it appears, he went into shock, that curious state which probably enabled him for a time to remain at his post, even though his condition was desperate. Lon could barely stand on his feet. Bleeding profusely, he was fast losing the strength to yell commands above the deafening racket. He called Sergeant Fuger to stand beside him and relay his orders to the artillerymen. Fuger demanded that he go to the rear. "No," replied Lon, "I stay right here and fight it out or die in the attempt!" One wonders if he simply had determined that death was near and that he would die at his post. Having been so badly mangled, he may well have been looking for a fatal missile.[53]

The bombardment was taking a toll on other Second Corps batteries as well. In the already depleted Battery B, 1st Rhode Island Light Artillery, one gun was struck by an exploding Confederate shell that killed two cannoneers. The number one cannoneer had stepped to his post in front, between the muzzle of the piece and the wheel on the right side; having swabbed the gun, he stood with the sponge staff reversed, waiting for the charge to be inserted in the bore. The number two cannoneer, in his place between the muzzle of the gun and the wheel on the left side, had taken the ammunition from the number five cannoneer, and was in the act of inserting it in the muzzle of the gun when the Confederate shell struck. The first cannoneer was killed instantly by a shell fragment that cut off the top left side of his head. He fell forward; his sponge staff was flung several yards ahead of him. The second man was hit in the left shoulder and his arm nearly torn from its socket. In a few minutes he died, shouting, "Glory to God! I am happy! Hallelujah!" The remaining cannoneers attempted to load the gun, but the shell became jammed in the muzzle. The gun, by then hit in three different places and almost dismounted, was withdrawn from the field and taken to the battery's wagon park in the rear. Brown's battery had only three guns remaining near the clump of trees.[54]

At Woodruff's battery in front of Ziegler's Grove, wrote Colonel Haskell, "the great oaks . . . heave down their massy branches with a crash, as if the lightning had smote them. The shells swoop down among the Battery horses, standing there apart,—a half a dozen horses start,—they tumble,—their legs stiffen,—their vitals and blood smear the ground. And these shot and shells have no respect for men either. We see the poor fellows hobbling back from the crest, or unable to do so, pale and weak lying on the ground, with the mangled stump of an arm or leg, dripping their life blood away, or with cheek torn open, or shoulder smashed. And many, alas! hear not the roar as they stretch upon the ground, with upturned faces, and open eyes, though a shell should burst at their very ears. Their ears, and their bodies this instant are only mud."[55]

Along Cemetery Ridge the scene was chaotic. It was not long before staff officers galloped down the Union lines exhorting the artillerymen to stop firing. An infantry attack was expected, and General Hunt determined that the batteries must husband their ammunition. Lon, hearing the horsemen, called to his gunners, "Cease firing!"[56] Just up the line from Lon, Little Dad Woodruff's battery too fell silent, though from across the fields, the Confederate bombardment continued with unabated fury. Woodruff walked by Colonel Pierce of the 108th New York. Little Dad was cool, calm, and totally self-possessed. "Pretty warm here isn't it, Colonel?" Woodruff asked. "Mighty hot," said Pierce. "Can you silence those fellows?" Little Dad shook his head. "Ammunition all gone." All of Woodruff's solid shot, shell, and spherical case had been expended; only canister remained in the limber chests and caissons. Woodruff then directed his section commanders to limber up the six Napoleons and move them to the rear in the hope of finding some shelter for his men and horses in the grove and ravine. In need of assistance because of the loss of horses, Woodruff asked for help from Colonel Pierce's infantrymen. With iron hail raining down upon the men, the six Napoleons were hitched to the limbers and hauled back through the 108th New York and into the grove, where they were halted among the rock outcroppings. Unfortunately, Woodruff was to find that the horses, men, and equipment were even more exposed to the Confederate artillery fire there than they had been along the stone wall.[57]

Back at the angle, General Webb was deeply concerned. Like almost everyone along Cemetery Ridge, he knew that the bombardment was but a prelude to an infantry assault, and that that assault would be directed toward the position of his brigade and its artillery support. Webb scanned his position. In the center, Cushing's battery was a wreck. With only two of its Ordnance rifles still in service, leaving it where it was would be an invitation to disaster; the battery was supposed to occupy an infantry regimental front. Lt. T. Fred Brown's battery on the left was also in shambles: two of its limbers and thirty of its battery horses were strewn across the fields in front of the stone wall; only three of its Napoleons remained in service; Lieutenant Brown was badly wounded; and the battery had lost many of its cannoneers. The Rhode Islanders could not hold their segment of the line in the defenses. At a minimum, Webb needed a fresh battery to replace Brown's guns.[58]

Down the line south of Webb's position, supporting the remnants of

General Newton's First Corps, and near Ransom's and McGilvery's brigades of the Artillery Reserve, was a battery from the Sixth Corps which had arrived along Cemetery Ridge earlier in the morning from the vicinity of Culp's Hill. It was Capt. Andrew Cowan's 1st New York Independent Battery of six three-inch Ordnance rifles. Captain Cowan was born in Ayrshire, Scotland, in 1841, the year of Lon's birth. His parents had brought young Andrew to the United States as a lad, settling in Auburn, New York, less than one hundred miles east of Lon's home county. Cowan had entered Madison College (formerly Hamilton Literary and Theological Institute, the school Lon's father had briefly attended) but left at the outbreak of the war to join the 19th New York, a three-month regiment. Returning to New York after his enlistment had expired, Cowan volunteered to raise an artillery company. On November 23, 1861, he was formally mustered into service with the 1st New York Independent Battery. By April 6, 1862, he had assumed command of the battery, having been promoted to the rank of captain in the volunteer service. Ever since then, the 1st New York Independent Battery had been known in the Army of the Potomac as "Cowan's battery." As part of the artillery complement of the Sixth Corps, Cowan's guns had fought through the battles of White Oak Swamp, Malvern Hill, Antietam, Fredericksburg, Chancellorsville, and Deep Run.[59]

Thus, when Webb called upon Capt. Charles H. Banes, his assistant adjutant general, to ride down the lines and bring back a battery to replace Brown's, Banes rode south and located Cowan's battery. A rider had just galloped past Cowan ordering him to cease firing, and the young captain had just delivered the order to his men, when Captain Banes rode through the dense smoke and dust, yelling to Cowan, "Report to General Webb at the right with your battery!" Cowan at first hesitated—he was still under orders from General Newton—but in a moment, he obeyed the command. Orders were shouted above the whistling and bursting shells: "Limber to the right, forward!" Whips cracked, horses neighed and snorted, and the 1st New York Independent Battery rumbled up Cemetery Ridge toward Lon's position. There was neither time nor space to bring the caissons, and they were left behind with the lieutenant in charge of them.[60]

Through the heavy smoke behind the copse of trees, Cowan saw an officer waving his hat. It was General Webb. The three remaining Napoleons of Brown's crippled battery were being withdrawn from their positions to the left of Cushing's Ordnance rifles and to the left of the clump of trees. Cowan's battery, directed by Webb's waving hat, wheeled into the position vacated by Brown's Rhode Islanders. Cannoneers unhitched the Ordnance rifles and rolled them forward into line about 125 feet from the stone wall. The battery had moved at such a furious gallop that one gun was carried to the right of the clump of trees and placed to the left and front of Cushing's battery.[61]

Confederate artillery fire had continued without letup for more than an hour and a half. By the time it subsided—after 2:30 P.M.—Lon could count only two Ordnance rifles remaining in his battery, number three and four. Dead and wounded artillerymen were strewn around the angle. The slain and wounded who belonged to Cushing's battery could be readily identified by the red flannel shirts so many of his men wore, shirts acquired by the cannoneers when they had marched through Maryland only a few days before. By then Pvts. Ansil Fassett, John Carl, Murray B. Headington, Lucas Henry, Edward Hill, Aaron Kope Jr., Rody Landregan, Daniel Lee, Robert Martin, William Miller, Charles Morison, John Olney, Frederick Patterson, Martin Scanlin, Charles Sprague, Hosea Stone, Charles Hubbs, David McWilliams, Artemis L.W. Decker, and blacksmith Benjamin Hacket of Cushing's battery had fallen. Most of the other cannoneers and drivers were scattered, having lost the guns, limbers, and caissons they had served.[62]

As the bombardment slackened, Lon, with the aid of Sergeant Fuger, hobbled over to confer with General Webb, who was still behind the clump of trees and in front of the 72d Pennsylvania, observing the placement of Cowan's Ordnance rifles. Webb could see that Lon was in desperate shape, and Lon acknowledged that he was ill but said he would remain at his post. Webb was in awe of the young man. Cushing, in obvious pain, reported that "pretty much all of my guns are disabled. If I had some men I could still work my guns." General Webb agreed to order men from his brigade to help service the remaining guns. "Cushing," Webb said, "it is my opinion that Confederate infantry will now advance and attack our position." Seeing that Cowan already had one of his Ordnance rifles positioned down near the stone wall in front of his remaining guns, Lon replied: "I had better run my guns right up to the stone fence and bring all my canister alongside each piece." "All right, do so," Webb responded.[63]

General Webb went to Col. R. Penn Smith of the 71st Pennsylvania and ordered him to detach some men to assist Lon's gunners in running the pieces to the wall and serving them. Colonel Smith called for some of his best men, including a hefty number of noncommissioned officers, to help the regular artillerymen. He ordered Sgt. Albert G. Bunn and Sgt. Paul Dubin of Company B; Sgt. George Donnelly, Cpl. Samuel Clawson, and Pvt. John Barnholt of Company D; Pvts. James L. Brown and Charles S. Olcott of Company E; Sgt. Isaiah Tapp and Pvts. Edward F. McMahon, Joshua Larnhoff, and Peter Rudoonff of Company F; Sgt. William J. Brown of Company G; and Cpl. George H. Elmer, Cpl. Richard Margerum, and Pvt. John Hope of Company H of his "California Regiment"—many Germans and Irishmen—to report to Cushing. To augment his thinned ranks and replenish his ammunition, Lon sent a private back to Corporal Moon, ordering him and the drivers attending the three caissons on the Granite School House Road to hurry them forward. The drivers would be able to assist the cannoneers in serving the remaining pieces.[64]

Captain Cowan, having observed his one Ordnance rifle come to halt north to the clump of trees, rode over to see whether it interfered with the placement of Lon's remaining pieces. Bleeding profusely and in obvious pain, Lon had just finished his conference with Webb and was standing near the clump of trees behind Cowan's stray gun. He assured Cowan that it was not crowding his battery, since his two remaining guns were going to be rolled down to the wall anyway. Lon faintly offered his assistance if Cowan needed it. The two young officers, both the same age and both hailing from the Empire State but born on opposite sides of the Atlantic Ocean, wished each other luck. They then parted.[65]

Lon hobbled over to Maj. John W. Moore, whose 99th Pennsylvania of Brig. Gen. Hobart Ward's Third Corps brigade had just reported to General Webb, along with the 3d and 4th Maine of Ward's brigade and Col. Charles Collis's 114th Pennsylvania of Brig. Gen. Charles K. Graham's Third Corps brigade, to help bolster the defenses. Lon asked Major Moore if his men would help pull the four disabled guns from the crest of the ridge to the rear to prevent them from falling into the hands of the enemy. Moore promptly obliged, and the Pennsylvania infantrymen pulled the four shattered Ordnance rifles by their prolonges through the ranks of Collis's colorful Zouaves to the low ground in front of the eastern face of Cemetery Ridge.[66]

Satisfied that he could keep the remnants of his battery effectively in the field, Lon turned to his faithful first sergeant and exhorted: "By hand to the front!" Fuger shouted the command to the smoke-blackened and sweating cannoneers and infantrymen. Immediately, the two remaining Ordnance rifles were rolled down to the low stone wall and halted between the 69th Pennsylvania's right (Company I) and the 71st Pennsylvania's left (Companies A and B), with all the canister piled alongside the position of the number two cannoneer at each piece. In addition, Lon ordered all twenty-eight of the handspikes of the battery brought down to the wall. He obviously expected hand-to-hand fighting; and as Sergeant Fuger recalled, "Those handspikes [were] the finest weapons for close contact." Lon's cannoneers manned the number four gun at the wall; the soldiers borrowed from Colonel Smith's 71st Pennsylvania manned number three. The infantrymen at the wall had to move aside in order to make room for the two guns and their detachments. Space was left—

about ten feet—between the muzzles of the Ordnance rifles and the stone wall to enable the number one and two cannoneers to work the pieces. The guns were positioned about nine yards apart. Cowan's lone Ordnance rifle on Cushing's left, north of the clump of trees, gave the angle the appearance of being occupied by three guns from the same battery.[67]

Out in front of Lon's guns, along the west side of the Emmitsburg Road, two companies and a detachment from the 106th Pennsylvania and two companies each from the 69th and the 72d Pennsylvania nestled behind piled fence rails as skirmishers; to Cushing's left and rear—behind the clump of trees—the rest of 72d Pennsylvania hugged the ground in reserve. Between Lon's guns and the 72d, General Webb paced up and down. The dense yellowish smoke still hung close to the ground. All eyes were on the distant Confederate lines.[68]

There were problems similar to Cushing's three hundred yards north of the angle. As soon as the bombardment ceased, Little Dad Woodruff again asked for the help of Colonel Pierce's infantrymen to bring his six Napoleons back out of the grove and into the defense lines. Unfortunately, the Confederate bombardment had penetrated what he had thought was the protective cover of trees and the ravine; a caisson had been hit and exploded, and many of the horses were dead or maimed and entangled in their harness. Nevertheless, moving forward one two-gun section at a time, Woodruff's cannoneers and Colonel Pierce's infantrymen methodically repositioned Battery I along the crest of the ridge.[69]

It was about 2:50 P.M., when the command from Confederate field and foot officers, "Fall in," "Fall in," rang through the Seminary Ridge woods. With those commands, nearly 10,500 infantrymen—Virginians, North Carolinians, Tennesseans, Alabamians, and Mississippians—moved into their positions and dressed ranks. The sulfurous smoke was dense. The lines were steadied. In all, forty-two regiments and battalions made up the assault force: nineteen from Virginia, fifteen from North Carolina, three each from Tennessee and Mississippi, and two from Alabama.[70] Pickett, his heart saddened by what he foresaw as a dreadful waste of life, tears filling his eyes, stood in front of his three brigades and said, "Charge the enemy, and remember Old Virginia." Then came the order: "Forward! Guide center! March!" The butternut and gray columns broke through the Seminary Ridge woods. Riding his horse, General Garnett, ill that day and wearing an old blue army overcoat, led his men out with Kemper's brigade abreast. The ranks were in nearly perfect alignment. Fifes and drums played "Dixie." Armistead and his men followed behind.[71] To the left of Pickett's Virginians, with drums rolling and cheers for the "Old North State" ringing in the air, Pettigrew's men moved out into the smoke-covered fields, dressed ranks, and methodically followed the advance of the Virginians with Trimble's North Carolinians behind them.[72]

Difficult at first to see from the Union lines, given the dense smoke and deep swales in the terrain, the Confederate advance soon came into view of the blue-clad cannoneers and infantrymen as a sudden puff of air somewhat thinned the sulfurous clouds. Near the waiting 15th Massachusetts a general's aide, observing the massive legions moving across the fields, called out, "Up boys, they are coming!" Soldiers in the 19th Massachusetts heard yells from all around them: "Here they come! Here they come! Here comes the infantry!" Up the lines, within the Third Division, some in the gallant 12th New Jersey had thought the battle was over when the Confederate artillery finally ceased. Then, almost at once, tired and dirty infantrymen began calling out, "Look! Do you see them coming?"[73]

To Lon and the others the sight through dense smoke was awe-inspiring. The enemy columns extended more than half a mile from flank to flank. Over the columns limply hung what seemed to be a sea of First National Confederate flags—the Stars-and-Bars—as well as the red St. Andrew's cross battleflags then in general use. The mass of rifles with bayonets attached seemed to Col. Frank Haskell a "sloping forest of flashing steel." General Webb shouted to his infantrymen not to fire until the enemy reached the fences along the Emmitsburg Road. Caught up in the moment, General Hays rode along his Third Division lines, exhorting, "They're coming boys; we must whip them!" In front of the 12th New Jersey, where some of its men were coming out from behind farmer Brian's hog pen, Hays reined his horse, pointed to the post-and-rail fence along the eastern side of the Emmitsburg Road, and said, "You men with buck and ball, don't fire until they get to that fence!" Hays rode on in front of Little Dad's six Napoleons, encouraging his cannoneers. Probably best summing up the feelings of the Union soldiers watching the spectacle was Lt. Tully McCrea's remark: "We thought that our chances for Kingdom Come or Libby Prison were very good."[74]

As a slight breeze fluttered the leaves of the chestnut oak trees near the angle, the smoke began to rise, and the tremendous assault columns became fully visible. They were marching at "route step," a deliberate march of about 110 paces per minute. With average thirty-inch strides, the enemy was advancing slightly less than a hundred yards every minute. As the butternut and gray legions moved forward, Confederate field officers could be heard steadying their commands, nervously beseeching the men to "close up the ranks, close up." Men speaking to one another within the ranks gave the advance a sound later described as a "murmur," accompanied by the "jingle" of canteens and accoutrements; the "rustle of [the] thousands of feet amid the stubble" in the fields stirred a cloud of dust "like the dash of spray at the prow of a vessel." Birds were "flushed out" before the heavy columns and flew into the sulfurous air.[75]

Lon called for spherical case and solid shot.

"Ready," his gunners reported. The lanyards were pulled tight.

"Number one, fire! Number two, fire!"

The two guns belched forth their death-dealing fury. Almost simultaneously all the artillery batteries along Cemetery Ridge opened fire. Thomas's and Weir's guns, Rorty's remaining guns, Cowan's battery, Lon's two pieces, and Arnold's guns relentlessly poured round upon round of case and solid shot into the advancing columns. With all his ammunition except canister exhausted, Little Dad had to wait until the approaching Confederate columns were within closer range. In the meantime, he ordered all his pieces loaded with canister.[76]

Midway between Seminary Ridge and Lon's position ran the Emmitsburg Road. On the west side of the road, at intervals, the fences had been broken down. In front of Pickett's columns on the east side of the road stood the red Codori farmhouse and barn, the terrain behind the house sloping upward to the crest from which frowned the Union defense lines. West of the road were the smoking remains of the Bliss barn and farmhouse, but once they were reached, more than half a mile of open fields still stretched before the Confederate assault force. Between Pickett's left front (Garnett's brigade) and Pettigrew's right (Fry's brigade), a slight ridge and fence line separated the columns until they came to the Emmitsburg Road. From the outset, it had been planned that Pickett's and Pettigrew's columns, followed by Trimble's, would step off the attack minutes apart from one another and follow the terrain; when they reached the Emmitsburg Road—and the long swale in the land which could provide some slight cover from Union artillery fire—Pickett's Virginians would perform a "left oblique" movement and dress upon Pettigrew's right flank; then the entire assault force would move forward in unison toward the Union lines.[77]

As the columns pressed through the smoke and dust toward the Emmitsburg Road, the fury of the Union artillery fire increased. Vast gaps were torn in the ranks by solid shot and shells. "A ponderous shell screams across the valley, striking the ground in front of the advancing line, bursts and 'cuts [a] swath' of ten men out of a company," recalled a soldier in the 8th Virginia. "Four of them all flat on their faces, nevermore to rise; five or six others limp away to the rear, or lie moaning and groaning in agony. 'Close up men!' shouts the captain and immediately the gap is closed; a new 'touch of elbows' is established, and the line moves on without faltering for an instant. 'Whizz-z!' whistles a grape shot, and the crashing bones tells that it has found a victim in the same captain who just spoke! 'Close up, men!' shouts the first lieutenant now

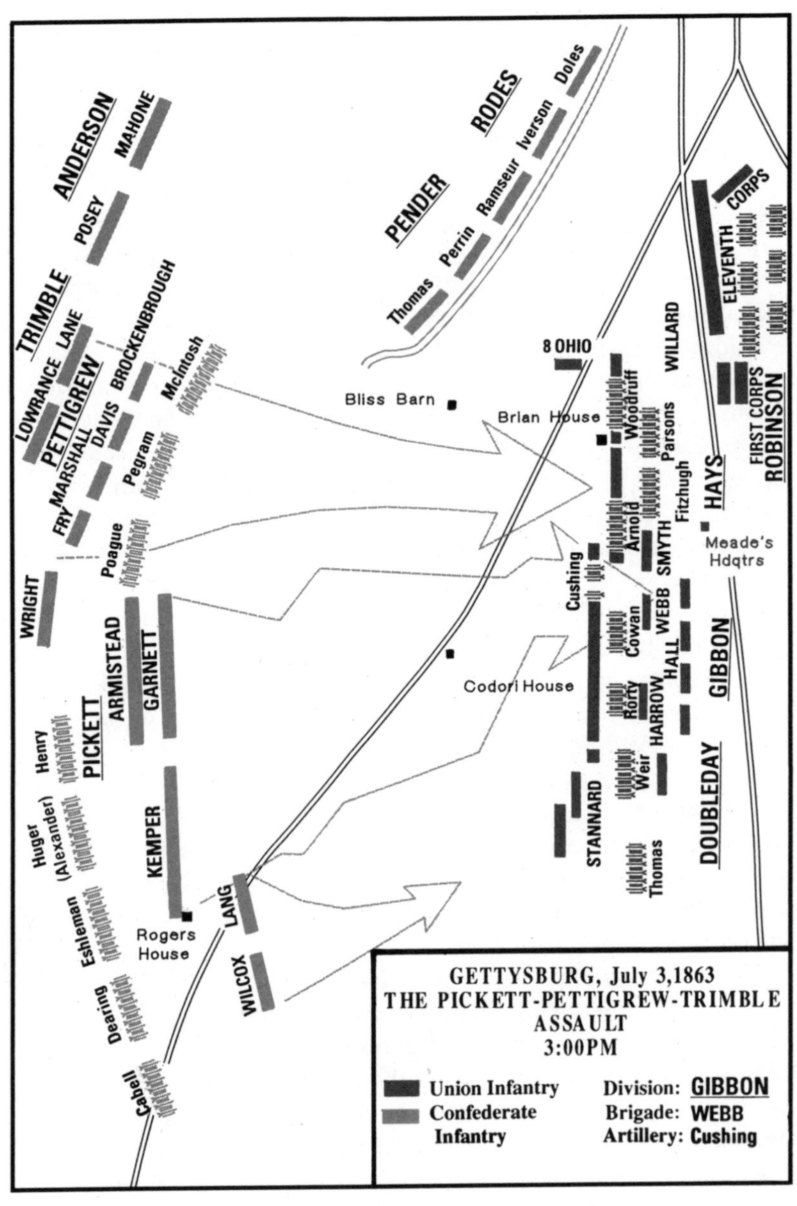
GETTYSBURG, July 3,1863
THE PICKETT-PETTIGREW-TRIMBLE ASSAULT
3:00PM
Union Infantry
Confederate Infantry
Division: GIBBON
Brigade: WEBB
Artillery: Cushing
Bliss Barn
Codori House
Rogers House
Meade's Hdqtrs
8 OHIO

in command. Another crash, and the regimental major falls dead. 'Close up, men!' and we step over the corpse, and march right on."[78]

Union skirmishers along the Emmitsburg Road poured a spattering fire into the columns but quickly fled back across the fields to the Cemetery Ridge defense works. As Pickett's three brigades reached the depth of the extensive swale west of the Emmitsburg Road, the air was pierced by shouts of field officers ordering "left oblique." As if on dress parade, the columns, line by line, before the murderous artillery fire, moved forty-five degrees to the left front and merged with Pettigrew's oncoming hosts. The assault force was now one gigantic column moving forward, one eyewitness wrote, "as with one soul." Artillery fire was thinning the oncoming ranks severely, and as they approached the Emmitsburg Road, the Union infantry opened up a galling fire from their muskets.[79]

"As the charging column neared the Emmitsburg Road," recalled a Tennessean in Fry's brigade, "volley after volley of small arms aided with dreadful effect in thinning our ranks. We reached the first plank or slab fence and the column clambered over with a speed as if in stampeded retreat. The time it took to climb to the top of the fence seemed to the men an age of suspense. It was not a leaping over; it was rather an insensible tumbling to the ground in the nervous hope of escaping the thickening missiles that buried themselves in falling victims, in the ground and in the fence, against which they rattled with the distinctness of large rain drops pattering on a roof. Every man that reached the road, in my view, sank to the ground. . . . In a moment the order to advance was given, and on we pressed across the next fence, but many of our comrades remained in the road and never crossed the second fence, many being wounded in crossing the first and in the road."[80]

Behind the attacking columns, just west of the Emmitsburg Road and south of the Codori house, batteries of artillery unlimbered, including Major B.F. Eshleman's, Lt. C.W. Motes's Troup (Georgia) Artillery, and Henry's battalion under Maj. John C. Haskell. Colonel Alexander had brought forward the guns from the right wing of his artillery line near the peach orchard. Within moments the Confederate artillery raked the Union lines. Exploding shells crashed into Cushing's position. Heavy smoke obscured the landscape, and the enormous assault columns in front of Lon's guns were lost behind a newly dense screen of sulfurous billows.[81]

Rumbling into position to Lon's right and rear—behind the 125th New York, 1st Delaware, and 14th Connecticut—came Capt. Robert H. Fitzhugh's Battery K, 1st New York Light Artillery (six three-inch Ordnance rifles), along with Lt. A.N. Parsons's Battery A, 1st New Jersey Artillery (six ten-pound Parrott rifles), from the Artillery Reserve. Soon those twelve guns were pouring shells into the advancing columns.[82]

Captain Rorty, who had kept his remaining two Parrott rifles in the action, was struck by a bursting Confederate shell and his bloody frame hurled to the ground alongside his number two gun. The brave and devoted Irishman was dead. In civilian life before the war he had complained of being sickly and affected by nervous disorders, including panic attacks, yet at the time of his death he exhibited as much valor and courage as any man on that bloody field. Just minutes later his second-in-command, Lt. A.S. Sheldon, fell desperately wounded. But with the Massachusetts infantrymen manning one gun, and the bloodied remnants of Rorty's cannoneers manning the other, the battery continued to fire at the enemy.[83]

Lon stood alongside his number four gun. With him were First Sergeant Fuger, Sgt. Edward Hurley, Pvts. Patrick Glascott, Christopher Smith, Patrick Mullen, and Simon Malinger, and Cpl. Thomas Moon. Three of the cannoneers were German-born and German-speaking, one was the son of a Swiss-born mother, and three were Irish-born; they were all that remained of the cannoneers of Battery A, 4th United States Artillery, at the stone wall. Lieutenant Milne and the infantrymen from the "California Regiment" continued to man the number three gun to the right.[84]

Gen. Webb could see the moment of crisis fast approaching. Cushing's battery would not be able to hold its position in the line, and the gap created by his silenced guns would cut Webb's infantry brigade in half if it were not closed. The tremendous Confederate columns continued up the forward slope toward Lon's position. Cushing called to Sergeant Fuger to order the cannoneers to fire canister.

"Canister!" yelled Fuger in his deep German voice.

The shot was rammed down the hot barrels of the two guns.

"Ready," the gunners replied. Lon nodded.

"Fire!" The two guns recoiled behind dense banks of smoke and sheets of flame.[85]

With the order "commence firing," the Ordnance rifles blasted forth round upon round of canister. The shot ripped gaping holes in the butternut ranks. Many of the men in the enemy assault columns were "bent in a half stoop as they marched up the slope, as if to protect their faces and dodge the balls." The Confederates "were at once enveloped in a dense cloud of smoke and dust," wrote the commander of the 8th Ohio, Col. Franklin Sawyer. "Arms, heads, blankets, guns and knapsacks were thrown and tossed into the air. Their track, as they advanced, was strewn with dead and wounded. A moan went up from the field, distinctly to be heard amid the storm of battle, but on they went, too much enveloped in smoke and dust now to permit us to distinguish their lines or movements, for the mass appeared more like a cloud of moving smoke and dust than a column of troops. Still it advanced amid the now deafening roar of artillery and storm of battle."[86]

Lon assisted his cannoneers in loading the number four gun. Finding the leather thumbstall charred and ruined through frequent use and no replacement anywhere to be found, he stoppered the gun's vent with his bare thumb. The escaping gases from the swabbing of the barrel burned his thumb to the bone. Lon grabbed his thumb, grimacing in pain. His agonies were indescribable.[87]

Midway up the slope, Pickett's brigades began yet another "left oblique" in the face of the blistering artillery fire from Thomas's, Weir's, Rorty's, Cowan's, Cushing's, Arnold's, Fitzhugh's, and Parsons's guns and an enfilading fire from Lt. Benjamin F. Rittenhouse's guns as far away as Little Round Top. Union flanking columns from Brig. Gen. George Stannard's infantry brigade—the 13th, 14th, and 16th Vermont—from the First Corps poured a devastating fire into the right flank of the Virginians. General Kemper went down in the smoke and fury; a bullet entered his groin and ricocheted up his spinal column. Farther up the slope, General Garnett, still steadying his men, was blasted from his horse, his body torn to pieces. Garnett's frightened and wounded mount sped to the rear. The general's remains were never found.[88]

The 16th Vermont, supported by four companies of the 14th, about-faced and struck the left flank of Wilcox's and Lang's brigades just east of the Emmitsburg Road. The Alabamians and Floridians had stepped off in the attack well behind and to the right of Pickett's, Pettigrew's, and Trimble's columns. The fire on their left flank and the incessant artillery fire from the Union Artillery Reserve batteries along Cemetery Ridge brought the two hapless Confederate brigades to a bloody halt.[89]

The Confederate infantrymen in Pickett's division, as they approached to within two hundred yards of Cushing's battery, leveled their rifles and, behind walls of flame and smoke, poured ragged volleys into the Union lines. Some of Lon's remaining cannoneers fell, among them Lieutenant Milne. Hit in the abdomen, he fell to the ground, writhing in pain. Lon, seeing the volunteer lieutenant fall, beckoned to Fuger to order some men nearby—probably infantrymen from the 71st Pennsylvania—to take Milne to the rear. He was in agony, bleeding profusely. Though not well liked by many of the regular artillerymen, the Rhode Island lieutenant had displayed much bravery. The wound was mortal; he would die six days later at the Second Corps hospital.[90]

Out from the rear of Pickett's bloodied columns came General Armistead, his hat placed on the tip of the blade of his upraised sword, urging his Virginians to follow him. Lon's two guns continued to fire round upon round of canister into the advancing hosts.[91] As the enemy columns came to within one hundred yards of Lon's guns, Little Dad, up the

Union line, observed through the dense smoke what appeared to him to be a Confederate breakthrough at Cushing's position. He quickly ordered Lt. John Egan to hitch up the two guns that made up the left section of the battery, and to move south to help his old classmate. He must have recalled how Lon had brought two brass guns to his assistance along the Smoketown Road at Antietam almost a year before. The guns were hitched to the limbers, and under the yells of drivers and the crack of whips the battery section left its position in front of Ziegler's Grove. Woodruff waved them on, calling to the drivers to hurry. Just as he turned around, a musket ball struck him in the spine, exiting near his lower rib. Little Dad crumpled to the ground. Egan saw him fall and ordered two of the cannoneers running alongside the limbers and guns to assist in carrying their commander to safety. "I ordered you to the left," Woodruff yelled to Egan above the din. "Do your duty, and leave me!" Desperately wounded and bleeding profusely, Woodruff was nevertheless moved by the two men into Ziegler's Grove, where he was propped up against a tree.[92]

Back down the Union lines, south of Lon's position, one of the Parrott rifles remaining in Rorty's battery was loaded with three rounds of canister and, in the frenzy of the moment, apparently overloaded with powder. When it was fired, the gun recoiled so violently that it broke the trail and completely overturned.[93]

The situation in the angle was critical. Faint from loss of blood and terribly ill, gritting his teeth in a vain attempt to withstand the severe pain, Lon asked Fuger to order the two remaining guns double-shotted with canister.[94]

"Double canister," shouted Fuger. The artillerymen, sweating and coughing in the dense smoke under the hot July sun, hastened to service the two pieces. The infantrymen from the 71st Pennsylvania manning the number three gun had to improvise; having expended all their ammunition, they emptied their cartridge boxes and scoured the ground, picking up jagged fragments of burst shells and rocks. Ramming home bullets, rocks, shell fragments, and even a bayonet, the infantrymen feverishly loaded the number three gun, then stepped back into their respective positions alongside the Ordnance rifle to await the order to fire.[95]

"Ready," yelled the gunners. The lanyards were stretched. Lon peered through his field glasses at the oncoming hosts. It seemed like an eternity. His face was distorted with pain when he turned to Fuger. "Fire!" he cried.

"Fire!" bellowed Fuger.[96]

As the lanyards were jerked, the two Ordnance rifles boomed and recoiled, belching forth their hail of iron through red sheets of flame and great clouds of smoke. Almost simultaneously, Fuger turned around and saw Lon lunge violently. His knees buckled; the field glasses fell from his hand. Fuger, then standing only about three feet ahead and a foot to the right, stepped over to catch his young commander. Cushing's arms stretched outward as if to catch his sergeant's shoulders; then he fell to his knees, and blood gushed from his nose and mouth, splattering Fuger's boots, trousers, and blouse. Lon's eyes rolled back in their sockets. His kepi fell from his head. A bullet had hit him just below his nose, drilling its way to the base of his brain. Fuger caught Lon's mangled and bloody frame in his right arm, momentarily holding it upright amid the torrent of gunfire. Then the loyal first sergeant gently lowered the body of his lieutenant, by now in its death convulsions, to the ground along the right side of the trail of the number four gun, the head toward the enemy. Lt. Alonzo Hereford Cushing was dead. From the time he had received his first ghastly wounds, Lon had remained on the field for over one and one-half hours![97]

Above the roar of gunfire, Sergeant Fuger yelled to his cannoneers to take Lon's body to the rear. Private Smith and, most likely, Sergeant Hurley—a German and an Irishman—carried their noble commander's body back beyond the crest of the ridge and laid it down behind a rock outcropping near the 114th Pennsylvania and 3d Maine. The two cannoneers then bravely ran back to the remaining guns at the wall.[98]

Fuger's heavy German accent boomed out the command "Treble canister!" The number four gun was swabbed and loaded for one last shot.[99] The dense mass of attackers was just over fifty yards from the stone wall. "Old Lo" Armistead, seeking a place to breach the Union defenses, saw ahead of him the disabled Battery A, 4th United States Artillery, and the massive gap it created in the defense lines. With his hat pierced by the blade and drooping over the hilt of his upraised and gesturing sword, Armistead beckoned to his men to follow him. "Give them the cold steel," he yelled. Through the din, the Confederates began their high-pitched "rebel yell." The sound sent chills of fright through the blue ranks as the depleted and bloodied yet confident butternut and gray columns stormed toward the wall.[100]

The two companies of the 71st Pennsylvania retired from the forward wall and, under orders from Colonel Smith, took up positions behind the perpendicular stone fence between the inner and outer angles in front of Battery A, 1st Rhode Island Light Artillery. They took with them the loaded muskets they had scoured from the bloody field the night before. The men of the 69th Pennsylvania, beneath their green Irish flag, unleashed ragged volleys of rifle fire from their similarly scavenged muskets. The rush of the enemy, though, was too great. With the infantrymen of the 69th Pennsylvania slowly giving up ground, the regimental line bent back through the slashing and into the copse of trees.[101]

The two Ordnance rifles of Cushing's battery stood silent. The cannoneers of the number four gun, after loading the three canister rounds, waited for the command to fire. The enemy steadily marched closer. The lanyard was stretched. Christy Smith motioned to Sergeant Fuger that the time had come to fire.

"Wait a minute," said Fuger. The enemy closed to well below point-blank range.

"Let 'em have it!"

The lanyard was jerked and with a "splitting report," the gun blasted forth its death-dealing charges into the faces of the enemy, recoiling and shaking the ground. Smoke seemed to envelop everything. Cries, shrieks, and a distinct moan could be heard above the roar and blast of gunfire. A massive gap had been torn in the butternut ranks. "For an instant," recalled Christy Smith, "the columns wavered and swayed." The attack did not halt, however; the brave attackers "with a savage yell" closed ranks and pressed onward toward their objective, their one remaining brigade commander in the lead.[102]

The number four gun in Cushing's battery was completely out of ammunition. Corporal Moon ran back to one of the unexploded limbers to look for more canister, but there was none. The cannoneers at the number four gun fought the swarming Confederate legions with pistols, sabers, handspikes, rammers, and even their hands. For the few remaining men of Cushing's battery, however, resistance was fruitless. The sheer numbers in the attacking enemy force were overwhelming. Sergeant Fuger, Private Smith, and the remaining artillerymen abandoned the last Ordnance rifle at the wall. Amid the roar of battle the Confederates yelled, "Stop, you Yankee devils!" Corporal Moon had started back to the line, but observing the cannoneers leaving the guns at the wall, he turned around and joined his fellow artillerymen in flight.[103]

Some of the soldiers from the 71st Pennsylvania remained alongside the number three gun as the dense masses of butternut and gray poured over the wall. Pvt. Charles Olcott of Company F swung a sponge staff at an approaching Virginia officer, hitting him squarely in the head. It was the last act of defense the thinned gun crew of infantrymen could offer. They quickly fled to the rear, and the gap in the Union lines at the outer angle was complete.[104]

Momentarily, General Webb was seized with panic. His brigade had fallen away from the forward stone wall; the front regiments were in a state of disorganization; the men were confused and frightened. Some were running. Cushing's battery, which should have been replaced before the assault began, was silent. Where the Philadelphia Brigade and its artillery support had held the center of the Union lines, a gnawing gap appeared, inviting the enemy to seize it. "The Army of the Potomac was never nearer being whipped than it was here," General Webb later remarked. "I almost wished to get killed." He felt at fault for having left Cushing's battery on the field. "Where I put Cushing I should have gone myself, and (remembering the hour and the day) I wanted the supports to take the place where I had placed [Cushing]," he asserted.[105]

The Confederates, having overtaken Cushing's guns at the wall, leveled their muskets and fired a volley at the retreating cannoneers. A bullet hit Hurley in the back. He leaped into the air and then fell to the ground, crying, "For God's sake, don't leave me here!" Fuger and Smith stopped in the pandemonium of battle, grabbed the desperately wounded Hurley, dragged him over the crest of the ridge, and laid him behind a fallen tree.[106] General Webb observed another of Cushing's gunners running to the rear. Moving in front of the terrified artilleryman, Webb pointed his sword at the soldier's breast and told him to stand where he was. "My God, General," the cannoneer exclaimed, "I can do nothing here alone!" Webb replied firmly, "You stay here and I will get you help." Just then a shell smashed into one of Cushing's caissons not far from the clump of trees. The shell exploded, hurling fragments of the chest, chassis, and wheels into the air, killing and maiming the horses harnessed to it.[107]

Webb turned around. Pandemonium reigned in the angle. Motioning with his sword and yelling at the top of his lungs, trying to be heard above the roar and roll of gunfire, he ordered the 72d Pennsylvania to advance toward the angle. The men could not hear him, but Colonel Baxter observed the young brigadier's motions and led the 72d obliquely to the right. The regiment came to a halt in line of battle facing the angle along the crest of the ridge, just behind the position occupied by Cushing's guns when the bombardment began.[108]

Ahead of the 72d Pennsylvania and in front of Cushing's wrecked battery, General Armistead mounted the stone fence. The cheering Confederates, beneath a sea of waving red flags, all tattered and shot-torn, advanced toward the outer angle. Steadying himself as he bounded off of the wall and onto the ground, Armistead placed his left hand on the left wheel of Cushing's number four gun, the one Lon had manned until his death.[109]

The 72d Pennsylvania, its men somewhat broken up into knots after it had been brought to a halt along the crest, began to fire ragged volleys into the approaching columns. The noise was deafening; bullets flew across the angle. General Webb ordered the 72d to advance toward the stone wall. "Charge bayonets!" he cried.[110] The 72d did not move. Webb tried to wrench the colors from the terrified bearer, but the soldier

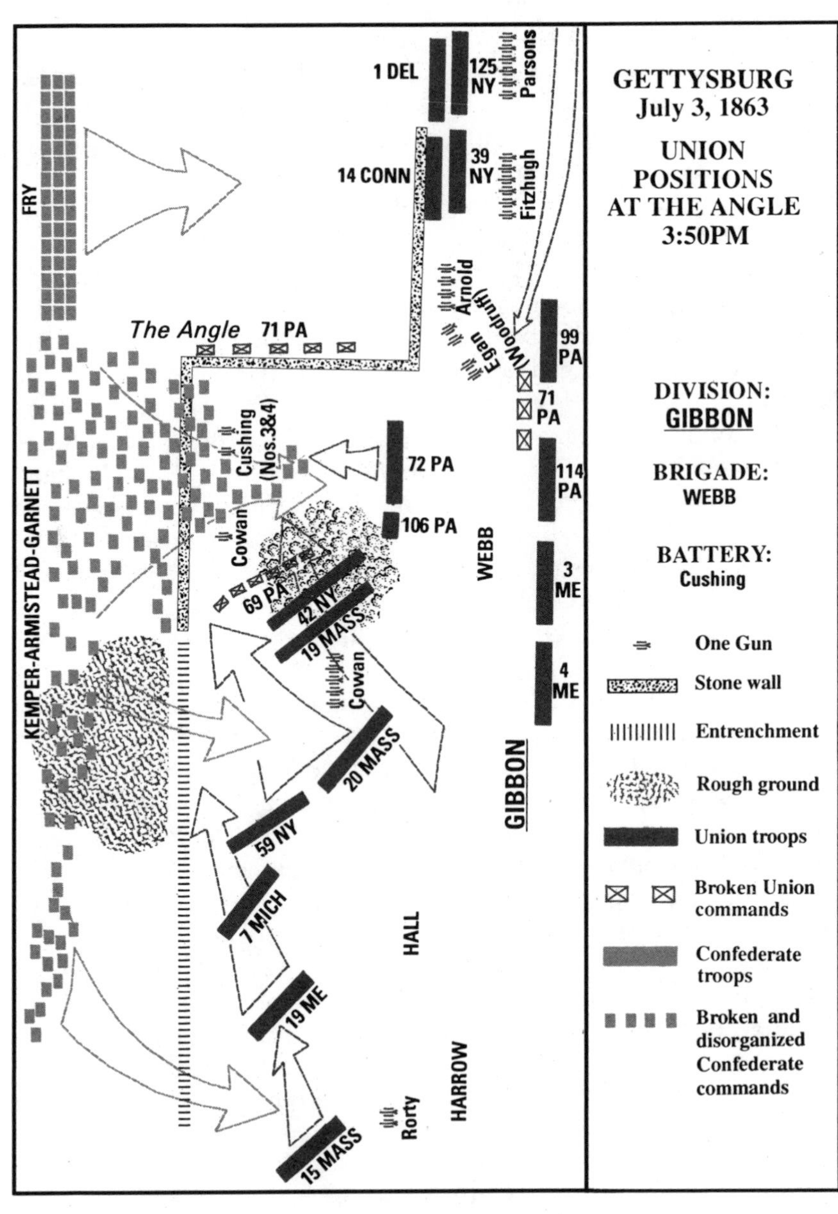
GETTYSBURG
July 3, 1863
UNION POSITIONS AT THE ANGLE
3:50PM
DIVISION:
GIBBON
BRIGADE:
WEBB
BATTERY:
Cushing
One Gun
Stone wall
Entrenchment
Rough ground
Union troops
Broken Union commands
Confederate troops
Broken and disorganized Confederate commands
FRY
KEMPER-ARMISTEAD-GARNETT
The Angle
71 PA
1 DEL
125 NY
Parsons
14 CONN
39 NY
Fitzhugh
Arnold
(Woodruff)
Egan
99 PA
71 PA
114 PA
3 ME
4 ME
Cushing (Nos.3&4)
72 PA
106 PA
Cowan
69 PA
42 NY
19 MASS
20 MASS
59 NY
7 MICH
19 ME
15 MASS
Rorty
WEBB
GIBBON
HALL
HARROW

impulsively resisted. The enemy, led by the intrepid Armistead, was massing inside the angle and in front of the clump of trees. Webb, looking over his right shoulder, saw remnants of the 69th Pennsylvania giving more ground. He left the 72d at the crest of the ridge, and coolly walked over to the Irish regiment to try to keep it from breaking.[111]

General Hancock, astride his horse behind the 19th Massachusetts and 42d New York, to the rear and south of the clump of trees, exhorted the men impatiently, "Forward, men! Forward! Now is your chance!" The men of the two regiments of Colonel Hall's fine brigade arose and ran, en masse, through Cowan's guns and into the clump of trees to bolster the terribly thinned and weakened 69th Pennsylvania. Their movement was made at almost a right angle to the rest of their brigade. In the excitement of the moment, the 7th Michigan, 59th New York, and 20th Massachusetts bent back around Cowan's guns as elements of Pickett's division massed ahead of them. General Hancock, after galloping to the left, fell with a nasty leg wound.[112]

Back in the angle, the soldiers of Companies A and B of the 71st Pennsylvania, forming a line behind the perpendicular fence between the inner and outer angles, fired two ferocious volleys into the oncoming Virginians. General Armistead had advanced only a few yards beyond Cushing's number four gun when the enfilading fire from the infantrymen of the 71st Pennsylvania tore through him and his men. In the dense gunsmoke, dust, and fire, "Lo" Armistead staggered and then crumpled to the ground, literally riddled with bullets, just beyond Cushing's battered number four gun. Large numbers of his exultant Virginians were also mowed down by the lead hail.[113]

At the crest of the ridge, the 72d Pennsylvania was given courage by the effect of the rapid fire of the two companies of the 71st. The standardbearer began to wave the national colors; Colonel Baxter yelled for his men to fire a volley into the attackers, and a sheet of flame erupted from the rifle barrels of Baxter's Fire Zouaves. A ragged volley was returned by the surging Virginians. In Baxter's regiment three color bearers fell in rapid succession. One of them was hit by thirteen bullets.[114]

Almost simultaneously, the left section of Arnold's battery, behind and to the right of the inner angle, was ordered by its captain to direct its fire into the angle where Armistead's legions swarmed through Cushing's silent guns. The two guns were double-shotted with canister and swung about forty-five degrees to the left. At the same time, Lieutenant Egan's two Napoleons of Woodruff's battery arrived at the angle under the direction of General Hays, who by that time had stripped off his blouse and was directing his men in shirtsleeves. The guns were unlimbered just to the left of Arnold's battery and in front of the 99th Pennsylvania and Collis's Zouaves. The cannoneers feverishly loaded two guns with double rounds of canister and opened fire. The deadly shot blasted the attackers, shattering their ranks. The canister shot hurled into the angle from Arnold's and Egan's guns ripped through the dense mass of attackers and mangled and splintered Cushing's silent Ordnance rifles at the wall to utter scrap.[115]

Another surge into the Union lines struck below the angle but was beaten back by Rorty's Parrott rifles and Cowan's Ordnance rifles, coupled with heavy fire from Hall's and Harrow's infantrymen.[116] With the attack against Cowan's guns crushed, the 20th Massachusetts, 59th New York, and 7th Michigan of Colonel Hall's brigade, almost on impulse, poured northward toward the angle. General Harrow's commands—the 19th Maine, 15th Massachusetts, 1st Minnesota, and 82d New York—crowded behind Hall's veterans after the enemy thrust against Rorty's battery had been crushed.[117] In the angle, artillery fire had been replaced by small arms fire and hand-to-hand combat as the 72d Pennsylvania, followed by the 114th Pennsylvania, swept through the remnants of Cushing's battery.

Pettigrew's columns had hit the Union lines as Pickett's thrust spent itself, but Davis's, Marshall's, and Fry's brigades approached the climax of the attack with their flanks hopelessly exposed. Mayo's (Brockenbrough's) Virginians on Pettigrew's extreme left had been stunned early in the attack by concentrated artillery fire and the fire of a flanking force made up of the 8th Ohio. Their organization had been broken up previously by the fact that their movement had taken them around the smoldering Bliss house, barn, outbuildings, and fences. Once disorganized, the brigade had broken apart under the heavy gunfire and fled to the rear. With their left flank completely melted away, the North Carolinians, Tennesseans, Alabamians, and Mississippians had raced toward the Union defense lines just as Pickett's columns on the right were overwhelmed. Pettigrew's butternut hosts, closely followed by Trimble's two Tar Heel brigades, had let out a yell and swarmed toward the wall.[118] Woodruff's battery—reduced to four guns—had been silent until the Confederate columns had approached to within five hundred yards; then it opened fire, together with blasts from Fitzhugh's, Parsons's and Arnold's guns. Pettigrew's commands were torn apart by the terrific artillery fire and infantry fusillades. The desperate Confederates fought near the wall with clubbed muskets and gouged with bayonets, but to no avail. The attack, launched without necessary support, melted away in the sulfurous smoke and dust. Brigades had been reduced to small regiments; regiments to mere squads.[119]

The battle was won. Rebel soldiers, hopelessly outnumbered, threw down their arms and surrendered in large numbers or withdrew back down Cemetery Ridge; many in the attacking force streamed back across the smoke-laden fields toward Seminary Ridge. Trimble's demi-division, the second wave behind Pettigrew's brigades, was the most nearly intact; it withdrew toward the Emmitsburg Road in some order. Pickett's and Pettigrew's commands, however, had been almost destroyed. Pickett's division of Virginians had lost 2,882 officers and men, a staggering 62 percent. Thirty-one of Pickett's colonels, lieutenant colonels, and majors were killed, wounded, or missing. All three brigade commanders were casualties. In front of Cushing's battery, Sergeant Fuger reported that his surviving cannoneers counted over six hundred dead, nearly all from Pickett's division—ghastly testimony of the effectiveness of Cushing's fire. Within Pettigrew's command the losses were equally staggering: 3,585 officers and men were casualties, nearly 56 percent. Almost all of Pettigrew's field grade officers were killed, wounded, or missing. Marshall's and Davis's brigades each lost nearly 70 percent of its effective force. To top it all, General Hancock reported that the men of his Second Corps had captured thirty-three Confederate battle flags.[120]

All who remained along the crest of Cemetery Ridge knew that at last there was victory. Many others never knew. Behind a large rock, on the eastern face of the ridge, lay Lon's body, bloody and stilled in death.

Epilogue: "Faithful until Death"

The Army of the Potomac indeed tasted victory on July 3, 1863. East of Gettysburg, Gen. J.E.B. Stuart's Confederate horsemen had been fought to a standstill by Union cavalry. One brigade particularly distinguished itself during the spirited engagement. The Michigan cavalry brigade—the 1st, 5th, 6th, and 7th Michigan and Battery M, 2d United States Artillery—was commanded by none other than Lon's classmate, Fannie Custer, who, since June 29, 1863, had been wearing the shoulder straps of a brigadier general of volunteers.[1]

Along Cemetery Ridge, General Meade and his son and aide-de-camp rode up to the center of the Second Corps lines. Dressed in his sack coat with the shoulder straps of a major general, a straight sword, heavy hightop boots, buff gauntlets, and broad-brimmed slouch hat, Meade was hardly the figure of a hero. But the attack had been repulsed; Confederate prisoners were being collected, and soon "a miserable, melancholy stream of dirty gray [poured] over the crest to [the] rear." The general, in a state of exultation, let forth a hearty "Hurrah!" His aides "roared out three 'Hurrahs,'" and the men of the Second Corps began to cheer. Immediately, Meade started giving orders for the replacement of troops along the forward line and the advancement of reinforcements.[2]

He could see that Cushing's battery had ceased to exist. All six of its Ordnance rifles had been dismounted and their carriages reduced to splinters. None of the limbers remained; all had been exploded or shot to pieces. Twenty-nine horses had been killed, and thirty-six were wounded or otherwise unfit for service. Fifty remained serviceable, and those were mostly in the teams pulling the baggage wagons and forge. Seven of the battery's officers and men had been killed and thirty-three wounded; one enlisted man was missing and presumed dead.[3]

Sergeant Fuger, the senior officer of the battery, assembled the men who remained. He was ordered by Captain Hazard to take them back up the Granite School House Road, beyond the Second Corps hospital site at the schoolhouse, to a site near the Baltimore Pike. In the wake of the fighting, Fuger had not been able to locate his horse; he even searched among the hundreds of dead horses along Cemetery Ridge without success. Giving up his quest, he walked with his men to the rear.[4]

Fuger called for Cpl. Thomas Moon, acting sergeant of the guard, to take the body of Lieutenant Cushing back beyond the Second Corps hospital to the bivouac site of the battery. Moon asked other members of the battery to help him. Pvts. Patrick Mullen, Simon Malinger, and John McCormack—Irish and German-born volunteers, formerly with the 116th Pennsylvania of the Irish Brigade—helped Moon carry Lon's bloody frame back to the rear. At the bivouac site, Fuger ordered Moon and the three privates to lay Lon's body on the ground nearby, where they covered it with "a piece of tarpaulin or a shelter tent."[5]

At the Second Corps hospital lay thousands of wounded from the old corps, including Lt. Joseph A. Milne, who was writhing in agony. That evening the desperately wounded Lt. George A. Woodruff was brought in and laid on a stretcher in the little stone schoolhouse. After clearing the field of wounded, ambulance crews scoured houses and barns along the Taneytown Road for wounded soldiers who had been carried there. The Second Corps chief of ambulances found one fellow lying on his face in a cowshed. He was an artilleryman from one of the Second Corps batteries, possibly Lon's. An artillery shell had carried away all of the flesh of his hams so that his bones were visible. He told the ambulance crews that, as an artilleryman, he had to stand with his side to the enemy fire, and the shell had torn through his hams from side to side. The poor soldier was taken to the Second Corps hospital.[6]

Along Cemetery Ridge the grim task of burying the dead continued. More than 1,800 bodies of Confederate soldiers lay in front of the low stone wall from Ziegler's Grove to below the clump of trees. Just to the left of the clump of trees, Capt. Andrew Cowan counted the casualties in his own battery, and with the help of infantrymen from the nearby 20th Massachusetts, he organized squads to bury the dead south of the angle. Cowan himself directed the interment of the remains of Capt James McKay Rorty, down along the stone wall—a Scotsman burying his Irish comrade-in-arms. Rorty's grave was marked with a board removed from a box of hardtack.[7]

After Sergeant Fuger and his exhausted men reached their bivouac site near the Baltimore Pike, rations were delivered. Someone gave the sergeant some hardtack and a piece of bacon. Fuger lay down beside the body of Alonzo Cushing and fell asleep with the hardtack and bacon still in his hands; he was simply too tired to eat.[8]

As darkness fell, a man awakened him. "Sergeant," he said, "your horse is here at the picket line." Fuger got up and followed the soldier. Sure enough, his horse "had found [its way to] the battery in some mysterious way." The animal was terribly wounded, however; one of its hips had been completely torn away by an artillery shell. Fuger ordered the poor brute put out of its misery.[9] Fuger and Moon guarded Lon's body all through the night. By the early morning of the "Glorious Fourth," it had begun to rain. It seemed always to rain after great battles. To avoid sleeping in the water, Moon placed a blanket over Lon's body and slept the rest of the morning on top of his lifeless commander.[10]

Later that morning Lt. Tully McCrea of Battery I, 1st United States Artillery, called the roll of what was left of Cushing's battery. Four noncommissioned officers and one hundred privates answered roll call. Afterward, Corporal Moon walked over to Lon's body. He removed the rent and bloody shell jacket and gave it to Henry, Lon's faithful cook and servant. Moon kept Lon's bloodstained shoulder straps.[11]

Little Dad Woodruff had passed the night in terrible pain, yet "not one groan or murmur escaped him." Lieutenant Egan visited with him all through the day. "Have we beaten the enemy?" Woodruff asked. "Yes," replied Egan. "There was an expression of gladness," Egan recalled of Woodruff's countenance, "that only a patriot's soul could stamp." At 4:00 P.M. on July 4, Lt. George A. Woodruff died. In the coat pocket of their lifeless commander, Egan and McCrea found an unopened letter from Little Dad's father. It announced the death of Woodruff's mother, Augusta. In the pouring rain, Egan and McCrea buried their brave little commander beneath an oak tree that had been ripped apart by a solid shot near the Granite School House.[12]

In Washington, Milton Buckingham Cushing, Jr., heard the news of Lon's death shortly after the fighting ended. He immediately set out for Gettysburg to try to locate his brother's body. Milton was fortunate; Sergeant Fuger and Corporal Moon had protected the remains of their commander. After procuring a wooden soldier's casket, Milton placed the body of his brother aboard a train and accompanied it all the way to West Point, where Lon had told his brothers he wanted to be buried.[13]

The naval squadron to which Lt. William Barker Cushing had been attached had been called back to Washington to bolster the defenses of the capital during Lee's invasion of Maryland and Pennsylvania. When he read in the press of the loss of his brother at Gettysburg, William was granted a leave of absence. Not knowing that his older brother had preceded him to the battlefield, he arrived in Gettysburg just days after Milton had departed for West Point with Lon's body. "The field, when I reached it," Will wrote, "was a sickening sight. Thirty thousand wounded men and thousands of unburied dead lay on the earth—in road, field, wood and orchard—and under the scorching sun on the bare hillside amidst all the wreck of a great battle. Dismounted cannon, dead horses, exploded caissons and broken muskets were everywhere—and the artillery position [of Cushing's battery] was almost paved with the rebel iron that had been hurled by the hundred and fifty guns massed against it previous to the final charge. My brother's battery was destroyed. Five out of the six guns were dismounted—all of the officers and most of the men were shot, and seventy of its horses stiffened upon the wooded knoll where they were placed. Our army had moved on in pursuit of the foe, and there was nothing left for me to do but return to naval duty."[14]

What remained of Battery A, 4th United States Artillery, was attached to Battery I, 1st United States Artillery; temporarily, Lon's and Little Dad's former commands were united. On July 16, 1863, the two units were separated again, Battery A becoming a horse artillery battery, equipped with two three-inch Ordnance rifles and two twelve-pound Napoleons, and later with four twelve-pound Napoleons. It was assigned to the First Brigade of Horse Artillery in the Cavalry Corps of the Army of the Potomac. Returning to take over the command of the battery was Lt. Rufus King, Jr. Lt. Arthur Morris was reassigned to the battery as the senior section commander.[15]

After the fall of Vicksburg, Pvt. Howard Bass Cushing had recuperated from a bout with the recurring symptoms of tuberculosis in the shell-pocked home of his cousin Judge Lawrence Sterne Houghton. Hearing of his brother's death at Gettysburg, Howard obtained a commission in the regular army and, with President Lincoln's endorsement, joined Lt. Rufus King's Battery A, 4th United States Artillery, in November 1863. He served with King's battery until the end of the war. Though court-martialed and suspended from service in 1865, Howard later returned to the army as a lieutenant in the 3d United States Cavalry, and was killed by the Apache Indians near Tucson, Arizona, in May 1871. Cannoneer Thomas Moon had given Lon's bloodstained shoulder straps to Howard when he joined Battery A in the fall of 1863. Presumably, Howard had them with him when he was killed.[16]

Lon's hope for his brother William's success was truly realized. On October 27, 1864, Will daringly guided a torpedo into the Confederate ram *Albemarle*, sinking the vessel and thereby opening the way for Union control of the Roanoke River in North Carolina. President Lincoln commended him for bravery, and Congress promoted him to the rank of lieutenant commander. His daring exploit against the *Albemarle* and his actions in the attack on Fort Fisher made him one of the most popular wartime heroes in his own lifetime. He eventually reached the rank of commander. He married Katherine Louise Forbes of Fredonia in 1870, and two daughters were born to the marriage. Will was never well, however; he died of tuberculosis at the age of thirty-two on December 17, 1874, and was buried in the Naval Academy Cemetery at Annapolis.[17]

Milton, Jr., also remained in the U.S. Navy. He married his longtime sweetheart, Ellen Douglas Grosvenor, in 1869. His health too remained precarious, however, and on January 4, 1887, after numerous leaves of absence from his navy duties, he died of tuberculosis at Dunkirk, New York.[18]

Mary Barker Smith Cushing died on March 26, 1891, at the age of eighty-four; she had been living with her daughter, Mary Isabel, and son-in-law in St. Joseph, Missouri. Mary was buried alongside her husband in Forest Hill Cemetery in Fredonia, New York. She died with the comfort of having visited the grave of her son Alonzo at least once. Accompanied by her oldest son, Milton, she stopped at West Point in October 1865 on her way from Fredonia to Chelsea to visit her sisters and their families. She saw the 1850 Barracks, the Academy Building, the Library and Post Headquarters and the Cadet Chapel. "After talking with the Adjutant of the post," she wrote to William, "I went in a carriage to dear, dear Lon's grave. Sadly neglected we found it. Not even sodden with nature's beautiful green, for in raising a costly monument to the memory of Gen. [John] Buford, Allie's grave had been trampled on, and nearly levelled with the Earth! So our country rewards her fallen sons; fallen in her defense! A nameless, neglected grave! We deposited there a beautiful wreath made by cousin Martha [Houghton Wheeler, sister of Judge Houghton] and I set out a white rose bud brought from Fredonia."[19]

The next morning Mary and Milton journeyed to New York City, and at a marble works there Mary purchased a lancet-shaped stone and pedestal for Lon's grave for one hundred dollars—a large sum for her, especially since she never received an adequate pension for the death of her son in spite of repeated appeals.[20] Mary composed the inscription herself. Although Lon's brevet ranks to major for his services at the Battle of Chancellorsville and lieutenant colonel for his services at the Battle of Gettysburg were never officially conferred until President Andrew Johnson signed the commissions in June 1868, Mary was aware of the recommendations. She thus included Lon's brevet rank of lieutenant colonel on the inscription, which read:

Brevet Lt. Colonel Alonzo H. Cushing
4th Artillery
Fell
July 3, 1863
at
Gettysburg

Faithful until Death

The stone stands over the grave today. Around it are the graves of many of those Lon knew well: Ranald S. Mackenzie, Joseph C. Audenreid, George Armstrong Custer, Hugh Judson Kilpatrick, John Buford, George Sykes, Erasmus Keyes, and Winfield Scott. Also buried nearby is Gulian V. Weir.[21] The backdrop to the cemetery is one of the most spectacular scenes in North America: the busy Hudson River and its impressive Highlands. Nearby stands the little Cadet Chapel, which in 1911 was moved, stone by stone, to the cemetery from its original location near the Library and Academy Building; it was the academy edifice Lon remembered most fondly from his years as a cadet. From the portals of that little Greek revival chapel, Lon had set out on his brief journey, which resulted in glory and immortality, as well as the rebirth of the nation into one that his Puritan and nativist ancestors never dreamed it would be.

Lon's real epitaph was written by his devoted first sergeant, a German immigrant and devout Roman Catholic. Years after the war, then Lt. Col. Frederick Fuger wrote: "Lieutenant Cushing, my commander, was a most able soldier, a man of excellent judgment, and great decision of character; devoted to his profession, he was most faithful in the discharge of every duty, accurate and thorough in its performance; possessed of mental and physical vigor, joined to the kindest of hearts, he commanded the love and respect of all who knew him. His superiors placed implicit confidence in him, as well they might. His fearlessness and resolution, displayed in numerous actions, were unsurpassed and his noble death at Gettysburg should present an example for emulation to patriotic defenders of the country through all time to come."[22]

Appendix

Roster, Battery A, Fourth United States Artillery, with Gettysburg Casualties

Officers

Capt. Charles H. Morgan (on detached service)
Lt. Alonzo H. Cushing (in command of battery) killed, July 3
Lt. Rufus King, Jr. (on detached service)
Lt. Arthur Morris (on detached service)

Attached Officers

Lt. Samuel Canby wounded, July 2
Lt. Joseph Milne (attached from Battery B, First Rhode Island Light Artillery) wounded, July 3

Noncommissioned Officers

1st Sgt. Frederick Fuger
Sgt. Louis Blockinger
Sgt. Thomas Whetston
Sgt. Angus Brenan
Cpl. Charles Au wounded, July 3
Cpl. Patrick Manley
Cpl. Edward M. Hurley wounded, July 3
Bugler Albert Keyser wounded, July 3
Bugler James H. Patterson

Daniel Wallace, artificer
Edward Hickey, artificer

Privates

Abraham, Francis
Ball, Daniel O.

Beal, John
Bender, Jacob
Benson, William E.
Benvenuti, Ausans
Bigby, John
Blankenmiller, George
Bowman, Jacob H.
Boyce, James
Boyce, Michael
Brong, William
Brookmire, James G.
Callahan, Daniel
Carl, John wounded, July 3
Carnorst, Jacob
Clark, Symonds
Clute, George W.
Colqui, Frank
Colwell, William
Conley, Henry
Corsey, William F.
Daniels, William
Decker, Frederick
Deckman, William
Degrote, George
Delcamp, Samuel
Deutscher, Henry
Devine, John
Devlin, Michael
Drummond, Edward
Eagan, Andrew wounded, July 3
Edmiston, Franklin
Ensign, Frederick wounded, July 2
Erline, Christian M.
Fassett, Ansil wounded, July 3
Ferguson, Joseph A.
Foster, Samuel
Garbison, Henry
Gaskill, Hays
Glascott, Patrick
Graham, Patrick
Grandon, William R. wounded, July 2
Griffin, Arsenal H. killed, July 3
Gu, Nicholas
Haffezinger, Sylvester
Harding, Cornelius
Hayden, James
Hays, John
Headington, Murray B. wounded, July 3
Heller, John A.
Henry, Lucas wounded, July 3
Hill, Edward wounded, July 3

Hoey, William
Hoslicher, Andrew
Jackson, Brantley
Johnson, Alexander
Jones, William B.
Kelly, Martin
Kelly, Patrick
Kibler, Joseph wounded, July 2
Klitt, Jacob
Kope, Aaron, Jr. wounded, July 3
Kuntz, John wounded, July 2
Landregan, Rody wounded, July 3
Laudenberger, Albert
Laudy, John
Lee, Daniel wounded, July 3
Lung, Henry
McConnell, Edward
McCormack, John
McGorson, Patrick
McKee, Byron
McMahan, James
McMahan, John
Malinger, Simon killed, July 3
Mandeville, Charles
Marris, Dennis
Martin, Robert wounded, July 3
Miller, William wounded, July 3
Missimer, Andrew killed, July 2
Moon, Thomas
Morrison, Charles wounded, July 3
Moses, John F.
Mullen, Patrick
Murphy, James killed, July 3
Nander, Joseph
Newbury, Miles F.
Newbury, Norton L. wounded, July 2, and missing
Noel, William
Noland, William
Olney, John wounded, July 3
O'Neil, Hugh
Page, John M.
Patterson, Frederick wounded, July 3
Patton, William killed, July 3
Pavier, James R.
Pense, Isaac
Romains, William H.
Samuels, Patrick
Scanlin Martin wounded, July 3
Schmidt, William
Schriner, Adam J. wounded, July 2
Shaffer, Richard

Sharky, Charles	
Sherman, Henry	
Slack, George W.	
Smedley, Edwin	
Smith, Charles	
Smith, Christopher	
Smith, Orlando M.	
Smith, William	wounded, July 2
Snow, Beverly W.	
Sprague, Charles	wounded, July 3
Stewart, William	
Stone, Hosea	wounded, July 3
Stork, Edward D.	
Strode, William H.	
Styles, Samuel A.	
Thompson, Charles	
Tracey, Francis	
Watson, Solomon B.	
White, John	
Whittington, William H.	
Wright, John J.	
Yocom, William	
Zellers, Henry	
Zimmer, Frederick	

Ordnance Men Attached

Adams, William, ordnance mechanic	
Hacket, Benjamin, ordnance mechanic	wounded, July 3
Hall, Oscar D., ordnance mechanic	
Whickam, James, ordnance mechanic	

Volunteers Attached **(1st Company Minnesota Sharpshooters)**

Barron, Norman	
Brown, Sylvester	killed, July 2
Burtruff, Henry	missing, July 2
Collins, Elliott F.	
Decker, Artemus L.W.	wounded, July 3
Heal, Morrison R.	
Hubbs, Charles L.	wounded, July 3
Kenny, Mark	
McWilliams, David	wounded, July 3
Merrill, Sumner	
Wood, Lunan S.	

Notes

Abbreviations

Repositories and Sources

ANMP	Antietam National Military Park Archives. Sharpsburg, Maryland.
CCHS	Chautauqua County Historical Society, Westfield, New York.
DAB	Arlen, Johnson and Dumas Malone, eds. *Dictionary of American Biography*, 20 vols. New York, 1928-37.
DRBL	Darwin R. Barker Library and Museum. Fredonia, New York.
GNMP	Gettysburg National Military Park Archives. Gettysburg, Pennsylvania.
KMB	Kent Masterson Brown Collections. Lexington, Kentucky.
LC	Library of Congress, Washington, D.C.
LS	Larry Sanford Collections. Beloit, Wisconsin.
MHS	Massachusetts Historical Society, Boston.
NA	National Archives, Washington, D.C.
OHS	Ohio Historical Society, Columbus.
OR	U.S. War Department. *War of the Rebellion: A Compilation of the Official Records of the Union and Confederate Armies*. Ser. I. 73 vols. Washington, D.C., 1880-1901.
RLL	Richard L. Leisenring, Jr., Collections. Kanona, New York.
USMA	United States Military Academy Archives. West Point, New York.
UWM	University of Wisconsin at Milwaukee.
WHS	Wisconsin Historical Society, Madison.

Persons

A.A.	Albert Alden
A.H.C.	Alonzo Hereford Cushing
E.T.	Elizabeth "Lizzie" Tupper
F.S.E.	Francis Smith Edwards
H.B.C.	Howard Bass Cushing
I.H.	Senator Ira Harris
J.G.H.	John G. Hazard
L.S.H.	Lawrence Sterne Houghton
M.B.C.	Milton Buckingham Cushing

M.B.C. Jr. Milton Buckingham Cushing, Jr.
M.B.S.C. Mary Barker Smith Cushing
M.L.C. Marie Louise Cushing
P.J.R. Col. Paul J. Revere
R.K. Jr. Lt. Rufus King, Jr.
W.B.C. William Barker Cushing
W.H.H. William H. Harris

Note: Full information for works cited will be found in the Bibliography, beginning on page 303.

Prologue: "In the Midst of Life We Are in Death"

1. Special Orders No. 16, July 11, 1863, Post Orders, 1861-66, USMA; Werstein, *July, 1863*, 23.

2. Cook, *Armies of the Streets*, 54. Col. Robert Nugent, who headed the provost marshal general's bureau in New York City, had set Saturday, July 11, as the day to begin drawing names for the draft in the powder-keg Ninth District of the bureau, which consisted of Manhattan above Fortieth Street. The Eighth District, which comprised the eighteenth, twentieth and twenty-first wards of the city, was to draw names on Monday, July 13. Although there were rumors of seizures of arsenals, riot, and arson on July 11 and 12, the draft riots did not begin in earnest until July 13. Werstein, *July, 1863*, 45-119; Tillman, "Academic History of the Military Academy," 1:381.

3. Sladen, "Uniform of Cadets," 1:518-19.

4. Cullum, *Biographical Register of West Point*, 2:556; Sergent, *They Lie Forgotten*, 77; Special Orders No. 16, July 11, 1863, Post Orders, 1861-1866, USMA; Heitman, *Historical Register*, 1:234, 311; DAB, s.v. "Scott, Winfield"; Parker, *Chautauqua Boy in '61*, 87. Parker, a boyhood friend of Alonzo H. Cushing and William B. Cushing, was told by Alonzo's oldest full brother, Asst. Paymaster Milton Buckingham Cushing, that Milton had taken Alonzo's body to West Point for burial.

5. Special Orders No. 16, July 11, 1863, Post Orders 1861-66, USMA.

6. *New York Times*, July 6, 1863.

7. Crary, *Dear Belle*, 92; Sergent, *They Lie Forgotten*, 100. The hymn, titled "Unity," was written by two Baptist clergymen, A.A. Watts and the Rev. S.F. Smith, and was set to music composed by Lowell Mason.

8. "Order for the burial of the Dead," in *Book of Common Prayer*, 241. French was an Episcopalian and the United States Army historically used the prayerbook of the Episcopal Church for Protestant services.

9. *Fredonia Censor*, July 29, 1863.

10. Special Orders No. 16, July 11, 1863, Post Orders, 1861-66, USMA; Heitman, *Historical Register*, 1:356.

11. Schaff, *Spirit of Old West Point*, 117-18. Morris Schaff recalled the funeral of Maj. Francis Taylor, class of 1825 and a hero of the Mexican War, and Lt. William Gaston, class of 1856, in the fall of 1859 at West Point; both had been killed in action with the Spokane Indians near Snake River, Washington Territory. The funeral of Alonzo H. Cushing would have been conducted like that of Taylor and Gaston.

12. *Book of Common Prayer,* 234; Quintard, *Doctor Quintard,* 57-58. Parsons would study for the ministry under the tutelage of former Confederate Chaplain Charles Todd Quintard, who from behind the lines of the right wing of the Confederate Army of the Mississippi had observed Parsons's heroic stand at Perryville. Parsons would become rector of St. Lazarus Episcopal Church, Memphis, Tennessee; he would die in Memphis aiding victims of the yellow fever epidemic in 1878.

13. DAB, s.v. "Scott, Winfield."

14. *Book of Common Prayer,* 244; Schaff, *Spirit of Old West Point,* 117-18.

15. Benet, *John Brown's Body,* 304-5. The poet's grandfather, Lt. Stephen Vincent Benet, began serving as librarian at West Point in the summer of 1863. Norton, *A History of the United States Military Academy Library,* 24; Sergent, *They Lie Forgotten,* 46.

1. "His Mother Is Poor but Highly Committed"

1. Cushing, *Genealogy,* 229; Marie Louise Cushing, "Our Grandmother: Mary Barker Smith Cushing" (1917), 5, CCHS.

2. Cushing, *Genealogy,* 21-22, 91-94, 103-4, 352-54; Secretary of the Commonwealth, *Massachusetts Soldiers and Sailors,* 4:283-305. Among the descendants of Matthew Cushing and his youngest son, John, were some of the early Republic's foremost public figures. Thomas Cushing (1725-88) became a member of the Provincial and Continental Congresses, lieutenant governor of Massachusetts, and acting governor in 1785. William Cushing (1732-1810) became attorney general and chief justice of Massachusetts, and associate justice of the U.S. Supreme Court for twenty years. Caleb Cushing (1800-1877) became a congressman, minister to China, regimental commander and hero in the Mexican War, justice of the Supreme Judicial Court of Massachusetts, and attorney general of the United States from 1853 to 1857. Milton Buckingham Cushing was a descendant of Matthew's son, Daniel Cushing.

3. *Fredonia Advertiser,* Jan. 15, 1864; Cushing, *Genealogy,* 132-33, 225-29; gravestone of Zattu Cushing, Old Pioneer Cemetery, Fredonia; Buckingham, *Ancestors of Ebenezer Buckingham,* 18-20. Zattu's father, Nathaniel Cushing, disposed of the family farm during the Revolution, accepting for its sale Continental currency, whose rapid depreciation left the Cushings penniless.

4. *Fredonia Advertiser,* Jan. 15, 1864; Young, *History of Chautauqua County,* 70-77, 482-83; Downs and Hedley, *History of Chautauqua County,* 2 vols. (Boston, 1921), 1:215; Cushing, *Genealogy,* 134, 229, 230. The ship Zattu Cushing helped to build was christened *The Good Intent* and launched at Presque Isle, Pennsylvania. On his way home from western Pennsylvania, Zattu passed through the holdings of the Holland Land Company in western New York and determined then to move there.

5. *Fredonia Advertiser,* Jan. 15, 1864; Young, *History of Chautauqua County,* 113; Crocker, *Yesterdays,* 1:18-19, 4:39. Zattu was originally named "Justice of the Peace and Overseer of the Poor" and later a county judge of Niagara County before the creation of Chautauqua County.

6. *Fredonia Advertiser,* Jan. 15, 1864; Hickey, *War of 1812* (Urbana, Ill., 1989), 141-43.

7. *Fredonia Advertiser,* Jan. 15, 1864; Cushing, *Genealogy,* 134; gravestone of Zattu Cushing.

8. Lee, *History of the City of Columbus*, 1:106-7. Gen. Rufus Putnam of Brookfield, Massachusetts, was one of Gen. George Washington's foremost engineer officers. He was commander of the 5th Massachusetts Continental Line and the 3d Massachusetts Brigade, veteran of the Saratoga campaign, senior officer in command of the garrison at West Point from 1778 to 1782, and senior Massachusetts Line officer at the Cantonment on the Hudson at New Windsor, New York, in 1783. Col. and Bvt. Brig. Gen. Benjamin Tupper of Chesterfield, Massachusetts, was the commander of the 10th Massachusetts Continental Line when it was garrisoned at West Point. He was a veteran of the Saratoga campaign, Valley Forge, and the operations at Fort Ticonderoga in 1778. Maj. Winthrop Sargent married Tupper's daughter, Rowena. Secretary of the Commonwealth, *Massachusetts Soldiers and Sailors*, 12:875-76, 16:144-45; Boatner, *Encyclopedia of the American Revolution*, 1129.

9. Cushing, *Genealogy*, 228-29; Edwards, *Commander William Barker Cushing*, 14. All the Cushing family histories record that Milton Buckingham Cushing was graduated from Hamilton Literary and Theological Institute with a degree of Doctor of Medicine, but it is doubtful that he studied there for more than one year; the school was founded in 1819, and by 1820-21 he had already migrated to Ohio. A search of the records of the registrar and alumni office of Hamilton and Colgate fail to reveal that Milton was actually graduated, though he does refer to himself as "Dr. Cushing" on the gravestones of his first wife, Abigail Browning (Tupper) Cushing, and his daughter, Abigail Elizabeth Cushing, in Woodlawn Cemetery, Zanesville, Ohio.

10. Catharenus Putnam Buckingham, "Recollections of C.P. Buckingham" (holographic memoir), 72, OHS; *Muskingum Messenger and Democratic Republican*, Oct. 9, 1821.

11. Buckingham, "Recollections," 42; *Muskingum Messenger and Democratic Repubican*, Dec. 2, 1832; Cushing, *Genealogy*, 227-28. Milton and Abigail were married by Rev. James Culbertson in the Presbyterian Meeting House at South and Fourth Streets, Zanesville.

12. Her gravestone records that Abigail Browning (Tupper) Cushing died of "consumption." In a letter to his second wife, Milton records his own bout with "consumption," as well as those of his children. M.B.C. to M.B.S.C., Nov. 29, 1846, CCHS; obituary of Benjamin Tupper Cushing, unidentified newspaper (Columbus, Ohio, December 1850), LS; Wintrobe et al, *Harrison's Principles of Internal Medicine*, 6th ed. (New York, 1970), 866-76, 870-71.

13. Buckingham, "Recollections," 73; Cushing, *Genealogy*, 227, 229-30, 230-31; L.S.H. to E.T., Nov. 6, 1857, LS. C.P. Buckingham recalled that "Milton had no money but had a new store building, and my father [Ebenezer Buckingham, Jr.] supplied him with the necessary capital for business." Milton purchased the Stone Academy from Henry Matthews on January 12, 1829, for $650. Marie L. Cushing, daughter of Commander William Barker Cushing, attended the Putnam Female Academy, which was started by Esther Cooley Buckingham and conducted in the Old Stone Academy until 1839, then moved to a new building on Woodlawn Avenue; she stated that her grandfather Milton and his first wife lived in the Old Stone Academy when they resided in Putnam ("Our Grandmother," 4).

14. Buckingham, "Recollections," 72-74, 79; Warner, *Generals in Blue*, 49-50. In Buckingham's class at West Point were Robert E. Lee and Joseph E. Johnston. After graduation, Buckingham surveyed the Green River in Kentucky and served as an instructor at West Point. He resigned his commission in the army after only

two years' service. His father, Ebenezer Buckingham, Jr., was killed during the construction of the second "Y" bridge.

15. Cushing, "Our Grandmother," 3; Schneider, *Y-Bridge City*, 200-201, 207-9; Lewis, *Zanesville and Muskingum County*, 1:247-48; *Zanesville Gazette*, March 27, 1833. Milton's uncles Austin A. Guthrie and George Guthrie concealed runaway slaves in their homes along Woodlawn Avenue in Putnam as did his brother-in-law Cyrus Merriam. At least twenty-five Muskingum County homes were stations on the underground railroad.

16. Cushing, *Genealogy*, 227-28; gravestone of Abigail Browning (Tupper) Cushing and Abigail Elizabeth Cushing.

17. Clerk, Court of Common Pleas, Muskingum County (Zanesville), Ohio, Chancery Record D, 608, *Goodcil Buckingham v. Milton Buckingham Cushing*, No. 102, February Term, 1845, Appearance Docket Q, 458, Rev. Goodcil (actually, Goodsell) Buckingham was the son of Stephen and Esther Cooley Buckingham.

18. Smith, *Memorial of the Rev. Thomas Smith*, 59-60, 78; Cushing, "Our Grandmother," 3. John Gillman Pillsbury had learned the printing business in Lowell, Massachusetts. In Columbus he opened a printing office, Cutler & Pillsbury, on North High Street. Mary Barker Smith opened a small, select female school in the cellar of the residence where she lived, the home of a Mrs. E. Campbell on Front Street. Lee, *History of the City of Columbus*, 1:376, 515.

19. Cushing, *Genealogy*, 227-28; Smith, *Memorial of the Rev. Thomas Smith* 60; Cushing, "Our Grandmother," 1-3.

20. Smith, *Memorial of the Rev. Thomas Smith*, 21-22, 26-32, 32-35. Joseph and Albert Smith were the sons of Mary's uncle Capt. Albert Smith and Ann Ellis Smith.

21. Rings, *Marriage Records of Franklin County*, 258; Lee, *History of the City of Columbus*, 1:375; Cushing, *Genealogy*, 228, 280; Cushing, "Our Grandmother," 3. Milton and Mary were married by Rev. T.R. Cressy and moved into the apartment over Milton's dry goods store in the Exchange Building. Mary advertised in the Columbus papers that she "conducted a school for young ladies and misses in the Exchange Building over the store of Cushing & Warner."

22. Smith, *Memorial of the Rev. Thomas Smith*, 85; Lee, *History of the City of Columbus*, 1:375. By 1837 Milton had dissolved the partnership of Cushing & Warner and entered into his own dry goods business, M.B. Cushing & Co., in "Goodale's Row" on High Street. Presumably, the Cushings lived in an apartment over the new store.

23. Remini, *Life of Andrew Jackson*, 338-39; Peterson, *Great Triumvirate*, 265, 274; Schneider, *Y-Bridge City*, 113; Quaife, *Wisconsin*, 1:409-39, 441-42.

24. Averill, *History of Gallia County*, iv, v, xv-xvi; Cushing, *Genealogy*, 227, 229-31; L.S.H. to L.T., Nov. 6, 1857, LS; Office of the Register of Deeds in and for Milwaukee County, Wisconsin, Deed Book L, 289; Office of the Register of Deeds in and for Waukesha County (Delafield), Wisconsin, Deed Book F, 207. Although the deed to Alonzo and Margaret Hereford Cushing was dated August 5, 1839, it was not recorded until January 23, 1844.

25. Haight, *Three Wisconsin Cushings*, Cushing, *Genealogy*, 381; Cushing, "Our Grandmother," 5.

26. Haight, *Three Wisconsin Cushings*, 13-15; Butterfield, *History of Waukesha County* 311, 383; Smith, *History of Wisconsin*, 2 vols. 2:354-81; Milwaukee County, Wisconsin, Deed Book L, 289; Waukesha County, Wisconsin, Deed Book F, 208; Milwaukee County, Wisconsin, Mortgage Book D, 387; Waukesha County, Wisconsin, Mortgage Book B, 30.

27. Tuttle, *Illustrated History of the State of Wisconsin*, 694-95; Butterfield, *History of Waukesha County*, 355-58.

28. Cushing, "Our Grandmother," 8; M.L.C. to Colonel Heimstreet (typescript), 2, CCHS.

29. Cushing, "Our Grandmother," 8; Smith, *Memorial of the Rev. Thomas Smith*, 83-84; Cushing, *Genealogy*, 226.

30. Cushing, *Genealogy*, 226, 227-28; Cushing, "Our Grandmother," 5.

31. Quaife, *Wisconsin*, 1:442-55.

32. Cushing, "Our Grandmother", 5, 8.

33. Ibid., 5.

34. Olsson, *Pioneer in Northwest America*, 1:166-71, 226-29. Swedish traveler Gustaf Unonius claimed that many of the settlers of Delafield he met in 1841 were bankrupts, escaping creditors.

35. Smith, *Memorial of the Rev. Thomas Smith*, 85-87.

36. Waukesha County, Wisconsin, Deed Book L, 593.

37. Milwaukee County, Wisconsin, Deed Book D, 389; Waukesha County, Wisconsin, Mortgage Book B, 32; Milwaukee County, Wisconsin, Deed Book K, 594, and Mortgage Book D, 388; Waukesha County, Wisconsin, Deed Book B, 199, and Mortgage Book B, 31; M.B.C. to A.A., Oct. 1, 1843, UWM.

38. Cushing, "Our Grandmother," 8-9.

39. *Goodcil Buckingham v. Milton Buckingham Cushing*.

40. Cushing, "Our Grandmother," 8; Cushing, *Genealogy*, 228-29; M.B.C. to M.B.S.C., Nov. 29, 1846, CCHS.

41. Obituary of Benjamin Tupper Cushing, LS; Lee; *History of the City of Columbus*, 1:4; Blue, *Salmon P. Chase*, 14-40; Cushing, *Genealogy*, 228; Buckingham, *Ancestors of Ebenezer Buckingham*, 47.

42. L.S.H. to L.T., Nov. 6, 1857, LS; Buckingham, *Ancestors of Ebenezer Buckingham*, 46, 114-15; Gordon Cotton, "Judge's Letters Describe Vicksburg," *Vicksburg Sunday Post*, June 1, 1987; Cushing, "Our Grandmother," 9.

43. Milwaukee County, Wisconsin, Mortgage Book 3, 522, 59, and Mortgage Book G, 110; Waukesha County, Wisconsin, Mortgage Book A, 227.

44. M.B.C. to M.B.S.C., Nov. 29, 1846, CCHS. The only letter extant between Milton and Mary during Milton's absence reveals that Mary and the children were then living in Chelsea, Massachusetts.

45. Smith, *Memorial of the Rev. Thomas Smith*, 57, 78-81, 83-84, 85-87.

46. Mary Barker Smith Cushing, "William Cushing" (holographic memoir), 2, CCHS.

47. M.B.C. to M.B.S.C., Nov. 29, 1846, CCHS.

48. Ibid.

49. Cushing, "Our Grandmother," 9; Cushing, *Genealogy*, 228; Hill, *Historical Notes about Gallipolis*, 3.

50. Cushing, *Genealogy*, 386.

51. Cushing, "William Cushing," 2; Cushing, "Our Grandmother," 9.

52. Gravestone of Eunice Elderkin Cushing, Old Pioneer Cemetery, Fredonia, New York; Cushing, *Genealogy*, 139, 225-26, 227, 229-31; Buckingham, *Ancestors of Ebenezer Buckingham*, 29-30; L.S.H. to L.T., Nov. 6, 1857, LS.

53. Cushing, "Our Grandmother," 9-10; letter of L.S. Higgins, Aug. 9, 1881, WHS; Crocker, *Yesterdays*, 1:38, 4:40. Green Street in Fredonia is now known as Cushing Street.

54. Map of Fredonia, New York, 1860, DRBL; Crocker, *Yesterdays*, 1:38, 47-50, 2:3-4, 4:6-9, 39-41; Adams, *Tales of Early Fredonia*, 38-43, 93-97.

55. Edwards, *Commander William Barker Cushing*, 32-37.

56. Ibid., 20; Haight, *Three Wisconsin Cushings*, 24-25; obituary of Mary Barker Smith Cushing, unidentified newspaper (Fredonia, New York, 1891), CCHS.

57. Quoted in Edwards, *Commander William Barker Cushing*, 29.

58. Cushing, "Our Grandmother," 14-15.

59. A.H.C. to W.B.C., Feb. 24, April 23, and April 27, 1863, CCHS (Alonzo signed the letters as "Lon" and one also as "Indian"); Edwards, *Commander William Barker Cushing*, 38, 98, 123. Julia Greenleaf and William Barker Cushing often called Alonzo Allie or Lon. Edward Anselm apparently gave most of his half-brothers their nicknames.

60. A.H.C. to M.B.C. Jr., June 5, 1862, CCHS.; A.H.C. to W.B.C., Nov. 12, 1862, CCHS.

61. Cushing, "William Cushing," 1-2; Edwards, *Commander William Barker Cushing*, 24-75; A.H.C. to W.B.C., Oct. 2, 1859 (William B. Cushing is referred to by Alonzo as "Willie"), April 23, 1860, Sept. 18, 1860, June 10, 1862, Nov. 12, 1862, April 23, 1863 (William B. Cushing is referred to by Alonzo as "Will"), Feb. 24, 1863, April 14, 1863, May 7, 1863 (William B. Cushing is referred to by Alonzo as "Coon"), all in CCHS.

62. Edwards, *Commander William Barker Cushing*, 26-27.

63. Ibid.

64. Parker, *Chautauqua Boy in '61*, 65-66.

65. Ibid., 66.

66. Cushing, "Our Grandmother," 11.

67. Freehling, *The Road to Disunion*, 458-62, 475-86.

68. Buckingham, *Ancestors of Ebenezer Buckingham*, 59-60; *Grape Belt*, (Dunkirk), May 14, 1951.

69. *Evening Observer* (Dunkirk), May 14, 1951.

70. Obituary of Benjamin Tupper Cushing, LS; Cushing, *Genealogy*, 228.

71. Haight, *Three Wisconsin Cushings*, 24-25, 27; obituary of Mary Barker Smith Cushing, CCHS.

72. *Fredonia Advertiser*, Jan. 15, 1864; Adams, *Tales of Early Fredonia*, 27-28, 31; Crocker, *Yesterdays*, 2:49, 5:49-50; Catalogue of Fredonia Academy, 1857-58, DRBL; Adams, *Tales of Early Fredonia*, 27-28.

73. Obituary of Mary Barker Smith Cushing, CCHS; *Fredonia Censor*, July 11, 1900; Edwards, *Commander William Barker Cushing*, 20.

74. Edwards, *Commander William Barker Cushing*, 22-23, 29-30, 39-40.

75. Ibid., 37-38.

76. Ibid., 38-39.

77. Potter and Fehrenbacher, *Impending Crisis*, 206-24.

78. Anbinder, *Nativism and Slavery*, 3-19; Miller, *Emigrants and Exiles*, 280-81, 323-44; Kamphoefner, Helbich, and Sommer, *News from the Land of Freedom*, 1-11.

79. Anbinder, *Nativism and Slavery*, 20-51; Potter and Fehrenbacher, *Impending Crisis*, 248; Miller, *Emigrants and Exiles*, 323-24; Kamphoefner, Helbich, and Sommer, *News from the Land of Freedom*, 17-19.

80. U.S. Senate, *Biographical Congressional Directory*, 624.

81. Edwards, *Commander William Barker Cushing*, 47-48.

82. Cushing, "Our Grandmother," 10-11.

83. Class records of Fredonia Academy, 1856-57, DRBL.

84. Potter and Fehrenbacher, *Impending Crisis*, 258-64; U.S. Senate, *Biographical Congressional Directory*, 624; Anbinder, *Nativism and Slavery*, 158. It appears that Congressmen Francis S. Edwards and William Welch were implicated in an influence-peddling scandal prior to Edwards's election defeat.

85. F.S.E. to J.B. Totten, Dec. 1, 1856, in Application Papers of Alonzo H. Cushing to the United States Military Academy, R.G. 94, NA.

86. A.H.C. ("Alfred A. Cushing") to Jefferson Davis, Jan. 1857, in Application Papers of Alonzo H. Cushing to the United States Military Academy, R.G. 94, NA.

87. Ibid.

88. Edwards, *Commander William Barker Cushing*, 47-48.

89. A.H.C. ("Alfred A. Cushing") to F.S.E., Feb. 9, 1857, in Application Papers of Alonzo H. Cushing to the United States Military Academy. R.G. 94, NA.

2. "I Am Boning Everything"

1. Young, *History of Chautauqua County*, 151; 1851 New York & Erie Railroad advertisement, DRBL

2. Schaff, *Spirit of Old West Point*, 22-23.

3. Heitman, *Historical Register*, 1:439; Schaff, *Spirit of Old West Point*, 22.

4. Sergent, *They Lie Forgotten*, 24.

5. W.H.H. to I.H., June 20, 1857, USMA.

6. Schaff, *Spirit of Old West Point*, 37-40.

7. Special Orders No. 90, June 20, 1857, Post Orders 1856-60, USMA.; Tillman, "Academic History of the Military Academy," 230-31; Sergent, *They Lie Forgotten*, 59-60.

8. "Bibliographies of the U.S. Military Academy," 2:116; Summary of Class Standings of Alonzo H. Cushing, USMA (hereafter cited as Class Standings).

9. A.H.C. to M.B.S.C., May 28, 1861, CCHS.

10. Register of Delinquencies, 1856-1861, "Alonzo H. Cushing," July 16, July 18, and August 21, 1857, USMA.

11. Drawing in George A. Woodruff, "A Collection of Cadet Songs and Other Writings Relating to the U.S. Military Academy at West Point, N.Y., 1859" USMA.

12. Sergent, *They Lie Forgotten*, 59-60.

13. Cushing, *Genealogy*, 467-68. Samuel Tobey Cushing was a direct descendant of Matthew Cushing and Matthew's youngest son, John.

14. Sergent, *They Lie Forgotten*, 156-57; Cullum, *Biographical Register of West Point*, 2:526-27; *Historical Register*, 1:603.

15. Sergent, *They Lie Forgotten*, 138-39; Lewis, *Zanesville and Muskingum County*, 1:332.

16. Sergent, *They Lie Forgotten*, 125-26; Cullum, *Biographical Register of West Point*, 2:564-65; Heitman, *Historical Register*, 1:374.

17. Bennett, "Ideal of a Soldier," 35-36; Schaff, *Spirit of Old West Point*, 31-34.

18. Schaff, *Spirit of Old West Point*, 26; Cullum, *Biographical Register of West Point*, 2:568-69.

19. Schaff, *Spirit of Old West Point*, 35; Cullum, *Biographical Register of West Point*, 2:568-69; "Memoirs of George A. Woodruff" by his sister, 9-10, USMA.

20. A.H.C. to W.B.C., Dec. 11, 1859, CCHS; Cullum, *Biographical Register of West Point*, 2:562, 566-67.

21. Cullum, *Biographical Register of West Point* 2:562, 566-67; Farley, *West Point in the Early Sixties*, 78-79.

22. Cullum, *Biographical Register of West Point*, 2:567-69.

23. Class Standings; Register of Merit, 1853-1865, "Alonzo H. Cushing, Fifth Class Year Ending June, 1858," USMA; Register of Delinquencies, 1856-61,

"Alonzo H. Cushing," Sept. 16, and Oct. 30, 1857; Jan. 22, and March 18, 1858, USMA.

24. Schaff, *Spirit of Old West Point*, 26-27.

25. Special Orders No. 89, June 19, 1858, Post Orders, 1856-1860, USMA.

26. Schaff, *Spirit of Old West Point*, 28.

27. Ibid., 29-30.

28. Ibid.

29. Register of Delinquencies, 1856-1861, "Alonzo H. Cushing," June 24, 1861, USMA.

30. Monaghan, *Custer*, 34; Kinsley, *Favor the Bold*, 10; Crary, *Dear Belle*, 42.

31. Woodruff, "Cadet Songs," 37-41.

32. Farley, *West Point in the Early Sixties*, 27.

33. Potter and Fehrenbacher, *Impending Crisis*, 326-27, 331-55.

34. A.H.C. to W.B.C., Dec. 11, 1859, CCHS; Crary, *Dear Belle*, 59; Sergent, *They Lie Forgotten*, 59.

35. Norton, *History of the USMA Library*, 19-23; Circulation Records, 1857-63, USMA; Register of Delinquencies, 1856-61, "Alonzo H. Cushing," April 30, 1861, USMA.

36. Class Standings; Register of Merit, 1853-65, "Alonzo H. Cushing, Fourth Class Year Ending June, 1859," USMA; Register of Delinquencies, 1856-61, "Alonzo H. Cushing," May 24, 1859, USMA; Staff Records, 7:70-71, USMA.

37. Roske and Van Doren, *Lincoln's Commando*, 64; Edwards, *Commander William Barker Cushing*, 54-55.

38. Woodruff, "Cadet Songs," 64-66.

39. Sergent, *They Lie Forgotten*, 72.

40. Parker, *Chautauqua Boy in '61*, 66-67.

41. A.H.C. to M.B.S.C., Dec. 24, 1861, CCHS.

42. Ibid.

43. A.H.C. to W.B.C., Oct. 16, 1859, CCHS.

44. Parker, *Chautauqua Boy in '61*, 66-68.

45. A.H.C. to W.B.C., Oct. 2, 1859, CCHS.

46. Ibid.

47. Ibid.

48. A.H.C. to W.B.C., April 23, 1860, CCHS.

49. Potter and Fehrenbacher, *Impending Crisis*, 254-59, 356-84; A.H.C. to W.B.C., Dec. 11, 1859, CCHS.

50. A.H.C. to W.B.C., Dec. 11, 1859, CCHS.

51. *Centennial History of the USMA*, 2:112; A.H.C. to W.B.C., Oct. 16, 1859, CCHS; Register of Delinquencies 1856-61, "Alonzo H. Cushing," June 18, 1861, USMA.

52. Class Standings; Register of Merit, 1853-65, "Alonzo H. Cushing, Third Class Year Ending June, 1860," USMA.

53. Register of Delinquencies, 1856-61, "Alonzo H. Cushing," Jan. 2, 1860, USMA.

54. Special Orders No. 79, June 16, 1860, and No. 120, Aug. 28, 1860, Post Orders, 1856-60, USMA.

55. A.H.C. to W.B.C., Sept. 18, 1860, CCHS.

56. Hughes, *General William J. Hardee*, 51-69.

57. Nichols, *Toward Gettysburg*, 22-68, 70-71; W.H.H. to I.H., Nov. 4, 1860, USMA.

58. Farley, *West Point in the Early Sixties*, 69-81.

59. Ibid., 82-88; Ness, *Regular Army*, 232, 243-44.

60. Sergent, *They Lie Forgotten*, 51; Farley, *West Point in the Early Sixties*, 63.

61. W.H.H. to I.H., Oct. 24, 1858, USMA; Fuger, "Cushing's Battery at Gettysburg," 409n.

62. Sergent, *They Lie Forgotten*, 8; A.H.C. to W.B.C., Sept. 18, 1860, CCHS.

63. Potter and Fehrenbacher, *Impending Crisis*, 405-29, 442.

64. Roland, *American Iliad*, 30-33.

65. Schaff, *Spirit of Old West Point*, 183, 207-8.

66. Williams, *P.G.T. Beauregard*, 2-3, 13-33, 44-47; Tillman, "The Academic History of the Military Academy," 236.

67. Schaff, *The Spirit of Old West Point*, 197-98.

68. Williams, *P.G.T. Beauregard*, 48-50.

69. A.H.C. to M.B.S.C., April 17, 1861, CCHS; Roland, *American Iliad*, 30-35.

70. Roske and Van Doren, *Lincoln's Commando*, 87-88.

71. A.H.C. to M.B.S.C., April 17, 1861, CCHS.

72. Bushong and Bushong, *Fightin' Tom Rosser*, 13; Milham, *Gallant Pelham*, 34; Parker, *General James Dearing*, 10; Schaff, *Spirit of Old West Point*, 246-48; Cullum, *Biographical Register of West Point*, 2:548-68.

73. A.H.C. to M.B.S.C., April 17, 1861, CCHS.

74. Special Orders No. 60, May 6, 1861, Post Orders, 1861-66, USMA.

75. Class Standings; Register of Merit, 1853-65, "Alonzo H. Cushing, Second Class Year Ending May, 1861," USMA.

76. W.H.H. to I.H., March 4, 1860, USMA; A.H.C. to W.B.C., Oct. 16, 1859, CCHS.

77. Special Orders No. 60, May 6, 1861, Post Orders, 1861-66, USMA.

78. Farley, *West Point in the Early Sixties*, 19.

79. A.H.C. to M.B.S.C., April 28, 1861, CCHS.

80. A.H.C. to W.B.C., May 28, 1861, CCHS; Register of Delinquencies, 1856-61, "Alonzo H. Cushing," May 27, 1861; A.H.C. to M.B.S.C., May 28, 1861, CCHS.

81. Haight, *Three Wisconsin Cushings*, 24-26; Personal Service Records of Lt. Howard B. Cushing, RG 94, NA; Reece, *Report of the Adjutant General of the State of Illinois*, 1:227-352, 8:607, 662. An examination of all the three-month troops failed to reveal Howard's name. As it is known he was present in the "Cairo Expedition," and that Battery B, 1st Illinois Light Artillery, was present as well, it is presumed he volunteered to serve with that command in April 1861. He appears on the rolls of the battery officially beginning on March 24, 1862.

82. A.H.C. to M.B.S.C., May 28, 1861, CCHS.

83. Class Standings; Register of Merit, 1853-1865, "Alonzo H. Cushing, First Class Year Ending June, 1861," USMA.

84. Monaghan, *Custer*, 42-43; Special Orders No. 114, July 17, 1861, Post Orders, 1861-1866, USMA. Cadet George A. Custer, while serving as officer of the guard on June 29, 1861, was cited by Lt. William B. Hazen for allowing two cadet candidates to engage in a fist fight. Custer was placed under arrest; whether he played a role in inviting the brawl is not clear. Lt. Stephen Vincent Benet presided at the hearing, where he pleaded guilty.

85. Sergent, *They Lie Forgotten*, 100.

86. A.H.C. to M.B.S.C., April 17, 1861, CCHS.

87. Special Orders No. 120, June 24, 1861, Post Orders, 1861-66, USMA.

3. "I Fancy I Did Some of the Prettiest Firing"

1. Farley, *West Point in the Early Sixties*, 100-101; Haight, *Three Wisconsin Cushings*, 32; A.H.C. to W.B.C., April 23, 1860, and A.H.C. to M.B.S.C., May 28, 1861, CCHS.

2. Rodenbough and Haskin, *Army of the United States*, 351-59.

3. Ibid., 359.

4. Farley, *West Point in the Early Sixties*, 100-101.

5. A.H.C. to Gen. Lorenzo Thomas, Oct. 10 and 30, 1861, in Personal Service Records of Lt. Alonzo H. Cushing, Record Group 94, NA; Edwards, *Commander William Barker Cushing*, 107; Haight, *Three Wisconsin Cushings*, 27; Parker, *Chautauqua Boy in '61*, 73.

6. Russell, *My Diary North and South*, 188-92; Leech, *Reveille in Washington*, 1-13.

7. Farley, *West Point in the Early Sixties*, 100-101; Leech, *Reveille in Washington*, 1-3, 5.

8. Farley, *West Point in the Early Sixties*, 101; Tarbell, *In the Footsteps of the Lincolns*, 1-16.

9. Cooling and Owen, *Mr. Lincoln's Forts*, 2-5; Leech, *Reveille in Washington*, 80.

10. McPherson, *Battle Cry of Freedom*, 335-40.

11. Ibid.

12. Warner, *Generals in Blue*, 297-99; Walcher, *Union Army*, 71-73.

13. McPherson, *Battle Cry of Freedom*, 335.

14. *OR*, 2:348-51, 372-73, 408-11, 436-37; W.H.H. to I.H., July 22, 1861, USMA.

15. A.H.C. to M.B.S.C., July 23, 1861, CCHS; Russell, *My Diary North and South*, 195-96.

16. Cooling and Owen, *Mr. Lincoln's Forts*, 89-92; Shaw, *Canals for a Nation*, 102-17; Russell, *My Diary North and South*, 195.

17. Russell, *My Diary North and South*, 196.

18. Walcher, *Union Army*, 71-73; A.H.C. to M.B.S.C., July 17, 1861, CCHS; *Fredonia Censor*, July 31, 1861, CCHS; Ripley, *Artillery and Ammunition*, 109-10.

19. *OR*, 2:315; Warner, *Generals in Blue*, 113-14; Phisterer, *New York in the War of the Rebellion*, 3:1912-22, 1946-58, 2089-2103, 2103-14.

20. *OR*, 2:315; Warner, *Generals in Blue*, 37; Phisterer, *New York in the War of the Rebellion*, 1:673-90, 3:1815-31, 2062-77, 2088-2213; Bates, *History of Pennsylvania Volunteers*, 1:382-417.

21. Kamphoefner, Helbich, and Sommer, *News from the Land of Freedom*, 402-3. One German immigrant, Peter Klein of Pottsville, Pennsylvania, wrote home to his family in Guchenbach, in Germany's Koller Valley, in 1861: "For us Germans the war is very good, for since the Germans have shown themselves to be the keenest defenders of the Constitution, and provide entire regiments of the best and bravest soldiers and officers, they're starting to fill the native Americans with respect. Now the Americans don't make fun of us anymore since they know that we are the mainstay of their country and their freedom."

22. Leech, *Reveille in Washington*, 88-89.

23. *OR*, 2:303-5; A.H.C. to M.B.S.C., July 17 and 23, 1861, CCHS.

24. *OR*, 2:305-8; A.H.C. to M.B.S.C., July 17 and 23, 1861, CCHS.

25. A.H.C. to M.B.S.C., July 17, 1861, CCHS; *OR* 2:306.

26. A.H.C. TO M.B.S.C., July 17, 1861, CCHS.

27. *OR*, 2:306-8, 310-12; Davis, *Battle of Bull Run*, 132-58.

28. A.H.C. to M.B.S.C., July 23, 1861, CCHS.

29. *OR*, 2:377-81, 424, 426-27, 436; A.H.C. to M.B.S.C., July 23, 1861, CCHS; Sanger and Hay, *James Longstreet*, 21-27.

30. *OR*, 2:326-27; 348-51, 383-87, 402-4; Rhodes, *All for the Union*, 33.

31. *OR*, 2:410-11.

32. Ibid., 394, 407; Aldrich, *History of Battery A, Rhode Island*, 14-31.

33. Davis, *Battle of Bull Run*, 204; *OR*, 2:348-51.

34. A.H.C. to M.B.S.C., July 23, 1861, CCHS; *OR*, 2:373-76, 377-81, 428-32, 436; Heitman, *Historical Register*, 1:333. The Confederate advance was led by Company H, 17th Virginia Infantry. Wise, *History of the Seventeenth Virginia Infantry*, 23-25.

35. *OR*, 2:394, 407.

36. Ibid.

37. Kinsley, *Favor the Bold*, 19-41.

38. A.H.C. to M.B.S.C., July 23, 1861, CCHS; *OR*, 2:334-36, 436-37.

39. A.H.C. to M.B.S.C., July 23, 1861, CCHS; *OR*, 2:436-37; W.H.H. to I.H., July 22, 1861, USMA.

40. Haight, *Three Wisconsin Cushings*, 34-35.

41. A.H.C. to M.B.S.C., July 23, 1861, CCHS; Cooling and Owen, *Mr. Lincoln's Forts*, 87-88.

42. *OR*, 2:436-37.

43. Edwards, *Commander William Barker Cushing*, 98.

44. Sears, *George B. McClellan*, 1-25, 50-67, 95-124.

45. A.H.C. to M.B.S.C., July 23, 1861, CCHS.

46. Ibid.

47. A.H.C. to Maj. S. Williams, accompanying certificate of J.J. Woodward, Asst. Surgeon, U.S.A., approved by Brig. Gen. Henry W. Slocum, Sept. 18, 1861, and A.H.C. to Brig. Gen. Lorenzo Thomas, Oct. 30, 1861, Records of U.S. Regular Army Mobile Units, 1821-1942, 4th United States Artillery, "Lt. Alonzo H. Cushing," RG 391, NA; Parker, *Chautauqua Boy in '61*, 73.

48. Journal of Lieutenant Commander William B. Cushing, May, 1861 to February, 1865, Microcopy T0794, NA (hereafter W.B.C. Journal); Edwards, *Commander William Barker Cushing*, 102-3.

49. A.H.C. to Brig. Gen. S. Williams and accompanying certificate of George M. Sternberg, Asst. Surgeon, U.S.A., Oct. 30, 1861, Records of U.S. Regular Army Mobile Units, 1821-1942, RG 391, NA; Edwards, *Commander William Barker Cushing*, 103-8.

50. Returns from Regular Army Artillery Regiments, June 1821 to January 1901, 4th Regiment of Artillery, July-Sept. 1861, Roll 29, NA

51. Ibid.; Rodenbough and Haskin, *Army of the United States*, 360.

52. Personal Service Records of Capt. Evan Thomas, RG 94, NA.

53. Personal Service Records of Maj. Rufus King, Jr., RG 94, NA; DAB, s.v. "King, Charles," and "King, Rufus."

54. Personal Service Records of Lt. Col. Frederick Fuger, RG 94, NA.

55. French, Barry, and Hunt, *Instruction for Field Artillery*; A.H.C. to M.B.S.C., Dec. 24, 1861, CCHS.

56. A.H.C. to M.B.S.C., Dec. 24, 1861, CCHS.

4. "It Was the Grandest Sight"

1. *Fredonia Censor*, Jan. 29, 1862; Haight, *Three Wisconsin Cushings*, 38.

2. Stanley, *E.V. Sumner*, 1-13; DAB, s.v. "Sumner, Edwin Vose."

3. A.H.C. to W.B.C., Feb. 24, 1863, CCHS.

4. Warner, *Generals in Blue*, 489-90; Teall, *Onondaga's Part in the Civil War*, 76-80.

5. Warner, *Generals in Blue*, 489-90; DAB, s.v. "Sumner, Edwin Vose."

6. Stanley, *E.V. Sumner*, 1-13; Bruce, *Onondaga's Centennial*, 2:1-6.

7. A.H.C. to M.B.S.C., Dec. 24, 1861, CCHS; Cooling and Owen, *Mr. Lincoln's Forts*, 65, 70-73; Monaghan, *Custer*, 79-80.

8. Sears, *George B. McClellan*, 147-67.

9. Ibid.

10. McPherson, *Battle Cry of Freedom*, 373; Smith, *Memorial of the Rev. Thomas Smith*, 27-32; Niven, *Gideon Wells*, 365, 404.

11. Lewis, *Admiral Franklin Buchanan*, 178-91; Niven, *Gideon Wells*, 404.

12. Niven, *Gideon Wells*, 404-7.

13. Walker, *History of the Second Army Corps*, 3; Sears, *George B. McClellan*, 160.

14. Walker, *History of the Second Army Corps*, 13.

15. Ibid., 4.

16. Ibid.; Lyons, *Brigadier-General Thomas Francis Meagher*, 9-41, 64-90.

17. Jones, *Irish Brigade*, 11-104. See also Kohl and Richard, *Irish Green and Union Blue*, 2, 10-11, 50, 65-67, 101; these letters to his wife from Peter Welsh of the 28th Massachusetts—which would become part of the famed Irish Brigade in the fall of 1862—articulately express the attitudes of most Irish soldiers toward the war.

18. Walker, *History of the Second Army Corps*, 4; Phisterer, *New York in the War of the Rebellion*, 3:2415-36, 2489-2502, 2648-60; Bates, *History of Pennsylvania Volunteers*, 2:92-134.

19. Walker, *History of the Second Army Corps*, 4.

20. Phisterer, *New York in the War of the Rebellion*, 3:1208; Teall, *Onondaga's Part in the Civil War*, 56-58.

21. Walker, *History of Second Army Corps*, 55; Phisterer, *New York in the War of the Rebellion*, 2:1789-1805.

22. Walker, *History of the Second Army Corps*, 6-8.

23. Ibid., 6; Phisterer, *New York in the War of the Rebellion*, 3:2125-37, 4:2897-2913; Ford, *Story of the Fifteenth Massachusetts*, 9-31; Holcome, *History of the First Minnesota*, 1-14.

24. Walker, *History of the Second Army Corps*, 6; Banes, *History of the Philadelphia Brigade*, 7-16.

25. Walker, *History of the Second Army Corps*, 6; Phisterer, *New York in the War of the Rebellion*, 3:2253-70; Waitt, *History of the Nineteenth Massachusetts*, 1-8; Bruce, *Twentieth Regiment of Massachusetts Volunteer Infantry*, 1-15; Robertson, *Michigan in the War*, 270-80.

26. Walker, *History of the Second Army Corps*, 6.

27. Haskin, *History of the First Regiment of Artillery*, 150-151; Crary, *Dear Belle*, 135.

28. Walker, *History of the Second Army Corps*, 6; Aldrich, *History of Battery A, Rhode Island*, 1-53; Rhodes, *History of Battery B, Rhode Island*, 5-46.

29. Heitman, *Historical Register*, 1:517; Personal Service Records of Capt. George Washington Hazzard, RG 94, NA.

30. Returns from Regular Army Artillery Regiments, 4th Artillery, Sept.-Dec. 1861, Jan.-Feb. 1862, Roll 29, NA.
31. Personal Service Records of Lt. Col. Edward Field, RG 94, NA.
32. Personal Service Records of Capt. Arthur Morris, RG 94, NA.
33. Cullen, *Peninsula Campaign*, 15.
34. Walker, *History of the Second Army Corps*, 3-15; Returns from Regular Army Artillery Regiments, 4th Artillery, March-April 1862, Roll 29, NA.
35. Returns from Regular Army Artillery Regiments, 4th Artillery, Roll 29, NA.
36. Walker, *History of the Second Army Corps*, 14-15.
37. Ibid., 15.
38. Cullen, *Peninsula Campaign*, 45-47.
39. Sword, *Shiloh*, 171-211; Reece, *Report of the Adjutant General of the State of Illinois*, 3:162, 169.
40. *OR*, 11 (1): 18-25.
41. Ibid.; Powell, *Fifth Army Corps*, 29.
42. *OR*, 11 (1): 18-25.
43. Ibid., 37-38, 812-18.
44. Ibid., 933-35, 939-41, 943-46.
45. Ibid., 763-64.
46. Ibid., 795-96; Haskin, *History of the First Regiment of Artillery*, 154.
47. *OR*, 11 (1): 763-64.
48. Ibid., 795-96; Haskin, *History of the First Regiment of Artillery*, 154.
49. A.H.C. to M.B.C. Jr., June 5, 1862, CCHS; *OR*, 11 (1): 795-96.
50. A.H.C. to M.B.C. Jr., June 5, 1862, CCHS; *OR*, 11 (1): 763-64, 791-793, 795-796.
51. A.H.C. to M.B.C. Jr., June 5, 1862, CCHS; *OR*, 11 (1): 763-64, 989-94.
52. A.H.C. to M.B.C. Jr., June 5, 1862, CCHS; *OR*, 11 (1): 764-66.
53. Warner, *Generals in Gray*, 191-92.
54. A.H.C. to M.B.C. Jr., June 5, 1862, CCHS; *OR*, 11 (1): 763-766.
55. A.H.C. to M.B.C. Jr., June 5, 1862, CCHS.
56. Ibid.
57. Cullum, *Peninsula Campaign*, 77-78.
58. Porter, "Hanover Court House and Gaines's Mill," 2:324.
59. A.H.C. to W.B.C., June 10, 1862, CCHS.
60. Personal Service Records of Lt. Evan Thomas, RG 94, NA.
61. *OR*, 11 (2): 489-91.
62. Ibid., 19-23, 489-94.
63. Sears, *George B. McClellan*, 215.
64. *OR*, 11 (2): 19-23, 49-50, 88-90; Rhodes, *History of Battery B, Rhode Island*, 97.
65. *OR*, 11 (2): 494, 664-65.
66. Ibid., 49-51, 53-55, 56-57, 57-60, 77-78, 82-86.
67. Ibid., 664-65.
68. Ibid., 49-51, 53-60, 82-86, 105.
69. Ibid., 664-65.
70. Ibid., 51, 53-60.
71. Ibid., 57-60; Rhodes, *History of Battery B, Rhode Island*, 96-99.
72. *OR*, 11 (2): 556-57.
73. Ibid., 22.
74. Ibid., 495-96.
75. Ibid., 53-55, 57-60, 72-75, 556-57.
76. Ibid., 53-55, 57-60.

77. Ibid., 53-55, 57-60, 70-75.

78. Returns from Regular Army Artillery Regiments, 4th Artillery, June-July 1862, Roll 29, NA.

79. *OR,* 11 (2): 22-23, 389-91, 402-4, 428-29, 756-61.

80. Ibid., 110-13; Aldrich, *History of Battery A, Rhode Island,* 106-7.

81. *OR,* 11 (2): 227-28, 389-94, 402-5.

82. Ibid., 229-31, 238-39.

83. Aldrich, *History of Battery A, Rhode Island,* 107-8.

84. *OR,* 11 (2): 495-97, 628-29, 817-20.

85. Hill, *Bethel to Sharpsburg,* 2:158-78.

86. Walker, *History of the Second Army Corps,* 88.

87. Ibid., Personal Service Records of Lt. Alonzo H. Cushing, RG 94, NA.

88. W.B.C. Journal; Edwards, *Commander William Barker Cushing,* 112.

89. W.B.C. Journal.

90. Ibid.

91. Ibid.

92. *OR,* 11 (1): 763-64; 11 (2): 52.

5. "My God! We Must Get Out of This!"

1. McPherson, *Battle Cry of Freedom,* 524-25; Pope, "Second Battle of Bull Run," 2:449-52; Warner, *Generals in Blue,* 447-48.

2. Pope, "Second Battle of Bull Run," 2:449-52.

3. McPherson, *Battle Cry of Freedom,* 525-26.

4. Walker, *History of the Second Corps,* 87.

5. McPherson, *Battle Cry of Freedom,* 526-32; Walker, *History of the Second Corps,* 88-89; Pope, "Second Battle of Bull Run," 2:468-70.

6. Walker, *History of the Second Corps,* 89-90.

7. McPherson, *Battle Cry of Freedom,* 526-32.

8. Ibid., 531-32.

9. Sears, *George B. McClellan,* 263-65.

10. Sears, *Landscape Turned Red,* 102-03.

11. Walker, *History of the Second Corps,* 87-98; P.J.R. to Mrs. P.J.R., Sept. 4, 1862, MHS.

12. Haskin, *History of the First Regiment of Artillery,* 540.

13. Personal Service Records of Capt. James McKay Rorty, RG 94, NA; Phisterer, *New York in the War of the Rebellion,* 2:1595.

14. Personal Service Records of Capt. James McKay Rorty, RG 94, NA; *Irish World,* June 18, 1887.

15. Sears, *Landscape Turned Red,* 91-99.

16. Walker, *History of the Second Corps,* 92-95.

17. *OR,* 19 (1): 210.

18. Ibid., 210-11, 283, 284, 293-95.

19. Ibid.; Hitchcock, *War from the Inside,* 46-48.

20. *OR,* 19 (1): 338-39, 418-19; Hitchcock, *War from the Inside,* 48-49.

21. Hitchcock, *War from the Inside,* 48-49; Waitt, *History of the Nineteenth Massachusetts,* 130-31; Taylor, *Taylor Sketchbook,* 296-99.

22. *OR,* 19 (1): 283. Lt. Evan Thomas's abbreviated report of Batteries A and C fails to mention any action on September 15 or 16. The returns for the batteries, however, indicate they expended ammunition on September 16. Clearly they

were engaged, with Pettit's battery. Returns from Regular Army Artillery Regiments, 4th Artillery, Sept. 1862, Roll 29, NA.

23. *OR*, 19 (1): 210, 283.

24. Ibid., 210.

25. Ibid., 287; Child, *History of the Fifth New Hampshire*, 117-19.

26. *OR*, 19 (1): 293, 304.

27. Ibid., 283, 293, 844-45, 1022.

28. Ibid., 283; Returns from Regular Army Artillery Regiments, 4th Artillery, Sept. 1862, Roll 29, NA.

29. *OR*, 19 (1): 338, 350; Walker, *History of the Second Corps*, 96-97.

30. *OR*, 19 (1): 53-55, 338-39.

31. Ibid., 29.

32. Ibid.; Crary, *Dear Belle*, 148.

33. *OR*, 19 (1): 29; Bruce, *Twentieth Regiment of Massachusetts Volunteer Infantry*, 159; Sears, *George B. McClellan*, 292-93.

34. *OR*, 19 (1): 54, 284; Powell, *Fifth Army Corps*, 269-71.

35. Child, *History of the Fifth New Hampshire*, 119; Reese, *Sykes' Regular Infantry Division*, 132-33.

36. *OR*, 19 (1): 283, 350-51, 844.

37. Hitchcock, *War from the Inside*, 51-54.

38. Crary, *Dear Belle*, 149.

39. *OR*, 19 (1): 350-51.

40. Ibid., 54-55, 206, 283, 342.

41. Hitchcock, *War from the Inside*, 51.

42. *OR*, 19 (1): 54-55.

43. Ibid., 55, 217.

44. Ibid., 283, 308.

45. Ibid., 218; Aldrich, *History of Battery A, Rhode Island*, 135; Rhodes, *History of Battery B, Rhode Island*, 121; Haskin, *History of the First Regiment of Artillery*, 158, 540; Antietam Battlefield Board, *Map of the Battlefield of Antietam* (hereafter cited as Antietam Map), "Daybreak," ANMP.

46. *OR*, 19 (1): 54-55.

47. Ibid., 148-49, 923, 955, 1022.

48. Ibid., 206, 226, 845.

49. Ibid., 475; Quaife, *From the Cannon's Mouth*, 125.

50. Hitchcock, *War from the Inside*, 54.

51. Murfin, *Gleam of Bayonets*, 212. Murfin credited the weather observations to R.L. Duncombe, director and nautical almanac officer, United States Naval Observatory, Washington, D.C.

52. *OR*, 19 (1): 218, 224, 234.

53. Ibid., 218, 223-25, 956.

54. Vautier, *History of the 88th Pennsylvania*, 74.

55. Ibid.; Cook, *History of the Twelfth Massachusetts*, 68; Hall, *History of the Ninety-Seventh New York*, 91; Dawes, *Service with the Sixth Wisconsin*, 90.

56. *OR*, 19 (1): 224-25, 956.

57. Ibid., 956, 1008.

58. Ibid., 475; Regimental Committee, *History of the One Hundred and Twenty-fifth Pennsylvania*, 65.

59. *OR*, 19 (1): 922-24, 927-38.

60. Ibid., 14, 475-76, 857-59, 914-15, 956.

61. Gould, *Joseph K.F. Mansfield*, 8-18; Hebert, *Fighting Joe Hooker*, 142-43.

62. *OR*, 19 (1): 504-6.

63. Ibid., 474-77, 504-6.

64. Ibid., 275.

65. Ibid., 284.

66. Ibid., 283, 308-9, 325-6; Antietam Map, "8:30 to 8:40 A.M."

67. *OR*, 19 (1): 191, 199.

68. Ibid., 275.

69. Walker, *History of the Second Corps*, 100-101, n.1.

70. Ibid., 102-3, *OR*, 19 (1): 305-6, 484-85; Regimental Committee, *History of the One Hundred and Twenty-fifth Pennsylvania*, 72-73; Chapin, *Brief History of the Thirty-Fourth Regiment, N.Y.S.V.*, 62-63.

71. *OR*, 19 (1): 857-59, 956.

72. Ibid., 308-9, 504-6, 865; Aldrich, *History of Battery A, Rhode Island*, 139-40.

73. Regimental Committee, *History of the One Hundred and Twenty-fifth Pennsylvania*, 75-76; Chapin, *Brief History of the Thirty-Fourth Regiment, N.Y.S.V.*, 62-63.

74. Bruce, *Twentieth Regiment of Massachusetts Volunteer Infantry*, 168-69.

75. *OR*, 19 (1): 858-59, 864-65, 874-75.

76. Ibid., 476; Ford, *Story of the Fifteenth Regiment Massachusetts Volunteer Infantry*, 194-95.

77. *OR*, 19 (1): 312-14, 318-19; Ford, *Story of the Fifteenth Massachusetts*, 195-97; Waitt, *History of the Nineteenth Massachusetts*, 136-37.

78. *OR*, 19 (1): 309-10; Haskin, *History of the First Regiment of Artillery*, 540.

79. *OR*, 19 (1): 309-10; Haskin, *History of the First Regiment of Artillery*, 540; Crary, *Dear Belle*, 151-52; Antietam Map, "9:00 to 9:30 A.M."

80. Ford, *Story of the Fifteenth Massachusetts*, 196-97; Waitt, *History of the Nineteenth Massachusetts*, 136-37.

81. *OR*, 19 (1): 306; War Department, Special Orders No. 299, Oct. 17, 1862 (granting leaves of absence to Lt. Col. Paul J. Revere and Capt. J.C. Audenreid), MHS; Higginson, *Harvard Memorial Biographies*, 1:124-35, 219-37.

82. *OR*, 19 (1): 309-10.

83. Ibid., 308.

84. Ibid., 476-77, 496, 502, 914-19.

85. Ibid., 309-310; Priest, *Antietam*, 164; Brady, *Hurrah for the Artillery*, 153.

86. *OR*, 19 (1): 284, 309-10. It is believed that the advanced section would have been the one commanded by the senior section commander of the battery, who at the time was Lt. Alonzo H. Cushing.

87. *OR*, 19 (1): 284, 308-9.

88. Ibid., 284, 308-9, 918; Priest, *Antietam*, 151-52.

89. *OR*, 19 (1): 284, 309-10, 515.

90. Ibid., 915-16; Graham, "Twenty-seventh Regiment," 2:433-37.

91. *OR*, 19 (1): 915-16; Graham, "Twenty-seventh Regiment," 434-36; Priest, *Antietam*, 155-56.

92. *OR*, 19 (1): 309, 326; Aldrich, *History of Battery A, Rhode Island*, 139-140.

93. *OR*, 19 (1): 310; Crary, *Dear Belle*, 153.

94. *OR*, 19 (1): 284, 477, 482; Brady, *Hurrah for the Artillery*, 153, 158-59; Capt. Frederick Fuger to Gen. H. Heth, Nov. 14, 1891, ANMP.

95. Graham, "Twenty-seventh Regiment," 435.

96. Priest, *Antietam*, 155-56.

97. *OR*, 19 (1): 323-24.

98. Ibid., 277-83.

99. Ibid., 277-83, 323-24.

100. Ibid., 277-83; Jones, *Irish Brigade*, 141-42.
101. *OR*, 19 (1): 279.
102. Ibid., 277-81, 284-87.
103. Ibid., 284; Graham, "Twenty-seventh Regiment," 434-36; Antietam Map, "Noon to 12:15 P.M."; Brady, *Hurrah for the Artillery*, 162.
104. *OR*, 19 (1): 284, 504-5; Graham, "Twenty-seventh Regiment," 435.
105. *OR*, 19 (1): 284, 323-24, 504-5; Graham, "Twenty-seventh Regiment," 435; Brady, *Hurrah for the Artillery*, 162.
106. *OR*, 19 (1): 284, 323-24, 504-5.
107. *OR*, 19 (1): 284, 409-12.
108. Phisterer, *New York in the War of the Rebellion*, 3:1958-70, 2378-99; Antietam Map, "1 P.M."
109. *OR*, 19 (1): 284.
110. Ibid., 277-83, 840.
111. Ibid., 280.
112. Ibid.
113. Ibid., 419-21, 840-41.

6. "The Army Is Extremely Disgusted"

1. *OR*, 19 (1): 32, 369; Walker, *History of the Second Corps*, 127.
2. *OR*, 19 (1): 32; 19 (2): 330-31.
3. Walker, *History of the Second Corps*, 127-28.
4. A.H.C. to Brig. Gen. Lorenzo Thomas, Sept. 21, 1862, in Personal Service Records of Lt. Alonzo H. Cushing, RG 94, NA; Frassanito, *Antietam*, 268-71.
5. *OR*, 19 (2): 342-43; Returns from Regular Army Artillery Regiments, 4th Artillery, Sept.-Oct. 1862, Roll 29, NA.
6. Walker, *History of the Second Corps*, 128-29; Sears, *Civil War Papers of McClellan*, 488.
7. Walker, *History of the Second Corps*, 128-29; Warner, *Generals in Blue*, 95-96.
8. Returns from Regular Army Artillery Regiments, 4th Artillery, Sept.-Oct. 1862, Roll 29, NA; Rodenbough and Haskin, *Army of the United States*, 360; A.H.C. to Gen. Lorenzo Thomas, Oct. 11, 1862, in Personal Service Records of Lt. Alonzo H. Cushing, RG 94, NA.
9. Walker, *History of the Second Corps*, 131; McClellan, *I Rode with Jeb Stuart*, 167-69; Neese, *Three Years in the Confederate Horse Artillery*, 129-30.
10. Records of the Adjutant General's Office, "Muster Rolls Pertaining to Battery A, 4th United States Artillery," Dec. 31, 1862, to Feb. 28, 1863, RG 94, NA; Rodenbough and Haskin, *Army of the United States*, 360; Kepler, *History of the Fourth Ohio*, 83; Roster Commission, *Official Roster of the Soldiers of the State of Ohio*, 2:88-120. Kepler indicates that some forty members of the 4th Ohio enlisted in the 4th United States Artillery, but his rosters are somewhat uneven; the official rosters show more than fifty members doing so. The soldiers in the 4th Ohio had seen significant combat experience in McClellan's successful western Virginia campaign and Gen. Nathaniel Banks's unsuccessful campaign against Stonewall Jackson in the Shenandoah Valley.
11. Records of the Adjutant General's office, "Muster Rolls Pertaining to Battery A, 4th United States Artillery," Dec. 31, 1862 to Feb. 28, 1863, RG 94, NA.
12. Rodenbough and Haskin, *Army of the United States*, 360; Ripley, *Artillery and Ammunition*, 161-62.

13. Personal Service Records of Lt. Samuel Canby, RG 94, NA.
14. McClellan, *McClellan's Own Story*, 645-50; *OR*, 19 (2): 685-86.
15. McClellan, *McClellan's Own Story*, 645-46; Walker, *History of the Second Corps*, 131-33.
16. McClellan, *McClellan's Own Story*, 647; Walker, *History of the Second Corps*, 136.
17. Returns from Regular Army Artillery Regiments, 4th Artillery, Oct.-Nov. 1862, Roll 29, NA; Rodenbough and Haskin, *Army of the United States*, 360.
18. Sears, *Civil War Papers of McClellan*, 519; Walker, *History of the Second Corps*, 136-37.
19. A.H.C. to Maj. I.C. Woodruff, Nov. 7, 1862, in Records of the Office of the Chief of Engineers, "Topographical Engineers," RG 77, NA.
20. Buckingham, "Recollections," 116-17, OHS.
21. Warner, *Generals in Blue*, 49-50; Thomas and Hyman, *Stanton*, 12; Buckingham, "Recollections," 106-14. When Catharenus P. Buckingham left Putnam, Ohio, he and his wife, along with Rachel Cushing, traveled to Fredonia, New York, to visit his uncle, Zattu Cushing. Buckingham stayed in the home of Zattu and Eunice Cushing for several days.
22. Buckingham, "Recollections," 114-15.
23. Ibid., 115-16.
24. Ibid., 116-17.
25. Ibid.
26. Ibid., 117-19.
27. Ibid., 119-20.
28. Ibid., 120.
29. McClellan, *McClellan's Own Story*, 651-52; Buckingham, "Recollections," 120-21.
30. Buckingham, "Recollections," 121.
31. A.H.C. to W.B.C., Nov. 12, 1862, CCHS.
32. Marvel, *Burnside*, 160-65.
33. Warren, *Generals in Blue*, 57.
34. McClellan, *McClellan's Own Story*, 647-48.
35. Teall, ". . . Ringside Seat at Fredericksburg," 20-21.
36. A.H.C. to W.B.C., Nov. 12, 1862, CCHS; *OR*, 21:220; Heitman, *Historical Register*, 1:672.
37. Teall, ". . . Ringside Seat at Fredericksburg," 21; Meriwether, *Raphael Semmes*, 12; A.H.C. to W.B.C., Nov. 12, 1862, CCHS.
38. W.B.C. Journal; Edwards, *Commander William Barker Cushing*, 113-19.
39. H.B.C. to M.B.S.C., May 29, 1862, CCHS; Reece, *Report of the Adjutant General of the State of Illinois*, 8:660-61.
40. A.H.C. to W.B.C., Nov. 12, 1862, CCHS.
41. *OR*, 21:48-61.
42. Ibid.
43. Ibid., 84-85, 550-52.
44. Ibid., 550-53, 568-69.
45. Ibid., 550-53, 630-31.
46. Ibid., 87-89, 550-51.
47. Ibid., 180-89.
48. Ibid., 88-89, 169-71, 175-77.
49. Ibid., 221, 253, 282.
50. Ibid., 552, 600-607. Barksdale's command consisted of his own 13th,

17th, 18th, and 21st Mississippi along with portions of the 8th Florida and 3d Georgia. Waitt, *History of the Nineteenth Massachusetts*, 165-68.

51. *OR*, 21:600-607.
52. Ibid., 183, 221-22, 282; Waitt, *History of the Nineteenth Massachusetts*, 166-68.
53. *OR*, 21:183, 221-22, 282-83; Waitt, *History of the Nineteenth Massachusetts*, 166-68.
54. *OR*, 21:221-22, 282-83, 285; Waitt, *History of the Nineteenth Massachusetts*, 166-69; Bruce, *Twentieth Regiment of Massachusetts Volunteer Infantry*, 193-201; Regimental Committee, *History of the 127th Pennsylvania*, 118-20.
55. *OR*, 21:221-22, 282-84, 285; Bruce, *Twentieth Regiment of Massachusetts Volunteer Infantry*, 199-205.
56. *OR*, 21:221-22, 262-63, 335, 536.
57. Couch, "Sumner's 'Right Grand Division,'" 3:108; Bruce, *Twentieth Regiment of Massachusetts Volunteer Infantry*, 206-8.
58. *OR*, 21:88-90; Walker, *History of the Second Corps*, 156-58.
59. Couch, "Sumner's 'Right Grand Division,'" 109-10; Bruce, *Twentieth Regiment of Massachusetts Volunteer Infantry*, 207.
60. Walker, *History of the Second Corps*, 159-64.
61. *OR*, 21:568-70, 578-81.
62. Walker, *History of the Second Corps*, 158-59.
63. *OR*, 21:224; Couch, "Sumner's 'Right Grand Division,'" 115; Walker, *History of the Second Corps*, 181.
64. *OR*, 21:222.
65. Ibid., 222-33.
66. Teall, ". . . Ringside Seat at Fredericksburg," 27.
67. *OR*, 21:222-23, 286-87, 290-99; Couch, "Sumner's 'Right Grand Division,'" 111-13; Aldrich, *History of Battery A, Rhode Island*, 160-61.
68. Couch, "Sumner's 'Right Grand Division,'" 113.
69. *OR*, 21:290-99.
70. Ibid., 300-304; Page, *History of the Fourteenth Connecticut*, 85-86.
71. Couch, "Sumner's 'Right Grand Division,'" 113.
72. *OR*, 21:629-30.
73. Ibid., 222-23, 226-32, 588-91, 607-8, 625-28.
74. Ibid., 227, 240-62; Jones, *Irish Brigade*, 152-56; Mulholland, *Story of the 116th Pennsylvania*, 43.
75. Walker, *History of the Second Corps*, 172, 175.
76. *OR*, 21:227, 233-39; Walker, *History of the Second Corps*, 172-73.
77. *OR*, 21:262-86; Regimental Committee, *History of the 127th Pennsylvania*, 126-31; Waitt, *History of the Nineteenth Massachusetts*, 178-81.
78. *OR*, 21:223; Couch, "Sumner's 'Right Grand Division,'" 113-15.
79. *OR*, 21:429-30; McNamara, "Gettysburg Centenary Recalls Heroism of Rochester."
80. *OR*, 21:223, 225, 232, 267; Couch, "Sumner's 'Right Grand Division,'" 113; Rhodes, *History of Battery B, Rhode Island*, 139-44; Haskin, *History of the First Regiment of Artillery*, 541-42.
81. Couch, "Sumner's 'Right Grand Division,'" 115-17; Walker, *History of the Second Corps*, 179-81.
82. *OR*, 21:355-57, 399-402, 430-35.
83. Couch, "Sumner's 'Right Grand Division,'" 116.
84. Walker, *History of the Second Corps*, 189.
85. *OR*, 21:224; Heitman, *Historical Register*, 1:347.

7. "The Elements Are at War with the Army"

1. *OR*, 21:224, 225, 264, 273, 415.
2. Ibid., 208-10, 212-13.
3. Ibid., 225, 416; Teall, ". . . Ringside Seat at Fredericksburg," 30; Galway, *Valiant Hours*, 64-65.
4. *OR*, 21:212, 264; Holcome, *History of the First Minnesota*, 270-72; Records of the Adjutant General's Office, "Muster Rolls Pertaining to Battery A, 4th United States Artillery," Dec. 31, 1862, to Feb. 28, 1863, RG 94, NA; Returns from Regular Army Artillery Regiments, 4th Artillery, casualties for Dec. 14, 1862, Roll 29, NA.
5. Teall, ". . . Ringside Seat at Fredericksburg," 30.
6. Ibid.; *OR*, 21:225, 415; Galway, *Valiant Hours*, 66.
7. Mulholland, *Story of the 116th Pennsylvania*, 51.
8. Ibid., 61.
9. Teall, ". . . Ringside Seat at Fredericksburg," 30; Galway, *Valiant Hours*, 66.
10. Teall, ". . . Ringside Seat at Fredericksburg," 30.
11. Ibid., 30-31; Cole, *Under Five Commanders*, 114.
12. Teall, ". . . Ringside Seat at Fredericksburg," 27-31; *OR*, 12:151-54.
13. Crary, *Dear Belle*, 178-80; Mulholland, *Story of the 116th Pennsylvania*, 63.
14. A.H.C. to Maj. I.C. Woodruff, Dec. 7, 1862, in Records of the Office of the Chief of Engineers, "Topographical Engineers," RG 77, NA.
15. Teall, ". . . Ringside Seat at Fredericksburg," 31.
16. Ibid.; Crary, *Dear Belle*, 178-79; Col. Patrick H. O'Rorke to General ——, Dec. 3, 1862, RLL. O'Rorke wrote even before the fiasco at Fredericksburg: "Since I have joined this portion of the army [the Fifth Corps] I have been very much grieved to find a very despondent feeling pervading it. This was the case before McClellan was removed, and it has been deepened and intensified since. I have heard the opinion expressed time after time by officers of volunteer regiments and batteries all through the war thus far, that we would not succeed in quelling this rebellion. Almost all of them despair of a successful termination of the war and do not hesitate to say so openly before their men."
17. Teall, ". . . Ringside Seat at Fredericksburg," 31.
18. Ibid.
19. Mulholland, *Story of the 116th Pennsylvania*, 72.
20. *OR*, 12:95, 697, 703, 704; Teall, ". . . Ringside Seat at Fredericksburg," 32-33.
21. *OR*, 12:95-96; Marvel, *Burnside*, 208-11. Among those officers who sought to undermine Burnside's attempted movement were Brig. Gens. John Newton and John Cochrane, division and brigade commanders respectively in Maj. Gen. William F. Smith's Sixth Army Corps of Franklin's Left Grand Division.
22. *OR*, 12:78, 96, 752-55.
23. Ibid., 96, 752-55.
24. Ibid., 752-55.
25. Ibid., 25 (2): 3.
26. Ibid.; Warner, *Generals in Blue*, 233-35; Hebert, *Fighting Joe Hooker*, 17.
27. Crary, *Dear Belle*, 183.
28. *OR*, 25 (2): 52.
29. A.H.C. to Col. J.A. Taylor, Jan. 26, 1863, in Personal Service Records of Lt. Alonzo H. Cushing, RG 94, NA; *OR*, 25(2): 52.
30. A.H.C. to W.B.C., Feb. 24, 1863, CCHS.

31. Ibid.

32. Warner, *Generals in Blue*, 490; Bruce, *Onondaga's Centennial*, 2:3.

33. A.H .C. to W.B.C., Feb. 24, 1863, CCHS; affidavit of Houghton Wheeler, Nov. 1863, in Pension Records, "Alonzo H. Cushing," MOC 11 871, NA.

34. A.H.C. to W.B.C., Feb. 24, 1863, CCHS.

35. Ibid.

36. Ibid.

37. Smith, *Memorial of the Rev.Thomas Smith*, 59, 74-89.

38. A.H.C. to W.B.C., Feb. 24, 1863, CCHS.

39. Ibid.

40. Ibid.; Parker, *Chautauqua Boy of '61*, 73.

41. A.H.C. to W.B.C., Feb. 24, 1863, CCHS; *Fredonia Censor*, July 11, 1900. The painting of Lt. Alonzo H. Cushing's death at Gettysburg by Henry Edwin Brown—pronounced by Gen. Alexander Stewart Webb, First Sergeant Frederick Fuger, and Mary Isabel Cushing Bouton, Alonzo's sister, to be the best likeness of him—portrays Cushing wearing a mustache and Vandyke beard.

42. A.H.C. to W.B.C., Feb. 24, 1863, CCHS; Records of the Adjutant General's Office, "Muster Rolls Pertaining to Battery A, 4th United States Artillery," Dec. 31, 1862 to Feb. 28, 1863, RG 94, NA; Personal Service Records of Lt. Arthur Morris, RG 94, NA; Typescript Statement of Thomas Moon, June 23, 1913, GNMP.

43. Records of the Adjutant General's office, "Muster Rolls Pertaining to Battery A, 4th United States Artillery," Dec. 31, 1862, to Feb. 28, 1863, RG 94, NA; Kepler, *History of the Fourth Ohio*, 19-24.

44. Roster Commission, Official Roster of the Soldiers of the State of Ohio, 120; Typescript Statement of Thomas Moon, GNMP.

45. *Buffalo Evening News*, May 29, 1894; Personal Service Records of Christopher Smith, RG 94, NA.

46. *OR*, 25 (2): 51, 52-53, 211-12.

47. Ibid., 176, 211-12; Warner, *Generals in Blue*, 237-39, 447-48; Carpenter, *Sword and Olive Branch*, 43.

48. *OR*, 25 (2): 582.

49. Catton, *Never Call Retreat*, 152-53. The correspondence of Major Henry Livermore Abbott, collected in Scott, *Fallen Leaves*, epitomizes the attitude of many native-born soldiers toward the Germans in the Eleventh Corps: in a letter blaming Gen. Hooker for failing to use all his corps at the Battle of Chancellorsville, Abbott spoke of "the disgraceful flight of those miserable Dutchmen, who every body knew would run away" (p. 181).

50. *OR*, 25 (2): 576-77.

51. Ibid., 152.

52. Ibid., 255-56, 262, 266-69, 273-77.

53. Edwards, *Commander William Barker Cushing*, 119-20.

54. Ibid., 120-21.

55. Ibid., 121-23.

56. A.H.C. to W.B.C., April 14, 1863, CCHS; Rhodes, *History of Battery B, Rhode Island*, 163; Aldrich, *History of Battery A, Rhode Island*, 172. In both Rhode Island batteries the men could tell as early as April 12 and 13 that a forward movement was at hand.

57. A.H.C. to W.B.C., April 14, 1863, CCHS.

58. Ibid.; Rhodes, *History of Battery B, Rhode Island*, 163.

59. A.H.C. to W.B.C., April 23, 1863, CCHS.

60. Ibid.

61. Ibid.

62. *OR*, 25 (2): 255, 262, 266-67, 268; *OR*, 25 (1): 305-8, 309-10.

63. A.H.C. to M.B.S.C., April 27, 1863, CCHS.

64. *OR*, 25 (1): 311.

65. Ibid., 305, 309, 311, 362.

66. Ibid., 305, 309.

67. Walker, *History of the Second Army Corps*, 218.

68. *OR*, 25 (1): 384.

69. Ibid., 305-7, 311, 525, 545-6, 669-70.

70. Ibid., 306-7.

71. Ibid., 796-97, 306-7, 309, 525, 541-42, 670; Aldrich, *History of Battery A, Rhode Island*, 175.

72. *OR*, 25 (1): 306-7, 311-12.

73. Ibid., 307, 385, 627-28, 670.

74. Ibid., 311-12; Walker, *History of the Second Corps*, 226-27.

75. *OR*, 25 (1): 798.

76. Couch, "Chancellorsville Campaign," 3: 162-63.

77. *OR*, 25 (1): 386-87, 798.

78. Ibid., 798.

79. Ibid., 634-35, 636, 645-46, 647-658; Trefousse, *Carl Schurz*, 133; Walker, *History of the Second Corps*, 228-29.

80. Personal Service Records of Lt. Alonzo H. Cushing, RG 94, NA. Lon's brevet to the rank of major would not be conferred until June 18, 1868, by then President Andrew Johnson.

81. *OR*, 25 (1): 309, 312-13, 322-23.

82. Ibid., 309-10.

83. Ibid., 798-99.

84. Ibid., 799-800; Couch, "Chancellorsville Campaign," 164-65.

85. *OR*, 25 (1): 309; Aldrich, *History of Battery A, Rhode Island*, 176; Haskin, *History of the First Regiment of Artillery*, 542.

86. *OR*, 25 (1): 307, 390-92, 799-800, 887-88, 943, 1005.

87. Ibid., 483-85.

88. Couch, "Chancellorsville Campaign," 167.

89. *OR*, 25 (1): 309-10; Aldrich, *History of Battery A, Rhode Island*, 176-77; Haskins, *History of the First Regiment of Artillery*, 542.

90. *OR*, 25 (1): 943, 1004-6.

91. Ibid. 313-23, 800, 826, 851.

92. Ibid., 723-25, 800.

93. Ibid., 307, 313-14, 390-93.

94. Ibid., 313.

95. Ibid., 309-10, 313-14.

96. Ibid., 259, 309-10; Maine Gettysburg Commission, *Maine at Gettysburg*, 107-10; Haskin, *History of the First Regiment of Artillery*, 542-43; "Memoirs of George A. Woodruff," 77-79, USMA.

97. *OR*, 25 (1): 307; Couch, "Chancellorsville Campaign," 168-70.

98. *OR*, 25 (1): 314-15; Walker, *History of the Second Corps*, 246.

99. *OR*, 25 (1): 314-15, 320-21.

100. Ibid., 800-801.

101. Stackpole, *Chancellorsville*, 373-75.

102. *OR*, 25 (1): 306; Diary of Patrick H. O'Rorke, May 5, 1863, RLL.

103. *OR,* 25 (1): 306.
104. A.H.C. to W.B.C., May 7, 1863, CCHS.
105. Illinois-Vicksburg Military Park Commission, *Illinois at Vicksburg,* 328-30.
106. Ibid.
107. Buckingham, *Ancestors of Ebenezer Buckingham,* 114-55; L.S.H. to E.T., March 25, 1859, LS. Theodosia Fredonia and Sara Lavina traveled to Fredonia in 1859, and Theodosia stayed there to attend Fredonia Academy.
108. L.S.H. to E.T., Aug. 19, 1863, LS.
109. Aldrich, *History of Battery A, Rhode Island,* 180-81; Rhodes, *History of Battery B, Rhode Island,* 177-78.
110. A.H.C. to J.G.H., May 24, 1863, "Requisitions," in Records of the United States Army Continental Commands, Second Army Corps Artillery Brigade, May 1863 to June 1865, vol. 68, bk. 357, RG 393, NA.
111. R.K. Jr. to A.H.C., May 27, 1863, "Letters and Endorsements," in ibid. bk. 354; Asa Bird Gardner to R.K., Jr., Nov. 5, 1897, in Personal Service Records of Maj. Rufus King, Jr., RG 94, NA.
112. A.H.C. to J.G.H., June 4, 1863, "Letters and Endorsements," Records of the United States Army Continental Commands, Second Corps Artillery Brigade, May 1863 to June 1865, vol. 68, bk. 354, RG 393, NA.
113. A.H.C. to J.G.H., May 27, and 30, 1863, "Requisitions," in ibid., bk. 357.
114. Schaff, *The Spirit of Old West Point,* 72-73.
115. "Memoirs of George A. Woodruff," 79-81, USMA.
116. Sergent, *They Lie Forgotten,* 160.
117. "Memoirs of George A. Woodruff," 78, USMA.

8. "Forward into Battery!"

1. Vandiver, *Mighty Stonewall,* 493-94.
2. *OR,* 25 (2): 814.
3. Roland, *American Iliad,* 67-87, 118-54.
4. Jones, "Gettysburg Decision," 332-40.
5. Ibid., 331-43; Jones, "Gettysburg Decision Reassessed," 64-66; *OR,* 27 (2): 293-94, 305, 313; 27 (3): 868-69, 880-82. Lee first notified the War Department by letter dated June 7, 1863, of the movements he began on June 3; the department did not receive Lee's letter until June 10. By that time Ewell's and Longstreet's corps had already reached Culpeper, Virginia.
6. *OR,* 25 (1): 30; 25 (2): 293; 25 (3): 859; 27 (3): 27-28.
7. Hebert, *Fighting Joe Hooker,* 237.
8. *OR,* 27 (3): 17.
9. Special Orders No. 14, June 6, 1863, "Special Orders, Circulars and General Orders," in Records of United States Army Continental Commands, Second Corps Artillery Brigade, May 1863 to June 1865, vol. 68, bk. 353, RG 393, NA.
10. Lewis, *History of Battery E, Rhode Island,* 224-25; *Buffalo Evening News,* May 29, 1894.
11. Lewis, *History of Battery E, Rhode Island,* 60-64, 224-25; *OR,* 11 (2): 168-69; Personal Service Records of Lt. Joseph A. Milne, RG 94, NA.
12. Hebert, *Fighting Joe Hooker,* 228-29; *OR,* 27 (3): 54-55. It appears that General Couch, along with General Slocum and Reynolds, actually visited President Lincoln to advocate Hooker's removal.

13. *OR,* 27 (3): 299; Warner, *Generals In Blue,* 202-3.
14. *OR,* 25 (2): 576-77.
15. Ibid., 577.
16. Ibid.
17. *OR,* 27 (2): 305-6, 313-15.
18. Ibid., 30-35.
19. Ibid., 38, 141.
20. Ibid., 36.
21. Ibid., 141.
22. Special Order No. 21, June 14, 1863, "Special Orders, Circulars and General Orders," in Records of the United States Army Continental Commands, Second Corps Artillery Brigade, May 1863 to June 1865, vol. 68, bk. 353, RG 393, NA.
23. Ibid.; *OR,* 27 (1): 141-42; Rhodes, *History of Battery B, Rhode Island,* 189. Lt. Samuel Canby, as senior subaltern in the battery, would have been placed in command of the rear two sections.
24. Rhodes, *History of Battery B, Rhode Island,* 189.
25. Beale, *Battle Flags of the Army,* "2nd Corps," n.p.
26. *OR,* 27 (1): 38, 40-41, 141-42; Rhodes, *History of Battery B, Rhode Island,* 190.
27. *OR,* 27 (2): 306, 314-15.
28. Aldrich, *History of Battery A, Rhode Island,* 185.
29. Ibid., 27 (1): 142; Rhodes, *History of Battery B, Rhode Island,* 190; Aldrich, *History of Battery A, Rhode Island,* 185.
30. *OR,* 27 (1): 142; Rhodes, *History of Battery B, Rhode Island,* 191; Aldrich, *History of Battery A, Rhode Island,* 185-86.
31. Aldrich, *History of Battery A, Rhode Island,* 185-86; Ford, *Story of the Fifteenth Massachusetts,* 256.
32. Rhodes, *History of Battery B, Rhode Island,* 191; Mulholland, *Story of the 116th Pennsylvania,* 115. The Irish 116th Pennsylvania took advantage of the opportunity to bathe in the Occoquan, but to their horror they found the creek "a mass of writhing, squirming serpents! Snakes of all sizes, short and long, thick and lean, in groups and tied in knots. Snakes single and by the dozen. Snakes by the hundred, countless and unnumerable." The men darted out of the water and scrambled for their clothes!
33. *OR,* 27 (1), 142; Rhodes, *History of Battery B, Rhode Island,* 191-92; Aldrich, *History of Battery A, Rhode Island,* 186.
34. Rhodes, *History of Battery B, Rhode Island,* 191-92; Aldrich, *History of Battery A, Rhode Island,* 186.
35. Rhodes, *History of Battery B, Rhode Island,* 191-92; Aldrich, *History of Battery A, Rhode Island,* 186.
36. Rhodes, *History of Battery B, Rhode Island,* 191-92; Aldrich, *History of Battery A, Rhode Island,* 186; Crary, *Dear Belle,* 202-3.
37. Rhodes, *History of Battery B, Rhode Island,* 191-92; Aldrich, *History of Battery A, Rhode Island,* 186; Banes, *History of the Philadelphia Brigade,* 172; Ward, *History of the One Hundred and Sixth Pennsylvania,* 173.
38. *OR,* 27 (1): 142-43; Rhodes, *History of Battery B, Rhode Island,* 192-93.
39. Rhodes, *History of Battery B, Rhode Island,* 193-94; "Memoirs of George A. Woodruff," 90, USMA.
40. Rhodes, *History of Battery B, Rhode Island,* 193-94; Records of the Adjutant General's Office, "Muster Rolls Pertaining to Battery A, 4th United States Artillery," April 30, 1863, to June 30, 1863, RG 94, NA.

41. Ibid., in addition to casualties, one caisson was upset and rendered useless.

42. Walker, *History of the Second Army Corps*, 259; Rhodes, *History of Battery B, Rhode Island*, 194-95.

43. *OR*, 27 (1): 143; "Memoirs of George A. Woodruff," 90, USMA; Rhodes, *History of Battery B, Rhode Island*, 195; Aldrich, *History of Battery A, Rhode Island*, 188-89.

44. Walker, *History of the Second Army Corps*, 260; Fleming, *Life and Letters of Alexander Hays*, 401.

45. *OR*, 27(1): 143; Rhodes, *History of Battery B, Rhode Island*, 195; Aldrich, *History of Battery A, Rhode Island*, 189.

46. Rhodes, *History of Battery B, Rhode Island*, 195; Aldrich, *History of Battery A, Rhode Island*, 189.

47. *OR*, 27 (2): 306-7, 315-16, 692.

48. *OR*, Ibid., 27 (1): 143; Rhodes, *History of Battery B, Rhode Island*, 189.

49. *OR*, 27(1): 143; Rhodes, *History of Battery B, Rhode Island*, 196-97; Aldrich, *History of Battery A, Rhode Island*, 189-90.

50. Walker, *History of the Second Corps*, 260; Banes, *History of the Philadelphia Brigade*, 173-74; Ward, *History of the One Hundred and Sixth Pennsylvania*, 78; Morning Reports of Co. B, 72d Pennsylvania Volunteers, Report for June 1863, remarks for July 1863, KMB.

51. Warner, *Generals in Blue*, 544-45.

52. *OR*, 27 (1): 143-44.

53. Herbert, *Fighting Joe Hooker*, 239-45; *OR*, 27 (3): 369.

54. *OR*, 27 (3): 369; Cleaves, *Meade of Gettysburg*, 123-26.

55. Warner, *Generals in Blue*, 315-17; McClellan, *McClellan's Own Story*, 140; Cleaves, *Meade of Gettysburg*, 3-9.

56. *OR*, 27 (1): 144; Rhodes, *History of Battery B, Rhode Island*, 197; Aldrich, *History of Battery A, Rhode Island*, 190; Bruce, *Twentieth Regiment of Massachusetts Volunteer Infantry*, 267.

57. Waitt, *History of the Nineteenth Massachusetts*, 217-22.

58. Ibid., 222.

59. *OR*, 27 (1): 144; Rhodes, *History of Battery B, Rhode Island*, 197-98; iron plaque, Uniontown, Maryland, Rt. 77, marking the location of the headquarters of the Second Corps, Army of the Potomac.

60. Crary, *Dear Belle*, 203-04.

61. Rhodes, *History of Battery B, Rhode Island*, 199; Records of the Adjutant General's Office, "Muster Rolls Pertaining to Battery A, 4th United States Artillery," April 30, 1863, to June 30, 1863, RG 94, NA.

62. *OR*, 27 (1): 144; 27 (2): 307, 316-17.

63. Rhodes, *History of Battery B, Rhode Island*, 199.

64. Ibid., 199-200.

65. *OR*, 27 (1): 243-48, 701-2; 27 (2): 307-8, 317-18.

66. Ibid., 27 (1): 249; 27(2): 317.

67. Ibid., 27 (1): 367; Tucker, *Hancock the Superb*, 129.

68. Cleaves, *Meade of Gettysburg*, 134-36.

69. *OR*, 27(1): 367; Tucker, *Hancock the Superb*, 130-31.

70. Tucker, *Hancock the Superb*, 130-131; Hancock, *Reminiscences of Winfield Scott Hancock*, 185-87.

71. *OR*, 27 (1): 369; Tucker, *Hancock the Superb*, 130; Rhodes, *History of Battery B, Rhode Island*, 199-200.

72. Personal Service Records of Lt. Alonzo H. Cushing, RG 94, NA; Records of the Adjutant General's Office, "Muster Rolls Pertaining to Battery A, 4th United States Artillery," June 30, 1863, to July 31, 1863, RG 94, NA; Hancock, *Reminiscences of Winfield Scott Hancock*, 188; Haight, *Three Wisconsin Cushings*, 44-45.

73. *OR*, 27 (1): 368; Hancock, *Reminiscences of Winfield Scott Hancock*, 188; Tucker, *Hancock the Superb*, 131.

74. Hancock, *Reminiscences of Winfield Scott Hancock*, 188-89.

75. Ibid., 189; *OR*, 27 (1): 252, 368, 704.

76. *OR*, 27 (1): 251, 702-5, 721; 27 (2): 307-8, 317-18.

77. Ibid., 27 (1): 252, 368-69; 704-5, 758-59.

78. Ibid., 27 (2): 318.

79. Ibid., 27 (1): 368; Hancock, *Reminiscences of Winfield Scott Hancock*, 191.

80. French, Barry, and Hunt, *Instruction for Field Artillery*, 281-82.

81. *OR*, 27 (1): 159; Personal Service Records of Capt. James McKay Rorty, RG 94, NA; New York Monuments Commission, *Final Report on the Battlefield of Gettysburg*, 3:1182; Teall, *Onondaga's Part in the Civil War*, 58.

82. *OR*, 27 (1), 369; Rhodes, *History of Battery B, Rhode Island*, 200.

83. *OR*, 27 (1): 478.

84. Coco, *Wasted Valor*, 79-86.

85. Fuger, "Cushing's Battery at Gettysburg," 406.

86. French, Barry, and Hunt, *Instruction for Field Artillery*, 277.

87. Ibid.; Records of the Adjutant General's Office, *Muster Rolls Pertaining to Battery A, 4th United States Artillery, December 31, 1862-December 28, 1863*, "Muster Rolls, June 30, 1863 to July 31, 1863," RG 94, NA; Typescript Statement of Thomas Moon, June 23, 1913, GNMP.

88. French, Barry, and Hunt, *Instruction for Field Artillery*, 107-8.

89. *OR*, 27 (1): 369, 416, 427, 477-78; Ward, *History of the One Hundred and Sixth Pennsylvania*, 199.

90. *OR*, 27 (1): 416, 419, 435-36.

91. Ibid., 453-54, 464-65; Seville, *History of the First Delaware*, 80.

92. Fuger, "Cushing's Battery at Gettysburg," 406; French, Barry, and Hunt, *Instruction for Field Artillery*, 336-37.

93. Fuger, "Cushing's Battery at Gettysburg," 406.

94. Ibid.; *OR*, 27 (2): 633.

95. *OR*, 27 (2): 308, 318-19, 358-59, 446, 607-8.

96. Ibid., 27 (1): 482-83, 531-32; de Trobriand, *Four Years with the Army of the Potomac*, 494-96.

97. *OR*, 27 (1): 234-36, 532.

98. Ibid., 416-17, 419, 423, 426; Ford, *Story of the Fifteenth Massachusetts*, 267-68; Rhodes, *History of Battery B, Rhode Island*, 200-201.

99. Cleaves, *Meade of Gettysburg*, 147-48; Taylor, *Gouverneur Kemble Warren*, 121-27; *OR*, 27 (1): 482.

100. Taylor, *Gouverneur Kemble Warren*, 126-27.

101. *OR*, 27 (2): 308, 320, 358-59, 404-5, 407-19.

102. Ibid., 27 (1): 592-93, 600-1, 607-8, 610-11; Norton, *Strong Vincent and His Brigade*, 6-8.

103. *OR*, 27 (1): 601-3; Gerrish, *Army Life*, 108.

104. *OR*, 27 (1): 659-60; Martin, "Little Round Top"; Roster Commission, *Official Roster of the Soldiers of the State of Ohio*, 2:45.

105. Martin, "Little Round Top"; Rittenhouse, "Battle of Gettysburg as Seen from Little Round Top," 1-14.

106. Martin, "Little Round Top"; Rittenhouse, "Battle of Gettysburg as Seen from Little Round Top," 1-14; Taylor, *Gouverneur Kemble Warren*, 129.

107. Taylor, *Gouverneur Kemble Warren*, 129.

108. Rittenhouse, "Battle of Gettysburg as Seen from Little Round Top," 1-14.

109. *OR*, 27 (1): 602-3; 27 (2): 391-96, 404-5; Norton, *Strong Vincent and His Brigade*, 8; Judson, *History of the Eighty-Third Pennsylvania*, 71; Coco, *Vast Sea of Misery*, 70-71.

110. *OR*, 27 (1): 634-35; Leeper, "Gettysburg."

111. *OR*, 27 (1): 634-35; Leeper, "Gettysburg."

112. *OR*, 27 (1): 634-35; Rittenhouse, "Battle of Gettysburg as Seen from Little Round Top," 1-14; Brainard, *Campaigns of the One Hundred and Forty-Sixth New York*, 118-20; Coco, *Vast Sea of Misery*, 70-71; Clinton Wagner to George Torney, Aug. 7, 1911, GNMP.

113. *OR*, 27 (2): 308, 320, 358-59, 366-75, 428-30; Gallagher, *Fighting for the Confederacy*, 238-42.

114. *OR*, 27 (1): 370-71, 379-80; Houghton, *Campaigns of the Seventeenth Maine*, 92; 493-94, 519-21; William Corby, C.S.C, to Col. John B. Bachelder, Jan. 4, 1879, GNMP.

115. *OR*, 27 (1): 371-72, 482-83, 472, 532-33, 879-80; Marbaker, *History of the Eleventh New Jersey*, 98-99.

116. *OR*, 27 (1): 879-80; Smith, *History of the Nineteenth Maine*, 69-70; Personal Service Records of Capt. Gulian V. Weir, RG 94, NA.

117. *OR*, 27 (1): 472-73; Willson, *Disaster, Struggle, Triumph*, 168-172; Simons, *Regimental History*, 110-14.

118. *OR*, 27 (1): 370-71, 417, 419-20, 423-24, 426, 879-80; 27 (2): 622-23; Ford, *Story of the Fifteenth Massachusetts*, 266-69.

119. *OR*, 27 (1): 422, 879-80; Smith, *History of the Nineteenth Maine*, 72; Capt. G.V. Weir to Gen. W.S. Hancock, Nov. 25, 1865, in Personal Service Records of Capt. Gulian V. Weir, RG 94, NA.

120. *OR*, 27 (1): 371, 417, 424-25; 27 (2): 617-19; Searles, *History of the First Minnesota*, 342-47; Centennial Committee, *Centennial History of Chautauqua County*, 1:215-16. William Colvill, Jr., who at the outbreak of the war was practicing law in Red Wing, Minnesota, was born in Forestville, Chautauqua County, New York; his father had been born in Scotland.

121. *OR*, 27 (1): 465, 470; 27 (2): 633-34; Ward, *History of the One Hundred and Sixth Pennsylvania*, 190-91.

122. Haines, *History of the Men of Co. F*, 38-39.

123. Ibid.

124. *OR*, 27 (1): 370-71, 478; 27 (2): 618-19; Rhodes, *History of Battery B, Rhode Island*, 201-2.

125. Rhodes, *History of Battery B, Rhode Island*, 202.

126. Personal Service Records of Lt. Samuel Canby, RG 94, NA; Fuger, "Cushing's Battery at Gettysburg," 406-7; Returns from Regular Army Artillery Regiments, 4th Artillery, July 1863, Roll 29, NA. Canby recovered from his wound and was transferred to the West, where he commanded Battery M, 4th United States Artillery, at the battles of Spring Hill, Franklin, and Nashville in the fall of 1864.

127. Fuger, "Cushing's Battery at Gettysburg," 407; Rhodes, *History of Battery B, Rhode Island*, 203.

128. *OR*, 27 (1): 427, 433-34; Ward, *History of the One Hundred and Sixth Pennsylvania*, 191-92.

129. *OR*, 27 (1): 372, 434, 456, 764; 27 (2): 446-47, 469-71, 479-81, 504; Ward, *History of the One Hundred and Sixth Pennsylvania*, 199.

130. *OR*, 27 (2): 624.

131. McKelvey, *Rochester in the Civil War*, 170.

9. "By Hand to the Front!"

1. *Philadelphia Times*, May 29, 1887; Carter, *Four Brothers in Blue*, 314; Norton, *Attack and Defense of Little Round Top*, 290. Lieutenant Hazlett's body was later located by his father, Robert Hazlett, and returned to Putnam, Ohio, where it was buried in Woodlawn Cemetery alongside his brother, Capt. John Hazlett, and only fifty paces from the graves of Abigail Browning (Tupper) Cushing, the first wife of Lon's father, and little Abigail Elizabeth Cushing, Lon's infant half-sister. Colonel O'Rorke's widow, Clara Bishop O'Rorke, journeyed to Gettysburg to find the grave of her husband; she had the remains exhumed and returned to Rochester, New York. There, on July 14, 1863, the day after Lon's funeral at West Point, Paddy O'Rorke was buried in the Old Catholic Cemetery on Pinnacle Hill after services in St. Bridget's Church. Clara entered a convent, taking her final vows in 1871 as a nun in the Order of the Sacred Heart of Jesus.

2. Rhodes, *History of Battery B, Rhode Island*, 203.

3. *Fredonia Censor*, July 11, 1900. Brown's painting of Cushing's death portrays him wearing a twelve-button shell jacket, a popular article of clothing among artillery officers, as well as an officer's kepi, cavalry boots, and a model 1860 cavalry saber. The photograph of Cushing taken at Warrenton, Virginia, in November 1862 shows him wearing cavalry boots and carrying a cavalry saber. When Brown's painting was unveiled, General Webb and Sergeant Fuger both described it as an accurate portrayal of Lieutenant Cushing at the time of his death.

4. *OR*, 27 (2): 320, 447, 504, 511, 519.

5. Ibid., 673-74; Wise, *Long Arm of Lee*, 665.

6. Page, *History of the Fourteenth Connecticut*, 144; Haines, *History of the Men of Co. F*, 39-40; Affidavit of Wilbur D. Fiske, Co. F, 14th Regiment Connecticut Volunteer Infantry, Oct. 9, 1887, GNMP.

7. *OR*, 27 (1): 467; Page, *History of the Fourteenth Connecticut*, 142-47; Affidavit of Wilbur D. Fiske, GNMP.

8. Page, *History of the Fourteenth Connecticut*, 142-47.

9. Page, *History of the Fourteenth Connecticut*, 146; Affidavit of Wilbur D. Fiske, GNMP.

10. Page, *History of the Fourteenth Connecticut*, 146-47; Affidavit of Wilbur D. Fiske, GNMP.

11. Fuger, "Cushing's Battery at Gettysburg," 407.

12. Ibid.; *OR*, 27 (1): 437, 438; Aldrich, *History of Battery A, Rhode Island*, 210.

13. *Buffalo Evening News*, May 29, 1894.

14. Ibid.

15. Ibid.

16. Hunt, "Artillery," 94.

17. Rhodes, *History of Battery B, Rhode Island*, 208; *Buffalo Evening News*, May 29, 1894.

18. Rhodes, *History of Battery B, Rhode Island*, 208; *Buffalo Evening News*, May 29, 1894.

19. *John Reed et al. v. Gettysburg Battlefield Memorial Ass'n.* (Court of Common Pleas, Adams County, Pa., 1889), Transcript of Testimony (hereinafter "Trial of the 72d Pennsylvania"), 258-59, GNMP.

20. *Buffalo Evening News*, May 29, 1894.

21. Cushing, "Our Grandmother," 2, CCHS.

22. Personal Service Records of Sgt. Frederick H. Fuger, RG 94, NA.

23. McDermott, *Brief History of the 69th Pennsylvania*, 5; Board of Commissioners, *Pennsylvania at Gettysburg*, 1:403; Banes, *History of the Philadelphia Brigade*, 14.

24. New York Monuments Commission, *Final Report on the Battlefield of Gettysburg*, 1:320-21; Bruce, *Twentieth Regiment of Massachusetts Volunteer Infantry*, 296.

25. Page, *History of the Fourteenth Connecticut*, 17, 131.

26. Time-Life Books Editors, *Echoes of Glory*, 90-91, 133, 140; "Trial of the 72nd Pennsylvania," 141; Rauscher, *Music on the March*, 11.

27. Byrne and Weaver, *Haskell of Gettysburg*, 144-47; Gibbon, *Personal Recollections of the Civil War*, 146; Rhodes, *History of Battery B, Rhode Island*, 208.

28. Notes of Rev. Dr. H.E. Jacobs, 35, GNMP.

29. Fuger, "Cushing's Battery at Gettysburg," 407; Records of the Adjutant General's Office, "Muster Rolls Pertaining to Battery A, 4th United States Artillery," April 30, 1863 to June 30, 1863, RG 94, NA; Typescript Statement of Thomas Moon, GNMP.

30. *OR*, 27 (2): 284, 308, 320-21, 359-60, 385-87; Stewart, *Pickett's Charge*, 172.

31. *OR*, 27 (2): 289, 608, 643-44, 650-51.

32. Ibid., 289, 666-67, 671-72.

33. Stewart, *Pickett's Charge*, 172-73.

34. *OR*, 27 (2): 320.

35. Ibid., 320, 608, 614-15, 619-20, 632-33.

36. Ibid., 320.

37. Ibid., 351-52, 359; Gallagher, *Fighting for the Confederacy*, 245-51; Wise, *Long Arm of Lee*, 651-53, 664-65.

38. Byrne and Weaver, *Haskell of Gettysburg*, 147; Wise, *Long Arm of Lee*, 677; Owen, *In Camp and Battle*, 248-49; *Buffalo Evening News*, May 29, 1894; Waitt, *History of the Nineteenth Massachusetts*, 234-35; Rhodes, *History of Battery B, Rhode Island*, 208.

39. *OR*, 27 (2): 352.

40. Letter of Cpl. Thomas Moon, in Haight, *Three Wisconsin Cushings*, 56.

41. *Buffalo Evening News*, May 29, 1894.

42. Fuger, "Cushing's Battery at Gettysburg," 408; Byrne and Weaver, *Haskell of Gettysburg*, 150.

43. Gibbon, *Personal Recollections of the Civil War*, 148.

44. Byrne and Weaver, *Haskell of Gettysburg*, 148.

45. *Buffalo Evening News*, May 29, 1894.

46. Ibid.

47. Letter of Cpl. Thomas Moon, in Haight, *Three Wisconsin Cushings*, 56.

48. Byrne and Weaver, *Haskell of Gettysburg*, 149; Bruce, *Twentieth Regiment of Massachusetts Volunteer Infantry*, 296.

49. Pvt. Homer Baldwin to his father, July 7, 1863, GNMP.

50. New York Monuments Commission, *Final Report on the Battlefield of Gettysburg*, 3:1183; Waitt, *History of the Nineteenth Massachusetts*, 234-36; *Irish World*, June 18, 1887.

51. *Buffalo Evening News*, May 29, 1894.

52. Ibid.; "Trial of the 72nd Pennsylvania," 147; Byrne and Weaver, *Haskell of Gettysburg*, 152.

53. Fuger, "Cushing's Battery at Gettysburg," 408; Ward, "Cushing's Battery at Gettysburg"; Records of the Adjutant General's Office, "Muster Rolls Pertaining to Battery A, 4th United States Artillery," June 30, 1863, to July 31, 1863, RG 94, NA; Returns from Regular Army Artillery Regiments, 4th Artillery, July 1863, Roll 29, NA. Although Fuger contended that Cushing received the two wounds when Pickett's division had come within four hundred yards of the stone wall, it is clear from the accounts of General Webb and Capt. Andrew Cowan that Lon was already wounded in the shoulder and groin when the bombardment ceased.

54. Rhodes, *The History of Battery B, Rhode Island*, 209-10; Typescript statement of Charles Tillinghast Straight, "The Gettysburg Gun, Battery B, 1st Rhode Island Light Artillery, Disabled at the Battle of Gettysburg—July 3, 1863," GNMP.

55. Byrne and Weaver, *Haskell of Gettysburg*, 151.

56. *OR*, 27 (1): 239, 480.

57. McKelvey, *Rochester in the Civil War*, 170-71; Haskin, *History of the First Regiment of Artillery*, 169, 544; Washburn, *Complete Military History and Record of the 108th N.Y.*, 50.

58. "Trial of the 72d Pennsylvania," 163.

59. *OR*, 27 (1): 428; Banes, *History of the Philadelphia Brigade*, 188-89; Brown, "Double Canister at Ten Yards," 293-99.

60. Brown, "Double Canister at Ten Yards," 293-99; New York Monuments Commission, *In Memoriam, Alexander Stewart Webb*, 65; "Trial of the 72d Pennsylvania," 272-73.

61. Brown, "Double Canister at Ten Yards," 293-99; New York Monuments Commission, *Final Report on the Battlefield of Gettysburg*, 3:1276.

62. *Buffalo Evening News*, May 29, 1894; Records of the Adjutant General's Office, "Muster Rolls Pertaining to Battery A, 4th United States Artillery," June 30, 1863, to July 31, 1863, RG 94, NA; Returns from Regular Army Artillery Regiments, 4th Artillery, July, 1863, Roll 29, NA.

63. "Trial of the 72d Pennsylvania," 128, 152; Fuger, "Cushing's Battery at Gettysburg," 408; New York Monuments Commission, *In Memoriam, Alexander Stewart Webb*, 65-66; Ward, "Cushing's Battery at Gettysburg."

64. *OR*, 27 (1): 432; *Philadelphia Times*, May 28, 1887.

65. New York Monuments Commission, *In Memoriam, Alexander Stewart Webb*, 65-66.

66. *OR*, 27 (1): 508-10, 513-14; "Trial of the 72d Pennsylvania," 42, 143.

67. Fuger, "Cushing's Battery at Gettysburg," 408-9; "Trial of the 72d Pennsylvania," 128-29, 243; *Philadelphia Times*, May 28, 1887; Ward, "Cushing's Battery at Gettysburg."

68. Ward, *History of the One Hundred and Sixth Pennsylvania*, 199; "Trial of the 72d Pennsylvania," 73.

69. Haskin, *History of the First Regiment of Artillery*, 169, 544; McKelvey, *Rochester in the Civil War*, 170; Washburn, *Complete Military History and Record of the 108th N.Y.*, 50.

70. Johnson, *Story of a Confederate Boy*, 204.

71. Lewis, *Recollections*; Hamilton, *Papers of Randolph Abbott Shotwell*, 2:9.

72. Clark, *Histories of the Several Regiments and Battalions from North Carolina*, 2:365.

73. Ford, *Story of the Fifteenth Massachusetts*, 276; Haines, *History of the Men of Co. F*, 41; Waitt, *History of the Nineteenth Massachusetts*, 238.

74. Byrne and Weaver, *Haskell of Gettysburg*, 158; Haines, *History of the Men of Co. F*, 41; Haskin, *History of the First Regiment of Artillery*, 544.

75. Dooley, *Confederate Soldier*, 106; Wood, *Reminiscence of Big I*, 46; Hamilton, *Papers of Randolph Abbott Shotwell*, 2:12; Shotwell, "Virginia and North Carolina in the Battle of Gettysburg," 80-97.

76. McKelvey, *Rochester in the Civil War*, 170; Haskin, *History of the First Regiment of Artillery*, 544-45.

77. Stewart, *Pickett's Charge*, 184.

78. Hamilton, *Papers of Randolph Abbott Shotwell*, 2:12.

79. Charles T. Loehr, *War History of the Old First Virginia*, 36; Stewart, *Pickett's Charge*, 184.

80. *Phildaelphia Times*, Nov. 4, 1892.

81. Wise, *Long Arm of Lee*, 684-85; Gallagher, *Fighting for the Confederacy*, 262.

82. *OR*, 27 (1): 895-96.

83. New York Monuments Commission, *Final Report on the Battlefield of Gettysburg*, 3:1183-84; Waitt, *History of the Nineteenth Massachusetts*, 235-37; *Irish World*, June 18, 1887.

84. *Buffalo Evening News*, May 29, 1894; Typescript Statement of Thomas Moon, June 23, 1913, GNMP; Mulholland, *Story of the 116th Pennsylvania*, 137; *Philadelphia Times*, May 28, 1887; Ward, "Cushing's Battery at Gettysburg"; "Trial of the 72d Pennsylvania," 242-43.

85. Fuger, "Cushing's Battery at Gettysburg," 408.

86. Hamilton, *Papers of Randolph Abbott Shotwell*, 2:13; Sawyer, *Military History of the 8th Ohio*, 131.

87. Letter of Cpl. Thomas Moon, in Haight, *Three Wisconsin Cushings*, 57.

88. *OR*, 27 (1): 349-50; Bright, "Pickett's Charge," 234; Peters, "Lost Sword of General Richard B. Garnett," 27-30.

89. *OR*, 27 (1): 349-50; 27 (2): 619-20, 632-33.

90. Fuger, "Cushing's Battery at Gettysburg," 408; Personal Service Records of Lt. Joseph A. Milne, RG 94, NA; *Buffalo Evening News*, May 29, 1894.

91. Martin, "Armistead at the Battle of Gettysburg." 186-87.

92. Haskin, *History of the First Regiment of Artillery*, 169-70; "Memoirs of George A. Woodruff," 92-93, 109-10, USMA; Crary, *Dear Belle*, 210.

93. New York Monuments Commission, *Final Report on the Battlefield of Gettysburg*, 3:1183-84.

94. Fuger, "Cushing's Battery at Gettysburg," 408.

95. "Trial of the 72d Pennsylvania," 243; *Philadelphia Times*, May 28, 1887.

96. *Buffalo Evening News*, May 29, 1894.

97. Fuger, "Cushing's Battery at Gettysburg," 408-9; *Buffalo Evening News*, May 29, 1894; Typescript Statement of Thomas Moon, GNMP; letter of Cpl. Thomas Moon, in Haight, *Three Wisconsin Cushings*, 56-57; *Fredonia Censor*, July 11, 1900. Brown's painting portrays Cushing's location alongside the number four gun and his reflex motion at the moment of his fatal wounding.

98. Fuger, "Cushing's Battery at Gettysburg," 408; Typescript Statement of Thomas Moon, GNMP.

99. Fuger, "Cushing's Battery at Gettysburg," 408.

100. Martin, "Armistead at the Battle of Gettysburg," 186-87.

101. *Philadelphia Times*, May 28, 1887; McDermott, *Brief History of the 69th Pennsylvania*, 31-32.

102. *Buffalo Evening News*, May 29, 1894.

103. Typescript Statement of Thomas Moon, GNMP; Fuger, "Cushing's Battery at Gettysburg," 409.

104. *Philadelphia Times*, May 28, 1887.

105. "Trial of the 72d Pennsylvania," 163.

106. *Buffalo Evening News*, May 29, 1894.

107. "Trial of the 72d Pennsylvania," 63.

108. Ibid., 35, 160, 273; *OR*, 27 (1): 428, 433.

109. Martin, "Armistead at the Battle of Gettysburg," 186-87; Typescript Statement of Thomas Moon, GNMP.

110. "Trial of the 72d Pennsylvania," 160-61, 273-74.

111. Ibid.

112. *OR*, 27 (1): 374, 437-39, 443, 448, 451; Waitt, *History of the Nineteenth Massachusetts*, 239-40.

113. *Philadelphia Times*, May 28, 1887; Poindexter, "Armistead at the Battle of Gettysburg," 186-89.

114. "Trial of the 72d Pennsylvania," 45, 60, 75-79, 172; Address of Comrade H.C. Barrows (7th Virginia), Presenting the Portrait of Col. Tazewell Patton to Lee Camp Gallery, Richmond, Va., November, 1901, KMB.

115. Arnold, *History of Battery A, Rhode Island*, 217; Haskin, *History of the First Regiment of Artillery*, 169-70; Address of Comrade H.C. Barrows, KMB. Among those who fell from the fire of the four guns was Col. Waller Tazewell Patton, commander of the 7th Virginia and the great-uncle of Gen. George S. Patton; he may well have been the last field grade officer in Pickett's division to fall in the attack. He was directing his men to fire on the color bearers of the 72d Pennsylvania ahead when the artillery fire struck him in the face, tearing away his lower jaw. He died at the College Hospital in Gettysburg on July 21, 1863.

116. New York Monuments Commission, *Final Report on the Battlefield of Gettysburg*, 3:1183-84, 1277.

117. *OR*, 27 (1): 374-75, 420, 423, 425, 426.

118. Hamilton, *Papers of Randolph Abbott Shotwell*, 2:19; Sawyer, *Military History of the 8th Ohio*, 130-32.

119. Haskin, *History of the First Regiment of Artillery*, 170-71; McKelvey, *Rochester in the Civil War*, 170-71.

120. Stewart, *Pickett's Charge*, 263; Fuger, "Cushing's Battery at Gettysburg," 409.

Epilogue: "Faithful until Death"

1. Monaghan, *Custer*, 133, 143-49.

2. Byrne and Weaver, *Haskell of Gettysburg*, 173-75.

3. Records of the Adjutant General's Office, "Muster Rolls Pertaining to Battery A, 4th United States Artillery," June 30, 1863, to July 31, 1863, RG 94, NA; Returns from Regular Army Artillery Regiments, 4th Artillery, July 1863, Roll 29, Fourth Regiment, Jan. 1861 to Dec. 1870, NA; Commonwealth of Pennsylvania, House of Representatives, *Revised Report of the Select Committee Relative to the Soldiers' National Cemetery*, 123. In the Gettysburg National Cemetery are buried four of Cushing's cannoneers who were killed or mortally wounded at Gettysburg: Pvts. Ansil Fassett, Martin Scanlin, William Patton, and James Murphy.

4. Carter, *Four Brothers in Blue*, 315.

5. Ibid.; Mulholland, *Story of the 116th Pennsylvania*, 137.

6. Livermore, *Days and Events*, 266-67; Personal Service Records of Lt.

Joseph A. Milne, RG 94, NA. It was said that just before Milne died, he was told that his mother was trying to get to Gettysburg. "Comfort my mother when she comes," he said, "and tell her that I died doing my duty." He was buried in Providence, Rhode Island. Lewis, *History of Battery E, Rhode Island*, 225.

7. New York Monuments Commission, *Final Report on the Battlefield of Gettysburg*, 3:1277-78; Byrne and Weaver, *Haskell of Gettysburg*, 186.

8. Carter, *Four Brothers in Blue*, 315.

9. Ibid., 315-16.

10. Ibid.; Typescript Statement of Thomas Moon, GNMP.

11. Returns from Regular Army Artillery Regiments, 4th Artillery, July 1863, Roll 29, NA; Typescript Statement of Thomas Moon, GNMP.

12. "Memoirs of George A. Woodruff," 110-15, USMA; Haskin, *History of the First Regiment of Artillery*, 169-70, 545.

13. Parker, *Chautauqua Boy of '61*, 87; Carter, *Four Brothers in Blue*, 315-16; Typescript Statement of Thomas Moon, June 23, 1913, GNMP; Letter of Cpl. Thomas Moon, in Haight, *Three Wisconsin Cushings*, 56-57.

14. W.B.C. Journal.

15. Haskin and Rodenbough, *Army of the United States*, 360; Haskin, *History of the First Regiment of Artillery*, 169-70, 545; Returns from Regular Army Artillery Regiments, 4th Artillery, July 1863, Roll 29, NA. Battery A, 4th United States Artillery, fought at Sulphur Springs, Sept. 11-12, 1863; Bristoe Station, Oct. 14, 1863; and Parker's Store, Nov. 29, 1863. In 1864 it fought at Todd's Tavern, May 5; Tiney Woods, May 6; Todd's Tavern, May 7; Pine Run, May 8; Ground Squirrel Church, May 10; Richmond, May 11; Mechanicsville, May 12; and Salem Church and Harrison's Store, May 28. In June 1864 the battery was sent to Washington and remained in the defenses of the capital until the end of the war. The remnants of Woodruff's Battery I were merged with Battery H, 1st United States Artillery, formerly commanded by Lt. Justin E. Dimick.

16. Personal Service Records of Lt. Howard Bass Cushing, RG 94, NA; Bourke, *On the Border With Crook* , 105-7; Typescript Statement of Thomas Moon, GNMP. The Houghtons' daughter Laura Winona died as a result of the long siege. The family moved to Winona, Minnesota, in hope that the climate would help the very ill and pregnant Jane Houghton; likely suffering from tuberculosis, she gave birth to a daughter there in November 1863, but by the end of the month both mother and daughter had died. L.S.H. to L.T., Aug. 19, 1863, LS; Buckingham, *Ancestors of Ebenezer Buckingham*, 114-15. While Battery A, 4th United States Artillery, was stationed in Washington, D.C., it was joined by Lt. Evan Thomas's Battery C. Thomas, it seems, was arrested after an altercation with the local police on November 4, 1863. Lts. Rufus King, Jr., and Howard B. Cushing, and other members of the batteries attempted to take Thomas out of jail by force on November 8. They were arrested, and after a lengthy court martial, Thomas, King, and Cushing were found guilty of a variety of offenses, including "conduct unbecoming an officer and a gentleman." The heavy sentences they all received, however, were commuted to suspension from rank and pay for one year. Thomas and King returned to the 4th Artillery. Thomas was killed by the Modoc Indians at Lava Beds, California, on April 26, 1873; King was dismissed from the service in 1871 for drunkenness and being "mentally and morally incompetent to fulfill the duties and responsibilities of an officer." After years of correspondence and through the efforts of powerful family members and friends, King obtained the Congressional Medal of Honor for his services at the Battle of White Oak Swamp; the medal was awarded in 1898. Personal Service Records of Capt. Evan Thomas, RG 94, NA;

Personal Service Records of Maj. Rufus King, Jr., RG 94, NA; Dillon, *Burnt-Out Fires.*

17. W.B.C. Journal; Edwards, *Commander William Barker Cushing*, 163, 170-74, 194-201; Cushing, *Genealogy*, 380-81. Will's two daughters, Katherine Louise Forbes and Marie Louise, were born in 1871 and 1873, respectively.

18. Abstracts of Service Records of Naval Officers (1789-1893), Microcopy No. 330, Rolls 9, 11, 13, 15, NA; Cushing, *Genealogy*, 380-81.

19. Cushing, *Genealogy*, 386. Mary Isabel married an Edward Francis Gale. Two children were born to the marriage: Alonzo Cushing and Grace Buckingham. After Gale died, Mary Isabel married Eli H. Bouton of St. Joseph, Missouri. Two children were born to the second marriage: William B. Cushing and Ferris Grosvenor. Mary Barker Smith Cushing had moved to St. Joseph to live with the Boutons. M.B.S.C. to W.B.C., Oct. 14, 1865, CCHS.

20. M.B.S.C. to W.B.C., Oct. 14, 1865, CCHS; Pension Records, "Alonzo H. Cushing," MOC 11 871, NA. Mary Cushing received fifty dollars per month as a pension for Lon's death.

21. Lon's West Point friends Joseph C. Audenreid and Ranald Slidell Mackenzie had distinguished military careers. Audenreid, after serving in the Atlanta campaign, was brevetted to the rank of lieutenant colonel. Mackenzie fought at Petersburg and at Cedar Creek. He later became a noted Indian fighter, rising to the rank of brevet major general. Heitman, *Historical Register*, 1:175, 672. Gulian V. Weir never recovered from the blame placed upon him for abandoning his guns on July 2, 1863, at Gettysburg. He remained in the army, rising to the rank of captain in the 5th United States Artillery. While in a state of deep depression, however, he shot himself in the head with a rifle while stationed at Fort Hamilton, New York, in 1886. Personal Service Records of Capt. Gulian V. Weir, RG 94, NA.

22. Fuger, "Cushing's Battery at Gettysburg," 409; Personal Service Records of Lt. Col. Frederick Fuger, RG 94, NA. Serving with Battery A, 4th United States Artillery, until war's end, Fuger went on to a distinguished military career. In 1897 he was awarded the Congressional Medal of Honor for his services at Gettysburg on July 3, 1863. By 1904 Fuger had risen to the rank of lieutenant colonel. He died in 1913.

Bibliography

Manuscripts

Adams County, Gettysburg, Pa., and Gettysburg College. Office of the Prothonotary, Court of Common Pleas. *John Reed et al. v. Gettysburg Battlefield Memorial Ass'n.*, 1889. Transcript of testimony.

Antietam National Military Park Archives, Sharpsburg, Md.

Battlefield Board: *Map of the Battlefield of Antietam*, 1904.

Photographic Collections.

Barker, Darwin R., Library and Museum, Fredonia, N.Y.

Fredonia Academy Catalogue and Class Records.

New York & Erie Railroad advertisement.

Photographic Collections.

Brown, Kent Masterson, Collections, Lexington, Ky.

"Address of Comrade H.C. Barrows (7th Virginia) Presenting the Portrait of Col. Tazewell Patton to Lee Camp Gallery, Richmond, Va., November, 1901."

Morning Reports of Co. B, 72d Pennsylvania Volunteers.

Chautauqua County Historical Society, Westfield, N.Y.

Letters of Alonzo Hereford Cushing, Howard Bass Cushing, Marie Louise Cushing, Mary Barker Smith Cushing; Papers of Milton Buckingham Cushing.

Marie Louise Cushing, "Our Grandmother: Mary Barker Smith Cushing." Holographic memoir.

Mary Barker Smith Cushing, "William Cushing." Holographic memoir.

Forest Hill Cemetery, Fredonia, N.Y. Milton Buckingham Cushing and Mary Barker Smith Cushing plots.

Gettysburg National Military Park Archives, Gettysburg, Pa.

Affidavit of Wilbur D. Fiske, Co. F, 14th Regiment Connecticut Volunteer Infantry.

Letter of Homer Baldwin to Father, July 7, 1863.

Letter of William Corby, C.S.C., to Col. John B. Bachelder, January 4, 1879.

Letter of Andrew Cowan to John P. Nicholson, December 5, 1913.

Letter of Clinton Wagner to George Torney, August 7, 1911.

Notes of Rev. Dr. H.E. Jacobs.

Photographic Collections.

Typescript Statement of Charles Tillinghast Straight, "The Gettysburg Gun, Battery B, 1st Rhode Island Light Artillery, Disabled at the Battle of Gettysburg—July 3, 1863."

Typescript Statement of Thomas Moon, June 23, 1913.

Groseclose, Richard, Collections, Hartland, Wis. Painting: *Death of Brevet Lieut. Colonel Alonzo Hereford Cushing, 1st Lieut., commanding Battery A, 4th U.S. Artillery, at Gettysburg, July 3, 1863,* by Henry Edwin Brown (Braun).

Leisenring, Richard L., Jr., Collections, Kanona, N.Y. Letters and Diary of Col. Patrick H. O'Rorke.

Library of Congress, Washington, D.C. Photographic Collections.

Massachusetts Historical Society, Boston, Mass. Papers of Col. Paul J. Revere.

Milwaukee County, Milwaukee, Wis., Office of the Register of Deeds. Deed Books and Mortgage Books.

Muskingum County, Zanesville, Ohio.

Clerk, Court of Common Pleas. *Goodcil Buckingham v. Milton B. Cushing,* Chancery Record D, 608, Appearance Docket Q, 458, February Term, 1845.

County Recorder's Office. Deed Books.

National Archives, Washington, D.C.

Abstracts of Service Records of Naval Officers (1789-1893). Microcopy No. 330, Rolls 9, 11, 13, 15.

Application Papers of Alonzo H. Cushing to the United States Military Academy. Record Group 94.

Journal of Lieutenant Commander William B. Cushing, May, 1861 to February, 1865. Microcopy T0794.

Pension Records, "Alonzo H. Cushing." MOC 11 871.

Personal Service Records of Lt. Samuel Canby; Lt. Alonzo H. Cushing; Lt. Howard B. Cushing; Lt. Col. Edward Field; Lt. Col. Frederick Fuger; Capt. George Washington Hazzard; Maj. Rufus King., Jr.; Lt. Joseph S. Milne; Capt. Arthur Morris; Capt. James McKay Rorty; Pvt. Christopher Smith; Capt. Evan Thomas; Capt. Gulian V. Weir. Record Group 94.

Photographic Collections.

Records of the Adjutant General's Office, Muster Rolls, Battery A, 4th United States Artillery, December 31, 1862-December 28, 1863. Record Group 94.

Records of the Office of the Chief of Engineers, "Topographical Engineers." Record Group 77.

Records of the United States Army Continental Commands, vol. 68, Second Army Corps Artillery Brigade, May 1863 to June 1865. Record Group 393.

Records of United States Regular Army Mobile Units, 1821-1942, 4th United States Artillery, "Lt. Alonzo H. Cushing." Record Group 391.

Returns from Regular Army Artillery Regiments, June 1821 to January 1901, Fourth Regiment of Artillery, Army of the United States. Roll 29.

New York Public Library, New York, N.Y. Photographic Collections.

Ohio Historical Society, Columbus, Ohio.

Catharenus P. Buckingham, "Recollections of C.P. Buckingham." Holographic memoir.

Photographic Collections.

Old Pioneer Cemetery, Fredonia, N.Y. Zattu Cushing, Rachel Buckingham Cushing, and Eunice Elderkin Cushing plots.

Sanford, Larry, Collections, Beloit, Wis.

Letters of Judge Lawrence Stern Houghton.

Letters of Pvt. Theodore P. Tupper.

Photographic Collections.

United States Army Military History Institute, Carlisle, Pa. Photographic Collections.

United States Military Academy Archives and Library, West Point, N.Y.
Circulation Records, 1857-60.
Letters of William H. Harris.
Letters of James H. Lord.
Letters of Tully McCrea.
Photographic Collections.
Post Orders, 1856-60, 1861-66.
Register of Delinquencies, 1856-61.
Register of Merit, 1853-65.
Staff Records, vol. 7.
Summary of Class Standings of Alonzo H. Cushing, supplied by Chief of Archives.
George A. Woodruff, "A Collection of Cadet Songs and Other Writings Relating to the U.S. Military Academy at West Point, N.Y." Holographic notebook.
"Memoirs of George A. Woodruff." Holographic memoir by a sister.

Waukesha County, Delafield, Wis. Office of the Register of Deeds, Deed Books and Mortgage Books.

West Point Cemetery, West Point, N.Y. Alonzo H. Cushing plot.

Wisconsin Historical Society, Madison, Wis.
Cushing Family, Miscellaneous Papers.
Letter of L.S. Higgins, August 9, 1881.
Photographic Collections.

Woodlawn Cemetery, Zanesville, Ohio. Abigail Browning (Tupper) Cushing and Abigail Elizabeth Cushing, Lt. Charles E. Hazlett, and Capt. John Hazlett plots.

Yale University, New Haven, Conn. Alexander Stewart Webb Papers, box 14. Frederick Fuger, "The Battle of Gettysburg and Personal Recollections of That Battle," typescript.

Zerwekh, Margaret E., Collections, Delafield, Wis. Collected Papers, including deeds and mortgages, of Milton Buckingham Cushing and Mary Barker Smith Cushing.

Books

Adams, Ellen E. *Tales of Early Fredonia*. Fredonia, N.Y., 1931.

Aldrich, Thomas A. *The History of Battery A, First Regiment Rhode Island Light Artillery*. Providence, R.I., 1904.

Anbinder, Tyler. *Nativism and Slavery: The Northern Know-Nothings and the Politics of the 1850s*. New York, 1992.

Averill, James P. *History of Gallia County*. Chicago, 1882.

Banes, Charles H. *History of the Philadelphia Brigade*. Philadelphia, 1876.

Bates, Samuel P. *History of Pennsylvania Volunteers, 1861-5*. 5 vols. Albany, N.Y., 1912.

Bauer, K. Jack. *The Mexican War, 1846-1848*. New York, 1974.

Beale, James. *The Battleflags of the Army of the Potomac at Gettysburg, Penna., July 1st 2d & 3d, 1863*. Philadelphia, 1885.

Benet, Stephen Vincent. *John Brown's Body*. New York, 1928.

Blue, Frederick J. *Salmon P. Chase: A Life in Politics*. Kent, Ohio, 1987.

Board of Commissioners. *Pennsylvania at Gettysburg: Ceremonies at the Dedication of the Monuments Erected by the Commonwealth of Pennsylvania*. 2 vols. Harrisburg, Pa., 1904.

Boatner, Mark Mayo. *Encyclopedia of the America Revolution*. New York, 1966.

The Book of Common Prayer. Oxford, 1869.

Bourke, John G. *On the Border with Crook*. New York, 1891.

Brady, James P., ed. *Hurrah for the Artillery: Knap's Independent Battery E, Pennsylvania Light Artillery*. Gettysburg, Pa., 1992.

Brainard, Mary Genevie Green. *Campaigns of the One Hundred and Forty-Sixth Regiment, New York State Volunteers*. New York, 1915.

Bruce, Dwight H. *Onondaga's Centennial: Gleanings of a Century*. 2 vols. Boston, 1896.

Bruce, George A. *The Twentieth Regiment of Massachusetts Volunteer Infantry, 1861-1865*. Boston, 1906.

Buckingham, James S. *The Ancestors of Ebenezer Buckingham Who Was Born in 1748 and of His Descendants*. Chicago, 1892.

Bushong, Millard K., and Dean M. Bushong. *Fightin' Tom Rosser*. Shippensburg, Pa., 1983.

Butterfield, C.W. *The History of Waukesha County, Wisconsin*. Chicago, 1880.

Byley, R. Carlyle. *The Old Northwest: Pioneer Period, 1815-1840*. 2 vols. Bloomington, Ind., 1951.

Byrne, Frank L., and Andrew T. Weaver, eds. *Haskell of Gettysburg: His Life and Civil War Papers*. Madison, Wis., 1970.

Carpenter, John A. *Sword and Olive Branch: Olive Otis Howard*. Pittsburgh, Pa., 1964.

Carter, Robert G. *Four Brothers in Blue*. Austin, Tex., 1978.

Catton, Bruce. *Never Call Retreat*. New York, 1965.

Centennial Committee. *The Centennial History of Chautauqua County*. 2 vols. Jamestown, N.Y., 1904.

The Centennial History of the United States Military Academy at West Point, New York, 1802-1902. 2 vols. Washington, D.C., 1904.

Chapin, L.N. *A Brief History of the Thirty-Fourth Regiment, N.Y.S.V. etc*. New York, 1902.

Child, William. *A History of the Fifth Regiment New Hampshire Volunteers in the Civil War, 1861-1865*. Bristol, N.H., 1893.

Clark, Walter. *Histories of the Several Regiments and Battalions from North Carolina in the Great War, 1861-1865*. 5 vols. Goldsboro, N.C., 1901.

Cleaves, Freeman. *Meade of Gettysburg*. Norman, Okla., 1960.

Coco, Gregory A. *A Vast Sea of Misery: A History and Guide to the Union and Confederate Field Hospitals at Gettysburg, July 1-November 20, 1863*. Gettysburg, Pa., 1988.

———. *Wasted Valor: The Confederate Dead at Gettysburg*. Gettysburg, Pa., 1990.

Cole, Jacob H. *Under Five Commanders; or, A Boy's Experience with the Army of the Potomac*. Paterson, N.J., 1906.

Commonwealth of Pennsylvania, House of Representatives. *Revised Report of the Select Committee Relative to the Soldiers' National Cemetery, etc*. Harrisburg, Pa., 1865.

Cook, Adrian. *The Armies of the Streets*. Lexington, Ky., 1974.

Cook, Lt. Col. Benjamin F. *History of the Twelfth Massachusetts Volunteers*. Boston, 1882.

Cooling, Benjamin Franklin, III, and Walton H. Owen. *Mr. Lincoln's Forts: A Guide to the Civil War Defenses of Washington*. Shippensburg, Pa., 1988.

Crary, Catherine S., ed. *Dear Belle: Letters from a Cadet and Officer to His Sweetheart, 1858-1865*. Middletown, Conn., 1965.
Crocker, Elizabeth L. *Yesterdays . . . in and Around Pomfret, N.Y.* 5 vols. Fredonia, N.Y., 1963.
Cullen, Joseph P. *The Peninsula Campaign, 1862*. Harrisburg, Pa., 1973.
Cullum, Bvt. Maj. Gen. George W. *Biographical Register of the Officers and Graduates of the U.S. Military Academy of West Point, N.Y.* 3 vols. New York, 1868.
Cushing, James S. *The Genealogy of the Cushing Family*. Montreal, 1905.
Davis, William C. *Battle of Bull Run*. New York, 1977
Dawes, Rufus R. *Service with the Sixth Wisconsin Volunteers*. Marietta, Ohio, 1890.
de Trobriand, Regis. *Four Years with the Army of the Potomac*. Boston, 1889.
Dillon, Richard. *Burnt-Out Fires*. Englewood Cliffs, N.J., 1973.
Dooley, John. *Confederate Soldier*. Georgetown, D.C., 1945.
Downs, John P., and Fenwick Y. Hedley, eds. *History of Chautauqua County, New York, and Its People*. 2 vols. Boston, 1921.
Edwards, E.M.H. *Commander William Barker Cushing of the United States Navy*. New York, 1898.
Ellis, David M., James A. Frost, Harold C. Syret, and Harry J. Corman. *A Short History of New York State*. Ithaca, N.Y., 1957.
Farley, Joseph Pearson. *West Point in the Early Sixties*. Troy, N.Y., 1902.
Fleming, George Thornton, ed. *Life and Letters of Alexander Hays*. Pittsburgh, Pa., 1919.
Ford, Andrew E. *The Story of the Fifteenth Regiment Massachusetts Volunteer Infantry*. Clinton, Mass., 1898.
Frassanito, William A. *Antietam: The Photographic Legacy of America's Bloodiest Day*. New York, 1978.
Freehling, William W. *The Road to Disunion: Secessionists at Bay, 1776-1854*. New York, 1990.
French, Capt. William H., Capt. William F. Barry, and Capt. Henry J. Hunt, eds. *Instruction for Field Artillery*. Philadelphia, 1863.
Gallagher, Gary W., ed. *Fighting for the Confederacy: The Personal Recollections of General Edward Porter Alexander*. Chapel Hill, N.C., 1989.
Galway, Thomas F. *The Valiant Hours*. Harrisburg, Pa., 1961.
Gerrish, Rev. Theodore. *Army Life: A Private's Reminiscences of the Civil War*. Portland, Me., 1882.
Gibbon, Brig. Gen. John. *Personal Recollections of the Civil War*. New York, 1928.
Gould, John Mead. *Joseph K.F. Mansfield, Brigadier General of the U.S. Army: A Narrative of Events Connected with His Mortal Wounding at Antietam*. Portland, Me., 1895.
Haight, Theron Wilber. *Three Wisconsin Cushings*. Madison, Wis., 1910.
Haines, William P. *History of the Men of Co. F, with Description of the Marches and Battles of the 12th New Jersey Vols*. Mickleton, N.J., 1897.
Hall, Isaac. *History of the Ninety-Seventh Regiment New York Volunteers ("Conkling Rifles") in the War for the Union*. Ithaca, N.Y., 1890.
Hamilton, J.G. R. ed. *The Papers of Randolph Abbott Shotwell*. 3 vols. Raleigh, N.C., 1931.
Hancock, Ada R. *Reminiscences of Winfield Scott Hancock*. New York, 1887.
Haskin, Bvt. Maj. William L. *The History of the First Regiment of Artillery*. Portland, Me., 1879.
Hebert, Walter H. *Fighting Joe Hooker*. Indianapolis, Ind., 1944.

Heitman, Francis B. *Historical Register and Dictionary of the United States Army*. 2 vols. Washington, D.C., 1903.

Hickey, Donald R. *The War of 1812*. Urbana, Ill., 1989.

Higginson, Thomas Wentworth, ed. *The Harvard Memorial Biographies*. 2 vols. Cambridge, Mass., 1866.

Hill, Daniel Harvey. *Bethel to Sharpsburg*. 2 vols. Raleigh, N.C., 1926.

Hill, Frank. *Historical Notes about Gallipolis, Ohio*. Gallipolis, Ohio, 1977.

Hitchcock, Col. Frederick L. *War From the Inside*. Philadelphia, 1904.

Holcome, R.I. *History of the First Regiment Minnesota Volunteer Infantry, 1861-1864*. Stillwater, Okla., 1916.

Houghton, Edwin B. *The Campaigns of the Seventeenth Maine*. Portland, Me., 1866.

Hughes, Nathaniel Cheairs, Jr. *General William J. Hardee: Old Reliable*. Wilmington, N.C., 1987.

Illinois-Vicksburg Military Park Commission. *Illinois at Vicksburg*. Springfield, Ill., 1907.

Johnson, David E. *The Story of a Confederate Boy in the Civil War*. Portland, Me., 1914.

Jones, Paul. *The Irish Brigade*. Washington, D.C., 1969.

Judson, A.M. *History of the Eighty-Third Regiment Pennsylvania Volunteers*. Erie, Pa., 1865.

Kamphoeforer, Walter D., Wolfgang Helbich, and Ulrike Sommer, eds. *News from the Land of Freedom: German Immigrants Write Home*. Ithaca, N.Y., 1988.

Kepler, William. *History of the Fourth Ohio Volunteer Infantry*. Cleveland, Ohio, 1886.

Kinsley, D.A. *Favor the Bold: Custer—The Civil War Years*. New York, 1967.

Kohl, Lawrence Frederick, with Margaret Cosse Richard, eds. *Irish Green and Union Blue: The Civil War Letters of Peter Welsh*. New York, 1986.

Latrobe, Charles J. *The Rambler in North America*. 2 vols. New York, 1835.

Lee, Alfred E. *History of the City of Columbus, Capitol of Ohio*. 2 vols. New York, 1892.

Leech, Margaret. *Reveille in Washington, 1860-1865*. New York, 1941.

Lewis, Charles Lee. *Admiral Franklin Buchanan*. Baltimore, Md., 1929.

Lewis, George. *The History of Battery E, First Regiment, Rhode Island Light Artillery*. Providence, R.I., 1892.

Lewis, John H. *Recollections from 1860 to 1865*. Dayton, Ohio, 1983.

Lewis, Thomas N. *Zanesville and Muskingum County, Ohio*. 2 vols. Chicago, 1924.

Livermore, Thomas L. *Days and Events, 1860-1866*. Boston, 1920.

Loehr, Charles T. *War History of the Old First Virginia Infantry Regiment*. Dayton, Ohio, 1978.

Lyons, Capt. W.F. *Brigadier-General Thomas Francis Meagher*. New York, 1870.

McClellan, George B. *McClellan's Own Story*. New York, 1887.

McClellan, H.B. *I Rode With Jeb Stuart: Life and Campaigns of Major General J.E.B. Stuart*. Bloomington, Ind., 1958.

McDermott, Adj. Anthony W. *A Brief History of the 69th Regiment Pennsylvania Veteran Volunteers*. Philadelphia, 1889.

McKelvey, Blake, ed. *Rochester in the Civil War*. Rochester, N.Y., 1944.

McPherson, James M. *Battle Cry of Freedom: The Civil War Era*. New York, 1988.

Maine Gettysburg Commission. *Maine at Gettysburg*. Portland, Me., 1898.

Marbaker, Thomas D. *History of the Eleventh New Jersey Volunteers*. Trenton, N.J., 1898.

Marvel, William. *Burnside*. Chapel Hill, N.C., 1991.

Meriwether, Colyer. *Raphael Semmes*. Philadelphia, Pa., 1913.

Milham, Charles G. *Gallant Pelham: American Extraordinary*. Washington, D.C., 1959.
Miller, Francis Trevelyan. *The Photographic History of the Civil War*. 10 vols. New York, 1911.
Miller, Kirby A. *Emigrants and Exiles: Ireland and the Irish Exodus to North America*. New York, 1985.
Monaghan, Jay. *Custer: The Life of General George Armstrong Custer*. Lincoln, Neb., 1959.
Mulholland, St. Clair, *The Story of the 116th Regiment, Pennsylvania Volunteers*. Phildaelphia, 1903.
Murfin, James V. *The Gleam of Bayonets*. New York, 1965.
Naisawald, L. Van Loan. *Grape and Canister: The Story of the Field Artillery of the Army of the Potomac, 1861-1865*. Washington, D.C., 1983.
Neese, George M. *Three Years in the Confederate Horse Artillery*. Dayton, Ohio, 1981.
Ness, George T. Jr. *The Regular Army on the Eve of the Civil War*. Baltimore, Md., 1990.
New York Monuments Commission. *Final Report on the Battlefield of Gettysburg*. 3 vols. Albany, N.Y., 1900.
———. *In Memoriam, Alexander Stewart Webb, 1835-1911*. Albany, N.Y., 1911.
Nichols, Edward J. *Toward Gettysburg: A Biography of General John F. Reynolds*. State College, Pa., 1958.
Niven, John. *Gideon Wells: Lincoln's Secretary of the Navy*. New York, 1973.
Norton, Aloysius A. *A History of the United States Military Academy Library*. Wayne, N.J., 1986.
Norton, Oliver W. *The Attack and Defense of Little Round Top, Gettysburg, July 2, 1863*. New York, 1913.
———. *Strong Vincent and His Brigade at Gettysburg, July 2, 1863*. Chicago, 1909.
Olsson, Nils William, ed. *A Pioneer in Northwest America, 1841-1858: The Memoirs of Gustaf Unonius*. 2 vols. Minneapolis, Minn., 1950.
Owen, William M. *In Camp and Battle with the Washington Artillery of New Orleans*. Boston, 1885.
Page, Charles D. *History of the Fourteenth Regiment Connecticut Vol. Infantry*. Meridan, Conn., 1906.
Parker, David B. *A Chautauqua Boy in '61 and Afterward*. Boston, 1912.
Parker, William L. *General James Dearing, C.S.A.*. Lynchburg, Va., 1990.
Peterson, Merrill D. *The Great Triumvirate*. New York, 1987.
Pfanz, Harry W. *Gettysburg: The Second Day*. Chapel Hill, N.C., 1987.
Phisterer, Frederick. *New York in the War of the Rebellion, 1861 to 1865*. 5 vols. Albany, N.Y., 1869.
Potter, David M., and Don E. Fehrenbacher. *The Impending Crisis, 1848-1861*. New York, 1976.
Powell, William H. *The Fifth Army Corps*. New York, 1896.
Priest, John M. *Antietam: The Soldiers' Battle*. Shippensburg, Pa., 1989.
Quaife, Milo M. *From the Cannon's Mouth: The Civil War Letters of General Alpheus S. Williams*. Detroit, Mich., 1959.
———. *Wisconsin: Its History and Its People*. 2 vols. Chicago, 1924.
Quintard, Charles Todd. *Doctor Quintard: Chaplain, C.S.A., and Second Bishop of Tennessee*. Sewanee, Tenn., 1905.
Rauscher, Frank. *Music on the March, 1862-1865: With the Army of the Potomac, 114th Regt. P.V., Collis' Zouaves*. Philadelphia, 1892.

Reece, Brig. Gen. J.N. *Report of the Adjutant General of the State of Illinois*. 8 vols. Springfield, Ill., 1901.

Reese, Timothy J. *Sykes' Regular Infantry Division, 1861-1864*. Jefferson, N.C., 1990.

Regimental Committee. *History of the One Hundred and Twenty-Fifth Regiment, Pennsylvania Volunteers, 1862-1863*. Philadelphia, 1906.

———. *History of the 127th Regiment, Pennsylvania Volunteers*. Lebanon, Pa., 1903.

Remini, Robert V. *The Life of Andrew Jackson*. New York, 1988.

Rhodes, Elisha Hunt. *All for the Union*. Lincoln, Neb., 1985.

Rhodes, John H. *The History of Battery B, First Regiment Rhode Island Light Artillery*. Providence, R.I., 1894.

Rings, Blanche Tipton, comp. *Marriage Records of Franklin County, Ohio, Early 1800s*. Columbus, Ohio, 1927.

Ripley, Warren. *Artillery and Ammunition of the Civil War*. New York, 1970.

Robertson, John. *Michigan in the War*. Lansing, Mich., 1882.

Rodenbough, Theodore F., and William L. Haskin. *The Army of the United States: Historical Sketches of Staff and Line with Portraits of General-in-Chief*. New York, 1896.

Roland, Charles P. *An American Iliad: The Story of the Civil War*. Lexington, Ky., 1991.

Roske, Ralph J., and Charles Van Doren. *Lincoln's Commando: The Biography of Commander William B. Cushing, U.S.N.* New York, 1957.

Roster Commission. *Official Roster of the Soldiers of the State of Ohio in the War of the Rebellion, 1861-1866*. 12 vols. Norwalk, Ohio, 1886.

Russell, William Howard. *My Diary North and South*. New York, 1954.

Sanger, Donald Bridgman, and Thomas Robson Hay. *James Longstreet*. Baton Rouge, La., 1952.

Sawyer, Franklin. *A Military History of the 8th Regiment, Ohio Vol. Inf'y*. Cleveland, Ohio, 1881.

Schaff, Morris. *The Spirit of Old West Point*. Boston, 1907.

Schneider, Norris F. *Y-Bridge City: The Story of Zanesville and Muskingum County, Ohio*. Cleveland, Ohio, 1950.

Scott, Robert Garth. *Fallen Leaves: The Civil War Letters of Major Henry Livermore Abbott*. Kent, Ohio, 1991.

Sears, Stephen W., ed. *The Civil War Papers of George B. McClellan: Selected Correspondence, 1860-1865*. New York, 1989.

———. *George B. McClellan: The Young Napoleon*. New York, 1988.

———. *The Landscape Turned Red: The Battle of Antietam*. New Haven, Conn., 1983.

———. *To the Gates of Richmond: The Peninsula Campaign*. New York, 1992.

Secretary of the Commonwealth. *Massachusetts Soldiers and Sailors of the Revolutionary War*. 17 vols. Boston, 1899.

Sergent, Mary Elizabeth. *They Lie Forgotten*. Middletown, N.Y., 1986.

Seville, William P. *History of the First Regiment Delaware Volunteers*. Wilmington, Del., 1884.

Shaw, Ronald E. *Canals for a Nation: The Canal Era in the United States, 1790-1860*. Lexington, Ky., 1990.

———. *Erie Water West: A History of the Erie Canal, 1792-1854*. Lexington, Ky., 1990.

Simons, Chaplain Ezra D. *A Regimental History: The One Hundred and Twenty-Fifth New York State Volunteers*. New York, 1888.

Smith, John Day. *The History of the Nineteenth Regiment of Maine Volunteer Infantry, 1862-1865*. Minneapolis, Minn., 1909.

Smith, Susan Augusta. *A Memorial of the Rev. Thomas Smith and His Descendants*. Plymouth, Mass., 1895.

Smith, William R. *The History of Wisconsin*. 2 vols. Madison, Wis., 1854.

Society of the Cincinnati. *Roster of the Society of the Cincinnati*. Washington, D.C., 1989.

Stackpole, Edward J. *Chancellorsville: Lee's Greatest Battle*. Harrisburg, Pa., 1958.

Stanley, F. *E.V. Sumner*. Borger, Texas, 1969.

Stewart, George R. *Pickett's Charge: A Microhistory of the Final Attack of Gettysburg, July 3, 1863*. Cambridge, Mass., 1959.

Sword, Wiley. *Shiloh: A Bloody April*. New York, 1974.

Tarbell, Ida M. *In the Footsteps of the Lincolns*. New York, 1924.

Taylor, Emerson Gifford. *Gouverneur Kemble Warren: The Life and Letters of An American Soldier, 1830-1882*. Boston, 1932.

Taylor, James E. *The James E. Taylor Sketchbook*. Dayton, Ohio, 1989.

Teall, Sarah Sumner. *Onondaga's Part in the Civil War: Annual Volume of the Onondaga Historical Ass'n. 1915*. Syracuse, N.Y., 1915.

Thomas, Benjamin P., and Harold M. Hyman. *Stanton: The Life and Times of Lincoln's Secretary of War*. New York, 1962.

Time-Life Books Editors. *Echoes of Glory: Arms and Equipment of the Union*. Alexandria, Va., 1991.

Trefousse, Hans L. *Carl Schurz: A Biography*. Knoxville, Tenn., 1982.

Tucker, Glenn. *Hancock the Superb*. Indianapolis, Ind., 1960.

Tuttle, Charles R. *An Illustrated History of the State of Wisconsin*. Madison, Wis., 1875.

U.S. Senate. *A Biographical Congressional Directory, 1774-1911*. Washington, D.C.

U.S. War Department. *The War of the Rebellion: A Compilation of the Official Records of the Union and Confederate Armies*. 73 vols. Washington, D.C., 1880-1901.

Vandiver, Frank E. *Mighty Stonewall*. New York, 1957.

Vautier, John D. *The History of the 88th Pennsylvania Regiment in the War for the Union, 1861-1865*. Philadelphia, 1894.

Waitt, E.L. *History of the Nineteenth Regiment Massachusetts Volunteer Infantry, 1861-1865*. Salem, Mass., 1906.

Walcher, Frank, J. *The Union Army, 1861-1865*. Bloomington, Ind., 1989.

Walker, Francis A. *History of the Second Army Corps*. New York, 1886.

Ward, Joseph R.C. *History of the One Hundred and Sixth Regiment Pennsylvania Volunteers*. Philadelphia, 1906.

Warner, Ezra J. *Generals in Blue*. Baton Rouge, La., 1964.

———. *Generals in Gray*. Baton Rouge, La., 1959.

Washburn, George H. *A Complete Military History and Record of the 108th Regiment, N.Y. Vols*. Rochester, N.Y., 1894.

Werstein, Irving. *July, 1863*. New York, 1957.

Williams, T. Harry. *P.G.T. Beauregard: The Words That Remade America*. New York, 1981.

Wills, Garry. *Lincoln at Gettysburg: The Words That Remade America*. New York, 1992.

Willson, Arabella M. *Disaster, Struggle, Triumph: The Adventures of 1000 "Boys in Blue" from August, 1862 to June, 1865*. Albany, N.Y., 1870.

Wintrobe, Maxwell M., et al., eds. *Harrison's Principles of Internal Medicine*, 6th ed. New York, 1970.

Wise, George. *History of the Seventeenth Virginia Infantry, C.S.A.*. Baltimore, Md., 1870.

Wise, Jennings Cropper. *The Long Arm of Lee*. New York, 1959.

Wood, W.N. *Reminiscence of Big I*. Jackson, Tenn., 1956.

Young, Andrew A. *History of Chautauqua County, New York*. Buffalo, N.Y., 1875.

Articles

Bennett, Brian. "The Ideal of a Soldier and a Gentleman," *Civil War: Magazine of the Civil War Society* 9, no. 2 (1992): 35-37, 64.

"Bibliographies of the U.S. Military Academy," *The Centennial History of the United States Military Academy at West Point, New York, 1802-1902*, II, 1-164.

Bright, Capt. R.A. "Pickett's Charge," *Southern Historical Society Papers* 31 (1903): 228-36.

Brown, Kent Masterson. "'Double Canister at Ten Yards': Captain Andrew Cowan at Gettysburg." *Filson Club History Quarterly* 59, no. 3. (1985): 293-326.

Cotton, Gordon. "Judge's Letters Describe Vicksburg." *Vicksburg Sunday Post*, June 1, 1987.

Couch, Maj. Gen. Darius N. "The Chancellorsville Campaign." In *Battles and Leaders of the Civil War*, ed. Robert Underwood Johnson and Clarence Clough Buel, 3:154-71. New York, 1956.

———. "Sumner's 'Right Grand Division.'" In *Battles and Leaders of the Civil War*, ed. Robert Underwood Johnson and Clarence Clough Buel, 3:105-20. New York, 1956.

Fuger, Frederick. "Cushing's Battery at Gettysburg." *Journal of Military Service Institution of the United States* 41 (November-December 1907): 404-10.

Graham, Capt. James A. "Twenty-Seventh Regiment." In *Histories of the Several Regiments and Battalions from North Carolina*, ed. Walter Clark, 2:424-63. Goldsboro, N.C., 1901.

Hunt, Bvt. Maj. Gen. Henry J. "Artillery." In Military Historical Society of Massachusetts, *Papers*, 13: chap. 3. Boston, 1918.

Jones, Archer. "The Gettysburg Decision." *Virginia Magazine of History and Biography* 68, no. 3 (1960): 331-43.

———. "The Gettysburg Decision Reassessed," *Virginia Magazine of History and Biography* 76, no. 1. (1968): 64-66.

Leeper, Joseph M. "Gettysburg: The Part Taken in the Battle by the Fifth Corps." *National Tribune*, April 30, 1885.

McNamara, Rev. Robert F. "Gettysburg Centenary Recalls Heroism of Rochester." *Catholic Council Journal* (Rochester, N.Y.), June 28, 1963.

Martin, Augustus P. "Little Round Top." *Gettysburg Compiler*, Oct. 24, 1899.

Martin, Dr. R.W. "Armistead at the Battle of Gettysburg." *Southern Historical Society Papers* 39 (1914): 186-87.

Peters, Col. Winfield. "The Lost Sword of General Richard B. Garnett, Who Fell at Gettysburg." *Southern Historical Society Papers* 33 (1905): 26-31.

Pope, Maj. Gen. John. "The Second Battle of Bull Run." In *Battles and Leaders of the Civil War*, ed. Robert Underwood Johnson and Clarence Clough Buel, 2:449-94. New York, 1956.

Porter, Maj. Gen. Fitz John. "Hanover Court House and Gaines's Mill." In *Battles and Leaders of the Civil War*, ed. Robert Underwood Johnson and Clarence Clough Buel, 2:319-43. New York, 1956.

Rittenhouse, Benjamin F. "The Battle of Gettysburg as Seen from Little Round

Top." In Military Order of the Loyal Legion of the United States, District of Columbia Commandery, *War Papers*, 3:1-14. (Washington, D.C., 1887).

Shotwell, Randolph Abbott. "Virginia and North Carolina in the Battle of Gettysburg." *Our Living and Our Dead*, no. 4 (March 1876): 80-97.

Sladen, Capt. Fred W. "The Uniform of Cadets, 1794-1902." In *The Centennial History of the United States Military Academy at West Point, New York, 1802-1902*, 1:508-21. Washington, D.C., 1904.

Teall, Col. William, ". . . Ringside Seat at Fredericksburg." *Civil War Times Illustrated*, no. 2. (May 1965): 17-34.

Tillman, Col. Samuel E. "The Academic History of the Military Academy, 1802-1902." In *The Centennial History of the United States Military Academy at West Point, New York, 1802-1902*, 1:223-466. (Washington, D.C., 1904).

Tuttle, Capt. Romulus M. "Unparalleled Loss." In *Histories of the Several Regiments and Battalions from North Carolina*, ed. Walter Clark, 5:599-603. Goldsboro, N.C., 1901.

Underwood, Asst. Surg. George C. "Twenty-sixty Regiment." In *Histories of the Several Regiments and Battalions from North Carolina*, ed. Walter Clark, 2:302-423. Goldsboro, N.C., 1901.

Ward, Joseph R.C. "Cushing's Battery at Gettysburg." *Grand Army Scout and Soldier's Mail*, Jan. 2, 1886.

Index

Regiments are alphabetized as though the number is spelled out.